Praise for Nassir Ghaemi's *A First-Rate Madness*

"[Ghaemi's] book is a readable layman's guide to depression, bipolar disorder, and other ills, with colorful case histories and well-chosen quotes. . . . A provocative thesis . . . Ghaemi's book deserves high marks for original thinking."

—*The Washington Post*

"Ghaemi is a remarkably disciplined writer, and he examines both psychiatry and history with impressive clarity and sensitivity. *A First-Rate Madness* will almost certainly be one of the most fascinating books of the year, not just because of the author's lucid prose and undeniable intelligence, but because of his provocative thesis: 'For abnormal challenges, abnormal leaders are needed.'" —NPR.org

"Enthralling." —*The American Scholar*

"On the surface, the thesis [of *A First-Rate Madness*] may seem counterintuitive. But Ghaemi provides exhaustive research and makes a compelling case for his point, which is perhaps best summed up by an aphorism from Martin Luther King, Jr.: 'Human salvation lies in the hands of the creatively maladjusted.'"

—*Scientific American*

"*A First-Rate Madness* is a sophisticated work of psychology, but it is also a gossipy work of celebrity history, a who's who of the eminently unhinged."

—*New York Observer*

"Provacative, fascinating." —Salon.com

"Insightful and extraordinary . . . Recommended." —*Seattle Post-Intelligencer*

"*A First Rate Madness* may have a daring and controversial thesis, yes, but its psychiatry and history are surprisingly first-rate and engaging." —*The Daily Kos*

"Plato said it first: We all have a degree of madness that can serve our creativity. Nassir Ghaemi has said it again in the language of psychiatry, in a book that is so well written and so full of engaging stories that you'll want to embrace his point of view. Dr. Ghaemi turns upside down our usual way of seeing. You will enjoy this challenging book and be thrown into wonder about the value of sanity and the perverse gifts of neurosis."

—Thomas Moore, author of *Care of the Soul* and *Care of the Soul in Medicine*

"With brilliance and courage, Ghaemi explores the relationship of mental illness to creative leadership in times of crisis. He explains with great clarity the myriad meanings of mood disorder and other illnesses and ties this analysis to compassionate historical discussions of many of the most—and least—successful major leaders of the past two hundred years. This is a first-rate book."
— Michael Fellman, professor emeritus of history at Simon Fraser University and author of *Citizen Sherman* and *In the Name of God and Country*

"Nassir Ghaemi reinvents psychohistory as a serious form of scientific inquiry. Along the way, he presents a bounty of startling facts about some of history's great heroes and villains. Under his highly informed and skeptical gaze, our burnished icons— Lincoln and Sherman, Churchill and Hitler, Kennedy and Nixon, and others—are in for some serious resculpting."
— Daniel Dennett, professor of philosophy at Tufts University and author of *Breaking the Spell*, *Freedom Evolves*, and *Darwin's Dangerous Idea*

"Considered together, and with such rigor and clarity as they are here, these stories are staggering. If so many leaders have suffered so hard, we may well ask: What is 'mental health' anyway? Certainly, we need to reconsider sentimental notions of greatness and heroism. With deft use of biographical and psychiatric detail, Ghaemi exposes a central current of human experience that badly needs this kind of careful and sensitive attention."   — Joshua Wolf Shenk, author of *Lincoln's Melancholy*

"Nassir Ghamei's book is a provocative examination of the link between leadership, depression, and mania. It will arouse enormous interest, together with anger and disagreement, and many people will want to read it."
— Paul Johnson, author of *Churchill*, *A History of the American People*, and *Modern Times*

"No one who reads this brilliantly insightful book will ever look at history or politics the same way. Ghaemi uses his deep knowledge of medicine and psychiatry to take readers on a fascinating voyage into the minds of great leaders. His conclusions are startling, provocative, disturbing, and deeply persuasive."
— Stephen Kinzer, author of *Reset*, *Overthrow*, and *All the Shah's Men*

PENGUIN BOOKS

A FIRST-RATE MADNESS

Nassir Ghaemi, MD, is a professor of psychiatry at Tufts University School of Medicine and director of the Mood Disorders Program at Tufts Medical Center in Boston. He trained in psychiatry at Harvard Medical School and also serves on the faculty there. He holds degrees in history (BA, George Mason University), philosophy (MA, Tufts), and public health (MPH, Harvard). He has published more than a hundred scientific articles and several books on psychiatry.

A FIRST-RATE
MADNESS

UNCOVERING THE LINKS BETWEEN
LEADERSHIP AND MENTAL ILLNESS

NASSIR GHAEMI

PENGUIN BOOKS

PENGUIN BOOKS
Published by the Penguin Group
Penguin Group (USA) Inc., 375 Hudson Street, New York, New York 10014, U.S.A. •
Penguin Group (Canada), 90 Eglinton Avenue East, Suite 700, Toronto, Ontario, Canada M4P 2Y3
(a division of Pearson Penguin Canada Inc.) • Penguin Books Ltd, 80 Strand, London WC2R 0RL,
England • Penguin Ireland, 25 St. Stephen's Green, Dublin 2, Ireland (a division of Penguin Books
Ltd) • Penguin Books Australia Ltd, 250 Camberwell Road, Camberwell, Victoria 3124, Australia
(a division of Pearson Australia Group Pty Ltd) • Penguin Books India Pvt Ltd, 11 Community
Centre, Panchsheel Park, New Delhi—110 017, India • Penguin Group (NZ), 67 Apollo Drive,
Rosedale, Auckland 0632, New Zealand (a division of Pearson New Zealand Ltd) • Penguin Books
(South Africa) (Pty) Ltd, 24 Sturdee Avenue, Rosebank, Johannesburg 2196, South Africa

Penguin Books Ltd, Registered Offices: 80 Strand, London WC2R 0RL, England

First published in the United States of America by The Penguin Press,
a member of Penguin Group (USA) Inc. 2011
Published in Penguin Books 2012

3 5 7 9 10 8 6 4 2

Grateful acknowledgment is made for permission to reprint an excerpt from "Home After Three
Months Away" from *Collected Poems* by Robert Lowell. Copyright © 2003 by Harriet Lowell and
Sheridan Lowell. Reprinted by permission of Farrar, Straus and Giroux, LLC.

Excerpt from Aristotle's *Problemata* from "The Paradox of Genius and Madness: Seneca and His
Influence" by Anna Lydia Motto and John R. Clark, *Cuadernos de Filología Clásica* (Editorial
Complutense, Madrid, 1992).

Excerpt from *On the Road* by Jack Kerouac (Penguin Books). Copyright © Jack Kerouac, 1955, 1957.

THE LIBRARY OF CONGRESS HAS CATALOGED THE HARDCOVER EDITION AS FOLLOWS:
Ghaemi, S. Nassir.
A first-rate madness: uncovering the links between leadership and mental illness / Nassir Ghaemi.
p. ; cm.
Includes bibliographical references and index.
ISBN 978-1-59420-295-7 (hc.)
ISBN 978-0-14-312133-6 (pbk.)
1. Depressed person—Psychology. 2. Depression, Mental. 3. Leadership—
Psychological aspects. I. Title.
[DNLM: 1. Mentally Ill Persons—psychology. 2. Mood Disorders. 3. Leadership.
4. Temperament. WM 171]
RC537.G479 2011   2011010232
303.3'4019—dc22

Printed in the United States of America
DESIGNED BY NICOLE LAROCHE

To my father, Kamal Ghaemi, MD,

and my mother, Guity Kamali Ghaemi,

and for

Heather, Valentine, and Zane

Why is it that all those who have become above average either in philosophy, politics, poetry or the arts seem to be melancholy, and some to such an extent that they are even seized by the diseases of black bile?

—*Aristotle*, Problemata, *section XXX*

The only people for me are the mad ones, the ones who are mad to live, mad to talk, mad to be saved, desirous of everything at the same time, the ones who never yawn or say a commonplace thing, but burn, burn, burn.

—*Jack Kerouac*, On the Road

CONTENTS

THE INVERSE LAW OF SANITY

"Genl Wm T Sherman Insane" ran the headline of the November 1861 *Cincinnati Chronicle*. General William Tecumseh Sherman had gone "stark mad" and been removed from Union command in Kentucky; his peers, family, and staff all agreed that he suffered from paranoid delusions. On his way home to Ohio, Sherman said with a shrug, "In these times it is hard to say who are sane and who are insane."

He would reclaim his commission and go on to become a symbol of the Civil War's horror and a spokesman for psychological terror—the man history remembers for decimating Atlanta and scorching a trail through Georgia on his devastating "March to the Sea." He is an iconic figure in American history, yet few Americans know about an essential aspect of the man whose "scorched earth" strategy informed modern warfare from London, Dresden, and the Battle of the Bulge to Vietnam, Bosnia, and Iraq.

Historical evidence suggests that Sherman suffered from manic-depressive illness, or bipolar disorder—extreme shifts in a person's mood, energy, and ability to function. Someone need have only one manic episode to be diagnosed as manic-depressive; in fact, most people with the illness suffer mostly from depression. In addition to the Kentucky breakdown, Sherman apparently had at least four other major depressive episodes, the first at age twenty-seven, with symptoms of hopelessness, inertia, insomnia, and loss of appetite. He'd been having trouble settling into a military career and feeling excessively controlled by his father-in-law. The second episode occurred around age thirty-seven, when Sherman was a struggling banker. Another followed a few years later, again involving financial hardship. Another, at age fifty-eight, thirteen years after the war, came after his oldest son, Tom, a deeply depressed and sometimes homeless man who ultimately died in an institution, refused to study law, as Sherman desired, and decided instead to become a Jesuit priest. (A paternal uncle of Sherman's also likely suffered from recurrent depression, a genetic link that supports this diagnosis.)

Sherman never admitted to a mental illness. In his *Memoirs*, published in 1875, he famously blamed others for his mistakes and finessed all questions about his mental health. Historians indulged his charitable self-image for more than a century. Only in 1995, with the work of historian Michael Fellman, were Sherman's moods more thoroughly documented. Retrospective psychiatric diagnosis is fraught with risk and never definitive. Yet this doesn't mean we shouldn't follow the documentary trail and, in Sherman's case, consider the likelihood that a man who caused so much suffering, suffered much himself.

MOST OF US make a basic and reasonable assumption about sanity: we think it produces good results, and we believe insanity is a problem. This book argues that in at least one vitally important circumstance *insanity* produces good results and *sanity* is a problem. In times of crisis, we are better off being led by mentally ill leaders than by mentally normal ones.

There are different kinds of leadership for different contexts. The *non-crisis leader* succeeds in ordinary times, but in times of crisis should be kept far away from the scepter of rule. As we'll see, the typical non-crisis leader is idealistic, a bit too optimistic about the world and himself; he is insensitive to suffering, having not suffered much himself. Often he comes from a privileged background and has not been tested by adversity; he thinks himself better than others and fails to see what he has in common with them. His past has served him well, and he seeks to preserve it; he doesn't acclimate well to novelty. We see the non-crisis leader all around us—the CEO, the department chief, your neighbor's boss, the bank president, the president. One more fact: he is quite mentally healthy. He has never suffered from depression or mania or psychosis. He has never seen a psychiatrist.

ARISTOTLE FIRST SPECULATED about the link between genius and madness twenty-five hundred years ago, and at the height of the Romantic era the nineteenth-century Italian psychiatrist Cesare Lombroso defined that link forcefully, which we might translate as a simple equation: insanity = genius. He believed you can't have one without the other. In contrast, the statistician and founder of behavioral genetics, Francis Galton, took the opposing view, which we can summarize as: sanity = genius. Galton argued that intelligence—the strongest indicator of a healthy brain—produced genius. Both men saw genius as biological in origin, but one believed it arose from illness, the other from health.

These two views have seeped into Western culture, with most of us reflexively preferring Galton over Lombroso. In this book, I take Lombroso's side, with some qualifications. Throughout I trace a basic law that emerges from studying the relation of mental illness to leadership. One might call it the *Inverse Law of Sanity:* when times are good, when peace reigns, and the ship of state only needs to sail straight, mentally healthy people function well as our leaders. When our world is in tumult, mentally ill leaders function best.

Four key elements of some mental illnesses—mania and depression—appear to promote crisis leadership: *realism, resilience, empathy,* and *creativity*. These aren't just loosely defined character traits; they have specific psychiatric meanings, and have been extensively studied scientifically. I use these terms in their scientific, not their common-sense, meanings. Among these qualities, psychologists have studied creativity and empathy most, but resilience and realism are just as important for leadership and have also been examined in some detail by recent researchers. Of these four elements, all accompany depression, and two (creativity and resilience) can be found in manic illness. Except for resilience, none are specific for other mental illnesses (like schizophrenia and anxiety disorders). Depression makes leaders more realistic and empathic, and mania makes them more creative and resilient. Depression can occur by itself, and can provide some of these benefits. When it occurs along with mania—bipolar disorder—even more leadership skills can ensue. In this book, I'll examine eight great political, military, and business leaders whose lives and work show various aspects of the link between leadership and madness: William Tecumseh Sherman, Ted Turner, Winston Churchill, Abraham Lincoln, Mahatma Gandhi, Martin Luther King Jr., Franklin D. Roosevelt, and John F. Kennedy. I also provide counterexamples of five mentally healthy "normal" leaders who failed in moments of crisis: Richard Nixon, George McClellan, Neville Chamberlain, and possibly George W. Bush and Tony Blair. These counterexamples are important: I am not just diagnosing illness everywhere; I see mental health in most of our leaders, and I see it as a potential impediment in times of crisis.

In the course of my research, it became clear to me that mental illness was even more influential in historical terms than I had first imagined. Several major Civil War leaders were mentally ill or abnormal: Lincoln and Sherman, as will be shown later, but also Ulysses S. Grant, the alcoholic; possibly Stonewall Jackson; even, according to some evidence of depression and a family history of mental illness, Robert E. Lee. All the major leaders of World War II can be shown, with reasonable evidence, to have been mentally ill or abnormal: Churchill,

FDR, and Hitler, as we will see; as well as Stalin and Mussolini, each of whom had severe depressive episodes and probable manic episodes. Two key figures in the American civil rights movement, John Kennedy and Martin Luther King, were also mentally abnormal.

I believe these examples are more than coincidence, and more than a historical oddity. They suggest a relatively consistent pattern that, if true, has been largely ignored by historians and the public, but that may have in fact shaped the second half of the twentieth century more than any other single force. Once we start to see history through this lens, the reach and import of madness and leadership become hard to deny.

THIS IS A BOOK of psychology and of history; it sits at the long-disputed intersection of two different disciplines. But this book is not psychohistory. Psychohistory is a discredited discipline, and with reason. One need only read the book that started it all, written by the founder himself, Sigmund Freud's *Woodrow Wilson*, cowritten with the American politician (and one of Freud's patients) William Bullitt. There one finds passages like this:

> [Wilson] carried great burdens during the war for a man whose arteries were in precarious condition; and, although he continued to be troubled as usual by nervous indigestion and sick headaches, he suffered no "breakdown." His Super-Ego, his Narcissism, his activity toward his father, his passivity to his father, and his reaction-formation against his passivity to his father were all provided with supremely satisfactory outlets by the war.

No wonder historians are allergic to psychological interpretation. The book was so weak psychologically that Freud's daughter and his closest disciples suppressed its publication, and when it finally appeared in 1967, they tried to argue that Freud wrote very little of it. For many historians, psychiatry and psychology are synonymous with psychoanalysis, and any psychological interpretation seems bound to end up in fruitless speculation about the early childhood traumas of historical figures. Indeed, until recently historians were correct. Psychiatry and psychology, in the United States, have long been infatuated with psychoanalysis. Only in the last two decades has psychoanalysis been put in its proper place—not simply discarded, but no longer seen as necessary and sufficient in itself. (Imagine if all of economics was thought to be contained in Marxism; psychiatry was that dependent on psychoanalysis until recently.)

This psychoanalytic obsession has been replaced by a perspective on mental illness that is scientifically and medically sound. This psychiatry, stripped of its psychoanalytic faith, can be an extremely useful tool for historians.

THE NEW PSYCHIATRY begins where modern medicine began, with the search for objective ways to diagnose illness. In internal medicine, doctors get a "case history"—a story of signs and symptoms and their course over time. Psychiatrists and historians do the same. Yet the internist has one resource that that historians and psychiatrists do not: pathology. Physicians have long disagreed with each other; one could diagnose a patient with a certain illness, and another could offer a quite different diagnosis, even given the same case history. But medicine changed dramatically when the pathologist could take a piece of tissue and determine which doctor's diagnosis was right. The doctors would discuss the case in an auditorium, with students watching, each providing a rationale for a diagnosis. At the end of an hour's debate, the pathologist would stand up, put a slide under a microscope, and reveal the right answer.

Sometimes other tests are done: an analysis of blood chemistry, or an MRI scan of an organ. Yet sometimes these tests don't give a definitive answer; sometimes tests can even be wrong. And good doctors know that tests help us get to the right answer by adding to the evidence gathered in the case history; alone they are hardly foolproof ways to diagnose illness. Of course, tests for physical conditions are often conclusive, but the problem with psychiatry—and with history—is that there's no conclusive test. One can't prove that a patient has schizophrenia with a blood test or a brain scan; and if this is true with a living patient sitting in front of me, it is obviously so with a dead historical figure.

Yet medicine has long faced and solved this problem. Many illnesses outside of psychiatry can only be examined based on the case history—migraine, for example, and rheumatoid arthritis, and many forms of epilepsy. In these cases, doctors are in the same boat as are those who study mental illness—there's no definitive test. The solution comes from the field of clinical epidemiology, the same discipline that teased out the link between cigarette smoking and lung cancer. When there's no single proof, the solution is to obtain several independent sources of evidence. No single source is enough to prove a diagnosis, but all of them can converge to make a diagnosis likely.

Four specific lines of evidence have become standard in psychiatry: symptoms, genetics, course of illness, and treatment.

Symptoms are the most obvious source of evidence: most of us focus only on this evidence. Was Lincoln sad? That symptom could suggest depression, but of course one could be sad for other reasons. Symptoms are often nonspecific and thus not definitive by themselves.

Genetics are key to diagnosing mental illness, because the more severe conditions—manic-depressive illness in particular—run in families. Studies of identical twins show that bipolar disorder is about 85 percent genetic, and depression is about half genetic (The other half, in the case of depression, is environmental, which is why this source of evidence is also not enough on its own.)

Perhaps the least appreciated, and most useful, source of evidence is the *course of illness*. These ailments have characteristic patterns. Manic-depressive illness starts in young adulthood or earlier, the symptoms come and go (they're episodic, not constant), and they generally follow a specific pattern (for example, a depressive phase often immediately follows a manic episode). Depression tends to start somewhat later in life (in the thirties or after), and involves longer and fewer episodes over a lifetime. If someone has one of these conditions, the course of the symptoms over time is often the key to determining which one he has. An old psychiatric aphorism advises that "diagnosis is prognosis": time gives the right answer.

The fourth source of evidence is *treatment*. This evidence is less definitive than the rest for many reasons. Sometimes people never seek or get treatment, and until the last few decades, few effective treatments were available. Even now, drugs used for mental illnesses often are nonspecific; they can work for several different illnesses, and they can even affect behavior in people who aren't mentally ill. Sometimes, though, an unusual response can strongly indicate a particular diagnosis. For instance, antidepressants can cause mania in people with bipolar disorder, while they rarely do so in people without that illness.

IT'S IMPORTANT TO NOTE that the psychiatrist's method is exactly the same as the historian's. In other words, what the psychiatrist does when evaluating a living patient is no different from what a historian can do when evaluating the psychological makeup of a dead historical figure. The case history approach is the same: one assesses the person's past, based on his or her own report and that of third parties (families and friends and colleagues). The only difference is that the living patient can speak to the psychiatrist, while the dead historical figure speaks only through documents like personal letters. This difference is not as much of a drawback to the historian as it might seem. Living patients are often inaccurate or reticent about their symptoms during interviews with psychiatrists. In fact, some mental illnesses are characterized by how difficult they are to diagnose through interviews: for instance, about half the time, people with bipolar disorder deny having manic symptoms that they've actually experienced. In medical parlance, a patient's "self-report" is often inadequate and insufficient; psychiatrists should get information from family and friends as well. Historians faced with a dead figure are only at a partial disadvantage; even if that figure were alive, much of what he or she might say about potential psychiatric symptoms would be wrong.

Whether dealing with the living or the dead, third parties are often better sources than subjects themselves. In that sense, historians and psychiatrists are working with the same material: the case history of a living person being evaluated by a psychiatrist isn't fundamentally different from the history of a dead person being studied by a historian.

THIS BOOK DESCRIBES conditions that have applied to many leaders throughout history, and no doubt the reader can think of contemporary leaders to whom they apply as well. I'll focus primarily on a handful of historical figures whose lives spotlight different aspects of the relationship between mental health and leadership, and for whom there is particularly strong documentary evidence. General Sherman and cable entrepreneur Ted Turner exemplify how the symptoms of bipolar disorder can enhance creativity. The careers of Abraham Lincoln and Winston Churchill show the special relationship between depression and realism. So too do Mahatma Gandhi and Martin Luther King Jr.; their lives also highlight the strong link between depression and empathy. Franklin D. Roosevelt and John F. Kennedy, both of whom had hyperthymic personalities (that is, mildly manic traits), demonstrate the close connection between mental illness and resilience. Kennedy's experiences with medication also show the dramatic power of drugs to enhance the positive aspects of mental illness—or to make those illnesses even worse. Adolf Hitler's treatments provided similar, and more horrible, lessons.

To sharpen our understanding of successful crisis leaders, I will compare several of them to well-known, mentally healthy contemporaries who failed in crises. So, for instance, I'll contrast Sherman with

General George McClellan, who thrived in the Union army before the Civil War but failed notoriously and repeatedly during the war. And I'll show how Churchill's realistic assessment of the Nazi threat contrasts with the infamous inability of his eminently sane colleague Neville Chamberlain to recognize that threat.

I focus on historical leaders because, as a psychiatrist, I am eager to understand the benefits, as well as drawbacks, that can accompany mental illnesses. Clinical research has demonstrated these benefits—resilience, realism, empathy, and creativity. Yet most people haven't taken much note of this research. Showing the link between these strengths and madness in several of our most celebrated leaders could raise our awareness about the strengths that some mental illnesses can bestow on anybody who suffers from them. Furthermore, going back into history, rather than simply discussing contemporary figures, offers the advantage of hindsight. We see the past more clearly than the present; our current biases and hopes and uncertainties make our grasp of today much less solid than our hold on yesterday. If I were to focus on the current president or prime minister, my readers and I would automatically apply many of our own biases to those people. On the other hand, we can all be more objective about Churchill and Lincoln, much more so than their contemporaries were. (This doesn't mean we can make no inferences at all about contemporary leaders, as I'll do in chapter 15, but that such inferences are less definitive than with prior historical figures.) Historical perspective may allow us to perceive the impact of mental illnesses on leadership more clearly, not less so, than analyzing today's leaders.

BEFORE WE EXPLORE the links between mental illness and leadership, it's essential to understand what mental illness is—and is not.

First and most important, mental illness doesn't mean that one is simply insane, out of touch with reality, psychotic. The most common mental disorders usually have nothing to do with thinking at all, but rather abnormal moods: depression and mania. These moods aren't constant. People with manic-depressive illness aren't always manic or depressed. Thus they aren't always insane; in fact, they're usually sane. Their illness is the *susceptibility* to mania or depression, not the fact of *actually* (or always) being manic or depressed. This is important because they may benefit as leaders not just directly from the qualities of mania or depression, but also indirectly from entering and leaving those mood states, from the alternation between being ill and being well.

Contrary to popular belief, the psychiatric concept of clinical depression is different from ordinary sadness. Depression adds to sadness a constellation of physical symptoms that produce a general slowing and deadening of bodily functions. A depressive person sleeps less, and the nighttime becomes a dreaded chore that one can never achieve properly. Or one never gets out of bed; better sleep, if one can, since one can't do anything else. Interest in life and activities declines. Thinking itself is difficult; concentration is shot; it's hard enough to focus on three consecutive thoughts, much less read an entire book. Energy is low; constant fatigue, inexplicable and unyielding, wears one down. Food loses its taste. Or to feel better, one might eat more, perhaps to stave off boredom. The body moves slowly, falling to the declining rhythm of one's thoughts. Or one paces anxiously, unable to relax. One feels that everything is one's own fault; guilty, remorseful thoughts recur over and over. For some depressives, suicide can seem like the only way out of this morass; about 10 percent take their own lives.

The most popular psychological theory about depression these days is the *cognitive-behavioral model*, which views depression as distorting our perception of reality, making our thoughts abnormally negative. This model, the basis for cognitive-behavioral therapy, is contradicted by another theory that has a growing amount of clinical evidence behind it: the *depressive realism hypothesis*. This theory argues that depressed people aren't depressed because they distort reality; they're depressed because they see reality more clearly than other people do.

The notion of depressive realism implies that the disease has an upside, but I don't want to misrepresent how deeply dangerous and painful depression is. If untreated, it becomes a game of Russian roulette, with nature pulling the trigger when she decides, and with suicide the outcome. "Depression is a terrifying experience," said one of my patients, "knowing that somebody is going to kill you, and that person is *you*." Suicidal thoughts occur in about half of clinical depressive episodes.

The anger and despondency of depression (as well as the impulsivity of mania) can also cut a person off from the people he loves most. Divorce and broken relationships are the rule. Said one patient, "The illness is a kind of robbery; it robs you of those you love. I don't want money or power or fame. I just want to keep those I love. And this illness robs them from me. They wake up one day, and I am not the same person, and they say, 'Who is this?' And they leave." The benefits of depression come at a painful, if not deadly, price.

IF THE NUANCES of depression are confusing, mania seems even more complicated. Here mood is generally elated, even sometimes giddy, often alternating with anger. One doesn't need to sleep much; four hours can do it. While the rest of the world is sleeping, one's energy level is as high as it might be at 11 a.m. Why not clean the entire house at 3 a.m.? Things need to get done, even if they don't. Redecorate the house; do it again; buy a third car. Work two or three extra hours every day: the boss loves it. One's thoughts pour forth; the brain seems to be much faster than the mouth. Trying to keep up with those rapid thoughts, one talks fast, interrupting others. Friends and coworkers become annoyed; they can't get a word in edgewise. This may make one more irritable; why can't everyone else get up to speed? "Mania is extremity for one's friends," Robert Lowell remarked, "depression for oneself."

Self-esteem rises. Sometimes it leads to great successes, where one's skills are up to the task at hand. But often it leads to equally grand failures, where one oversteps one's bounds. But for someone in a manic state, there is no past; there is hardly today; only the future counts, and there, anything is possible. Decisions seem easy; no guilt, no doubt, just do it. The trouble is not in starting things, but in finishing them; with so much to do and little time, it's easy to get distracted.

Mania often impairs one's judgment, and bad decisions typically fall into four categories: sexual indiscretions, spending sprees, reckless driving, and impulsive traveling. Sex becomes even more appealing; one's spouse may like it, or tire of it. The urge is so strong that one might look to satisfy it elsewhere; affairs are common; divorce is the norm; HIV rates are high. Divorce, debt, sexually transmitted diseases, occupational instability: mania is the perfect antidote to the cherished goals of most people—a family, a home, a job, a stable life. The depressed person is mired in the past; the manic person is obsessed with the future. Both destroy the present in the process. In the worst-case scenario, the depressed person takes her life, the manic ruins hers. In manic-depressive illness, one suffers from both tragic risks.

Yet for all its dangers, mania can confer benefits that psychiatrists and patients both recognize. A key aspect of mania is the liberation of one's thought processes. My patients are sometimes eloquent when describing this freedom of thought (which psychiatrists label "flight of ideas"):

"Everything was swirling like a whirlwind; you just had to reach up to grab a word. You could see it, but you couldn't say it, like the word 'flower.' But when it got faster, you couldn't even see it."

Or: "My thoughts were like fireworks, going up and then exploding in all directions."

This emancipation of the intellect makes normal thinking seem pedestrian: "It felt like my mind was a fast computer," said one patient.

This produces the swell of creativity that only great poets who have themselves been manic can describe. Like William Blake:

> *To see a world in a grain of sand*
> *And heaven in a wild flower*
> *Hold infinity in the palm of our hand*
> *And eternity in an hour.*

Or Robert Lowell:

> *For months*
> *My madness gathered strength*
> *To roll all sweetness to a ball*
> *In color, tropical . . .*
> *Now I am frizzled, stale and small.*

THEORIES OF MANIA do not abound. It's as if traditional psychiatry saw the condition as too superficial to merit explanation.

The psychoanalytic view, which sees mania as a defense against depression, is the most coherent but probably the most wrongheaded. Some of my own patients offer a version of this explanation. "Sometimes I think I make myself become manic to ward off a depression," one patient told me. "I make myself be happy about everything and I do a lot of things and I stop sleeping because I know if I don't do this, I'll become depressed." Such rationales seem logical, but I'm skeptical about them. Mania often occurs without any preceding depression, and in fact more commonly, depression follows mania, suggesting that mania causes depression, rather than the reverse.

For psychoanalysts, depression was respectable; mania was not. Freud at least was honest about this: he wrote practically nothing about mania, and he admitted that psychoanalysis had no role in understanding or treating manic-depressive illness. His followers spoke where he was silent, blaming manic patients for being too childish to face their depressions. Mania does seem to hamper self-awareness, perhaps another reason why psychoanalysts looked askance at it. In my practice, I often see patients who are manic but don't realize it. Some others only see the benefits of mania: enhanced creativity, energy, sociability. Mania becomes a kind of temporary "personality transplant" where people take on the kind of charisma that our society rewards. But they don't fully realize the negative aspects of the disease, which are usually even more pronounced than its benefits: irritability, promiscuous sexuality, and lavish spending.

Mania is like a galloping horse: you win the race if you can hang on, or you fall off and never even finish. In Freudian terms, one might say that mania enhances the id, for better or worse. All energies, sexual and otherwise, overwhelm the usual controls that we learn to impose over a lifetime. The core of mania is *impulsivity with heightened energy*. If to be manic means to be impulsive, then perhaps the expression of mania depends on how far the civilized veneer that holds our lives together is stretched. If it is stretched only a little, manic-depressive persons may function fine and actually be rewarded for their creativity and extraversion. If it is stretched too much, society disapproves, and tragedy may ensue.

SOME PEOPLE ARE neither depressed nor manic, but they aren't mentally healthy either. They have *abnormal personalities or temperaments*. Personality or temperament is just as biological as mental illness, though most of us think otherwise. Our basic temperaments are set by the time we reach kindergarten; studies show that those basic temperaments measured at age three persist and predict adult personality at age eighteen. From then onward as well, despite what many intuitively believe, our basic personality traits change little throughout adulthood and into old age. We may get wiser as we get older, but we do not become less introverted, or more open to experience, or less neurotic (to mention three basic personality traits).

Usually we don't think about personality in relation to mental illness. Indeed, my main focus in this book will be to apply the psychiatric concepts of depression and mania to history. But many leaders, though not manic-depressive, have abnormal temperaments that are mild versions of manic-depressive illness.

Personality traits are like height and weight—variables that describe the shape of our minds, just as height and weight describe the shape of our bodies. A century of research on personality has produced some consensus. Most studies on personality identify at least three basic traits common to all people: neuroticism, extraversion, and openness to experience. One of these traits is anxiety—we're all more or less anxious (neuroticism). Another is sociability—some of us are more extraverted, some more introverted (extraversion). Another is experience seeking—some of us are curious and take risks, others are more cautious (openness to experience). We each have more or less of these traits, and, with well-designed psychological tests, one can establish how they're distributed among thousands of normal people. One can then know where any single person stands on each trait, near the middle of a normal curve—and thus near the average—or toward the extremes.

These traits can combine to form specific personality types. Some people are always a little depressed, low in energy, need more than eight hours' sleep a night, and introverted. This personality type is called *dysthymia*. Other people are the opposite: always upbeat, outgoing, high in energy. They need less than eight hours' sleep a night and have more libido than most of us. This type is called *hyperthymia*, and it occurs often in great leaders, like Franklin Roosevelt and John F. Kennedy. And some people are a little of both, alternating between lows and highs in mood and energy. This type is called *cyclothymia*.

These abnormal temperaments are mild versions of depression, mania, and bipolar disorder; as such, they're abnormal personality traits, which a person has all the time, not mood episodes that come and go. They can occur by themselves, without any episodes of mania or depression, or they can occur alongside bipolar disorder or severe depression (for instance, someone might have episodes of mania or depression every other year, and in between those episodes have a dysthymic personality). In fact, these abnormal personalities occur more often in those with bipolar disorder or severe depression than they do in people without mental illness. They also occur much more frequently in relatives of people with severe depression and mania than in the normal population.

These temperaments were described by the early-twentieth-century German psychiatrist Ernst Kretschmer, the first modern researcher on abnormal personality, who also noted the link between insanity and genius. He recognized the benefit of a little mental abnormality, either in "the initial stages" of severe mental illness, or in "mild, borderline states of mental disease," which is what I mean by abnormal personalities or temperaments. If we removed the insanity from these people, Kretschmer said, we would convert their genius into merely ordinary talent. Insanity is not a "regrettable . . . accident" but the "indispensable catalyst" of genius.

SURPRISINGLY, MENTAL HEALTH can be as challenging to define as mental illness, because our sense of one is informed by our sense of the other. To keep it simple, I define mental health as *the absence of mental disease, plus being near the statistical average of personality traits.* Thus, *mental illness* means the presence of disease, like manic-depressive illness; and *mental abnormality* means being at the extremes, not near the average, of personality traits. Mental abnormality means having abnormal temperaments—like dysthymia, cyclothymia, hyperthymia—that don't occur in the vast majority of normal people. Therefore, these conditions aren't part of mental health; they are essentially milder versions of mental illness.

With these definitions, the theme of this book can be stated this way: *The best crisis leaders are either mentally ill or mentally abnormal; the worst crisis leaders are mentally healthy.*

In times of peace, mental health is useful. One meets the expectations of one's community, and one is rewarded for doing so. In times of war or crisis, it is the misfits who fill the bill. Kretschmer noticed this pattern and explained it using the metaphor of bacteria, which replicate and survive only in times of crisis. "The brilliant enthusiast, the radical fanatic and the prophet are always there, just as the tricksters and criminals are—the air is full of them," but they flourish only during crisis. In peacetime, they are our patients, he famously wrote; we rule them. In crisis periods, they rule us.

Great crisis leaders are not like the rest of us; nor are they like mentally healthy leaders. They're often intelligent, prone to poor physical health, the products of privileged backgrounds, raised by parents in conflict, frequently nonreligious, and ambitious. All these personality traits and experiences are also associated with mental illness, like mania and depression, or with abnormal temperaments, like hyperthymia. Much of what passes for normal is not found in the highly successful political and military leader, especially in times of crisis. If normal, mentally healthy people—what I will later define scientifically as "homoclites"—run for president, they tend not to become great ones.

A FINAL DISCLAIMER: the true mark of science (as opposed to its many masquerades) is an attempt to refute one's hypothesis, to be self-critical, to examine one's assumptions, and to point out ways to further test one's theory. I will strive to do all of these things throughout this book. Science makes probabilistic claims; it is not usually about proving that something is *always* the case, or *never* the case. Almost all science is about showing a greater probability that something is *usually* the case. On most scientific matters, especially in medicine and on the topic of disease, no single exception is a disproof. The preponderance of the evidence represents scientific knowledge.

I don't claim that depression *invariably* leads to realism, nor that mania *always* enhances creativity, nor that depression *on every occasion* increases empathy, nor that hyperthymia *inevitably* promotes resilience. Rather, I argue that, *on the whole, more often than not, those mental illnesses enhance or promote those qualities more frequently than is the case in the absence of those mental illnesses.* Some people with manic-depressive illness are unrealistic (even psychotic), unempathic, and unresilient. We shouldn't romanticize this condition; in its most extreme forms, it is highly disabling and dangerous. But most people have less severe forms of these illnesses; there will be many more manic-depressive leaders showing the beneficial traits discussed in this book than manic-depressive leaders who are dangerously crazy.

We will see that our greatest crisis leaders toil in sadness when society is happy, seeking help from friends and family and doctors. Sometimes they're up, sometimes they're down, but they're never quite well. Yet when calamity occurs, if they are in a position to act, they can lift up the rest of us; they can give us the courage we may have temporarily lost, the fortitude that steadies us.

Their weakness is, in short, the secret of their strength.

PART ONE
CREATIVITY

CHAPTER 1

MAKE THEM FEAR AND DREAD US

SHERMAN

In the brutal aftermath of the First World War, an American publisher asked British military historian B. H. Liddell-Hart to write a book on a key Civil War general, preferably Robert E. Lee. Liddell-Hart, who had concluded that European trench warfare in the recent conflict had replicated Lee's Virginia campaigns, chose another general. Lee's brand of battle had failed in the Great War, but Sherman had foreseen the future of warfare. In Virginia, Lee and Grant had fought a traditional war: one army sought to destroy the other using the Napoleonic concept of "strategic concentration," repeatedly trying to mass forces in central frontal assaults, repeatedly failing, and trying again. Napoleonic strategy in the era of modern weaponry produced only carnage. Sherman took a different approach: his assault on Georgia and the Carolinas delivered a decisive, fatal blow to the economic and moral heart of rebellion.

Sherman transformed warfare from its nineteenth-century incarnation into the total war that became endemic in the twentieth century and beyond. Sherman's forces burned one-third of the South and destroyed Atlanta; he is famous, and infamous, for his cruelty. But he wasn't *just* cruel. Many Civil War leaders spent most of their postwar lives defending their decisions, or attacking their foes, or glorifying the whole experience. Not Sherman: he always taught the harshness of war. Our view of the postwar Sherman is distorted by the prism of his actions during wartime. For instance, he never said, "War is hell"—a declaration that is usually quoted to suggest that he blithely embraced the brutality of armed conflict. During an 1879 military graduation speech, he did tell the young men in the audience, representatives of a generation that had never known battle, "There is many a boy here who looks on war as all glory. But boys"—he paused—"war is all hell. You can bear this warning voice to generations to come."

That voice has been lost in the mists of history. Reconstructing the real Sherman, with his coercion as well as his complexity, means recognizing that he had manic-depressive illness. In fact, of all the leaders in this book, I would say that Sherman is the prototypical mentally ill leader. In different aspects of his bipolar disorder, he displayed many of the powers of mental illness to improve leadership: depressive realism, empathy for the South (before and after the war), resilience beyond measure, and unique military creativity. Yet until recently, no historian had carefully assessed whether Sherman himself suffered from deep, indeed sick emotions. This task was taken up by Michael Fellman, a gregarious American, self-exiled in Canada since the 1960s, where he is professor emeritus of history at Simon Fraser University. A specialist in the American Civil War, Fellman had been taught traditional history: trace the documents of who did what, who said what, and what happened; pull it together for the reader; and let it go. Such history seldom made well-grounded analyses about the abnormal mental states of the people it studied.

Having himself suffered a painful depression, Fellman realized that traditional history was mistaken because such conditions have an enormous impact on people—famous, infamous, and obscure. He became attuned to evidence of abnormal mental states among the Civil War figures he studied. Besides Lincoln's melancholy, Fellman discovered depressive tendencies in Robert E. Lee, and outright mental illness in General Sherman. What followed was a biography—researching and reporting facts based on primary sources—that a century after Sherman's own memoir unmasked the whole man: greater than we thought, in part because he was much sicker than we knew.

PROBABLY THE OLDEST LINK between mental illness and a desirable personality trait was the one Aristotle first drew between creativity and depression. He noticed that poets tend to be melancholic, a finding that long ago became conventional wisdom; the depressed poet is an iconic stereotype. But the nature of the link—what causes what—has been a source of controversy, and few have asked how mental illness and creativity might be linked to leadership.

To understand the link, we should first figure out what creativity is. One definition of creativity is "divergent thinking"—generating many unusual solutions to a problem. There are several standard tests for divergent thinking; one asks the subject to "think of many different and unusual uses for a common item, such as a tin can or a brick." Other tests use word association or partially drawn figures that test subjects must complete.

Some people question whether studies like these really reflect original, real-life creativity, the kind that makes famous people famous. We might also question whether the divergent thinking model has its terms reversed. Creativity may have to do less with *solving* problems than with *finding* the right problems to solve. Creative scientists sometimes discover problems that others never realized. Their solutions aren't as novel as is their recognition that those problems existed to begin with. Newton's theories left most physicists untroubled until a young Zurich patent office employee realized they didn't work when applied to light; Albert Einstein saw problems others hadn't seen and asked new questions that replaced old solutions. Creativity may be about identifying problems, not solving them.

Or perhaps it's about both. Psychologists Richard Mansfield and Thomas Busse propose a two-phase process: First, "the selection of the problem," a creative activity dependent on personality traits of the scientist (individual autonomy, independent-mindedness, personal flexibility, and openness to experience). Second, the "extended effort to solve the problem," where persistence matters—the ability to keep going even when one's views are unpopular or unrewarded (here again one benefits from independence of character). Though I focus on the cognitive aspects of creativity—divergent thinking and the ability to find the right problems—the role of persistence is well worth noting. Darwin famously attributed his success to his "doggedness," not his genius. Here again mania, with its high energy (especially in hyperthymic personality), is advantageous; the energetic manic tends to be dogged—a trait General Sherman exemplified on his march through Georgia.

CREATIVITY, THEN, involves finding novel problems and solving them. Following the thinking of Aristotle and the nineteenth-century psychiatrist Cesare Lombroso, I believe that mental illness—and specifically mania—is a fine advantage in this process. Think of a classic manic symptom: flight of ideas. One's thoughts seem to literally fly in many different directions; they may or may not make sense, but they certainly get around. Divergent thinking is a daily experience in mania. Manic people are also hyperactive; they think quickly, talk rapidly, and need little sleep; they write much; they draw, plan, propose, implement. The psychologist Kay Redfield Jamison, drawing from her personal experience, puts it like this:

"Exuberant behavior and emotions—whether displayed in love, manifested in laughter and play, or kindled by music, dance, and celebration—have in common high mood and energy. They act on the same reward centers in the brain as food, sex, and addictive drugs, and they create states of mental and physical playfulness." She also noted the role of exuberance, as happens with mania, in leadership: "In times of adversity, inspired leadership offers energy and hope where little or none exist, gives a belief in the future to those who have lost it, and provides a unifying spirit to a splintered populace."

A final, and maybe the most important, aspect of creative thinking that we see in mania is the ability to think broadly; psychologists call this "integrative complexity." Creative people see farther and wider; their cognitive peripheral vision is clearer; they make connections between seemingly disparate things that many of us miss.

One way to measure this ability is the "paragraph complexity test," which asks subjects to complete sentences like: "When I am in doubt, I . . ." or "When I am criticized, I . . ." Then researchers see if responses take more than one perspective versus being simplistic. Applying this method to the speeches and letters of Civil War generals, one study found that Robert E. Lee set the standard: his writings demonstrated high complexity, and the differences between his paragraphs and those of opposing generals correlated with battlefield success. Lee was much more complex in his thinking than those he defeated handily—McClellan, Ambrose Burnside, Joseph Hooker; and only somewhat better than the opponent who matched him at Gettysburg—George Meade. He was lower than only one man: the general who defeated him—Ulysses Grant. General Sherman's writing was not included in this study, but reading the complex and emotional letters he wrote his wife and family, I suspect he would have been the most integrative-thinking general of them all.

This integrative complexity happens with mania, though patients often find it hard to describe. One who has tried is Tom Wootton—who is in treatment for bipolar disorder and gives seminars about the benefits of the illness. He likens human experience to seeing only part of a painting; normally, we see just the middle of the canvas, but some-one with bipolar disorder experiences oscillations in her view that allow her briefly to see larger parts of it. But the experience is vertiginous; it cannot be sustained without causing psychosis in mania, or abject despondency in depression. Only the great mystics, Wootton suggests, after years of spiritual training, can stand to see most of the painting, all at once, for extended periods of time. This all-encompassing view isn't feasible for most mortals.

Those brief insights stay with you after you return to normal. When not manic or depressed, those with bipolar disorder are normal, just like everyone else, but they retain an awareness that makes their perception just different enough to be unusually creative.

A NATIVE OF OHIO, William Tecumseh Sherman attended West Point, graduated in 1840 near the top of his class (despite demerits for misbehavior), went straight into the army, and married his childhood sweetheart, Ellen Ewing, whose father was in President Zachary Taylor's cabinet. Much was expected of the young Lieutenant Sherman; the president and key political figures such as Henry Clay and Daniel Webster attended his wedding. Yet in 1853, the low wages and lack of prospects for fame in a peacetime army made Sherman leave the military and pursue a career in business.

To his wife's exasperation, he frequently moved from city to city (a very common habit among those who experience mania). He accumulated debt by borrowing large sums of money for his investments, and except for happy events like the birth of his son, he was usually glum. In San Francisco he started a bank. Within four years, after the 1857 depression, this venture failed, leaving him bankrupt, $136,000 in debt (equivalent to over $3 million in today's currency), and despondent. "I am of course used up root and branch," he wrote to his brother-in-law, adding in another letter to Ellen, "I am afraid of my own shadow." He wished his asthma would kill him.

For the next two years he struggled on Wall Street, in San Francisco, and in St. Louis. Finally he moved to Kansas, where his in-laws owned land, and sold corn to prospectors headed west in search of gold. Much of the time he was alone; Ellen preferred the comforts of her father's Ohio home. Sherman's moods meanwhile fluctuated with every attempt to settle into a stable, remunerative job. "I am doomed to be a vagabond and I shall no longer struggle against my fate," he wrote to Ellen. In 1859, he reentered the army, taking a position as superintendent of a new military college in Louisiana.

Sherman obtained the Louisiana position partly through the recommendation of old West Point classmates, future Confederate generals Joseph Johnston and Pierre G. T. Beauregard. Though he now worked in the South, Sherman maintained an antiwar, antisecession stance throughout the increasingly tense years before the Civil War. His brother, John, a congressman from Ohio, gave fiery abolitionist speeches, provoking criticism from Sherman's Louisiana friends. Sherman was sympathetic to Southern concerns and was not critical of slavery. He saw fault on both sides: He blamed all politicians—abolitionist and proslavery alike—for stoking the North-South conflict. Before the war, he was rather friendly to the South and its culture; his support for the Northern cause was based on the principle, shared by many Unionist Southerners, of opposing secession.

Sherman's disgust with politicians and his postwar refusal to ever enter politics ("If nominated, I will not accept; if elected, I shall not serve"), even when the presidency was repeatedly offered him, stemmed from this prewar experience. Until the actual fall of Fort Sumter, Sherman hoped that the politicians could pull back from the brink. His repeated pleas to his brother and others were futile; the election of 1860 entailed a clear choice: slavery or war. Sherman declined to vote.

THE WAR SOON CAME. The first battle, Bull Run, was a Northern debacle, which Sherman witnessed firsthand. Afterward, he was appointed second in command in Kentucky. Soon his superior was transferred, and he took responsibility for the key border state. He was filled with anxiety. That October, in a routine reconnaissance with 4,000 soldiers, Sherman suddenly became convinced that he was surrounded by spies and that his troops were about to be overrun. He begged his superiors for 200,000 more men, a staggering number; he expressed his fears so vehemently that other officers, the secretary of war, and his family became concerned about his mental health.

In *Citizen Sherman*, Fellman describes how two reporters, Henry Villard and William Shanks, "shared the Louisville telegraph office with Sherman nearly every night from about 9 p.m. *until 3 a.m.* All would pore over Associated Press reports as they came in. Sherman *unceasingly talked*, paced, smoked cigars. . . . He seemed to smoke not from pleasure but as if it were a duty to be finished in the shortest imaginable time. . . . Sherman puffs furiously." Fellman, paraphrasing Shanks, noted that Sherman "would *never finish* a cigar. . . . Sherman simply never sat still . . . his fingers were always busy. . . . While sitting he would *cross and uncross his legs continuously*. And *on and on he talked*, nervously and obsessively. . . . He must talk quick, sharp . . . making odd gestures, which . . . emphasizes his language. He never hesitates at *interrupting* anyone, but he *cannot bear to be interrupted* himself. . . . Sherman had a *bad temper* but what is worse, he makes no attempt to control or correct it. . . . He expressed himself entirely *without reserve* about men and matters . . . and I could not help thinking that in doing so he said *more than was wise and proper*." (italics added)

The italicized phrases illustrate classic signs of mania: irritable mood, decreased need for sleep (sleeping little but being a bundle of energy), distractibility, rapid speech, increased talkativeness, hyperactivity, physical agitation, and inability to function at work. Villard added that after the general's frenetic behavior ended he would "lapse into long silent moods . . . and literally brood day and night. . . . It was soon whispered about that he was suffering from mental depression."

"I am up all night," Sherman wrote, always under "the quiet observation of spies." He lost his appetite and began to drink, which worsened his depression. He was convinced his life would end soon. "The idea of going down in History with a fame such as threatens me nearly makes crazy—indeed I may be so now," he wrote to his wife.

Sherman's staff took the unusual step of writing to his family and asking that they visit him in the Kentucky field. By the time his wife arrived, he was practically mute. "He has had little or no sleep or food for some time," Ellen Sherman wrote from Kentucky. She knew insanity to run in the Sherman family and had seen her husband in severe melancholic states. "Several of the army officers are staying at the hotel and all seem deeply interested in him," she wrote. "He however pays no attention to them, or to anyone, and scarcely answers a question unless it be on the all-engrossing subject [of the war]. He thinks the whole country is gone irrevocably and ruin and desolation are at hand."

Sherman's brother John, now a U.S. senator, questioned the general's grasp of reality: "You are not only in error but are laboring under some strange delusions. . . . Your mind casts a somber shadow on everything. . . . Your manner is abrupt and almost repulsive." Sherman was in despair: "I see no hope at all. You can trust in Providence [but] why he has visited me with this terrible judgment is incomprehensible." Sherman's superior, General Halleck, ordered a medical examination; a physician concluded that there was "such nervousness that [Sherman] was unfit for command." Halleck sent Sherman home to Ohio.

In retrospect, Sherman's mania seemed to have lasted about two weeks. It was followed by two months of deep depression with likely paranoid delusions. In his memoirs he made much of the fact that the reporters who publicized concerns about his mental health disliked him; historians later dismissed the manic episode as a concoction of his enemies. Yet even his family clearly feared for his sanity, and Sherman himself wrote to his brother a few months after the danger had passed: "I should have committed suicide were it not for my children."

SIX MONTHS LATER Sherman was feeling better, though wearied by his recent despair. His wife and brother had done much to rehabilitate his public image, including personally visiting President Lincoln, who was sympathetic—indeed, perhaps empathetic—to his plight. The Union still needed Sherman, but top leaders, including Ulysses S. Grant, his new immediate superior, ensured that when he returned to service he was no longer placed in sole command. Under Grant's supervision he fought effectively in his next great battle, Shiloh. Formerly so self-disparaging, he experienced "an abrupt spiritual rebirth," in Fellman's words. In July 1863, Sherman and Grant sealed the first real Union military success with the brutal siege of Vicksburg.

After Vicksburg, Sherman began to engage in the kind of war that would make him famous. "We are absolutely stripping the country of corn, cattle, hogs, sheep, poultry, everything," he reported to Grant on his operations around Jackson, Mississippi. "The wholesale destruction to which the country is now being subjected is terrible to contemplate, but it is the scourge of war." He even mocked the earlier accusations of insanity leveled against him: "To secure the safety of the navigation of the Mississippi River I would slay millions. On this point I am not only insane but mad."

Grant proved to be Sherman's savior, believing in Sherman despite the latter's past mental instability. ("He stood by me when I was crazy, and I stood by him when he was drunk," Sherman would say after the war.) Under Grant's watchful but approving gaze Sherman was let loose in Georgia. The strategy of destroying the economic heart of the South was planned with Grant, yet the specifics were left up to Sherman. Initially, upon crossing into Georgia from Tennessee, Sherman conducted conventional flanking actions, avoiding direct conflict with the Confederate army under General Joseph Johnston, focused on the goal of destroying Atlanta. When, after some minor engagements around Atlanta, the Northern troops entered the city, Sherman was merciless. All citizens were forced from their homes and given one-way rail tickets northward; then he burned it all. Atlanta remains the last U.S. city ever destroyed in warfare. Grant had not ordered the evacuation and destruction of Atlanta, but once Sherman started the process,

Grant did not stop him. (In his *Memoirs*, Grant credits Sherman with the entire plan of the march, and notes that he agreed with Sherman, having to convince numerous other generals and a reluctant president that Sherman's campaign was worthwhile.)

Sherman stated his goal clearly, explicitly telling the South what he intended to do. He knew that the prospect of his attacks was as much a weapon as the attacks themselves. His Confederate counterpart John Bell Hood, who had replaced Johnston, wrote him bluntly when Sherman announced the depopulation and planned destruction of Atlanta, "The unprecedented measure you propose transcends, in studied and ingenious cruelty, all acts . . . in the dark history of war. In the name of God and humanity I protest." "God will judge us in due time," Sherman replied.

In a letter responding to the mayor of Atlanta, Sherman offered a remarkable explanation for his strategy, one that chides Southerners for their lack of empathy with the civilians their own armies had made homeless, and that even shows a kind of empathy for the Southerners he was about to make homeless:

> *Gentlemen:*
>
> *. . . You might as well appeal against the thunder-storm as against these terrible hardships of war. They are inevitable, and the only way the people of Atlanta can hope once more to live in peace and quiet at home, is to stop the war, which can only be done by admitting that it began in error and is perpetuated in pride.*
>
> *We don't want your negroes, or your horses, or your houses, or your lands, or any thing you have, but we do want and will have a just obedience to the laws of the United States. That we will have, and, if it involves the destruction of your improvements, we cannot help it. . . .*
>
> *I myself have seen in Missouri, Kentucky, Tennessee, and Mississippi, hundreds and thousands of women and children fleeing from your armies and desperadoes, hungry and with*

bleeding feet. In Memphis, Vicksburg, and Mississippi, we fed thousands upon thousands of the families of rebel soldiers left on our hands, and whom we could not see starve. Now that war comes home to you, you feel very different. You deprecate its horrors, but did not feel them when you sent car-loads of soldiers and ammunition, and moulded shells and shot, to carry war into Kentucky and Tennessee, to desolate the homes of hundreds and thousands of good people who only asked to live in peace at their old homes and under the Government of their inheritance. . . .

But, my dear sirs, when peace does come, you may call on me for any thing. Then will I share with you the last cracker, and watch with you to shield your homes and families against danger from every quarter.

Now you must go, and take with you the old and feeble, feed and nurse them, and build for them, in more quiet places, proper habitations to shield them against the weather until the mad passions of men cool down, and allow the Union and peace once more to settle over your old homes at Atlanta. Yours in haste,

> *W. T. Sherman, Major-General*
> *commanding*

Sherman then turned south, ignoring the attempts of General Hood and the Confederate army to coax him back into battle. The March to the Sea began, and now Sherman came into his own. Generals had always protected their links with headquarters, which they needed to give and receive orders, food, and ammunition. Knowing he would now go deep into Southern territory, and that he could not defend his supply lines, Sherman cut them loose. (He let Grant know his intentions, and Grant said he preferred otherwise, wishing Sherman to attack Hood; but he left the final decision to Sherman.) Said the British military experts of the *Army and Navy Gazette*, "If Sherman has really left his army up in the air and started off without a base to march from

Georgia to South Carolina, he has done either one of the most brilliant or one of the most foolish things ever performed by a military leader." For three tense months, Sherman was entirely on his own; Grant and Lincoln had no clue what he was doing, whether he was winning or losing, alive or dead. (When Sherman was close to Savannah, Grant even sent orders by messenger for him to break off the march and come to Virginia by sea. Sherman, upset, did not respond and intensified his assault on Savannah; when it finally fell, he persuaded Grant to rescind the new orders and allow him to continue the march through the Carolinas.)

Sherman now started his innovative attack on civilian morale and property. His men foraged off the land, forced to do so by lack of supplies, but also as part of Sherman's new military strategy. Attack and destroy property, not soldiers; ruin the ability to wage war—by decimating crops, farms, cities, and, most important, civilian morale. With their base of support thus ravaged, even the most gallant warriors would have to submit. When Sherman was finished, the South would have neither the food nor the will to keep up the fight. At about this time, a Russian anarchist, Mikhail Bakunin, had divined what was in Sherman's psyche: all destruction, Bakunin taught, is also a creative destruction. Sherman was unapologetic then and later: "If the people raise a howl against my barbarity and cruelty, I will answer that war is war." "War is cruelty, and you cannot refine it," he had told Atlantans. After the war, he reflected on the emotional impact of his warfare, the suffering he may have known from his own personal depression: "My aim then was to whip the rebels, to humble their pride, to follow them to their inmost recesses, and make them fear and dread us. 'Fear of the Lord is the beginning of wisdom.'"

SHERMAN WAS IN a high-strung, high-energy, hyperthymic state (which appeared to be his usual personality when he was not severely manic or depressed), but he was not disconnected from reality as he had been in Kentucky. A Grant emissary reported Sherman engaged in "a marvelous talk about a march to the sea. His mind, of course, was full of it. He seemed the very personification of nervous energy." Sherman "rocked back and forth in his chair, his hands were at work shredding the newspaper they held, while his stockinged feet darted in and out of their slippers."

During the next three months Sherman's troops slowly moved toward Savannah, systematically tearing up railroad tracks and heating and twisting the rails into spirals ("Sherman's neckties"), often shaping the metal into the letters "US." Troops lived off whatever they found en route to the Atlantic, and though Sherman had ordered them not to take more than the mission required, and not to harm or even insult civilians, but to burn the property of anyone who defied them, once the destruction began it was difficult to rein in. Soldiers looted homes, and there were reports of rape, torture, and killing. When rebel guerrillas began planting explosives in the roads, Sherman used Confederate prisoners as minesweepers.

As he advanced on Savannah he assured superiors of the value of the "total war" strategy that his march would make famous. "I attach much more importance to these deep incisions into the enemy's country, because this war differs from European wars in this particular," he later telegraphed Henry Halleck, the chief general in Washington. "We are not fighting armies, but a hostile people, and must make old and young, rich and poor, feel the hard hand of war." When he got to South Carolina, the state that started the whole conflict with its secession and takeover of Fort Sumter, Sherman was merciless. Wrote a Michigan soldier in his army, "In South Carolina, there was no restraint whatever in pillaging and foraging. Men were allowed to do as they like, *burn and destroy*." Historian Michael Fellman notes that though Sherman opened the door to total war, he did not fully practice it. After Atlanta, he did not evacuate any city; rape of women was not practiced; no concept of genocide existed. All these practices came later, especially with the Second World War. For his time, Sherman was brutal. But compared with what would later come, he was mild.

This future misery gave no succor, of course, to the people of the South who stood in Sherman's path. Nor did Sherman think much about restraining his men; he mostly focused on destroying as much property and instilling as much fear as feasible. The general paid attention to how his victims reacted; years later he commented that Georgians at least "bore their afflictions with some manliness," but South Carolinians "whined like curs." By the time Sherman reached North Carolina in March 1865, he was steps away from meeting up with Grant in Virginia and forcing Lee's surrender. The manic general eased off, ordering one of his generals, "It might be well to instruct your brigade commanders that now we are out of South Carolina and that a little moderation would be of political consequence to us in North Carolina." A month later, the war was over.

WITH ALL THIS military success, Sherman had rehabilitated his image from crazy failure to insane genius. Another military leader, George McClellan, as we will see later, evolved in the opposite direction—from precocious sensation to plain dud. Almost no psychiatric contrast in history stands out more clearly, side by side, than these two men.

The American Civil War lays out the stark contrast: the greatest generals in war are often abundant failures during peacetime, and vice versa. McClellan and Sherman are the sharpest contrasts; but there is also Grant the peacetime drunkard, and Stonewall Jackson the barely tolerable military professor. Only Lee stands out as effective in both peace and war (and even he had a mentally unstable father, and Lee himself may have been dysthymic in his general personality).

The contrast reflects, I think, the different psychological qualities of leadership needed in different phases of human activity, peace and war being two extremes. A civilian analogy might be when a president takes office in peacetime versus wartime, or in a strong economy versus an economic crisis. Another might be when a businessman manages an already successful company well, versus starting, building, and growing a new enterprise. The same kind of leader can be a successful Calvin Coolidge in one setting, a failed Herbert Hoover in the other. Or the very same person—a Ted Turner, as we'll see next—can be a bust in one context, a hit in the other.

FOR LEADERS IN any realm, creativity is not just about solving old problems with new solutions, it's about finding new problems to solve. Mania enhances both aspects of creativity: the divergence of thought allows one to identify new problems, and the intense energy keeps one going until the problems are solved. We can see these features in bipolar leaders as different from each other as William Tecumseh Sherman and Ted Turner. The problem for Sherman was not how to better attack and defeat the Confederate armies: many Northern generals had tried many approaches, without victory. Sherman gave up on that problem. He came up with a new one: How can you break the morale of the Southern people? If you can do that, then you might weaken the Confederate armies enough so that they will gradually dissolve. His solution: Destroy cities and farms, attack the economy, target people and property, and you will win by undermining the army's base of support.

The problem for Turner was not how to become a big mogul in the traditional news media. There was a standard solution to that problem: move to New York and work your way up the corporate ladder. Instead, Turner saw that the cable medium provided a new mechanism for news, and his solution was to start an all-day news provider in that medium.

None of this is to suggest that we should glorify Sherman or Turner. They solved old problems by creating new ones. Sherman solved the problem of brutal face-to-face army combat, which had produced the carnage of Antietam and Gettysburg, but he created a new and greater problem: targeting civilians in wartime. Turner ended the news monopoly of New York corporations, but he created a new problem: the twenty-four-hour news cycle and the endless punditry that treats opinion as news.

These leaders were creative, manic originators: they answered questions nobody had yet asked, but in so doing they produced other questions nobody can yet answer.

CHAPTER 2

WORK LIKE HELL— AND ADVERTISE

TURNER

The classic entrepreneur founds entirely new notions: Henry Ford and the mass-produced automobile, Thomas Edison and the light bulb, Bill Gates and personal computer software, Ted Turner and twenty-four-hour cable television news. Given the theme of this book, Turner is especially relevant because he has been somewhat open about his mental health.

In his recent autobiography, Turner describes a difficult childhood in which his father, Ed Turner, constantly moved the boy from one boarding school to another. Forever the new kid, Turner faced more than typical childhood harassment from his peers; at one point, when he was sent away from home at age four, he felt completely abandoned. When Ted was home, Ed Turner worked his son hard and sometimes beat him. The boy was once expelled from elementary school ("I was a restless kid and got in trouble a lot. I didn't do anything really bad," Turner explains) and had poor grades, which he now attributes to his painful home life. ("Today's schools would probably jump to the conclusion that I had Attention Deficit Disorder, but that wasn't the case. After being isolated and alone for so long I was simply craving attention.")

After his father placed the troublemaker in a high school military academy, Turner evolved into an academic and social success. Urged by his father to go to the Ivy League, Turner did well at Brown initially, but then partied his way to becoming a dropout. (He attributes this reversion to conflict with his father, who refused to support him financially after Turner chose to major in classics.) Around this time, Turner also describes potentially manic symptoms, such as reckless driving. He routinely drove about 120 miles per hour from his father's vacation home in South Carolina to visit friends in Savannah, Georgia. On one such occasion, while crossing a railroad track, he narrowly missed being run over by a train. He was also a highly energetic person, a personality trait that he acknowledges. (And explains away: "I have always had a lot of energy. Every since I was little, my mind and body were active and I couldn't stand sitting around. Even today, I'm constantly moving. Purgatory for me would be spending twenty-four hours with nothing to do but to be alone with my thoughts.") His ex-wife Jane Fonda psychoanalyzes away this manic personality trait: "As a result of his upbringing, for Ted there's fear of abandonment that is deeper than with anyone I've ever known. As a result he needs constant companionship and keeping up with him can be exhausting. It's not just all the constant activity—it's his nervous energy that almost crackles in the air. He can't sit still because if you sit still the demons catch up with you. He has to keep moving."

TURNER'S SYMPTOMS ARE put into relief by his family history: Ed Turner committed suicide at the peak of his professional success, after he had built up a thriving billboard advertising company in Atlanta. Turner explains the act as the paradoxical aftermath of success; his father had achieved all his goals and was left with no new ambitions. But Turner also describes, sometimes in literal terms, a sick mind: "The fall of 1962 was an exciting time. Dad was elated—the most energized I'd ever seen him. . . . Unbeknownst to all of us, this upbeat behavior came just as he was approaching the brink of collapse. He was like an engine that runs at its fastest right before stripping the gears. My dad had always had his mood swings, but almost overnight his behavior became significantly more erratic and unpredictable. One day he'd be high as a kite and the next he'd be in a state of abject depression."

These mood swings were accompanied by paranoid and nihilistic thoughts: "My father knew the billboard business cold and while most of his advisers assured him that he wouldn't have trouble meeting his [debt] obligations, an irrational fear of losing everything began to consume him." He also began drinking and smoking more, and eventually went to a psychiatric hospital in Connecticut. Turner's recollection at this point seems to get cloudier, and he attributes his father's worsening mental state and eventual suicide to having been prescribed the wrong medicines at the hospital. "He said they were for 'his nerves,' and I'm pretty sure they included Quaaludes and a variety of other uppers and downers. In effect, my dad basically swapped alcohol and tobacco for prescription drugs." This may be true, since in 1962 antidepressants were barely known, antipsychotics were rarely used for mania, and lithium (which likely would have saved his father's life) still languished in unread journals, unused until a decade later. The most common treatments in that era were amphetamines ("uppers," which would worsen mania), and barbiturates or benzodiazepines ("downers," which could exacerbate depression but lessened anxiety and encouraged sleep). His father finally decided to sell his growing, successful company at a large discount to a competitor. Turner, who had joined the family business, argued forcefully against this, but his father signed a letter promising to sell the company, and a few days later shot himself.

Faced with his father's death, and the impending loss of the family business, twenty-one-year-old Ted, to the surprise of many, rallied the company staff, hired lawyers, negotiated with his father's competitor, and settled the agreement to sell by giving company stock to the competitor. Turner not only kept the billboard enterprise going and growing, but eventually he expanded it to radio and television.

IN LATER YEARS, Turner himself saw a psychiatrist, but now he denies severe depression or clear mania, unlike his father, attributing most of his own mental symptoms to anxiety triggered by the stresses of an active life:

> I'd had some problems with mood swings when I was a kid—probably because of being sent away at such a young age and the anxiety that my life produced. . . . Still, in the 1980s a doctor diagnosed me with bipolar depression and put me on lithium. I took this medication for a couple of years but I couldn't tell that it made much of a difference. When I switched psychiatrists, I had a thorough interview that led to a completely different diagnosis. My new doctor asked me questions like whether I ever went for long stretches without sleep (only when I was sailing, I told him), and whether I ever spent inordinate amounts of money. (We both got a chuckle out of that one. . . .) He concluded that while I definitely had an uncommon drive and still do struggle with occasional bouts of anxiety, I don't have depression, and he canceled the lithium.

The differing views of Turner's doctors reflect the state of our knowledge. Many psychiatrists in the 1980s and 1990s did not diagnose bipolar disorder: about 40 percent of people with bipolar disorder were misdiagnosed as not having it (and usually given anxiety disorder or depression labels instead, as Turner was).

For Turner, the evidence for at least some bipolar condition seems strong if we apply the four lines of diagnostic evidence, not just symptoms, but also course of illness, family history, and treatment response. His father likely had severe bipolar disorder; his mood symptoms began quite early in childhood (which is uncommon in mood conditions besides bipolar disorder); Turner's specific symptoms included decreased need for sleep (constant high energy), distractibility (self-described since childhood), agitation (being unable to sit still), notable self-confidence, rapid speech, impulsive behaviors like his reckless driving, and sexual indiscretions as documented in Jane Fonda's memoir. One might add excessive spending, but this criterion is difficult to assess in a billionaire. His self-described lack of response to lithium doesn't support the bipolar diagnosis, but it hardly rules out that interpretation either. Many people with bipolar disorder don't respond to lithium, and Turner's self-reported nonresponse would need to be verified by others, such as family and friends, who might have witnessed a change in his behavior he didn't pick up on himself. (Indeed, in 1992, Turner's female companion stated that for Turner, "lithium is a miracle"; at that time, both his ex-wife, Janie, and his wife-to-be, Jane Fonda, confirmed the benefits of lithium for Turner. Now Turner denies such benefit.) Based on Turner's own report (which can be wrong, since patients often have little insight into their own manic symptoms), his symptoms were constant, not episodic. This *course of illness*, if true, is consistent with hyperthymic personality (which is genetically related to bipolar disorder but less severe).

Though I believe Turner was a success because of, rather than despite, his bipolar symptoms, we will see below that in the long run a touch of lithium wouldn't have hurt.

HOW DID TURNER'S CONDITION, whether hyperthymic personality or bipolar disorder, affect his leadership? One might cite resilience, after his father's suicide, but in this chapter I will focus on the creativity he displayed throughout his career.

Turner likes to analogize business decisions to military methods. He compares the launch of CNN in 1980, for instance, to the methods of World War II German general Erwin Rommel: "On several occasions, the German general attacked the British when he knew he didn't have enough fuel to conduct an entire offensive. What he intended to do was strike when they weren't expecting it, overrun their lines, and then capture their fuel dumps. At that point, he could refuel his panzers and continue the offensive. My vision for financing CNN was similar." With little cash on hand, and no chance of getting decent loans, Turner launched CNN knowing he only had enough funds to run it for about a year. After that, he hoped, correctly, that it would generate enough attention that new sources of funding (through advertising, cable fees, and new loans) could be found. It was an audacious risk, certainly not standard practice in the business world. It reminds me of Sherman sending his army into southern Georgia and the Carolinas, cutting off his supply lines behind him, planning on living off the land that he would despoil along the way.

Another example of Turner's manic creativity occurred soon afterward. In its early years, when CNN survived and grew, the networks took notice. ABC planned a direct competitor to CNN, as well as a cable headline news network that would repeat the main stories hourly, as opposed to CNN's in-depth coverage. Turner saw this competition as potentially fatal to his new company: "We had already invested about $100 million in CNN and were still far from breaking even. Now, two multibillion-dollar corporations [ABC in partnership with Westinghouse] were coming at us with a dagger pointed at our heart. . . . I once again thought in military terms and reasoned that I could not afford to engage in a long, protracted war against opponents with such superior resources. I had to knock them out, and quickly." So Turner created CNN2 (now called Headline News) almost spontaneously, working feverishly to get the new channel on the air in only four months, so as to preempt ABC's proposed channel by six months. By establishing his channel first, he made ABC's plans for a headline news station more competitive and costly; ABC decided to scrap its second channel. Then to fight off the direct competitor (ABC's Satellite News Channel), Turner used his personal contacts with cable providers to get preferential exposure for CNN2. Eventually, Turner bought out ABC's channel and got rid of his competition; in so doing, he protected CNN for another decade of competition-free growth.

TURNER CLEARLY SEES HIMSELF as a divergent thinker: "Confronted with a problem, I've always looked for an unconventional angle and approach. Nothing sneaky, nothing illegal or unethical, just turning the issue on its head and shifting the advantage to our side." His great achievement—cable media (not just news, but also the first national cable station, and all-sports, all-movie, and all-cartoon networks)—entailed recognizing a new medium at its inception and jumping into it without inhibition, when others either failed to see the opportunity or hesitated to take advantage of it.

On the one hand, Turner seems to have been realistic: he saw a new field about to explode. Yet, as Shelley Taylor, the psychologist who described the notion of positive illusions, notes, entrepreneurs are unrealistic, at least initially, taking chances that may or may not work out. Whether Turner was more realistic than others because of his depression is uncertain; but his manic energy and creativity are relatively clear.

In later years (after coming off lithium), Turner made his great mistake: he joined forces with Time Warner in 1995, hoping to garner enough funds to buy one of the major networks, a lifelong goal of his. But the Atlanta entrepreneur couldn't survive within the confines of a New York corporation. He could no longer make decisions himself: his audacious moves were now vetoed by the corporation's board. By merging his business, he had lost control of it, a fact that became clear when, at the peak of the new Internet market, Time Warner merged with AOL, without consulting Turner. Within months of the announcement, the Internet stock bubble peaked, then crashed. Turner watched his net worth fall by $10 million daily, without (given his contractual obligations to Time Warner) being able to do anything about it. He waited out an 80 percent loss of his wealth, eventually sold all his stock in AOL Time Warner, and resigned.

CNN lives on, but it is no longer Ted Turner's CNN. In 1991, on Turner's personal orders, and despite pleas from the White House, the network refused to remove its reporters from Baghdad when George H. W. Bush bombed the city, thereby showing the American public the truth about what was happening there. A decade later, after Turner's exit, CNN went meekly along with other networks, "embedding" its reporters for the attack of another George Bush on Iraq, this time presenting only what the military allowed journalists to see. In the buildup and the immediate aftermath, CNN, like most of the media, followed the administration's line; there was little independent journalism or critical thinking. As Turner writes in his memoirs, he would never have let that happen if he'd still been in charge.

TED TURNER'S SUCCESSES and setbacks demonstrate how a person's mental condition fosters different kinds of leadership in the business world, just as it does in the other contexts we examine in this book. In a strong economy, the ideal business leader is the corporate type, the man who makes the trains run on time, the organizational leader. He may not be particularly creative, but he doesn't need new ideas; he only needs to keep going what's going. Arthur Koestler called this kind of executive the Commissar; much as a Soviet bureaucrat administers the state, the corporate executive administers the company. This is not a minor matter; administration is no easy task; but with this approach, all is well only when all that matters is administration.

When the economy is in crisis, when profits have fallen, when consumers no longer demand one's goods or competitors produce better ones, then the Commissar fails; the corporate executive takes a back-seat to the entrepreneur, whom Koestler called the Yogi. This is the crisis leader, the creative businessman who either produces new ideas that navigate the old company through changing times or, more often, produces new companies to meet changing needs. David Owen, a neurologist and British politician, has observed political leaders up close, and also served on corporate boards. He notes that the skills needed by successful businessmen may exceed those of great statesmen. The goals of businessmen, unlike politicians, are "defined almost exclusively in terms of growth . . . doing little or even on rare occasions nothing is sometimes a wise course in politics; that is rarely the case in business."

The Commissar is the peacetime business leader; the Yogi the crisis business leader. The best business leaders combine both qualities—doers, like Commissars, and thinkers, like Yogis—but such specimens are rare. Most leaders lean more in one direction or the other, mainly based on how they are mentally primed. In business, it seems that Ted Turner may not have understood that his mental makeup prepared him to be an excellent Yogi, but a poor Commissar. The entrepreneurial winner was a corporate failure.

PART TWO

REALISM

CHAPTER 3

HEADS I WIN, TAILS IT'S CHANCE

The psychologist Martin Seligman first set forth the highly influential "learned helplessness" theory of depression in 1967. He reasoned that depressed people see the world too negatively because they are scarred by early hardship and learn to feel helpless. Studies on animals had supported the theory, and in 1979 two of Seligman's students, Lauren Alloy and Lynn Abramson, decided to test it on undergraduates. They asked their test subjects to press a button and observe whether it turned on a green light. The subjects effectively had no control over the light; the researchers would decide whether or not to turn it on when the subjects pressed the button. In several different trials, the researchers varied how often the light came on after the button was pressed: in one experiment, it lit up 75 percent of the time; in another experiment, 50 percent; in a third, only 25 percent. Students were divided into two groups, based on tests they'd previously taken: those with no symptoms of depression, and those with some depression.

Alloy and Abramson made an unwelcome discovery: their teacher was wrong. Depressed students didn't underestimate how much control they had; normal students *overestimated* it. This observation, which they called "depressive realism," was strongest when the green light came on most often. When the light came on only 25 percent of the time after they pressed the button, about half of both depressed and normal groups realized they had no control over it. But when the light came on 75 percent of the time, only 6 percent of normal students realized they had little control versus 50 percent in the depressed group.

Aware that this artificial test didn't replicate real-world decisions because there were no performance-based rewards or penalties, the researchers introduced motivation—money. Students were told they would gain or lose up to five dollars (which was worth a lot more in 1979 than it is now) each time the green light went on. As before, the experimenters manipulated the frequency of the light. When they made money off the green light, normal students again thought they had more control over it than they actually did. But when the light meant losing money, the normal students were more realistic. In all cases, depressed students accurately judged how much control they had.

Alloy and Abramson had discovered something new: depression led to more, not less, realistic assessments of control over one's environment, an effect that was only enhanced by a real-world emotional desire, like making money. In the decades since they published their paper, their results have been replicated many times in other experiments. As counterintuitive as the idea of depressive realism may be, it is hard to deny.

A FEW YEARS EARLIER, psychologists Ellen Langer and Jane Roth had tested the concept of an "illusion of control" in our daily decisions. They devised an experiment in which ninety Yale students were asked to call out heads or tails just before thirty coin tosses. Unbeknownst to the students, the results were rigged. One group was told repeatedly, *early* in the thirty coin tosses, that their guesses were *correct* even when they weren't; this was called the *descending outcomes* group. Occasionally, researchers would show the coin to the students when they guessed right in order to reinforce the impression that they were being told the truth. The opposite, *ascending* group, was repeatedly told that their guesses were *incorrect* (even when they were right) *early* in the thirty tosses, and then more and more correct as the study went on. A third group was told the truth throughout the thirty coin tosses. Afterward, students were asked how good they thought they were at predicting coin tosses and whether they thought they could improve with practice.

The ascending and random groups were realistic: they were convinced the results were the product of chance, that they hadn't done especially well, and that they wouldn't do better with practice. But, the *descending* group thought they'd done rather well, and would do better with practice.

Langer and Roth found it remarkable that highly intelligent students at a prestigious college, who clearly knew that coin tosses are completely random events, could be fooled by early apparent success into consistently overestimating their sense of control. The researchers titled their paper "Heads I Win, Tails It's Chance" and concluded that normal people have an illusory sense of control, especially if things seem to go well for them.

Building on this work, Shelley Taylor, a psychologist at the University of California at Los Angeles, spent much of her career developing the concept of "positive illusions." Studying how we react to sickness, she first thought that normal people who became ill and then recovered would return to their former worldviews. But she found that breast cancer patients saw the experience of serious illness and subsequent recovery as transformative; they didn't just go back to being who they were. They became different, and two-thirds of them said they'd changed for the better. But this sense of well-being came at a price. Taylor dryly noted, "From many of their accounts there emerged a mildly disturbing disregard for the truth." The women emerged with a greater sense of control over their disease or their recovery than was actually the case. The typical patient consistently overestimated her likely survival compared to the known statistics and her own medical status. Interviewing the oncologists and psychotherapists who cared for these patients, the researchers found that their unrealistically optimistic attitudes correlated with *better* psychological adjustment. That is, *the psychologically healthier patients were the most unrealistic.* Taylor had discovered "positive illusion"—the opposite of depressive realism, a kind of healthy illusion found not just in a trivial button-pushing test, but in life-threatening illness.

If all this is correct—if there is depressive realism, and if there are normal illusions that have positive effects—then we have to reconsider what it means to be mentally healthy. We tend to see mental health as "being normal"—happy, realistic, fulfilled. Yet Taylor showed that we sacrifice realism in the interest of happiness. These counterintuitive data lead me to two conclusions about what it means to be normal:

1. *The skew of happiness:* Under normal conditions, normal people overestimate themselves. We think we have more control over things than we do; we're more optimistic than circumstances warrant; we exaggerate our skills, beauty, and intelligence. "Heads I win; tails it's chance" is our unconscious philosophy of life. More than a hundred separate studies have documented that people estimate themselves as more likely to experience positive events than their peers.

   One study even quantified this principle. Standardizing sixteen studies of life satisfaction on a 0 to 100 scale—with 0 reflecting abject misery and 100 bliss—the average score was 75 percent, meaning that most people are mostly happy about their lives. More important, the spread of scores was very tight: almost everyone scored between 70 and 80 percent. In fact, 90 percent of people scored above 50 percent (which would theoretically be an average level of satisfaction). In other words, there is a skew to normal life: most everyone feels happier than average, which means that "average" satisfaction is uncommon.

2. *The perils of success:* Leston Havens, a wise psychotherapist, once commented to me that he had known many people who had been improved by failure, and many ruined by success. Failure deflates illusion, while success only makes illusion worse, as shown in the coin toss and button-pushing studies (in which believing one was correct early on, or winning money, enhanced the illusion of control). Most normal, mentally healthy people have these features: they overestimate how happy they are; and when things go well, this illusion only gets worse.

This isn't a settled debate, and these interpretations could be proven wrong. But if they're correct, they raise several questions. Why do positive illusions occur? Can we only arrive at realism through personal hardship? Or are some of us inherently more likely than others to become realistic? Is depression the royal road to realism?

We tend to assume linear relationships about most things. If some is good, we presume that more is better. But for many things, there is a curvilinear relationship: too little is harmful, so is too much; in the middle is just right. Scientists call this the inverted U-curve, but we can also see it in the fairy tale about Goldilocks and the three bears, where the girl is choosing between bowls of porridge or beds until she finds the ones that are just right. We might call this the *Goldilocks principle*.

In biology, it's generally accepted that anxiety is curvilinear. A moderate amount is good for the organism, keeping it vigilant, ready to defend itself or flee. Too little would make an organism vulnerable to predators or other danger; too much would cause excessive stress, making the organism less capable of handling danger. Illusion may play a similar role, suggests Taylor, noting that most of the patients in her studies of physical illness were not completely out of touch with reality; they were far from psychotic, or even neurotic. They were basically normal people, in touch with reality, who, in relation to their medical illness, were overly optimistic. They were, in short, only *a little* unrealistic. Too little illusion, she suggests, makes us all too realistic, seeing the stark hopelessness of the facts, leading us to give up. Too much illusion, as Freudians argue, renders us unable to respond properly to the world's challenges. Positive illusion in people with medical illness is a moderate, in-between amount that helps them cope with adversity even better, to prepare responses to life's challenges and to meet them.

WHETHER ONE SUCCEEDS by luck or skill, the absence of early hardship often has a later negative effect; when difficult times arrive, one is vulnerable. Early triumph can promote future failure.

In contrast, early failures repeatedly experienced by a person predisposed to depression inoculate against future illusion. Like the ascending group in the Yale experiment, later success fails to swell one's head because one remembers one's failures and respects the role of chance in life. The philosopher Karl Jaspers once said that how a man responds to failure determines who he will become. Through suffering, one becomes more realistic about the world, and thus better able to change it. Lincoln suffered immensely; Churchill suffered much; so did Sherman. Others who were luckier in their early lives—including, as we'll see later in the book, McClellan and Neville Chamberlain—failed where the mentally ill leaders succeeded.

Of course, everyone suffers. But life's pain can come harshly or gently, earlier or later. For the lucky, suffering is less frequent, less severe, and delayed until it can't be avoided. The unlucky, who, early in their lives, endure hardships and tragedies—or the challenge of mental illness—seem to become, not infrequently, our greatest leaders.

CHAPTER 4

OUT OF THE WILDERNESS

CHURCHILL

We remember Winston Churchill the orator, the fiery leader, the man who refused to submit to tyranny, and in whose stubborn refusal a nation, and then the world, found the strength to resist and ultimately prevail. Other prominent British statesmen had failed to fill the role that Churchill rode to glory. Churchill alone emerged as the great leader, the wartime genius, the deliverer of democracy. And although some acknowledge that he had mental problems, few appreciate the relevance of those problems to his prodigious leadership abilities. I believe that Churchill's severe recurrent depressive episodes heightened his ability to realistically assess the threat that Germany posed.

One might suppose that such a great man would have to be especially whole, healthy and fit in mind and body, full of mental and spiritual capabilities that escape average men. But Churchill belied this notion. In fact, he was quite ill, and his story, if belonging to a middle-class American living in the twenty-first century, would seem a sad but typical tale of mental illness.

AS WE'VE SEEN, mental illnesses are partly genetic, and rare is the person with a severe illness who doesn't have some evidence of the same in her family. In Churchill's case, we don't have to search far: his father died insane. Lord Randolph Churchill, the eighth Duke of Marlborough, had attained political prominence quickly, as his son would later, becoming chancellor of the Exchequer by his thirties. In normal circumstances, he would have been marked for the premiership, but Lord Randolph had character flaws that would disqualify him. One of these was a special fondness for sex; he had many dalliances throughout his life, and his will provided £20,000 to a Lady Colin Campbell, known as the "sex goddess" of Victorian England.

Lord Randolph probably developed neurosyphilis (called "General Paralysis of the Insane"), which can cause manic and psychotic symptoms. In the nineteenth century, such cases were indistinguishable from schizophrenia, as defined by modern medicine. (Penicillin was used from the 1940s onward to cure neurosyphilis, hence it could be considered the most effective drug ever used for psychiatric symptoms.) Until the later development of laboratory tests for the bacterium that causes neurosyphilis, it was impossible to determine which patient had psychosis caused by syphilis and which had schizophrenia.

It complicates matters that manic-depressive illness, which also causes psychosis, and was often mistaken for schizophrenia in the past, can make patients sexually impulsive and overactive during manic episodes, often engaging in prostitution, unsafe sex, or other indiscretions. Sexually transmitted diseases (like neurosyphilis) are thus more common in people with manic-depressive illness than in the general population. Cause and effect are difficult to disentangle. Was Lord Randolph insane because he had neurosyphilis, or was he insane because he was manic-depressive, or both?

Neurosyphilis isn't genetic. Yet we'll see that Lord Randolph's son Winston had a different mental illness, as did Winston's daughter

Diana, who had a major depressive episode in 1952 and committed suicide in 1963 by barbiturate overdose (despite being active in suicide prevention efforts). Churchill's first cousin, called "Sunny," also suffered severe depressive episodes throughout his life. Thus we find a familial predisposition to severe depression among Churchill's relatives, and the presence of suicide indicates that this familial mood condition was more than a mild hereditary taint.

THE NEXT STEP is to examine Churchill's actual symptoms. There is no doubt that he had severe periods of depression; he was open about it—calling it, following Samuel Johnson, his "Black Dog." Apparently his most severe bout of depression came in 1910, when he was, at about age thirty-five, home secretary. Later in his life, he told his doctor, Lord Moran, "For two or three years the light faded from the picture. I did my work. I sat in the House of Commons, but black depression settled on me." He had thoughts of killing himself. "I don't like standing near the edge of a platform when an express train is passing through," he told his doctor. "I like to stand right back and if possible get a pillar between me and the train. I don't like to stand by the side of a ship and look down into the water. A second's action would end everything. A few drops of desperation." The desperate man of thirty-five was no different from the hero at seventy. In 1945, soon after Churchill lost his bid for reelection, Lord Moran visited his patient to find him complaining about the balcony of his new flat. "I don't like sleeping near a precipice like that," he said. "I've no desire to quit the world, but thoughts, desperate thoughts, come into the head."

Blaming someone's sadness on external events is common sense, but that approach can be as often wrong as right. In Churchill's case, it would certainly be wrong; there is no question his sadness came from within. In 1910 he was at the peak of success, one that he would not better until three decades later, after having presumed that his best days were behind him. In 1910 he was happily married, wealthy, famous, politically powerful, and widely respected. He had no reason to be depressed, much less suicidal, and he never claimed otherwise.

Churchill suffered from more than depression, though. Many historians now acknowledge his depression, but they generally don't appreciate that when he was not depressed, Churchill's moods shifted frequently. He was never "himself," because his "self" kept changing. When his depressive episodes subsided, he became another person—disagreeable and aggressive. His friend Lord Beaverbrook noted that Churchill was always either "at the top of the wheel of confidence or at the bottom of an intense depression." Said his military chief of staff, General Ismay, "He is a mass of contradictions. He's either on the crest of the wave, or in the trough: either highly laudatory, or bitterly condemnatory: either in an angelic temper, or a hell of a rage: when he isn't fast asleep he's a volcano. There are no half-measures in his make-up."

This frequent alternation between being somewhat up and somewhat down is exactly what psychiatrist Ernst Kretschmer meant by *cyclothymic* personality. Numerous physicians who knew Churchill or studied him have concurred on the view that he likely had a cyclothymic personality, which, as we now know, is biologically and genetically related to bipolar disorder. For instance, Lord Russell Brain, a famed British neurologist, knew Churchill for almost two decades and saw him as a patient for twenty visits. Lord Brain concluded that Churchill had "the drive and vitality and youthfulness of a cyclothyme." ("We are all worms," Churchill once commented, "but I do believe I am a glowworm.")

These observations suggest that when he wasn't depressed, Churchill probably had hypomanic (mild manic) symptoms: he was high in energy, highly sociable and extraverted, rapid in his thoughts and actions, and somewhat impulsive. He would routinely stay awake late into the night, with a burst of energy after midnight when in his bathrobe, he would dictate his many books and conduct much of his other work. He was incredibly productive, not only serving as a minister or prime minister for decades, but writing forty-three books in seventy-two volumes (not to mention an immense body of correspondence). There is also his courageous military service as a young man, fighting in India and the Sudan, and (when working as a journalist) even becoming a prisoner of war in South Africa during the Boer War (he escaped). Churchill was a famed, sometimes infamous, conversationalist; he dominated social settings even years before his fame, talking incessantly, vigorously, interminably. His mind never stopped; he was always thinking, always plotting and planning, whether or not he had reason to do so. Franklin Roosevelt observed this feature of Churchill's personality after the landings at Normandy, part of which involved creating artificial harbors made by sinking old ships filled with concrete one on top of the other to break the rough coast. Said FDR, "You know, that was Churchill's idea. Just one of those brilliant ideas that he has. He has a hundred a day and about four of them are good."

Since cyclothymic personality involves the constant alternation between mild manic (hypomanic) and mild depressive symptoms, and since Churchill also clearly had multiple severe depressive episodes, it seems to me that he meets the official current definition of biopolar disorder, type II (hypomania alternating with severe depression). It is also possible that he had more severe manic episodes, which we cannot fully document yet, in which case he would meet the diagnostic definition of standard bipolar disorder (also called type I).

THE *COURSE* OF his depressive episodes is also consistent with an illness because it was recurrent. His first severe episode occurred in Cuba in his early twenties; the next came in his mid-thirties as home secretary, another at age forty-one during World War I after failing in the naval battle of Gallipoli, and at least two episodes per decade into his forties and fifties, which included the famed Wilderness years. His fifties were a particularly dark decade, when he was seen as politically washed up, rejected by his own Conservative Party as well as his enemies. Like Lincoln, he seemed less symptomatic during his period of greatest renown, in his sixties and onward. Yet by then doctors were treating him with amphetamines, and he actively self-medicated with alcohol. Even so, there is some documentation of manic-like symptoms, and depression, even when the war was going well. In July 1943, Anthony Eden's private secretary noted, "The PM was in a crazy state of exultation. The battle has gone to the old man's head. The quantities of liquor he consumed—wine, brandies, whiskies—were incredible." In late spring 1944, Roy Jenkins notes that Churchill showed "great fluctuation of mood, with bursts of energy and indeed brilliance of performance intervening in a general pattern of lassitude and gloom. . . ."

Churchill never fully evaded his melancholic attitude, even after he became a legend. Toward the end of his life, he considered himself a failure. Montague Brown, a companion in his later years, wrote, "He felt that everything he had done had ended in disaster. He had won the war but lost the Empire, communism had swallowed up half of Europe, and socialism was threatening the world he loved at home." In his seventies, he told his daughter, "I have achieved a great deal to achieve nothing in the end."

Treatment is the last source of evidence, and Churchill was treated for his moods throughout his life. We have no evidence that he received much treatment that was specifically psychiatric, mainly because the first psychiatric medications weren't discovered until the 1950s. However, his doctor, Lord Moran, gave Churchill amphetamines at least in the 1950s, and possibly earlier. Amphetamines are effective antidepressants and were the most commonly used drugs for depression in the 1930s and 1940s; they're sometimes prescribed for depression even now.

He also self-medicated with liquor. "I have taken more out of alcohol," he averred, "than alcohol has taken out of me." In fact, most historians have seen alcohol as a rationale for his moodiness, making a cause out of what may have been an effect. His daily routine involved drinking whiskey and soda soon after breakfast, having champagne at lunch, another whiskey and soda in late afternoon (followed by a nap), then dinner at eight, usually with multiple drinks. After midnight,

Churchill would do most of his writing, with the help of some night-caps. ("I could not live without champagne," he said. "In victory I deserve it. In defeat I need it.") Once, when he was hit by a car and suffered a concussion during a visit to Prohibition-era New York, he even obtained a doctor's note to certify medical necessity for alcohol consumption. People with bipolar disorder often abuse alcohol. When they're depressed, anxious, and restless, alcohol soothes them; when they're manic and they can't control their impulses, alcohol serves them—along with sex and spending—as an appetite to be indulged.

Most historians have also ignored Churchill's mood swings. The psychiatrist Anthony Storr took the view that Churchill's manic depression helped him by making him a bit grandiose, luckily for England:

In 1940, when all the odds were against Britain, a leader of sober judgment might well have concluded that we were finished. . . . In 1940, any political leader might have tried to rally Britain with brave words, although his heart was full of despair. But only a man who had known and faced despair within himself could carry conviction at such a moment. Only a man who knew what it was to discern a gleam of hope in a hopeless situation, whose courage was beyond reason, and whose aggressive spirit burned at its fiercest when he was hemmed in and surrounded by enemies, could have given emotional reality to the words of defiance which rallied and sustained us in the menacing summer of 1940. Churchill was such a man: and it was because, all his life, he had conducted a battle with his own despair that he could convey to others that despair can be overcome.

I think Storr misses a deeper wisdom in Churchill's mental illness: not the supposed grandiosity of his manic temperament, but rather the realism of his depressive suffering. Perhaps the key to finding a link between this melancholic Churchill and his political realism can be found in the era of his political exile, the Wilderness years.

In the period between the two world wars, Winston Churchill, out of power and sidelined by his own Conservative Party, was seen as a peripheral and somewhat curmudgeonly political has-been. In 1924, in his last cabinet post as chancellor of the Exchequer, he showed minimal understanding of economics, and was off target (as with his strident opposition to the rising labor unions) in his domestic policies. His foreign policy fared little better: a war-weary nation cringed when Churchill wanted to send more troops to India rather than negotiate peaceful independence with that "half-naked little fakir," Mohandas Gandhi.

Churchill did not fit the times. In the 1920s and 1930s, the leader of the Conservative Party, Stanley Baldwin—a man esteemed by all, including Churchill—appeased his conservative base while also compromising with the Labour leader, Ramsay MacDonald, who exuded the same basic attitude (some leftists called MacDonald the "Boneless Wonder" for his penchant to compromise). For about a decade, the two men led a government of national unity, one that excluded Winston Churchill.

CHURCHILL WAS NOT part of the national unity club of the interwar peace primarily because his military views conflicted sharply with those of his peers. Churchill wanted to rearm England to prepare for the Nazi threat; he foresaw war. His peers opposed military spending and couldn't fathom the reality of the German danger. For instance, the Duke of Westminster—best man in Churchill's wedding, and widely viewed as England's richest man—was an openly anti-Semitic supporter of Nazi Germany. Lord Londonderry—a cousin to Churchill and head of the Air Ministry in the years 1931–1935—consistently rejected Churchill's calls to expand British air forces. Londonderry even hosted Hitler's aristocratic emissary, Count von Ribbentrop, during a 1935 visit to England. Sir John Simon, Baldwin's foreign secretary, called Hitler "an Austrian Joan of Arc with a moustache." Even Churchill's closest political mentor, the former World War I prime minister David Lloyd George, called Hitler "a born leader, a magnetic dynamic personality with a single-minded purpose," and concluded, "I only wish we had a man of his supreme quality at the head of affairs in our country." The royal family itself had pro-German sympathies; the Prince of Wales (the future King Edward VIII) told a German prince in 1933, "It was no business of ours to interfere in Germany's internal affairs either [regarding] Jews or anything else. . . . Dictators are very popular these days and we might want one in England before long." King George V was explicit: "I will not have another war. I will not. The last one was none of my doing and if there is another one, and we are threatened with being brought into it, I will go to Trafalgar Square [where demonstrators traditionally gathered] myself sooner than allow the country to be brought in."

Baldwin was ambivalent about Churchill. When Churchill sent signed copies of his books to Baldwin, the prime minister would write letters of praise in return. But deep down, the Conservative leader looked askance at the unpredictable Churchill, telling a friend in 1936, "When Winston was born lots of fairies swooped down on his cradle gifts—imagination, eloquence, industry, ability, and then came a fairy who said 'No person has a right to so many gifts,' picked him up and gave him such a shake and twist that with all these gifts he was denied judgment and wisdom . . . [which is why] while we delight to listen to him in this House we do not take his advice." Many assume that Churchill's isolation made him depressed; it may be that Churchill's depression made him isolated. Churchill was relegated to the Wilderness, by Baldwin and others, because his unconventional persona (partly reflecting his mood illness) provided an excuse to ignore his sadly realistic political judgment. Baldwin groomed another successor: Neville Chamberlain.

The contrast between Churchill and Chamberlain in their approach to Nazism is well known. Where Churchill began to warn about the Nazi threat as early as October 1930, Chamberlain remained oblivious as late as his fateful Munich visit in 1938. Chamberlain wanted to establish personal relations with Hitler, to meet him, to rationally *convince* him of the need to avoid war.

After his first meeting with Hitler, Chamberlain convinced himself that he had been right: "In spite of the hardness and ruthlessness I thought I saw in his face, I got the impression that here was a man who could be relied upon when he had given his word." Chamberlain met Hitler three times in all; before the third trip, as he announced his plan in the House of Commons, most members stood and cheered. A few, like Churchill, remained seated, despite angry reproaches from nearby colleagues. In September 1938, while Chamberlain had dinner with Hitler in Munich, Churchill supped with two anti-Nazi MPs and steamed, "How could honourable men with wide experience and fine records in the Great War condone a policy so cowardly? It is sordid, squalid, sub-human, and suicidal."

What made Churchill see the truth where Chamberlain saw only illusion? A key difference was that Chamberlain was mentally healthy (which we'll discuss more in chapter 14), while Churchill was clearly not.

Churchill never surrendered to the black dog that gnawed at him from the inside. Having survived thus far, he didn't intend to surrender to other dogs, whether Hitler or Mussolini. He had courage beyond reason, as Storr put it, because he had faced death many times before 1940, and not only during pitched battles fought in exotic lands, but within his daily life. His doctor, Lord Moran, relates a discussion with Viscount Brendan Bracken, a longtime Churchill friend, who remarked, "Winston has always been a 'despairer.' Orpen, who painted him after the Dardanelles debacle, used to speak of the misery in his face. He called him the man of misery. . . . Then, in his years in the wilderness, before the Second War, he kept saying, 'I'm finished.' He said that about twice a day. He was quite certain that he would never get back to office, for everyone seemed to regard him as a wild man. . . . Winston has always been wretched unless he was occupied. You know what he has been like since he resigned [the office of prime minister in 1946]. Why, he told me that he prays every day for death."

———

A SKEPTICAL READER might argue that Churchill was just a pessimist, always imagining the worst; his negativism just happened to be correct in the 1930s. Or one might think of him as an anomaly, an exception to the conventional wisdom that mental illness impairs leadership. Neither is the case.

Churchill is hardly the only example of depressive realism; we'll meet others elsewhere in this book—Lincoln, Gandhi, and Martin Luther King Jr. among them. One can see depressive realism playing out in a wide variety of circumstances: it guided Churchill and Lincoln to realize that war was necessary; it led Gandhi and King to reject violence. It is mistaken to focus only on Churchill, as some do, and view realism as a rationale for war, a logic for jingoism. Our greatest proponents of peace were also depressive realists.

CHAPTER 5

BOTH READ THE SAME BIBLE

LINCOLN

Historians have written more books about Abraham Lincoln than any other American political leader, and yet they hadn't fully studied his depression until recently. In *Lincoln's Melancholy*, Joshua Wolf Shenk lays out the case for the beneficial impact of depression on Lincoln's leadership, especially in how the disease fostered empathy and tenacity. Here we'll focus on how Lincoln's depression enhanced his political realism.

First, as with Churchill, we should establish the reality of Lincoln's mental illness. Lincoln undeniably experienced *symptoms* of depression. Historians only disagreed about whether such depression represented mental illness. Here is an account of his most severe depressive symptoms, which began shortly after his proposal of marriage was spurned: "In early January 1841, Abraham Lincoln was in very poor shape. He began to miss votes in the legislature. . . . The next week he missed many sessions. . . . 'Lincoln you know as desponding and melancholy . . .' wrote Edwin Webb. . . . 'He has grown much worse and is now confined to his bed sick in body and mind.'"

Just before this episode, Lincoln had pseudonymously published a poem on suicide. Earlier, in 1835, after the death of a young woman whom he loved, he had been actively suicidal:

> Lincoln "told me that he felt like committing suicide often," remembered Mentor Graham, and his neighbors mobilized to keep him safe. One friend recalled, "Mr. Lincoln's friends . . . were compelled to keep watch and ward over Mr. Lincoln, he being from the sudden shock somewhat temporarily deranged. . . ." Another villager said, "Lincoln was locked up by his friends . . . to prevent derangement or suicide." People wondered whether Lincoln had fallen off the deep end. "That was the time the community said he was crazy," remembered Elizabeth Abell. . . . After several weeks of worrisome behavior—talking about suicide, wandering alone in the woods with his gun—an older couple in the area [Mr. and Mrs. Bowling Green] took him into their home. . . . When he had improved somewhat, they let him go, but he was, Mrs. Green said, "quite melancholy for months."

In the 1840s, Lincoln admitted to a fellow politician that he "was the victim of terrible melancholy" at times, and thus never carried a pocketknife; he couldn't trust himself with it.

REGARDING *FAMILY HISTORY*, insanity and melancholy abounded in the Lincoln clan. Lincoln's father was gloomy; a neighbor commented that he "often got the 'blues,' and had some strange sort of spells, and wanted to be alone all he could when he had them." As Shenk recounts, other Lincolns also suffered:

> His great-uncle once told a court of law that he had "a deranged mind." His uncle Mordecai Lincoln had broad mood swings, which were probably intensified by heavy drinking. And Mordecai's family was thick with mental disease. All three of his

sons—who bore a strong physical resemblance to their first cousin Abraham—were considered melancholy men. . . . One of these Lincoln cousins swung wildly between melancholia and mania and at times had a tenuous grip on reality, writing letters and notes that suggest madness. Another first cousin of Lincoln's had a daughter committed to the Illinois State Hospital for the Insane. . . . One family member who had frequent spells of intense mental trouble referred to his condition as "the Lincoln horrors."

Regarding the *course* of his illness, Lincoln suffered his first severe depressive episode early in life, at age twenty-six, which is typical for this disease. He would recover from each episode (also typical), be well for a time, and then suffer another episode. (The next severe depression occurred at age thirty-two.) Life experiences triggered the episodes (the death of his love interest in the first episode, the refusal of a marriage proposal in the second, his imminent marriage in a third). For a century, historians mistook these environmental triggers as the sole causes of Lincoln's melancholy. In middle age, his depressive episodes tapered off, leaving him at a mildly depressed baseline personality. As the Civil War dragged on, he became more morose, and then, after he lost his eleven-year-old son Willie to typhoid fever in 1862, he probably went into a final severe depression. In April 1865, when he went to see a play at Ford's Theater, he was only beginning to recover.

Doctors also *treated* Lincoln's mental illness. In 1841, Dr. Anson Henry intensively medicated the thirty-two-year-old state legislator. A friend related, "The Doctors say he is within an inch of being a perfect lunatic for life. He was perfectly crazy for some time, not able to attend to his business at all. They say he don't look like the same person." Doctors apparently told Lincoln that he suffered from "hypochondriasm," then as now a descriptor of physical symptoms originating from mental causes. In an age of "great and dangerous cures" based on little science, the most common treatment for mental illness—whether termed hypochondriasis, melancholia, or insanity—was *bleeding:* the removal of blood by the application of leeches to suck, or by using a lancet to cut. The theory, going back to the ancient Roman physician Galen, was that bleeding would put the body's "humors" (fluids or substances: blood, phlegm, black bile, and yellow bile) back into balance. Other approaches that sought to balance the humors involved purgatives (which induced vomiting) or laxatives. Doctors also recommended extremely cold showers. Dr. Henry adhered to these views and prescribed mercury tablets (Lincoln called them "my blue pills") for their purgative and laxative effects. He probably also bled Lincoln. Doctors treated Lincoln intensively, but they could not help him; no Prozac existed to lift his gloom even for a day, and he knew it. He wrote in 1841, "I am now the most miserable man living. If what I feel were equally distributed to the whole human family, there would not be one cheerful face on the earth. Whether I shall ever be better I can not tell; I awfully forebode I shall not. To remain as I am is impossible; I must die or be better, it appears to me."

LINCOLN SUFFERED FROM severe depression, probably a version of manic-depressive illness (as was common in his relatives), more severe on the depressive side, with only mild symptoms, in his younger years, of high energy and "fun and hilarity without restraint" (according to a fellow politician).

Most of the time, Lincoln was a highly depressed, even suicidal man. Yet his depression conferred upon him, I believe, realism and empathy that helped make him a superb crisis leader. In his personal letters of the 1850s, one sees Lincoln's notable empathy when he describes seeing shackled slaves on a steamboat in 1841, and when he reacts to the white supremacist attitudes of the 1840s "Know-Nothing" movement:

> As a nation, we began by declaring that "*all men are created equal.*"
> We now practically read it "all men are created equal, *except*

Negroes." When the Know-Nothings get control, it will read "all men are created equal, except Negroes, *and foreigners, and Catholics.*" When it comes to this I should prefer emigrating to some country where they make no pretense of loving liberty—to Russia, for instance, where despotism can be taken pure, and without the base alloy of hypocrisy. (italics in original)

This natural empathy was tempered with hardy realism, even ruthlessness. The great man was not a consistent abolitionist. Lincoln opposed slavery, but until 1863 he also opposed abolishing it. He was the compromise Republican candidate in 1860, seen as a moderate who might still reach a peaceful accord with the South.

Lincoln saw a harsh and complex reality: the Constitution specifically sanctioned slavery. The South was fully within its constitutional rights to insist that slavery be protected. Lincoln the lawyer understood the law; but Lincoln the man believed that slavery was wrong; and Lincoln the politician realized that abolitionist views were spreading. Sooner or later, the Constitution would have to be altered and slavery outlawed; *how* was the problem.

Lincoln strongly opposed what actually happened, the violent ending of slavery in the South. He had preferred a containment strategy, preventing its expansion to the West, after which it would die out gradually. In a counterfactual world, if there had been no Civil War, slavery probably would have withered away within a few decades. It had been outlawed in the British Commonwealth by the 1840s after public opinion gradually but inevitably turned against it, and it ended in its last outpost, Brazil, by 1888. It would have died in the South eventually, with or without war. Lincoln was realistic in his attempt to compromise: his policy of "containment" might well have worked if given a chance.

It is no accident that Lincoln's greatest political hero was Senator Henry Clay, from the border state of Kentucky, the great compromiser of 1850. Lincoln, like Gandhi, admired compromise. Gandhi thought that sincere negotiation—extensive efforts at compromise—needed to fail fully before any nonviolent action began. Nonviolent resistance, like war, was a last resort, not an initial tactic. Lincoln pursued a similar philosophy throughout the 1850s, to the exasperation of abolitionists. After Fort Sumter, he realized that compromise was lost. He had hoped that slavery could be ended peacefully, but he was not given that option.

Before the war, then, Lincoln tried to be a truly national leader, sympathizing with both North and South, and thus distrusted by both. Despite his efforts, and a realistic assessment of what could have been, both extremes in North and South united to bring on a war that Lincoln had feverishly striven to avoid. When it came, Lincoln realistically turned to winning it.

LIKE MOST NORTHERNERS, the new president initially hoped the war could end speedily—an aberrant revolt quickly put down, like the Whiskey Rebellion of 1786. So he continued to push his moderate agenda: maintain the Union; limit, but do not abolish, slavery. He tried not to provoke greater Southern resentment than already existed, especially in the border states. Said the realist president, "I would like to have God on my side, but I must have Kentucky." (Kentucky remained in the Union, despite being a slave state.) He believed that though slavery was evil, its solution did not entail equal civil rights. Instead, he proposed returning American blacks to their "homeland," the new state of Liberia in West Africa. In August 1862, black leaders who met with Lincoln in the White House were struck by his insensitivity. He called slavery the "greatest wrong inflicted on any people," but denied any possibility of racial equality. It was a fact, he stated, not a matter for debate that "you and we are different. . . . It is better for us both, therefore, to be separated." His visitors felt he was lecturing them on this subject, rather than discussing it with them. Frederick Douglass wasn't present at this meeting, but when he was told about it, he felt compelled to write a scathing attack on Lincoln.

This is not the Abraham Lincoln of schoolbook lore: this realistic president was shrewd, even harsh. He was the ultimate politician, trying to keep all sides happy. He also could be a ruthless politician, willing to sacrifice his natural allies to mollify his strident enemies.

Yet one year after this meeting, Lincoln would issue the Emancipation Proclamation; he would give up all pretense of saving slavery anywhere or of avoiding hurt feelings among its sympathizers; he never spoke of repatriation to Africa again; and beginning in 1863, he began to arm American blacks, eventually putting about 150,000 former slaves in the Union army, along with another 40,000 blacks who had been free before the war; in total, blacks would eventually compose more than 10 percent of the Union force. Douglass became a Lincoln supporter, and in 1864 the first black invitee to a presidential inaugural ball. In the East Room of the White House, amid many prominent celebrants, Lincoln called out, "Here comes my friend Douglass. I am glad to see you. I saw you in the crowd today, listening to my inaugural address; how did you like it?" When Douglass briefly replied positively, Lincoln announced to all around him, "There is no man in the country whose opinion I value more than yours."

Lincoln's power should not be overstated: Congress, pushed by the abolitionist radicals, led the way on emancipation. Emancipation was already a reality: tens of thousands of Southern slaves liberated themselves by deserting to the Union lines. But Lincoln saw this reality, and he was enough of a realist to know that he must change his position quickly to adapt to it.

Some historians think the war changed Lincoln, making him more empathic with American blacks. Equally important, I think, was Lincoln's evolving realistic assessment of what racial relations would become in postwar America. Between the cold 1862 meeting with black leaders and the Emancipation Proclamation a year later, much blood was shed: Chancellorsville, Fredericksburg, Antietam. Lincoln realized that this war had only just begun, and that no rapid resolution and reconstruction was possible. The Union had been dissolved, as a matter of fact, and it would not be restored easily.

LINCOLN CLEARLY EMPATHIZED with slaves, yet his equally strong realism had prevented him from subscribing to radical abolitionism. His war experiences, in particular the gallantry of black soldiers in the Union army, made him empathize even more with blacks. In March 1864, he gave a speech to Indiana soldiers in which he commented, "Whenever I hear anyone arguing for slavery, I feel a strong impulse to see it tried on him personally." Meanwhile, the real political and social facts had also changed forever.

By 1864, Lincoln knew that the status quo ante could not be restored: Southern slavery could never return. And yet the South would not accept pure equality. How were these two opposing realities to be reconciled? Lincoln struggled with this conundrum in his final year, as all of America would for decades thereafter.

Perhaps Lincoln would have done no better than Andrew Johnson and President Grant and others. We cannot say. There were so many problems to wrestle with: profound racial hatred, an exhausted nation, a demobilizing army; so many wounds, so little balm. But Lincoln's second inaugural address at least suggests a general line of thinking that seems to interweave realism and empathy in a manner rarely seen among American presidents. Even after Gettysburg and Vicksburg and the destruction of Atlanta, in the face of approaching military victory, Lincoln unfurled no "Mission Accomplished" banners. He did not bask in success; instead, he reached out to his enemies, tried to commune with them, presaging Martin Luther King's advice that when your enemy is most vulnerable, when you could hurt him badly, *that* is when you must not do it. A psychological wisdom, a mix of realism and empathy, lay behind these classic words:

> Both read the same Bible and pray to the same God, and each invokes His aid against the other. . . . The prayers of both could not be answered. That of neither has been answered fully. The Almighty

has His own purposes. . . . If God wills that [the war] continue until all the wealth piled by the bonds-man's two hundred and fifty years of unrequited toil shall be sunk, and until every drop of blood drawn with the lash shall be paid with another drawn by the sword, as was said three thousand years ago, so still it must be said "the judgments of the Lord are true and righteous altogether."

With malice toward none, with charity for all, with firmness in the right as God gives us to see the right, let us strive on to finish the work we are in, to bind up the nation's wounds, to care for him who shall have borne the battle and for his widow and his orphan, to do all which may achieve and cherish a just and lasting peace among ourselves and with all nations.

IN RECONSTRUCTION YEARS, an us-against-them mentality evolved in both North and South. The few leaders of unimpeachable stature, like Lee in the South and Sherman in the North, refused to risk their reputations to heal festering resentments. An exception was ex-Confederate General James Longstreet, then a New Orleans–based Republican, who, after publicly expressing support for voting rights for blacks, was branded a "traitor" and a "scalawag" in an 1867 editorial in the *New Orleans Times*, which was widely reprinted throughout the South. The problems of Reconstruction seemed intractable, among them: How could black civil and voting rights be protected, while Southern white opinion was gradually directed toward incorporating the black minority into its civic life?

In the end, the Civil War replaced slavery with segregation. The nation would have to wait for another depressive leader to end another century of racism. Only the radically empathic politics of Martin Luther King's nonviolent resistance movement would complete that great task that remained. Lincoln had ended slavery legally; King would end it morally. The first had required military force; the second needed soul-force.

PART THREE
EMPATHY

CHAPTER 6

MIRROR NEURON ON THE WALL

Love, *agape*, *empathy*—whether in English, Greek, or modern jargon, human life entails this basic principle: dependence of everyone on everyone else, the existential equality of all persons. When depressed, one *knows* the truth of empathy—that our fundamental similarities make us feel similarly—more viscerally and painfully than normal people do. We've already seen the extent to which Lincoln and Sherman drew on their empathy. A few leaders, like Mahatma Gandhi and Martin Luther King Jr., who were intimately familiar with depression, made empathy the core of their political method. The *politics of radical empathy*, I believe, is the psychological underpinning of nonviolent resistance. Depression reveals the truth of empathy, and empathy, in turn, engenders unexpected powers of leadership.

Negative emotions like pain and suffering have generated more psychiatric interest than positive ones like empathy. Putting the self-help genre aside, serious works on empathy are rare. What little we know scientifically is of recent vintage. The very term didn't exist until the 1850s (originally to express how one appreciates a work of art, like a painting), and was applied to psychology in 1903 by the German physician Theodor Lipps. *Einfühlung* was the word he applied: *Ein* means "into," and *Fühlung* means "feeling." Thus empathy was *feeling into* another person's experience. Though this has been the usual interpretation, empathy can be equally interpreted to mean "one feeling," reflecting not so much imagining oneself in another person's place but actually experiencing what the other person is experiencing. Though the concept of empathy originated in an aesthetic sensibility of beauty, Lipps adapted it to the realm of human suffering. Indeed, the English translation, made by 1910, captures this usage from Greek roots: *em* means "into," *pathos* is "suffering"—"into suffering." Ten years after Lipps, Karl Jaspers made empathy central to psychiatry, a revolutionary idea at the time. (Jaspers divided all mental illness into those conditions with which one could empathize, such as depression and anxiety, and those with which one could not empathize, like schizophrenia.) Jaspers's insight was ignored by psychoanalysis and behaviorism, the two strongest currents of twentieth-century psychology. In recent years, though, empathy has made a comeback, sparked from an unexpected quarter for such a touchy-feely concept: neuroscience.

THE NEUROBIOLOGY OF EMPATHY begins with the observation that only 3 percent of animals are monogamous. Besides humans, the only other monogamous primate species is the orangutan; chimpanzees, our closest evolutionary cousins, are highly polygamous. Researchers have long wondered about this disparity, and what might constitute the biological basis of monogamy. These questions led them to the biology of empathy.

The humble vole (genus *Microtus*) proved centrally important. The prairie vole (*Microtus ochrogaster*) is monogamous, but the montane vole (*Microtus montanus*) is polygamous. Thomas Insel and associates at the National Institute of Mental Health found that the brain hormone oxytocin affects the bonding and sexual habits of these rodents.

The brain of the monogamous prairie vole contains many oxytocin receptors, especially in regions involving emotion processing. In contrast, the polygamous montane vole has few oxytocin receptors, and they occur in brain regions less involved with processing emotions. These neurological differences may produce changes in behavior: montane voles live by themselves; prairie voles live together as male/female pairs. The only time montane voles briefly cohabit is immediately after the birth of babies, when the mother nurses and raises her offspring. During that period, oxytocin receptors markedly increase in the mother montane vole's brain.

Oxytocin is the sex hormone par excellence: its levels spike during sexual activity between voles. But oxytocin has broader social effects; it is a kind of glue that bonds living things together. If oxytocin is injected into prairie voles, they have sex. If researchers prevent them from having sex, and then give them a shot of oxytocin, the voles groom and snuggle each other. (These effects are less visible in the montane vole, because of its relatively few oxytocin receptors.) In mice, one can remove the entire oxytocin receptor gene experimentally, producing animals without any oxytocin receptors at all. In these poor creatures, social memory is absent: such a mouse can't recall another mouse it met before, and each mouse isolates itself from other mice. In humans, as in voles, oxytocin activity peaks during orgasm, and is high during childbirth and breastfeeding.

In short, oxytocin is something like a love drug that produces feelings of emotional attachment in socially significant moments—like sex or breastfeeding. Its constant presence is associated with sociability, its absence with isolation. One might well wonder whether people with great empathy naturally have lots of oxytocin receptors.

THE NEXT HINT about empathy came from studying macaques, long the subjects of research by Giacomo Rizzolatti and his associates at the University of Parma, Italy. The NIMH scientists discovered *how* empathy worked in the brain; the Italian scientists discovered *where* empathy worked in the brain. When a macaque moved his arm or leg, the motor cortex of its brain lit up as expected; the motor cortex oversees the body's movements. But a few other parts of the brain lit up as well: the insula, which is involved in processing emotions, and the anterior cingulate gyrus, a large collection of fibers at the center of the brain that unite its two hemispheres. This was interesting; why were these extra parts of the brain lighting up, even though they didn't control any muscle movement?

Even more interesting, the researchers discovered that when one of them moved his hand in view of the macaque, the monkey's insula and cingulate gyrus lit up, *but not the motor cortex*. Then one monkey was placed in front of another: monkey A moved his hand; in the brain of *monkey B, a different monkey*, again the insula and cingulate gyrus became active, but not the motor cortex. The brain acted *as if* the experimental monkey were moving his hand when in fact the monkey was only watching someone else moving his hand. These neurons "mirrored" the activity of another being. Similar research has since shown that some of the neurons that fire when one feels pain will also fire when he witnesses someone else in pain. Here is empathy itself, lighting up on a brain scan. Coining the term "mirror neuron system," researchers found that 10 percent of the human brain is wired to turn on as if it is *doing* what it is only *observing*.

One-tenth of the brain is wired for empathy.

ALL OF THIS RESEARCH adds up to one conclusion: empathy is not a vague concept; it is a neurobiological fact. We are wired, literally, to feel the movements, emotions, and pain of others. So we should take empathy seriously, including its psychological effects. Psychologists divide empathy into different parts—cognitive, affective, motor, and sensory—distinctions that, though a bit abstract, are useful. *Cognitive* empathy means thinking another person's thoughts: I recognize that you have your own set of thoughts, and I try to understand what those thoughts are. *Affective* empathy involves feeling an emotion that another person feels: I am sad when I see that you're sad; one baby starts to cry, others follow suit. *Motor* empathy relates to moving the way another moves: the infant sees an adult smile, and she smiles. *Sensory* empathy means feeling a physical sensation that another person feels: you're in pain, and then I am; you're nauseated, and I feel it too. This experience happens sometimes during pregnancy, when the male partner can experience a woman's morning sickness, bloating, and even pain during contractions. Doctors call it pseudocyesis, or false pregnancy—the ultimate empathy.

There's a reason we're wired for empathy. We can't understand each other through words alone; we need to touch, to feel, to stroke each other emotionally and even physically. It is generally estimated that at least one-half of human communication is nonverbal. This is an incredible and underappreciated fact. No wonder emotionally charged emails and text messages are so easily misunderstood; they tell only half the story. Just as important as the content of one's message is the tone with which one delivers it, the expression on one's face, even one's posture. Without empathy, we can barely communicate with each other. Empathy is, it seems, central to the human (and rodent and primate) experience.

BESIDES BEING BORN with plenty of oxytocin receptors, how can one attain a high degree of empathy? One answer, I believe, is to be depressed. In one study, severely depressed patients had much higher scores on empathy scales than a college student control group; the more depressed patients were, the higher their empathy scores. This enhanced empathy was emotional, not cognitive; it reflected an actual sensation of sharing others' feelings, not merely an intellectual understanding of those feelings. This research suggests an important conclusion: when the depressive episode is over (and, short of suicide, all depressive periods end, usually within a year after they start), the intense experience of emotional identification with others might leave a lasting mental legacy. Emotional empathy, produced by the severe depressive episode, may prepare the mind for a long-term habit of appreciating others' points of view.

This is suggested by another study, in which patients with various psychiatric illnesses (depression, schizophrenia, personality and anxiety disorders) completed an empathy scale and measures of current or past suicidal thoughts or attempts. Various scales have been developed to measure empathy; they involve self-description of how often one appears to understand the emotions or thoughts of others. The Interpersonal Reactivity Index, used in this study, consists of twenty-eight questions that measure four behaviors: "perspective taking" or "the tendency to spontaneously adopt the psychological view of others in everyday life"; "empathic concern" or "the tendency to experience feelings of sympathy or compassion for unfortunate others"; "personal distress" or the "tendency to experience distress or discomfort in response to extreme distress in others"; and "fantasy" or "the tendency to imaginatively transpose oneself into fictional situations." These patients were in standard outpatient treatment and had few if any symptoms of their disease at the time of the study. They then read a brief story about a woman who committed suicide by overdose. Researchers expected that those subjects who were or had been suicidal would sympathize with the woman in the story, but in fact those who had never been suicidal were more sympathetic. The exceptions were depressed subjects with past suicidality; they were especially sympathetic to the story.

This correlation between depression and empathy shouldn't surprise mental health professionals. Maybe nothing is more important than empathy in the daily work of the mental health specialist;

nothing—not drugs or any specific psychotherapeutic technique. Subsequent studies have found that patients' ratings of their psychotherapists' empathy predict improvement for depression, even with treatments (like cognitive-behavioral therapy) that do not emphasize empathy.

Empathy seems central to the experience of depression, and just as central to its treatment. You are wired to experience it in your brain and in your body, and it thereby becomes central to your mental life. This is how things are for most of us, and perhaps more so for those who experience depression.

DEPRESSION DEEPENS our natural empathy, and produces someone for whom the inescapable web of interdependence (one of Martin Luther King's phrases) is a personal reality, not a fanciful wish. Depression cultivates empathic experience, ripens it, until, in a select few, it blooms into exemplary abilities.

Thus arises the empathic leader, a person sometimes so arresting that the rest of us become convinced he must be an otherworldly saint, a uniquely great soul, an anomalous event. He may be all those—but perhaps his secret is more prosaic: the common yet profound imprint of depression.

Mahatma Gandhi and Martin Luther King are the bookends of depressive activism, the innovators of a new politics of radical empathy that didn't exist before Gandhi and hasn't persisted after King. Though their countries and the world remain deeply influenced by their legacies, neither India nor the United States could now be said to exemplify the nonviolent ideals of these men. Their politics of radical empathy could not be maintained by leaders who lacked their vision—and their illness. They both attempted suicide as teenagers, endured at least one depressive episode in midlife, and suffered a very severe depressive episode in their final years, before they were killed. They each pushed the politics of empathy to its limits, and found their followers—the mass of normal humankind—unable to keep up with them.

Each man is now sanctified in the public mind, but few of us really appreciate them for who they were, for their weaknesses as well as their strengths, for the rejection they faced during their lives, and the depression they repeatedly endured and—in their empathy for others' suffering—ultimately overcame.

CHAPTER 7

THE WOES OF
MAHATMAS

GANDHI

Mahatma Gandhi was depressed. He also pioneered the politics of nonviolent resistance. I believe these two facts are related. His global impact is well known, but his depression is less so. As we'll see in this chapter, he suffered from at least three major depressive episodes, and he had a dysthymic personality, an abnormal temperament of chronic mild depression and anxiety, which is genetically and biologically related to severe depressive illness.

To say that Gandhi was mentally unusual is not news. The psychoanalyst Erik Erikson saw the Mahatma's inclusive and peaceful approach as a "maternal" politics, related to his identification with his mother. Such psychoanalytic speculation aside, no historian has seriously examined the potential effects of Gandhi's depression on his politics and worldview.

FIRST, LET'S QUICKLY ESTABLISH the fact of Gandhi's depression, using the four indicators we've used earlier in this book: symptoms, genetics, course of illness, and treatment. Beginning with *symptoms*, Gandhi clearly suffered a severe depressive episode in the final two years of his life. He was open about this bout of depression, even mentioning it in his speeches. Most historians attribute this episode to disillusionment with Hindu-Muslim partition. It may not be so simple. Said one aide, "I watched day after day the wan, sad look on that pinched face, bespeaking an inner anguish that was frightening to behold." Another aide noted that he "was literally praying that God should gather him into his bosom and deliver him from the agony which life had become."

This final severe depression was preceded by what likely was Gandhi's first depressive episode as a teenager, during which he attempted suicide. In his 1931 *Autobiography*, Gandhi himself describes this incident (unlike Martin Luther King, who similarly attempted suicide in adolescence but never wrote or spoke about it publicly). Yet the Mahatma may have concealed more than he revealed. He downplayed the event, focused more on the shame of stealing cigarettes than the suicide attempt. Erikson, for one, took Gandhi's cue when summarizing the Mahatma's childhood:

> He was very shy and withdrawn, unable to be critical of his elders. . . . Married too early, he was driven by a carnal desire which might have debilitated and even killed both him and his wife had they not lived separately for prolonged periods. . . . [He was] trying desperately to reform a Muslim boy who, in turn, went to unbelievable lengths to make young Mohan [Gandhi] eat meat and prove his manhood in brothels. Incidents of smoking and stealing and a spurious "suicide attempt" are followed by the crowning tragedy: the father whom he had nursed diligently died in an uncle's arms while the negligent boy lay with his (pregnant) wife.

Erikson skips quickly over the suicide attempt, which he further minimizes by putting it in quotes. Here, cited in full, is what Gandhi himself wrote about it, admitting what happened while at the same time explaining it away. First he describes how he and a friend smoked cigarettes surreptitiously, and even began to steal money to pay for the secret habit:

> Our want of independence began to smart. It was unbearable that we should be unable to do anything without the elders' permission. At last, in sheer disgust, we decided to commit suicide!
>
> But how were we to do it? From where were we to get the poison? We heard that *Dhatura* seeds were an effective poison. Off we went to the jungle in search of these seeds, and got them. Evening was thought to be an auspicious hour. We went to *Kedarji Mandar*, put ghee in the temple-lamp, had the *darshan* and then looked for a lonely corner. But our courage failed us. Supposing we were not instantly killed? And what was the good of killing ourselves? Why not rather put up with the lack of independence? But we swallowed two or three seeds nevertheless. We dared not take more. Both of us fought shy of death, and decided to go to *Ramji Mandir* to compose ourselves, and to dismiss the thought of suicide.
>
> I realized that it was not as easy to commit suicide as to contemplate it. And since then, whenever I have heard of someone threatening to commit suicide, it has had little or no effect on me.
>
> The thought of suicide ultimately resulted in both of us bidding good-bye to the habit of smoking. (italics in original)

Gandhi proceeds to describe how he confessed to his ailing father:

> I decided at last to write out the confession, to submit it to my father, and ask his forgiveness. . . . I was trembling as I handed the confession to my father. . . . He read it through, and pearl-drops trickled down his cheeks, wetting the paper. For a moment he closed his eyes in thought and then tore up the note. He had sat up to read it. He again lay down. I also cried. I could see my

father's agony. . . . Those pearl-drops of love cleansed my heart, and washed my sin away. Only he who has experienced such love can know what it is.

Gandhi clearly meant to minimize the suicide attempt, ascribing it to adolescent impulsivity and peer pressure. Such denial is facile, but the statistics suggest that any teenage suicide attempt should be taken seriously: only about 2 percent of children try to kill themselves, which shows that it is hardly a normal adolescent act. Indeed, 90 percent of children who attempt suicide have a psychiatric disorder, most commonly clinical depression.

Based on these facts, it is highly likely that Gandhi experienced depression during his adolescence, which manifested in a suicide attempt. Given that he ended his life with another depressive episode, it is statistically probable that Gandhi suffered from episodic depression throughout his life. This probability is confirmed by a careful study of his life.

Though he wrote letters continually, gave many speeches, and penned innumerable newspaper articles—constituting in total about ninety volumes of collected works—Gandhi provided little detail about his moods. Thus, between the severe depressive periods that bracketed his adult life, Gandhi himself provides sparse psychiatric evidence. But what evidence we have is consistent with dysthymia, or chronic mild depression (or possibly, given some hypersexuality, cyclothymia).

Throughout his life Gandhi was anxious, extremely shy, and prone to negative and pessimistic moods. In his *Autobiography*, he gives glimpses of these dysthymic traits, especially in young adulthood. Speaking of his high school years, he writes, "I was a coward. I used to be haunted by the fears of thieves, ghosts, and serpents. I did not dare to stir out of doors at night. Darkness was a terror to me. . . . I could not therefore bear to sleep without a light in the room." Of his twenties studying law in London: "I always felt tongue-tied. [A British vegetarian society colleague commented], 'You talk to me quite all right, but why is it that you never open your lips at a committee meeting? You are a drone.' . . . Not that I never felt tempted to speak. But I was at a loss how to express myself. . . . Even when I paid a social call the presence of half a dozen or more people would strike me dumb." This kind of social anxiety is typical of depression. For Gandhi, it was constant and chronic, as happens with dysthymic personalities: "It was only in South Africa that I got over this shyness, though I never completely overcame it. It was impossible for me to speak impromptu. I hesitated whenever I had to face strange audiences and avoided making a speech whenever I could. Even today I do not think I could or would even be inclined to keep a meeting of friends engaged in idle talk."

Dysthymia increases the chances of becoming severely depressed when stressful events happen, as in Gandhi's later years, and as occurred when he became physically ill. The vegetarian Mahatma refused most medications because of their animal origins. In his mid-forties, he had dysentery, a medical problem that quickly devolved into a psychiatric crisis, complete with suicidal thoughts. "I felt the illness was bound to be prolonged and possibly fatal. . . . One night I gave myself up to despair. I felt that I was at death's door. . . . [His doctor said,] 'Your pulse is quite good. I see absolutely no danger. This is a nervous break-down due to extreme weakness.' But I was far from being reassured. I passed the night without sleep. The morning broke without death coming. But I could not get rid of the feeling that the end was near. . . . I was incapable of reading. I was hardly inclined to talk. The slightest talk meant a strain on the brain. All interest in living had ceased." Ulti-mately, he got over his dysentery and his depression.

Gandhi made virtues out of necessities. For instance, he saw his nat-ural shyness as encouraging spiritually useful silence. Similarly, he interpreted his introversion as reflecting the ascetic virtues of detach-ment from the material world. He made even his crankiest, strangest qualities into exemplary behaviors. His obsession with sexual absti-nence, his insistence on making his own clothes, his rejection of the material comforts of Western life all were celebrated as the self-abnegation of the ascetic who devoted himself single-mindedly to the battle for justice and peace. Not coincidentally, these values also harmonize with his dysthymic personality.

GIVEN HIS LIFELONG depressive symptoms, the *course* of Gandhi's illness is also consistent with dysthymic personality, superimposed by a few major depressive episodes, probably at least three (adolescence, his mid-forties, and the end of his life). Of the four indicators of depression, only treatment cannot be applied to the Mahatma because he rejected most Western treatments, and in any case, few were available during his lifetime.

A more telling line of diagnostic evidence is *genetics*. Here we are faced with the unfortunate life of Gandhi's eldest son, Harilal, mentioned only once in the Mahatma's autobiography. During his life, Harilal caused Gandhi much pain; he did everything his father famously disavowed. Harilal converted to Islam briefly, ate meat, visited prostitutes, drank alcohol, and committed petty crimes such as embezzlement. In an open letter, Harilal accused Gandhi of ignoring his children's well-being, as when Gandhi refused Harilal's request to study law in London, as the Mahatma himself had done.

Most historians have blamed these problems on an eldest son's defiance toward a famous father. No historian has made a different suggestion: perhaps Harilal was mentally ill. He was clearly an alcoholic: he became homeless and destitute toward the end of his life, and he died of cirrhosis in his sixties. When Harilal attended Gandhi's funeral, the haggard, dirty son went unrecognized. Two months later, he died in a tuberculosis sanitarium, though he did not have tuberculosis. (Such sanitaria were also used in India to house the mentally ill.)

Gandhi's many descendants are not public regarding the presence of mental illness in the family. But if Gandhi's own depression, and his son's fate, indicate mental illness, it is quite possible that others in the family have suffered the same illness.

IF GANDHI INDEED suffered from depressive episodes and a dysthymic personality, we can ask how this depression might have influenced his politics. There is, as we've seen, a connection between depression and empathy. One sees the psychological concept of empathy prominently displayed in many of Gandhi's political statements. For instance:

> My attitude towards the English is one of utter friendliness and respect. I claim to be their friend, because it is contrary to my nature to distrust a single human being or to believe that any nation on earth is incapable of redemption. I have respect for Englishmen because I recognize their bravery, their spirit of sacrifice for what they believe to be good for themselves, their cohesion and their powers of vast organization. . . . By a long course of prayerful discipline I have ceased for over forty years to hate anybody. I know this is a big claim. . . . But I can and do hate evil wherever it exists. I hate the system of Government the British people have set up in India. I hate the domineering manner of Englishmen as a class in India. . . . But I do not hate the domineering Englishmen as I refuse to hate the domineering Hindus. I seek to reform them in all the loving ways that are open to me. My non-cooperation has its root not in hatred, but in love.

Both his allies and his enemies imposed limits on their love; Gandhi struggled to expand those limits. He tried to persuade Indians to value their British rulers even while they sought to free themselves from British rule; he attempted to sway his Hindu followers to respect the Untouchable caste and to live tolerantly with Indian Muslims.

Despite failing in the end to preserve a united India, he never compromised his method of radical empathy: "We can do nothing without Hindu-Moslem unity and without killing the snake of untouchability. . . . No man of God can consider another man as inferior to himself. He must consider every man as his blood brother. It is the cardinal principle of every religion."

He realized that empathy was the secret ingredient of nonviolence:

Three-fourths of the miseries and misunderstandings in the world will disappear if we step into the shoes of our adversaries and understand their standpoint. We will then agree with our adversaries quickly or think of them charitably. In our case there is no question of our agreeing with them quickly as our ideals are radically different. But we may be charitable to them and believe that they actually mean what they say. . . . Our business, therefore, is to show them that they are in the wrong, and we should do so by our suffering. I have found that mere appeal to reason does not answer where prejudices are age-long and based on supposed religious authority. Reason has to be strengthened by suffering, and suffering opens the eyes of understanding. (italics added)

As this passage makes clear, Gandhi understood the mechanics of empathy so deeply that he could apply it as a strategy. By understanding—and feeling—the mental state of his adversaries, he realized that they could be moved viscerally by the suffering of his people, even when the reason and justice of his people's cause failed to move them. This deep psychological insight, born of an extremely pronounced ability to empathize, was also his crucial political innovation.

GANDHI WOULD LEARN, however, that empathy had its limits, an insight previously reached by the psychiatrist/philosopher Karl Jaspers, famous for making empathy central to his thinking. Jaspers boldly resisted Nazism and was one of the few prominent anti-Nazi philosophers who stayed in Germany after Hitler took power. In both his psychiatric and political experience, Jaspers discovered the limits of empathy. In psychiatry, he found that the inability to empathize was a sign of psychosis, the loss of touch with reality that characterizes bizarre delusions or hallucinations. The psychotic's inability to empathize with others is mirrored by our inability to empathize with his delusions. If you firmly believe that your entrails are being invaded by Martians, no matter how much I try to understand your life and feelings and thoughts, I cannot make sense of—or empathize with—your delusion.

Just as Jaspers argued that there are limits to empathy in psychiatry, he found that he could not empathize with the Nazi evil; it was the political equivalent of a delusion—a pure falsehood with which he could not conceivably empathize. His discovery would be repeated by Gandhi's experience during the last decade of his life, and, initially, with the same challenge: Adolf Hitler.

At first, Gandhi took a clear anti-Nazi stand. Before the Second World War, he had criticized Chamberlain's appeasement: "Europe has sold her soul for the sake of a seven days' earthly existence," he declared. "The peace that Europe gained at Munich is a triumph of violence." After Hitler invaded Poland, he defended the Polish resistance. But as the war progressed, the Mahatma wavered. When he heard about the mass internment of Jews, he recommended that Jews commit collective suicide, in order to arouse the world's moral outrage. When Hitler had overtaken France and was threatening England, Gandhi again counseled countrywide passive resistance in an open letter to the British people: "Let them take possession of your beautiful island with your many beautiful buildings. You will give all these, but neither your souls, nor your minds."

He vacillated about whether Hitler could be redeemed, infamously penning a series of letters to the Nazi leader (all addressed to "My friend"). Gandhi's critics commonly use these letters now to deride him. They repeat the conventional wisdom that his nonviolent strategy could only work against a democracy like Britain; Hitler or Stalin would have defeated satyagraha. The conventionally wise error here lies in making only political judgments. Gandhi devised satyagraha not to gain Indian independence (which would have occurred with or without satyagraha), but rather because he wanted to influence *how* independence happened, to affect the collective psyches of India and Britain and thereby their relations after independence. As with Martin Luther King, Gandhi's nonviolent method sought to achieve psychological, not just political, ends.

I believe that Gandhi's letters to Hitler should be read psychologically. While they were naïve politically, they reflected a deep psychological commitment to a politics of *radical* empathy. The failure of this radical politics with Hitler does not negate the method; it merely suggests that, in politics as in psychiatry, empathy has its limits.

GANDHI WOULD SOON SEE these limits within India itself.

If we judge ideas by their consequences, then Gandhi's satyagraha ultimately failed. It had its successes—Indian independence, less stigma for the Hindu Untouchables—but it could not resolve the Hindu-Muslim conflict, a central goal of Gandhi's. The key players were Jawaharlal Nehru and Mohammad Ali Jinnah, previously allies in the Indian Congress Party, which Gandhi led. Though he was himself a secular Muslim, Jinnah harnessed religious tensions to maneuver himself toward political power. Gandhi tried to persuade Nehru and other Hindu leaders to compromise, even arguing that Jinnah be made prime minister of a united India. Jinnah rejected this offer in 1946, partly because the majority of the cabinet would still be Hindu; Nehru, though devoted to Gandhi, was also unenthusiastic about such an arrangement.

The results of this failed compromise were bloody. In 1947–1948, the Hindu-Muslim riots that preceded, accompanied, and followed partition caused at least a million deaths. From October 1946 to his death in January 1948, Gandhi moved constantly from province to province, frequently living with Muslim families, seeking to end the violence. He boldly reached out to Muslims, even persuading the newly independent Indian government to give Pakistan £44 million as its share of united India's assets.

Despite, or perhaps due to, all these efforts, Gandhi painfully concluded that India had failed to learn true nonviolence. "There was a time when people listened to me because I showed them how to give fight to the British without arms when they had no arms. . . . But today I am told that my non-violence can be of no avail against the [Hindu-Muslim riots] and, therefore, people should arm themselves for self-defence. If this is true, it has to be admitted that our thirty years of non-violent practice was an utter waste of time."

On India's Independence Day—August 15, 1947—a disheartened Mahatma refused to send any formal message to the nation. An aide noted in her diary, "He said, there was a time when India listened to him. Today he was a back number. He was told that he had no place in the new order where they wanted machines, navy, air force, and what-not. He could never be party to that."

Gandhi realized that satyagraha, the soul-force of nonviolence, had never truly occurred in India. Nonviolent when weak, his followers became violent once independence had strengthened them. When given a flag and an army, they immediately made war on one another. When they could have chosen nonviolence, they refused to do so. Two weeks before his death, he remarked despondently to an interviewer that "what he had mistaken for Satyagraha was not more than passive resistance, which was a weapon of the weak."

This collapse of the politics of radical empathy would be repeated two decades later when Martin Luther King's nonviolence gave way to the aggressive tactics of the Black Power movement. This trend shows how hard empathy is to maintain among the mass of humanity, whose normal psychology prevents them from developing true empathy with other groups even after they have suffered themselves. Again, it required the unusually acute psychological insight of two depressive men to envision and enact a political movement based on empathy.

Gandhi saw the inevitable end coming—for himself and his movement. When he received copious seventy-eighth-birthday homages in 1947, he despaired: "Where do congratulations come in? Would it not be more appropriate to send condolences? There is nothing but anguish in my heart. Time was whatever I said the masses followed. Today, mine is a lone voice in India."

"The woes of Mahatmas," he once said, "are known to Mahatmas alone." In January 1948, a young Hindu walked up to Gandhi in a prayer service and shot him. In the assassin's words, India thus averted "a dark and deadly future if left to face Islam outside and Gandhi inside."

GANDHI'S MELANCHOLY colored his life and his politics. He gave up a life of ease, rejected material prosperity, became an ascetic. He also invented a new nonviolent politics, an approach based on radical empathy—empathy for all: Hindus, Muslims, British. India's masses responded at first, but ultimately rejected his call; their empathy had limits. In contrast to his people, Gandhi appears an anomaly: a saint who could empathize without limits. The difference could be much more prosaic: Gandhi was depressed; India's populace was normal. That distinction may explain it all.

A decade later, another depressed man, a young black minister from Georgia, placed a wreath on the old Indian's grave.

CHAPTER 8

PSYCHIATRY FOR
THE AMERICAN SOUL

KING

After World War I, W. E. B. DuBois, a founder of the NAACP and a leading black intellectual, heard about a strange leader in India who fought injustice by refusing to fight. DuBois was intrigued. He and his colleagues debated the idea of using Gandhi's methods, but, as published in a 1924 symposium in the NAACP magazine, they concluded that an American Gandhi would be met with a "blood bath." But DuBois and other black leaders remained intrigued by the Mahatma. In 1935, a delegation headed by Howard Thurman, dean of Rankin Chapel at Howard University, visited Gandhi. Journalist Lerone Bennett movingly recounts the meeting:

> For several minutes, Gandhi and his guests discussed Christianity, oppression, and love. Then, unexpectedly, Gandhi asked the American Negroes to sing one of his favorite songs, "Were You There When They Crucified My Lord?" The old sad words rose and swelled like a benediction, like a curse, like a prayer, the more terrible, the more poignant perhaps for the strange setting.

Were you there when they crucified my Lord?
Were you there when they nailed him to the tree?
Oh, sometimes it causes me to tremble, tremble, tremble.
Were you there when they crucified my Lord?

The words weighted down with centuries of accepted and transmuted sorrow, winged their way to Gandhi's heart, and Gandhi lived through the words to the experience the words mediated. . . . When, at last, the words were done, Gandhi sat for a moment, silent. Then he said: "Perhaps it will be through the Negro that the unadulterated message of nonviolence will be delivered to the world."

By the 1940s, American black leaders had become deeply interested in satyagraha. By the time Martin Luther King used nonviolent resistance in the Montgomery bus boycott of 1956–1957, DuBois realized that Gandhi had revolutionized the black movement:

The black workers led by young, educated ministers began a strike which stopped the discrimination, aroused the state and the nation and presented an unbending front of non-violence to the murderous mob which hitherto has ruled the South. The occurrence was extraordinary. It was not based on any first-hand knowledge of Gandhi and his work. Their leaders like Martin Luther King knew of non-resistance in India; many of the educated teachers, business and professional men had heard of Gandhi. But the rise and spread of this movement was due to the truth of its underlying principles and not to direct teaching or propaganda. In this aspect it is a most interesting proof of the truth of the Gandhian philosophy.

DuBois then made a prophetic judgment: "The American Negro is not yet free. He is still discriminated against, oppressed and exploited.

The recent court decisions in his favour are excellent but are as yet only partially enforced. It may well be that the enforcement of these laws and real human equality and brotherhood in the United States will come only under the leadership of another Gandhi"—a second Gandhi, who would encounter similar failures, and successes, as the original.

THE SECOND GANDHI PROVED to be about as depressed as the first. Martin Luther King's depression is eerily parallel to Gandhi's, though more difficult to decipher. Unlike Gandhi, King left no autobiography and few introspective writings. An edited collection of his papers, published after his death as an authorized autobiography, gives little insight into his mental state. His letters and other personal papers are carefully guarded still, and not fully accessible to scholars. Those that are available give little information about his psychological state.

Yet absence of evidence is not evidence of absence. Like Gandhi, King tried to commit suicide as a teenager; in fact, King made two attempts. It is surprising how little this fact is recalled. *Time* magazine reported in its 1963 "Man of the Year" article on King as follows:

Raised in the warmth of a tightly knit family, King developed from his earliest years a raw-nerved sensitivity that bordered on self-destruction. Twice, before he was 13, he tried to commit suicide. Once his brother, "A.D.," accidentally knocked his grandmother unconscious when he slid down a banister. Martin thought she was dead, and in despair ran to a second-floor window and jumped out—only to land unhurt. He did the same thing, with the same result, on the day his grandmother died.

Lerone Bennett, who knew King personally, published a similar account during King's lifetime: "The first incident occurred after his beloved grandmother, Jennie Williams, was accidentally knocked unconscious. King, thinking she was dead, ran upstairs and leaped from a second-story window. For a moment, it seemed that he had killed himself. He lay motionless, oblivious to the screams of relatives. Then, as though nothing had happened, he got up and walked away. In 1941, on the death of the grandmother, King again leaped from the second-story window, and, again, he survived."

As we saw in the previous chapter, teenage suicide is both rare and strongly suggestive of depression. And it isn't the only evidence of King's mental illness. Like Gandhi, he endured his most unambiguous severe depression in his life's final years. The year 1966 marked King's last major civil rights march, the "Meredith march" in Mississippi, organized to support activist James Meredith, who had been shot when he tried to march by himself for voting rights. The weeklong procession would be the last hurrah of a unified nonviolent civil rights campaign. After the march ended, and following weeks of violent harassment by police, young activists (led by Stokely Carmichael of the Student Nonviolent Coordinating Committee) explicitly rejected nonviolence, raising, for the first time, the slogan of "Black Power" instead. Along with the defection of these young militants, King faced a very different challenge that derived from his success. He had achieved most of what he had wanted—voting rights and desegregation were now the law. What should he do next?

Jesse Jackson recalls that King mentioned in meetings that he felt depressed, that perhaps he should resign, that he had achieved his life's work and should now retire. But new challenges soon showed themselves: responding to the radicalization of black youth, and fighting the rise in domestic and foreign violence (especially the Vietnam War).

In the two years before his death, King spoke out against the war, antagonized President Johnson and his liberal allies in the Democratic Party, and confronted young black radicals. He turned his focus from racism to poverty, and overtly advanced a socialist agenda. This MLK was too radical for many, too conservative for some. He was increasingly damned, and increasingly depressed—not just sad, but clinically depressed.

Historian Stephen Oates recounts King's mental state at the time:

By 1968, King was working at a frenzied pace.... Unable to sleep, he would stay up all night thrashing out ideas or testing speeches on his weary staff.... It was as if he were cramming a lifetime into each day. Yet even his frantic pace could not assuage the despair he felt, a deepening depression that left him morose, distracted. His friends and aides did not know what to make of it or to do for him. One confidant recommended that he consult a psychiatrist. But King was personally hostile to psychoanalysis—had been since his Boston University days—and rejected the advice. He drove himself harder than ever, plunging into the planning and organization of the poor people's campaign like a man possessed.

Just before his death, King visited New York for private meetings with liberal and radical supporters, among them Bayard Rustin, Harry Wachtel, and Bernard Lee. Oates describes what happened:

"Bayard," King said [to Rustin] when they were alone, "I sometimes wonder where I can go from here. I've accomplished so much. What can I do now?" Rustin told Wachtel, "You know, Harry, Martin really disturbs me." Both thought something was happening to him, a kind of psychological deterioration that was hard to describe. "It got scary," Rustin recalled. "It was a very strange thing. When you would sit and talk philosophy with him or anything, it was the same old Martin. His judgments were not affected. But he was terribly preoccupied with death. And this flaw of 'will I continue to develop, will I continue to do things?'" Of course, given the tension and danger he was under, Rustin conceded that "he had some very good reasons to feel anguished." But Lee thought it was more than the pressure and lack of sleep. "It was deeper than that." His friends couldn't quite fathom what it was.

Alvin Poussaint, a psychiatrist who had marched with King repeatedly (and stayed in touch with him in the final years), saw a changed man:

After the Meredith march, there were fewer marches, and the funding started drying up, and people felt the movement was over. King felt we needed to go to the next stage, to social economic desperation. He seemed disappointed, where was the support now? He was more alone, and had trouble mobilizing people and fundraising. And the government lost interest too: civil rights they could support, but going beyond civil rights was not of interest to them.

He was depressed at the end, I would say, just based on what I saw on television. Especially in that April 3 speech in Memphis, where he said he had been to the mountaintop and he probably would not get there with his audience. He was depressed but he was still on mission. He looked troubled. When he talked about not caring about longevity, that was a depressive statement, he did not talk like that before. He was always upbeat, like in the march on Montgomery, where I was present, he was saying we will be victorious. But at the end he began to feel some of the despair, the fatigue of pushing this, and not getting the support he was used to getting. But he wasn't going to stop.

THE *COURSE* OF DEPRESSION is episodic and repetitive. The severe periods of melancholy come and go, and they usually happen more than once or twice in a lifetime. Looking for other periods of clinical depression (besides adolescence and the final years), I believe there's evidence of at least one other episode.

In 1959, three years after beginning his public life, King felt depleted: "What I have been doing is giving, giving, giving, and not stopping to retreat and meditate like I should—to come back. If the situation is not changed, I will be a physical and psychological wreck. I have to reorganize my personality and reorient my life. I have been too long in the crowd, too long in the forest." King's state met the definition of clinical depression: he was sad in his mood, uninterested in his usual activities, low in energy, unable to concentrate, suffering from insomnia, and had increased appetite (gaining twenty pounds; physicians told him that too much stress was making him ill). Those symptoms, in an average man, would be diagnosed as a major depressive episode.

Thus the course of his illness supports a depressive disease: probable episodes with suicide attempts in adolescence, another episode at age thirty, and a final one at age thirty-eight. While it is true that we can attribute external causes to each of these episodes, as we can with most mental illnesses, it's important to bear in mind that such apparent "causes" are neither necessary nor sufficient. The *recurrence* of episodes indicates an underlying biological *susceptibility* to depression; this susceptibility is, in essence, mental illness.

AT KING'S SIDE during many a march walked a young doctor with a black bag. Stand close to King, Andrew Young told the young volunteer for the Medical Committee for Human Rights. Never be more than a few people away. Inside the bag, Dr. Alvin Poussaint carried first aid material, in case King was shot. Poussaint also provided medical and psychological support for the marchers. A medical car (usually Poussaint's own car with an affixed red cross) trailed each march.

Dr. Poussaint, now a child psychiatry professor at Harvard, gave me a firsthand assessment of King's mental state in the final years of his life. Poussaint knew Dr. King reasonably well from the marches. He recalls an intense period of interaction with King in 1966 during the Meredith march, the beginning of the end of the civil rights movement. "King had a fearlessness about him. . . . He set the pace in marches, he was strolling, not walking fast, nor slow, but strolling, and always right in the front line, which put him at risk. Anyone could run out from the bushes and shoot him." Poussaint describes how terribly afraid he was many times during the marches, but how King always maintained his composure. Once King marched to a courthouse in Philadelphia, Mississippi, after some civil rights workers had been killed. He was met by two sheriffs on the sidewalk. Don't take another step, one of them said; they had their hands on their guns. "King was standing there, with his chest out, like he always stood. I thought he was going to walk onto the lawn, and they would then beat or kill him and us." King knelt on the ground to pray, and everyone around him did the same. Says Poussaint, "You have to realize there was a constant sense of fear on those marches. The marchers never knew if and when they might be attacked or even killed, and since they were enjoined never to fight back, they sometimes felt like lambs going to sacrifice. This constant fear was an extreme test of character, one which King passed, while others . . . did not."

Poussaint emphasizes that even in the face of all this anxiety, fear, and violence, King projected an abnormally calm sense of "serenity" and "peacefulness." Some of this may have been a show, to buck up his followers; in private, King would drink and get tipsy, or engage in hilarious jesting. Poussaint did not observe hyperthymic personality traits, such as being hyperactive, talking or walking fast. In fact, he saw the reverse: "He talked slow, and even walked slow, not only during marches, but I remember walking casually with him, just chatting, about nothing of consequence, and he walked slowly." Poussaint was unaware of King's adolescent suicide attempts, and when asked what he thinks as a child psychiatrist now, he replied, "It sounds like an impulsive grief reaction. I'll join [my grandmother] who's dead. I agree that one would be more likely to do that if depressed already." Despite the possibility of an adolescent period of depression, Poussaint doubted, from his own experiences and from speaking to others in King's circle, that Dr. King suffered from much depression otherwise.

I think we can conclude from the firsthand observations of Dr. Poussaint, and from the historical record, that—unlike Gandhi—King did not have a baseline dysthymic personality (with sadness, shyness, anxiety, and introversion). He was not chronically depressed. But, exactly as with Gandhi, King experienced at least three probable depressive episodes in the beginning, middle, and end of his life, the first associated with suicide attempts.

Of the four diagnostic validators of mental illness, symptoms and course both point toward depressive illness, but we can say nothing about *genetics* and *treatment*. Regarding genetics, King's family is private, and the presence or absence of psychiatric diagnoses among family members is not publicly available knowledge. Regarding treatment, during his final depression, some of King's aides urged their leader to get psychiatric help, but he never did so.

AS WITH GANDHI, King's depression may well have generated his politics of radical empathy. In fact, King drew an analogy between his politics and psychiatric treatment: the patient was America; the disease was racism. For example, in a 1957 interview with journalist Martin Agronsky, King said, "Psychologists would say that a guilt complex can lead to two reactions. One is repentance and the desire to change. The other reaction is to indulge in more of the very thing that you have the sense of guilt about. And I think we find these two reactions. I think much of the violence that we notice in the South at this time is really the attempt to compensate, drown the sense of guilt, by indulging in more of the very thing that causes the sense of guilt." Agronsky asked, "You really feel that, you prefer to make this sort of a psychiatric interpretation?" King replied, "Yes."

This view was widely held in King's circle, most explicitly by James Bevel, who, as Andrew Young recounted, "put our outrage into perspective when he said that we had to become 'political psychiatrists' and view our oppressors as our patients. 'A psychiatrist doesn't get angry with his patients when they are violent towards him; the doctor must help his patients to realize that their violence grows out of sickness and insecurity. We must help them, not hate them.'" (Bevel's insight was hard earned: his behavior was erratic, and his colleagues unsuccesfully tried to commit him more than once to mental hospitals.) Alvin Poussaint confirms that the movement leaders saw their mission this way: "By nonviolence, we were trying to cure white people of a sickness. . . . Nonviolence, [King] always said, was a way of life, not just a political movement. It was the way you treat other people. I felt he was trying to model it [in his personal demeanor]."

King's nonviolent movement was a cure for racism, not a political strategy. Like many treatments, it has healed rather than cured, leaving scars behind. It was a medical metaphor, a political psychiatry, based on the healing power of empathy.

But what was the treatment? How exactly does empathy heal? When faced with injustice, King taught, there are three options: violent resistance, nonviolent resistance, and acquiescence. Resistance of any kind is preferable to acquiescence (which is why Gandhi and King weren't pacifists; they didn't oppose violence under all circumstances), but violent resistance usually fails to achieve its goals. What is the nonviolent resistance option? *Loving* your enemies, King instructed, is not about actually *being in love* with another (the Greeks called this *eros*, "a sort of aesthetic or romantic love"), nor is it about even *liking* another (*philia*, "a reciprocal love and the intimate affection between friends"): it is about having goodwill toward another (*agape*, "understanding and creative, redemptive good will for all men"). The difference between *agape* and *philia* is why Jesus counseled us to *love*, not *like*, our enemies. Despite hate, anger, harm, spite, one reacts with goodwill, seeking to appreciate the good in others, trying to see another's perspective. King insisted that this goodwill is redemptive: by treating others this way, we change them.

A SKEPTICAL READER might say: Empathy is fine, but King and Gandhi certainly seem like idealists. If depression entails both realism and empathy, where is the realism? This attitude is understandable today.

The Martin Luther King of popular mythology is a cardboard icon, brought out once a year on a holiday, with little resemblance to the real historical man. The cardboard King was a pacificist idealist; he wanted everyone to make peace and hold hands. The real King was an aggressive, confrontational realist; he believed that all men were evil in part, including himself; he thought that violence was everywhere and unavoidable, including within himself. "Nonviolence" did not mean the absence of violence, but the control of violence so that it was directed inward rather than outward.

These are not my views; these are the explicit views of Gandhi and King, as I will show, and they are a reflection of their realistic views of evil and aggression as part of human nature. During a Howard University conference on nonviolence in 1963, the comments of Jerome Frank, a prominent psychiatrist at Johns Hopkins, represent an example of the misinterpretation of King's attitude toward violence:

> What do nonviolent fighters do with their impulses to violence? The continual humiliations and threats to which they are exposed must arouse intense anger which they must repress. Psychiatrists believe from clinical experience that emotions that are blocked from direct expression tend to manifest themselves obliquely. . . . [We should not expect] more of nonviolent methods of fighting than of violent ones. No form of waging conflict always wins. The most one can ask for nonviolent techniques is that where they fail, and they certainly will fail sometimes, violent methods would have failed more completely.

Frank's views, influenced by Freud, ran counter to King, who disliked Freudian ideology. King understood what Freud and Frank did not—that nonviolence is not pacifism; King and Gandhi had found a way to use aggressive impulses to resist injustice without hurting others. Where did the aggression go? The answer, as King would later tell Poussaint, was this: into the courage needed to resist without fighting back physically. Gandhi had clearly seen nonviolence this way (one of his followers termed it "war without violence"). For instance, Gandhi said, "My creed of nonviolence is an extremely active force. It has no room for cowardice or even weakness. There is hope for a violent man to be some day non-violent, but there is none for a coward. I have, therefore, said more than once . . . that, if we do not know how to defend ourselves, our women and our places of worship by the force of suffering, i.e., nonviolence, we must, if we are men, be at least able to defend all these by fighting."

King felt similarly: he called nonviolent resistance one of three options in response to injustice, along with violent resistance and passive acquiescence. If given a choice between violent resistance and passive acceptance, King and Gandhi both accepted violence. But they saw nonviolent resistance as a better alternative. Like violence, it was aggressive, but it was spiritually, not physically, so. It was active, refusing to accept evil, standing up and resisting without inflicting harm. King stated these ideas many times and in slightly different ways. Here is one example from a 1956 sermon: "The nonviolent resister is just as opposed to the evil that he is protesting against as a violent resister. Now it is true that this method is nonaggressive and passive in the sense that the nonviolent resister does not use physical aggression against his opponent. But at the same time the mind and the emotions are active, actively trying to persuade the opponent to change his ways and to convince him that he is mistaken and to lift him to a higher level of existence. This method is nonaggressive physically, but it is aggressive spiritually." King did not reject violence per se.

Freud and Frank were right, I think, that violent reprisal is a more natural response to injustice. When one fails to respond violently, he pays a psychological cost. Alvin Poussaint, who was fully committed to King's movement, came to the same conclusion in a 1967 *New York Times Magazine* article. Poussaint observed that the civil rights marchers—constantly fearing attack, abidingly alert to danger, with orders not to fight back—were angry; they wanted to fight back, but were taught by

King not to do so. "I used to sit there and wonder," wrote Poussaint, "'Now what do they really do with their rage?'" What they did was fight each other: "After a period of time it became apparent that they were directing it mostly at each other and the white civil-rights workers. Violent verbal and sometimes physical fights often occurred among the workers. . . . While they were talking about being nonviolent and 'loving' the sheriff that just hit them over the head, they rampaged around the project houses beating up each other. I frequently had to calm Negro civil-rights workers with large doses of tranquilizers for what I can describe clinically only as acute attacks of rage."

Another black political leader, also a psychiatrist, Frantz Fanon, argued that to overcome psychological servitude, blacks must violently attack their white oppressors. Fanon, a favorite of Black Power advocates, saw violence not only as political necessity but as psychological imperative. Violence was the cure for the disease of racism. Poussaint was inching toward that view in his article, expressing the standard psychiatric view (shared by Fanon and Freud) that it is better to express one's aggression than to repress it; otherwise depression ensues. The Black Power movement was an expression of these psychiatric facts, Poussaint concluded.

To remain allied to King, Poussaint needed a way out. He called it "constructive assertiveness": "James Meredith . . . said: 'If Negroes ever do overcome fear, the white man has only two choices: to kill them or let them be free.'. . . Since this assertive response appears to be growing more common among Negroes, the implications for American society are clear: stop oppressing the black man, or be prepared to meet his expressed rage."

Shortly afterward, when King visited Boston, he complimented Poussaint on the article, expressing agreement with it. Here we see the coming together of apparent irreconcilables: rage and peace, violence and nonviolence, Frantz Fanon and Martin Luther King. But seeing this convergence as a paradox reflects misunderstanding of King's philosophy. King did not advocate an attitude of peaceful beatitude toward others; he was an angry man, affronted by injustice; he just advocated expressing that anger in a nonviolent way. As King's close friend Harry Belafonte said, "Martin always felt that anger was a very important commodity, a necessary part of the black movement in this country." Thus as documented above, King's nonviolence is not about being nonaggressive; it is about being aggressive in a nonviolent way. Rage is natural, part of being human; one cannot deny it without painful psychic consequences. But rage can be channeled in a constructive manner, going outside insofar as it resists injustice, and going inward insofar as it supports the higher courage needed to suffer rather than inflict suffering. This cure for racism benefits both the oppressed and the oppressor.

LIFE IS FULL OF EVIL, King believed. All of us have to decide, again and again, how we are going to react to the plethora of evil in the world. The two most common reactions are violent resistance or passive acquiescence. Either approach is conformism; the masses of men acquiesce all the time to all kinds of evil and injustice; some resist violently, only adding more evil to the evil that already exists. King's advocacy of nonviolence was a third way that required, above all, nonconformism with the other two accepted paths. This is why King emphasized the need for nonconformism, not just as a feature of leadership, but for everyone, as a basic human attitude. These ideas are expressed most directly in a sermon that interprets the biblical phrase "Be not conformed to this world: but be ye transformed by the renewing of your mind" (Romans 12:2). Said King:

> Many people fear nothing more terribly than to take a position which stands out sharply and clearly from prevailing opinion. The tendency of most is to adopt a view that is so ambiguous that it will include everything and so popular that it will include everybody. . . . The saving of our world from pending doom will come,

not through the complacent adjustment of the conforming majority, but through the creative maladjustment of a nonconforming
minority. . . . [We are reminded] of the danger of overstressing
the well-adjusted life. Everybody passionately seeks to be well-
adjusted. We must, of course, be well-adjusted if we are to avoid
neurotic and schizophrenic personalities, but there are some
things in our world to which men of goodwill must be maladjusted. . . . Human salvation lies in the hands of the creatively
maladjusted.

Psychiatrists ask: Where does the aggression go? By trying to repress
it, we become maladjusted, unhealthy, abnormal. We must, above all,
be normal, mentally healthy. King disagreed: we must accept unhappiness, suffering, depression, even—God forbid—becoming maladjusted. His friend Reverend Joseph Lowery understood. To achieve
social change, he remarked recently, "you have to be a little crazy. All
the leaders of the movement were a little crazy. Including Martin."

PART FOUR
RESILIENCE

CHAPTER 9

STRONGER

In our first appointment, Liza barely spoke. Suffering from severe depression, she could not think or talk logically; it seemed to me she barely heard and understood every third word I spoke. Her daughter tried to explain her sixty-year-old mother's life to me.

"Mom had a horrendous childhood," the daughter began.

I saw her depression and had read about manic periods in her chart, so I knew Liza had bipolar disorder. But since childhood trauma is not a particular cause of bipolar disorder, I was only mildly interested in starting with childhood, especially as the clock ticked along and I knew we had complex decisions to make about which medications to prescribe for her condition. But I recalled the old lesson I learned in my residency: *Meet patients where they are.* So I listened:

"Her parents moved her twenty-three times."

I looked at Liza, who sat impassively. "Twenty-three times?" I repeated, afraid to ask why.

Liza finally spoke. "Yes. Mother couldn't keep still . . . manic, just like me."

As a child, Liza had also endured unwanted sexual attention from siblings and other relatives. I'd heard enough about her childhood to know that it was not one any child should experience. And yet here she was at age sixty, depressed, yes, but alive and whole—a mother herself, with a normal adult daughter beside her as well as four other healthy children and ten grandchildren, none of whom suffered as she had.

THIS IS WHAT psychologists mean by resilience—"good outcomes in spite of serious threats to adaptation or development." Resilience isn't simply something one is born with; it grows out of an *interaction* between factors that promote it (like hyperthymic personality) and harmful life events—producing a good outcome in the end. In psychology research, two lines of evidence support this notion. First, when people experience harmful events, some are injured psychologically, but others are not. Second, sometimes people even get *stronger* after such events, a "steeling" effect that protects them against future stresses.

Resilience is the mind's vaccine. Think how vaccines work: exposed to tiny amounts of virus, the body mounts an immune response; when the virus infects one later in life, the body, already prepared, kills off the infection before it can do serious harm. Just a few generations ago, a dozen illnesses often killed children or, like FDR's polio, paralyzed adults; nowadays, we routinely prevent such tragedies. Like a mental vaccine, resilience develops when, under certain circumstances, we experience harmful events, we survive, and then prosper. Nietzsche famously pointed out that what does not kill you makes you stronger. He understood resilience.

Resilience can grow out of the experience of illness, whether mental or physical. Mental illnesses like manic depression may especially promote resilience because people experience episodes that come and go. Manic depression is recurrent by nature; the episodes go away, but they always come back. Thus people have "breaks" in between the experience of illness, when they can reflect upon and try to understand what just happened, whether the severe depression that made the world seem hopeless or the ecstatic mania that made life so joyous for a while. They also know that they will go through those episodes again, and so they may learn to develop coping styles, ways to recognize the episodes when they begin, or to help control them. People with manic depression often become resilient, as we've already seen in the cases of General Sherman and Winston Churchill.

But there is another source of resilience. Some people are just born resilient; it's an inherent part of their personality. Why this is so is still open to question, but some research, which I will describe below, suggests that hyperthymic temperament is especially associated with resilience. The historical examples that follow, FDR and JFK, display perhaps the perfect cocktail of resilience: hyperthymic personality plus chronic physical illness. In Kennedy's case, this cocktail is topped off by his use of mind-altering medications (especially steroids) for a beneficial effect—enhancing physical and emotional resilience.

ALTHOUGH NIETZSCHE'S OBSERVATION is over a century old, the notion of resilience dawned much more recently upon modern psychologists. The first inklings came during the Second World War. Psychiatrists newly trained in Freudian methods began screening draftees before combat to gain a baseline knowledge of the troops' preexisting mental state. Once deployed, the troops experienced what all warriors since Achilles have encountered: intense fear, extreme physical hardship, gruesome injuries, the deaths of their brothers in arms.

These conditions had already been identified as the cause of a mental disorder that has gone by various names in various wars: shell shock (First World War), war neurosis (World War II), post-traumatic stress disorder (Vietnam/Iraq/Afghanistan). PTSD involves the presence of nightmares or flashbacks, meaning the physical reexperiencing of a traumatic event; these symptoms occur over and over again, and cause much anxiety and depression.

At the start of World War II, the American psychiatrist charged with minimizing this disorder was Harry Stack Sullivan, a brilliant psycho-analyst. Homosexual, leftist, probably bipolar himself, and an icono-clast in professional terms—he believed that all mental illness was ultimately about social relationships, not psychological trauma or biology—he was an unusual choice for the military brass to make. But on the basis of his clinical reputation, he was given a free hand to screen draftees carefully and remove anyone with any hint of succumbing to war neurosis. If Sullivan had applied Freudian belief in its purest for-mulation, namely that all people are neurotic to some degree, then he would have had to exclude everyone from the army; this was, of course, not an option, so Sullivan did as much as a good Freudian could do. Army psychiatric evaluators followed Sullivan's instructions and excluded a wide swath of potential conscripts, including "low-grade morons," "psychopaths," "the eccentric, the leader in subversive activi-ties, the emotionally unstable, the sexually perverse, those with inade-quate personalities that do not adapt readily and those who are resentful of discipline." Neither the aggressive nor the passive was fit to serve, according to Sullivan's guidelines. The general attitude of Sullivan's psychiatric evaluators was "when in doubt, reject," and 25 percent of draftees were rejected. Still, of the remaining soldiers, about half devel-oped war-related psychiatric problems. By 1943, 112,500 enlisted men had been discharged for psychiatric reasons. General George Marshall stepped in, expressing his skepticism about Sullivan's methods: "To the specialists, the psychoneurotic is a hospital patient," he remarked. "To the average line officer, he is a malingerer." Sullivan was fired.

The army brought in a new leader, Dr. William Menninger—a more orthodox psychiatrist than Sullivan, and a more typical American too (midwestern, WASP, heterosexual, middle-of-the-road politically). By this time, the war had become brutal. U.S. military deaths were reach-ing Civil War levels; the army couldn't afford mass psychiatric casual-ties too. Marshall gave Menninger new instructions: screen out only the most clearly insane draftees and, rather than finding reasons to bring soldiers home, try to keep them at the front. The results were amazing: more draftees passed their psychiatric evaluations, but fewer soldiers developed war neurosis.

Why was this the case? It turned out that all those personality traits—narcissism, dependence, avoidance, schizoid personality—that Sullivan thought would predict war neurosis didn't do so at all. The mass of American soldiers displayed many variations on normal personality, and most of them handled combat well.

One explanation may simply be that Freudian psychiatry was wrong; the theories about who needed to be screened out, and why (such as homosexuals, and those who did not meet the standards of Freudian ideology), were scientifically wrongheaded. This may be why they failed in practice. When Menninger was forced to apply more commonsense notions, psychiatrists observed that most soldiers were able to experience trauma without much mental hardship. When the psychiatrists were looking for war hysteria, they found it; when they stopped looking, they found less of it.

This is the case with all hysteria, that is, with all psychological symptoms that seem to be caused by trauma. In a classic example from medical history, the nineteenth-century French neurologist Jean-Martin Charcot developed an interest in hysterical epilepsy. Young women in Paris would present with highly unusual movements during seizures, quite different from most cases of epilepsy. These movements often mimicked sexual intercourse. Charcot was convinced that this was a unique form of epilepsy with a special lesion in the brain. One of his students, Freud, thought these women had experienced sexual trauma and were unconsciously expressing those traumatic symptoms through the physical symptoms of seizure-like movements. While Charcot was active, many women in Paris presented to doctors with hysterical epilepsy; his clinic was full. After Charcot died and his successors showed less interest in the topic, the frequency of hysterical epilepsy dropped sharply in his clinic. A similar pattern happened in the 1980s and 1990s with multiple personality; a sharp rise in professional interest led to a spike in diagnoses. Later, when professional

interest declined, patients apparently stopped having multiple personalities.

So by shifting the doctor's focus, the patients' symptoms can change.
This especially happens with trauma-related symptoms. And it seemed
to occur in the different approaches taken by Sullivan and Menninger.
As we will soon see, Menninger's approach probably approximates the
actual rates of PTSD; only a small minority of people exposed to
trauma actually have PTSD.

After World War II, psychiatrists began to realize that the relevant
question wasn't what caused war neurosis, but why more soldiers
weren't suffering from it. The doctors began to shift their focus from
risk factors to resilience.

IN THE INTERVENING half century, we've learned that war is hardly the
only source of psychological trauma. Childhood sexual abuse, physical
abuse, crime, and major car accidents can have similar effects. In fact,
about half of the U.S. population experiences a major trauma at least
once; but only 10 percent of those people meet the diagnostic definition of PTSD. So most people who experience trauma do *not* develop
PTSD.

The fact that trauma doesn't always lead to PTSD has recently led
some resilience researchers, like George Bonanno of Columbia University, to examine all the varieties of response to trauma. Bonanno
identifies four major types. First, there is the classic PTSD response:
some people experience severe psychological symptoms right after the
trauma, and consistently thereafter. This kind of chronic PTSD occurs
in only about 5 to 10 percent of people who are exposed to trauma.
Then there is delayed PTSD—the Freudian model. In Freud's famous
cases, young ladies suffered from severe hysteria, manifesting as physical paralysis of unknown causes. Then, in the course of psychoanalysis,
they recovered repressed memories of childhood sexual abuse, after

which their hysteria ceased and they were no longer paralyzed. As Bonanno notes, it is rare to actually observe anyone who displays the patterns seen in Freud's famous patients—that is, first suffering a psychological trauma, showing no psychiatric symptoms immediately afterward, but then later developing PTSD. (Instead, people usually experience psychiatric symptoms soon after trauma that get worse over time.) A third "recovery" group suffers initial PTSD symptoms that gradually go away. For instance, after the September 11 attacks, 7.5 percent of New Yorkers met full PTSD criteria initially, but only 1.7 percent at four months, and 0.6 percent at six months. Similarly, in Gulf War veterans with initial PTSD, 62.5 percent no longer had any symptoms a year after their initial trauma. A fourth "pure resilient" group suffers no symptoms of PTSD at any time—either right after trauma or months later. Traditionally this group has either been ignored by researchers or, in the Freudian tradition, thought to have latent symptoms that simply haven't shown themselves yet. And yet people in this fourth group seem able to withstand trauma and continue living normal lives. They aren't happy automatons, ignoring the misery around them; they just don't develop PTSD. The third and fourth groups together characterize what we mean by overall resilience: the experience, following trauma, of some psychiatric symptoms, which eventually go away—or no symptoms at all.

WHAT MAKES PEOPLE in these two groups more resilient to trauma than people in the other groups? Efforts to answer this question range widely, from studies of inner-city children, to healthy adults with past childhood sexual abuse, to combat veterans, to civilian populations exposed to war and terrorism. I will have to pick and choose among studies, some of which are inconsistent with others, to give a concise narrative, but interested readers can find more detail in the endnotes.

Taken together, this research suggests that resilience emerges from a combination of social support (good friends and family), hardship (bad luck), and certain personality traits (especially hyperthymia). Let's consider each of these factors.

Social support: Many children raised in socially and economically poor backgrounds grow up to be well-adjusted adults. They are resilient. Researchers find that a common feature in these resilient kids is strong social supports—good relationships with at least one parent and a large circle of childhood friends. (Some psychologists call this "ordinary magic" to emphasize the point that psychological resilience grows out of simple human experiences, such as having a loving parent.) Similarly, in studies on World War II veterans, those with greater social supports before war (meaning intact and supportive families) and during war (meaning intact military units with strong emotional bonds between soldiers) experienced less PTSD. This is the standard view. But there is another possibility based on a study of childhood adversity.

Hardship: In an uncommon project, unique in that it sought to study resilience and health (rather than illness), trauma researchers advertised for adults who had experienced sexual trauma but hadn't had any psychiatric problems in later life. Many people responded, eager to tell their stories, and researchers picked thirty-one adults—middle-aged, upper middle class, and well educated—as the resilient group, compared with a nonresilient control group, people from similar backgrounds whose earlier traumas had produced severe psychiatric consequences. Friends or family were used to confirm what the subjects themselves described about their lives. Surprisingly, the resilient group reported that they'd had little social and parental support in childhood. In contrast, the nonresilient group reported good social and parental support in childhood. A harsh childhood predicted adult resilience; a more benign childhood produced PTSD.

Perhaps the most common childhood hardship is loss of a parent, by death or divorce, a proven risk factor for adult depression. Studying predictors of greatness in 699 historical figures, psychologist Dean Keith Simonton found that 61 percent of great leaders lost a parent before age thirty-one, 52 percent before age twenty-six, and 45 percent before age twenty-one.

Apparent conflict in the above studies may relate to the difference between hardship and trauma. Trauma is more intense and acute, while hardship is less intense but more long lasting. Poverty is often a hardship, a chronic problem, not a brief intense trauma. It may have different effects, especially in relation to resilience, than a one-time severe trauma (such as battle or rape). In both cases, though, as we'll see, trauma and hardship interact with personality to determine whether or not a person becomes resilient and survives, maybe even thrives, or succumbs.

Personality: Personality traits that reflect biological temperament are usually set by age three or so, and persist throughout adulthood. They are not themselves produced by trauma. Adults who have higher neuroticism scores experience more PTSD than those with low scores, despite the presence in all cases of childhood sexual abuse. As we saw in the introduction, neuroticism is one of three major personality traits; it measures a person's general level of anxiety. If one tends to worry a lot, one has high scores; if one is usually calm and serene, one has low scores. People with hyperthymic personalities generally have low neuroticism.

Besides low neuroticism, hyperthymia enhances resilience. For example, one study examined psychiatric evaluations from seventy-two terrorist attacks in Russia between 1994 and 2005, during which time 7,416 hostages were taken, 1,609 people were killed, and 2,401 people were wounded. PTSD was more common in those hostages with neuroticism traits ("diffident, doubting, closed persons"), and least likely in hostages with hyperthymic personality traits.

Studies of normal populations may also point to the influence of hyperthymic traits. For instance, "positive emotions" (like gratitude, interest in others, sociability, friendliness, love, a sense of humor) are associated with greater psychological resilience to trauma. These traits are also present to a high degree in people with hyperthymic personalities. In one study of forty-six college students before and after the September 11 terrorist attacks in 2001, presence of positive emotions before the trauma predicted less depression afterward. Similarly, in young adults with childhood sexual abuse, positive emotions predicted better long-term outcomes. Building on this work, Bonanno has used the term "hardiness" to explain resilience, which he defines as "being committed to finding a meaningful purpose in life, the belief that one can influence one's surroundings and the outcome of events, and the belief that one can learn and grow from both positive and negative life experiences." This is a good description of how people with hyperthymic personality think, and such a worldview might do even more to influence resilience by affecting the kind of social support one receives. Having a circle of supportive friends and family—which Bonanno and others have identified as contributing to resilience—can be seen partly as the *result* of an extraverted, sociable, hyperthymic personality that draws people toward you. Genetic studies with identical versus fraternal twins support this paradoxical link—your genes and your personality partly determine the environment you will experience.

Of all these positive personality traits associated with resilience, I would emphasize humor. Roosevelt and Kennedy were famously witty, a hallmark of hyperthymic personality. Indeed, humor is a central ingredient to resilience. Psychoanalysts have long noted that a good sense of humor is a strong sign of psychological maturity. Freud wrote an entire book about wit, and the psychoanalyst George Vaillant, in his classic fifty-year study of mental health, concluded that humor was the best hallmark of mental health. If so, hyperthymic people, who are often seen as funny, may be the healthiest ones around. Their wit is not accidental to their resilience.

WE NOW COME TO the paradox of trauma—its *steeling* effect. Not only can it make a person psychiatrically ill, but it can make someone psychiatrically healthier. There is post-traumatic *growth:* trauma itself might not harm some people psychologically at all; it might in fact help them. It is not a matter of getting better *despite* the trauma, but rather *because* of it.

One source of evidence for the steeling effect is a classic study that followed children of the Great Depression into adulthood, which found that those who had experienced *more* childhood poverty grew up to be *more* psychologically healthy (based on standard psychological tests). Here is another way of testing the steeling affect: Are people with past PTSD more, or less, prone to experiencing future PTSD when exposed to new traumas? This question, rarely asked, answered itself in a project run by a research group, with which I was associated, at Massachusetts General Hospital. Given that PTSD symptoms had increased in New York City after the September 11 terrorist attacks, we were interested in the impact of the 9/11 trauma on people with mental illness, specifically those with bipolar disorder. From an earlier study, we'd already gotten data on PTSD prevalence in New York–based bipolar patients before 9/11, so we went back and tested them after the attacks. Just as in the general population, PTSD symptoms rose in people with bipolar disorder after 9/11, except for one group—those who'd *already had* PTSD and recovered from it before 9/11. Without intending to do so, we showed that past PTSD could, like a vaccine, protect against future PTSD.

There's other evidence for the steeling effect. For instance, in a study of well-being in two thousand adults, thirty-seven common harmful life events were studied, like losing a loved one, or divorce, or a serious illness. Subjective well-being, one's sense of personal happiness, was highest in those with some (two to six) but not too many or too few (zero to one) life traumas. Other research suggests that we might learn from trauma. One study began with the observation that although stress generally increases symptoms of depression, some people do not experience much depression, even with severe stress. So in seventy-eight women who had experienced a serious life event in the prior three months (such as sudden unemployment, a new serious illness, or the death of a family member or friend), researchers studied how depressed those subjects became after watching a sad film clip. The main factor being studied was the ability of subjects to interpret what had happened in a positive way (called "cognitive reappraisal"). In other words, it is not just what happens but how one feels about what happens that makes it a seriously negative or harmful experience. Some people are able to see an event as less harmful than others: after the death of an old beloved pet, for instance, one might focus on the many good years that had been spent together. The researchers found that those subjects who showed good cognitive reappraisal ability (using a standard measure, the Emotion Regulation Questionnaire) showed very little increase in depression after viewing the sad film clips, while those with poor cognitive reappraisal became much more depressed. One might thus think of depressive episodes as being learning experiences where one learns, or is forced to learn, how to reinterpret and reframe harsh life experiences if one is to survive. When future life stresses are faced, the depressed person may be in a better position, armed with methods of cognitive reappraisal, to face them.

Resilience grows out of exposure to, not complete avoidance of, risk. Recall the vaccine metaphor: trauma itself is not a disease, just as a virus is not itself an infection. Many of us get exposed to viruses or bacteria without developing any symptoms of disease. Similarly, we can experience traumas without developing any symptoms of PTSD. And yet that trauma can vaccinate us against future problems (like PTSD) when faced with future, perhaps more severe, traumas.

The vaccine metaphor leads to another metaphor (Nietzsche once said that truth is a mobile army of metaphors): immunity. The reason a virus itself fails to produce infection is dependent on the "host response," meaning how the body reacts to the virus. If one's immune system is strong, even a lot of virus exposure is harmless. If one is immune compromised, even a little virus can cause disease. So it is with hyperthymic personality. With that temperament, one can withstand a great deal of trauma, and even get stronger, whereas someone with a highly neurotic temperament may succumb to PTSD after being exposed to relatively slight trauma.

Hyperthymic personality is like an innate immunity to trauma. It is a harbinger of resilience. So too, often, are mental illnesses like manic depression. Mental illness and biologically abnormal temperaments may give great leaders—like Churchill and, as we'll now see, Franklin Roosevelt and John Kennedy—just such controlled exposure to risk throughout their lifetimes, perfecting the cocktail of resilience.

CHAPTER 10

A FIRST-RATE TEMPERAMENT

ROOSEVELT

On March 8, 1933, four days after the inauguration, one era paid its respects to another when a newly elected President Franklin Roosevelt called on Oliver Wendell Holmes. The elderly Supreme Court justice (who turned ninety-two years old that day) was a Civil War veteran, a man who as a child had played at the knee of Ralph Waldo Emerson and had come of age with the philosopher William James. As a Civil War officer, he had even accompanied Abraham Lincoln on a visit to the battlefront. (When a Confederate sharpshooter's bullet almost shot off the president's stovepipe hat, Holmes yelled at Lincoln, "Get down, you fool!") Roosevelt's wheelchair couldn't easily maneuver the narrow doorway of Holmes's house, so he put on his braces and struggled into a parlor, where Holmes rose slowly with the aid of a cane to greet him. Despite the dire depression that gripped the country, their conversation was light and banal: reminiscences about Harvard and mutual friends. FDR asked Holmes if he could do anything for him; Holmes requested permission to remove some of his money from the bank. At the end, FDR, facing the greatest economic crisis of American history, asked Holmes if he had any advice to offer. Holmes thought back to his army days and mentioned that when the troops were in retreat, all one could do was "blow your trumpet" and "give the order to charge. And that's exactly what you are doing." It is often held that soon after Roosevelt left, the old judge, turning to an aide, gave this verdict: "A second-class intellect, but a first-rate temperament."

The old judge was inerrant. FDR's first-rate temperament—or in psychological terms his personality—was hyperthymic. He was high in energy, extremely talkative, outgoing, extraverted—in short, very good company. When the journalist John Gunther first met FDR, the president was so buoyant that Gunther concluded, "Obviously that man has never had indigestion in his life." His talkativeness was famed. After Gunther made a trip to Latin America in 1937, the State Department asked him to brief the president in six or seven minutes set aside from the president's busy morning schedule; Roosevelt's appointments ran over, and the meeting was rescheduled for midafternoon. When Gunther finally got into the office, Roosevelt greeted him effusively and then proceeded to talk almost without interruption for forty-six minutes. Even when he wasn't speaking, his face was "never at rest, almost hyperthyroid." When the journalist mentioned that he had visited all twenty countries in Latin America, FDR asked the only question of this supposed briefing: "What are the bad spots?" When Gunther mentioned Panama, whose president was from Harvard, he triggered a thirty-minute monologue that began with FDR's alma mater ("Not really, is he a *Harvard* man?"), and proceeded to a discussion of the president of Haiti, the notion of colonizing Argentina, how FDR once rode through Montevideo, how Iquitos, Peru, should become a free port, how FDR told the president of Brazil to nationalize the utilities industry, the need for tourism in Chile, how Gunther should meet a certain chap in Puerto Rico who liked dry martinis, and on and on. Then he shifted to Europe, and by the time FDR was interrupted by a telephone call, Gunther was "acutely embarrassed" that he had taken up so much of the president's time. He got up to leave, but FDR waved him to stay, finally saying goodbye after the phone conversation ended a while later.

"FDR's extreme loquaciousness" was not limited to this one occasion. One general, during his first meeting with the president, could not find the opportunity to speak a single word. White House visitors developed special techniques to get Roosevelt to stop talking. "My own method," a well-known judge reported, "was to let him run for exactly five minutes, and then to cut in ruthlessly." A cabinet secretary commented: "The simplest way to get at the President was to be invited to lunch. Then you could talk while he ate." There seemed to be a method to Roosevelt's distractibility. He would change topics suddenly, as if to test or unnerve visitors, by, for instance, "asking somebody who had never been in Latin America what was the best hotel in Peru."

Some observers thought that Roosevelt purposefully digressed at the beginning of meetings to loosen up often tense sessions. For instance, after Pearl Harbor, during a special meeting of six senior military and political advisers where all expected FDR to get right to the urgent question of war, the president launched into a twenty-minute story about lobster fishing in Maine.

His verbosity reflected a generally high energy level. Says Gunther, "His vitality was, as everybody knows, practically unlimited. . . . In one campaign he traveled 13,000 miles in about seven weeks, and made 16 major and 67 second-string speeches—not to mention innumerable back platform appearances . . . and never stopped having a wonderful time." In twelve years of presidency, he made 399 trips by rail, covering about 545,000 miles. In 1936, the strenuous campaign exhausted the physically healthy Republican candidate, Alf Landon; doctors advised him to take to bed in its final days. The paralyzed president, in contrast, showed no strain. Thinking also of FDR's distant cousin, the exuberant Theodore Roosevelt, journalist (and FDR critic) H. L. Mencken reflected, "The Roosevelt family is completely superhuman. No member of it ever becomes tired."

Despite this high energy, FDR did not have a short sleep pattern (unlike many people with hyperthymic personality, like his cousin Theodore, who wrote about 100,000 letters during seven years of presidency and could read three or four books per night: Franklin once noted that TR needed only six hours' sleep nightly, while FDR felt he needed eight). It is said that throughout the war, Roosevelt maintained a regular sleep schedule, usually going to bed by 10 p.m. and waking around 7 a.m. One source reports that throughout his presidency he had only two sleepless nights, one on the day the banks closed and another on a night when Churchill was a houseguest. (Pearl Harbor did not keep him awake.)

Roosevelt was full of nervous energy, but not depressed or angst-ridden: Gunther wrote, "He was often restless, even agitated, but once a decision was made, he seldom worried. . . . 'He must have been psychoanalyzed by God,' one of his early associates told me. He almost never showed serious dubiety, disappointment, or depression. He was full of nerves and conflicts . . . but these did not end in any 'neurotic stagnation'; his buoyancy, gay resilience, and capacity to withstand shocks made him seem made of rubber."

HE WAS HIGHLY SOCIABLE. On his Harvard alumni questionnaire, when asked his aversions, he replied, "None." He spent about a quarter of the working day on the telephone. A circle of about one hundred advisers knew they could call him at any time on the telephone without means of an intermediary. He knew how to get people to do what he needed, even if they did not agree with him about why. Once, when asked why he asked political opponents to serve in his administration, he commented, "You know, a man will do a lot of right things for the wrong reasons."

His longtime associate and secretary of labor Frances Perkins called him "incurably sociable," even needing to read books aloud to others rather than by himself. His close aide Robert Jackson, who served him as attorney general and later as a Supreme Court justice, viewed FDR's sociability as his strongest asset: "It was here that Roosevelt was irresistible and inimitable. He liked people, almost any people. He liked their company, liked to pick their minds and see what they were thinking, liked to know the details of their lives and problems." Jackson contrasts FDR with Woodrow Wilson, whom FDR had served and admired. In personality, though not in politics, Franklin resembled his Republican relative, the dynamo Theodore, rather than the professorial Wilson. For instance, Jackson recounts meeting in the 1930s with one of Wilson's old aides, who described how they advised Wilson to meet with American businessmen in order to ramp up the war effort in the early months of World War I:

"[Wilson] refused to see most of them, saying they were specialists who had nothing to teach him with his general problems affecting the whole nation. Finally they prevailed upon him to see Henry Ford, and after the interview, [an aide] entered and said to the President, 'What do you think of Henry Ford?' Wilson impatiently answered, 'I think he is the most comprehensively ignorant man I ever met.' He had complete contempt for Ford. Two or three days after that lunch with [Wilson's old aide], I noticed that Ford was President Roosevelt's luncheon guest. I happened to be at the White House that afternoon late and opened the conversation by saying, 'Mr. President, I see you had lunch with Henry Ford.' 'Yes,' he said, 'I had a grand time with Uncle Henry.'" Then FDR launched into an extensive account of how he tried to get Ford to discuss the problem of low wages, despite Ford's constant efforts to avoid that topic. "But he liked Ford and respected him for the things in which he was able." The temperamental contrast with Wilson was sharp.

This sociability had its downside—a wish to be liked by everyone, which, in the context of his official responsibilities, led to some administrative disarray. Jackson viewed this as the president's main deficiency: "There was always considerable conflict of policy within the Administration and different factions favored different courses. . . .

There were always those who were trying to get him to commit himself in a hurry, and too often he yielded. The remedy, instead of squarely backing up and undoing what he had done, was to promulgate some sort of compromise. He was reluctant to dismiss or demote anyone he liked, and he liked nearly everybody. Instead of dismissing someone who was pursuing a course inconsistent with his policy, he would create an additional layer of authority, which usually merely complicated matters." Jackson draws a conclusion that reflects, I think, a core argument of this book: "Roosevelt certainly was not accomplished as an administrator and in normal times, when his office demanded only an orderly and efficient administration of settled affairs, it is doubtful if he could have been a distinguished President. He was just not a routine executive." Frances Perkins confirms that FDR was not "a careful, direct-line administrator"; rather his method of "not giving direct and specific orders to his subordinates released the creative energy of many men. . . . His four-track mind proved invaluable . . . he could keep many activities operating at top efficiency." Roosevelt was a whirlwind of a leader, an entrepreneurial president, always thinking ahead. (After the first wave of New Deal laws, Vice President John Garner advised the impatient leader, "Mr. President, you know you've got to let the cattle graze.") He would never have made a good corporate boss, nor would he have left the country alone in good times, as Coolidge did. Roosevelt was too unhealthy to be a good leader in normal times; but in abnormal times he was just right.

FOR BETTER OR WORSE, Roosevelt's sociable charm also attracted women. Many have noted that FDR had numerous female friends and that he loved to flirt. Later researchers have shown, with reasonable documentation, that some of these relations were sexual and extramarital (such as those with White House aides Lucy Mercer and Missy LeHand), although, unlike John Kennedy, as we will see, FDR's relations were fewer and of longer standing (one to two decades with each of the women mentioned). That FDR was highly attractive to women, especially before polio, is without doubt. But another source of his energetic libido may have been his hyperthymic personality.

His renowned sense of humor, another hyperthymic trait, often proved useful at strategic moments. In the Tehran summit, for instance, Stalin said that after the war fifty thousand German officers and leaders should be shot without trial. Churchill objected: after a fair trial, a thousand or so might be proven innocent. Tempers flared. Then FDR had an idea: why not just shoot forty-nine thousand instead? Stalin laughed, and the subject was dropped. Another time, Roosevelt was scheduled to talk to the Daughters of the American Revolution—a speech he dreaded. After a long and staid introductory ceremony, FDR—whose Dutch ancestors had come to New York in the seventeenth century—struggled to the stage in his braces, clutched the podium, and, smiling broadly at the audience of stiff matronly DAR members, began, "My fellow immigrants . . ."

Roosevelt's addiction to press conferences represents the consummate blending of his hyperverbal and energetic temperament. Though no president other than Nixon faced such hostile media, no president engaged the press like FDR. In FDR's era, the media was largely conservative. It has been estimated that in the New Deal years, editorial pages of about 60 to 80 percent of newspapers opposed him. Regions now liberal, such as New England, were reliably Republican in those days; not a single Boston newspaper endorsed him in 1932. (Two decades later, little had changed; before John Kennedy became the first post–Civil War Democratic senator from Massachusetts, only one Boston daily, to which his father had recently given a large donation, endorsed him. As JFK commented, "You know, we had to buy that fucking paper.")

Despite, or perhaps because of, such hostility, FDR launched a media charm offensive unrivaled until Kennedy, and never approximated since. He held casual, cordial press conferences, with around a hundred to two hundred reporters attending, about twice weekly throughout his presidency (excluding vacations and campaign months); over twelve years, there were almost a thousand press conferences in all (about seventy-seven per year). (This was not new for him; as New York governor, he held press conferences twice *daily*.) Hearty laughter was common. For Roosevelt, reporters were potential friends to be won, rather than enemies to be avoided.

By the end of the 1930s, after this long and intensive campaign, FDR had won the media over. In the meantime, he had enjoyed himself immensely.

A KEY ASPECT of hyperthymic personality is "openness to experience" (one of the three major personality traits, along with neuroticism and extraversion). People with hyperthymic personality tend to score very high on openness to experience; they are curious, inventive, experimental souls. (They also tend to score low on neuroticism and high on extraversion.)

Roosevelt's high level of openness to experience is most visible intellectually. He was an omnivore and an innovator. Despite Holmes's verdict about a second-rate intelligence, Roosevelt's intellect was hardly inferior. He was open-minded and keen: "Innovations never frightened him, and he liked nothing better than a new idea. . . . The President's omniscience and erudition covered a very wide arc indeed; he knew a little about almost everything, from where to get a good beer in Georgetown to which wives of Cabinet ministers gossiped most. The three subjects about which he knew most were politics, American history, and geography in general." He loved to read, as Gunther put it, in four basic areas: American history, nautical works, "trash," and newspapers—all of six to eight papers daily. He spoke French fluently, could read German, and was semiliterate in Spanish.

An anecdote brings out both his broad, inventive intellect and his insatiable curiosity. After Yalta, FDR was headed to Saudi Arabia. Flying low over the sandy desert, he asked an aide why no one had ever irrigated that land to create farms. There is no water, the aide replied. None at all, Roosevelt asked? Just in oases and some wells. Wells mean there is a water table, the president surmised; how far down is it? About fifty feet, replied his aide. The president wondered: We can give them good pumps to bring it out, can't we? Yes, but the water would evaporate in the desert heat, said the aide. Why not irrigate at night, then, asked FDR? The questions never ended. A few days later, Roosevelt made the same inquiry with King Ibn Saud. "I am an old man," the king protested. "Agriculture is not for me." FDR was not satisfied; he later said privately that after his retirement he wanted to go to the Middle East and teach them to grow their own food ("an operation like the Tennessee Valley system"), the lack of which he saw as the main cause for the "explosiveness" of that region.

Roosevelt's intellectual openness was evident in his invention of the concept of a "brain trust" during the 1932 campaign, a reliance on academic expertise that has since become commonplace but at the time was quite unusual. Though he might or might not eventually agree with them, Roosevelt always sought out a wide range of ideas. He once said, "You sometimes find something pretty good in the lunatic fringe. In fact, we have got as part of our social and economic government today a whole lot of things which in my boyhood were considered lunatic fringe, and yet they are now part of everyday life." Roosevelt thought ahead, once writing a memorandum addressed to whoever would be president in 1956. "That fellow in the White House," his 1940 presidential opponent, Wendell Willkie, once remarked, "is just too smart to live."

FDR's intellect was not of the academic variety, as Justice Holmes perhaps realized. Roosevelt read hardly any philosophy or poetry, preferring history. When pressed to engage in intellectual discussion, he demurred. Once, a young reporter asked somewhat peremptorily, "Mr. President, are you a Communist?" "No." "Are you a capitalist?" "No." "Are you a Socialist?" "No," FDR said with a look of surprise. "Well, what is your philosophy then?" "Philosophy?" asked the president, puzzled. "Philosophy? I am a Christian and a Democrat—that's all."

Though not well versed in philosophy per se, Roosevelt was curious about human nature. In 1944, he invited a young Washington theologian to a private White House dinner. The conversation veered toward theology, and the visitor mentioned the nineteenth-century existentialist philosopher Søren Kierkegaard. Roosevelt admitted that he'd never heard of that name. The theologian explained that Kierkegaard was becoming popular, especially for his insights about the inherent sinfulness of humanity. Faced with Nazism, Roosevelt was intrigued, read some of Kierkegaard's works, and thereafter recommended reading the philosopher as a way to understand the Nazi evil.

Roosevelt's special expertise was geography, a skill developed when, confined to bed by polio and no longer able to play his beloved golf, he became a philatelic fanatic. With each new country's stamp, FDR read books and articles about its geography, eventually acquiring expertise on even the remotest lands. Once, in a meeting about Japan's attacking China's coast, while advisers searched for a map, FDR scribbled on a piece of paper China's coastal contours, cities, and ports. When the advisers produced a map, it matched his depiction.

FAMILY HISTORY PROVIDES some evidence, though not definitive, for FDR's hyperthymic personality. Theodore, probably manic-depressive and famously superenergetic, was a fifth cousin. Closer relations also displayed unusual temperaments. One neighbor called FDR's grandfather, Isaac Roosevelt, who trained as a physician but never practiced, "a queer duck." His father, James Roosevelt, was something of an adventurer: he left New York to fight alongside Giuseppe Garibaldi in the unification of nineteenth-century Italy. This brief family history obviously does not demonstrate frank insanity, such as psychosis, mania, or severe depression. But it does suggest that FDR's relatives had personalities abnormal enough to arouse the attention of average people. Hyperthymic personality is inherited not just in families where full-blown mania or depression occurs but also in those where there is a lot of hyperthymic personality. In fact, in some genetic studies of bipolar disorder, the most common condition seen in relatives is hyperthymic personality or low-level manic symptoms (hypomania). Full mania and severe depression, though present more than in the general population, are less common than hyperthymic personality.

We don't have much documentary evidence of others in Roosevelt's family who may have had full-blown severe mania or depression, but what limited evidence we have is consistent with hyperthymic personality. Even if this is not the case, the other sources of evidence (symptoms and course in particular) are consistent with hyperthymic personality. (In diagnosing mental illness, *all* four diagnostic validators don't have to be present; it is the preponderance of the evidence that counts. The more positive evidence there is, the more confident one can be in the diagnosis.)

Married at age fifty-two, James died in 1900 when FDR was eighteen, leaving Franklin alone with his famously imperious mother, Sara Delano. Sara, the strongest presence in FDR's life, later engaged in a long twilight struggle with his wife, Eleanor; as with most of his relationships, FDR refused to choose sides or let either one go.

Coming from such a prominent family, FDR grew up close to power. When he was four or five, his father took him to the White House, where President Grover Cleveland, beset by troubles, offered this advice: "I have one wish for you, little man, that you will never be President of the United States." When he married Eleanor, Theodore's niece, in 1905, President Teddy gave the bride away amid much Manhattan society. Great things were expected of him.

UNTIL 1921, Franklin Roosevelt had led a charmed life. Thirty-nine years old, with five children, a recent vice presidential nominee, a member of the presidential cabinet only three years earlier, he seemed ready to follow his cousin Teddy to the White House. Then fate intervened. After a summer swim in a pond, he got a chill, then a high fever.

His legs felt numb and tingly; then they stopped moving. His frantic family called the best doctors, who quickly recognized the terrible reality: he had contracted "infantile paralysis," or polio.

Roosevelt and his family were devastated. All his political plans were put on hold. He just wanted to walk again, to play and run and swim with his children, to resume golfing with his college chums. For three years, he focused only on halting the advance of his disease and rehabilitating his legs. He spent many months at various mineral spas—his favorite being Hot Springs, Georgia—where he exercised his legs. Though he ultimately recovered some strength, he remained highly disabled, and struggled emotionally. "It's ridiculous to tell me that a grown man cannot conquer a child's disease," he complained.

If his progress was to continue, he still needed to focus on physical rehabilitation, so he refused calls from old New York friends in 1924 to return to the political arena. But New York governor Al Smith, who was then running for president, could wait no longer; he intensified efforts to draft FDR for governor. Smith phoned Hot Springs over and over again; FDR kept avoiding the calls. The governor then lobbied Eleanor, the children, and Roosevelt's friends. Eleanor came around; so did FDR's daughter. Despite knowing that his physical recovery would stall, Roosevelt reluctantly agreed to run for the office Smith now held.

He returned to public life. But the man who came back was not the same one who swam in that pond in 1921.

ONE MAJOR CHANGE in FDR's life was that now almost all physical activity involved great effort. When he gave a speech, he was wheeled to the platform, then lifted on braces to the podium, on which he leaned his whole weight to avoid falling. His aides made certain that each podium was anchored securely to withstand his weight. Even so, he fell, or almost fell, about five times over twenty years of political speechmaking. Roosevelt was challenged and humbled by his paralysis.

At one campaign event in New York in 1928, when no one had noticed that Roosevelt could only enter the crowded auditorium by way of a high fire escape, he had no choice but to accept, in Frances Perkins's words, the "ultimate humility which comes from being helped physically." He had to allow himself to be carried in front of the crowd in the arms of other men. Then "he got up on his braces, adjusted them, straightened himself, smoothed his hair, linked his arm to his son Jim's, and walked out on the platform as if this were nothing unusual."

The sheer physical effort of trying to live an active life despite his paralysis was immense. His daughter told a similar story that illustrates the courage and resilience that so endeared him to his supporters. Roosevelt was going to speak in a huge hall in Brooklyn, but the only way inside was through the main entrance, with many broad steps and no railing. Not wanting to make a labored entrance in front of the audience, FDR chose to go up a steep iron fire escape to the stage. He climbed slowly, using his arms and shoulders to swing each leg up. Recalled his daughter, "When he reached the top, his face was streaming with perspiration, and his white shirt was soaked. He paused just long enough to mop his face and catch his breath. Then he walked out on to the stage and faced the audience with a humorous remark about the fact that it was quite warm in the hall."

He could never be left alone, except when he slept. This complete absence of privacy, he once said, was the worst aspect of his disability.

POLIO CHANGED FRANKLIN ROOSEVELT in ways that went well beyond the physical. He remained energetic and motivated, but he carried a different attitude. Pre-polio FDR was "an untried rather flippant young man," according to one political friend. Roosevelt was *disciplined* by his illness, future Supreme Court justice Robert Jackson remarked. Frances Perkins had known Roosevelt since 1910, and was close to him throughout his presidency until his last days. She was well positioned to know him before and after polio, and she was convinced there was a huge change: "Roosevelt underwent a spiritual transformation during the years of his illness. I noticed when he came back that the years of pain and suffering had purged the slightly arrogant attitude he had displayed on occasion before he was stricken. The man emerged completely warmhearted, with humility of spirit and with a deeper philosophy. . . . I saw Roosevelt only once between 1921 and 1924, and I was instantly struck by his growth. He was young, he was crippled, he was physically weak, but he had a firmer grip on life and on himself than ever before."

Before polio, he was a successful patrician: assistant secretary of the navy in Wilson's administration, vice presidential candidate in 1920, poised to run for senator or governor. After three years of seclusion, he returned to the national limelight at the 1924 Democratic convention, leaner, older, wheelchair-bound, speaking not as a candidate, as many had expected pre-polio, but as Smith's campaign manager. After hours of mediocre, self-serving speechifying, interspersed with tepid applause, Roosevelt held the delegates spellbound for seventeen minutes with an address that would become famous as the "Happy Warrior" speech. Describing Smith, Roosevelt cited lines from Wordsworth: "This is the Happy Warrior; this is he that every man in arms should wish to be." The delegates gave him a twelve-minute standing ovation, followed by an hour of singing, cheering, and clapping.

Four years later, running against the New York City Democratic machine of Tammany Hall, Roosevelt won the New York governorship, and four years after that, the presidency. FDR's hyperthymic personality steeled him for the challenges that his polio and later his presidency would make him face. And his polio seems to have given him a degree of empathy that we've seen in other leaders who endured depression. This combination of nature and circumstance made him unusually fit for the unprecedented series of crises that would mark his years in the White House.

Without hiding his disability, Roosevelt never used it to garner sympathy. It was, if anything, a political handicap. Some wondered, when he first ran for governor, whether a paralyzed man was fit to govern. (Al Smith responded, "A governor does not have to be an acrobat. We do not elect him for his ability to do a double back flip or a handspring.") In 1932, a rumor spread that polio eventually would affect the brain, making Roosevelt insane. FDR responded by authorizing three physicians to fully examine him and his medical records. Their report was frank in describing his physical disability, and his psychological strength: "Ten years ago, Governor Roosevelt suffered an attack of acute infantile paralysis, the entire effect of which was expended on the muscles of his lower extremities. There has been progressive recovery of power in the legs since that date; this restoration continues and will continue."

IN SUM, hyperthymic personality is key to Roosevelt's psychology. It made him open to new ideas, and charismatic, but also, in the face of polio, hyperthymia helped him to be resilient, to rise above and better understand human suffering. This psychological evolution may have helped him handle the huge crises of economic depression and world war. His mind was agile and he did not recoil from the most terrible of decisions. He had imbibed the pragmatic philosophy that Justice Holmes had helped invent—the view, as Perkins put it, that "nothing in human judgment is final. One may courageously take the step that seems right today because it can be modified tomorrow if it does not work well." She thought this attitude freed Roosevelt to act. Indeed it did. But it was not just a philosophical judgment that FDR made; rather, this approach was part of his hyperthymic temperament, the always active mind that would never have given him the option of standing still. (In contrast, normal, mentally healthy leaders like George W. Bush make decisions, but refuse to modify them when they do not work well. This inflexibility, I hold, is a feature of not being hyperthymic, that is, of *not* being mentally abnormal, as we'll see.)

Roosevelt never sought an overarching ideology to guide his decisions. He made each decision step by step, backing off where things did not work, forging ahead when they did. After a while, he was building a new approach to government, though he probably had not foreseen it clearly. In 1929, he saw that the Great Depression was "the end of an era" and that "recovery was not enough." He had declared something entirely new, a philosophy that remains controversial in American politics—the notion that government had a duty to create jobs and take care of its citizens, for a government "that cannot take care of its old, that cannot provide work for the strong and willing, that lets the black shadow of insecurity rest on every home is not a government that can or should endure."

Of all his programs, Roosevelt took the most pride in Social Security, though even there he refused to take an ideological approach. When the program was being prepared, one proposal would have covered everyone at the time, but it would have left a deficit to be handled by the U.S. government in 1980. "We can't sell the United States short in 1980 any more than in 1935," Roosevelt objected. Still, he faced critics who assumed there must be an ulterior motive. Frances Perkins, then secretary of labor, recalled appearing before a Senate committee, where Senator Thomas Gore from Oklahoma, blind and elderly, a former progressive Democrat, asked sarcastically, "Isn't this Socialism?" "Oh, no," Perkins replied. "Then, smiling, leaning forward and talking to me as though I were a child, he said, 'Isn't this a teeny-weeny bit of Socialism?'"

Franklin Roosevelt wasn't worried about any accusation, nor even of bringing about piecemeal socialism in the United States. He knew only that people were hurting; he knew what it was like to hurt; and his personality would not allow him to sit still. He tried whatever worked, and with that method he achieved astounding success. This wasn't just because of an intellectual pragmatism, as many presume. Though he studied at Harvard from 1900 to 1904 when the influential founder of philosophical pragmatism, William James, taught there, FDR did not take a class with James, and, as previously noted, he hardly read philosophy. His pragmatism was not intellectual; it was temperamental.

(James had the view anyway that one's philosophy is determined by one's personality.) It was not an overstatement when, long after Justice Holmes, another elderly American statesman, John Kenneth Galbraith—a member of FDR's administration, and a later confidant of Kennedy and Johnson—could conclude that FDR was "the greatest political personality of the century."

All this would not have happened had his hyperthymic temperament been different, as Holmes rightly saw. Nor would it have happened had he not been tried by the adversity of illness and, with his hyperthymic energy and spirit, grown from the experience. Frances Perkins saw this ability to grow, this "viability," as the hallmark of Roosevelt's personality. So too did the president's wife. Asked years later whether FDR's polio affected his politics, Eleanor summed it up well: "He would certainly have been President," she remarked, "but a president of a different kind."

CHAPTER 11

SICKNESS IN CAMELOT

KENNEDY

John F. Kennedy should never have survived into his thirties, much less become a great president. His success in becoming America's youngest president is in itself more remarkable than many realize. He overcame great adversity, like FDR, because of his hyperthymic personality.

Psychologically, young John Kennedy was a highly energetic, charming, hypersexual rebel—marked all over by traits of hyperthymic personality. At prestigious Choate Academy, where his brother Joe had been a star student-athlete, John posted middling grades and belonged to a misfit gang called the "Muckers," whose rebellious antics led to his temporary expulsion, reversed after a conference between the headmaster, George St. John, and Joseph Kennedy Sr. (After getting young John to promise Mr. St. John that he would behave, Joe Sr., himself a rebel, admonished the boy privately, "If that crazy Muckers club had been mine, you can be sure it wouldn't have started with an M!") Years later, when Choate planned a book about his school years, President Kennedy responded laconically, "I do not think it particularly helpful to go through the monthly reports, etc. It might have an adverse effect on the work of students who might think it necessary to work hard and do well at school in order to become President." The book did not advertise that headmaster St. John had been concerned enough about the mental state of the future president that he had arranged for a psychological evaluation of the seventeen-year-old, which, besides documenting an IQ of 119, concluded that Kennedy was "a very able boy, but definitely in a trap, psychologically speaking. He has established a reputation in the family for thoughtlessness, sloppiness, and inefficiency, and he feels entirely at home in the role."

AFTER HIS OLDER BROTHER Joe was killed in World War II, Jack was given the family mantle to bear. But before the adult Jack could deliver, the teenage Jack had to survive. John Kennedy was sick most of his life, and almost died multiple times before he was assassinated. In his teen years, Kennedy experienced the first of many lifelong physical illnesses that, inexplicable at the time, probably reflect onset of Addison's disease and related immune system illnesses. In Addison's disease, the adrenal glands do not produce steroids, which are essential for the proper functioning of the immune system. Like other immune system deficiencies, such as AIDS, Addison's disease makes its sufferers unable to resist infections. Along with adrenal problems, other immune system abnormalities in the body can lead to inflammation in the bowels, leading to belly pain and diarrhea, or inflammation in the muscles, leading to back pain. Kennedy was to suffer all these illnesses, without ever fully realizing how they were connected.

At age thirteen he was hospitalized with severe abdominal pain, which would recur throughout his life. Because of his weak immune system, even a knee scrape would lead to severe infection, a long healing process, and the need for crutches. He had frequent colds, ear infections, and influenza. Jack was sick so often that his brother Robert joked that if a mosquito bit Jack, the mosquito would die. At age seventeen, he had his worst infection ever, with high fever, hives all over his body, very low white blood cell count (probably due to inadequate steroid levels), and jaundice. He was diagnosed with fatal leukemia and given a 5 percent chance of survival.

His father, unwilling to accept this death sentence, sought a second opinion—a month of testing at the Mayo Clinic, after which the best doctors of the era confessed that they had no idea what illness had almost killed the young man. Nevertheless, the doctors prescribed strict diet and limits on physical exertion.

Like manic-depressive illness, Addison's disease is episodic; crises are followed by natural recovery, and later relapse into another episode. Probably because of nature, rather than the doctors' advice, Kennedy improved in his final year of high school and graduated. In the next few years, though, the episodes increased in frequency and severity: on a trip to London after graduation, after entering Princeton, and following his withdrawal from Princeton. Months of hospitalization were inconclusive; tests were still mostly normal. Symptoms were nonspecific: jaundice, weight loss, fatigue, diarrhea. Kennedy knew his condition was serious, and seriously confusing. While he was at Brigham Hospital, he wrote to a friend that "they have not found out anything as yet except that I have leukemia + agranulocytosis. Took a peak [*sic*] at my chart yesterday and could see that they were mentally measuring me for a coffin." He felt ashamed of his illnesses and weakness, it seems, competing even there with his brother Joe. "Joe's blood count was 9400," he wrote in a letter to his brother Robert, "mine for comparison was 4000 which makes him twice as healthy."

As psychoanalytic concepts became popular, one of Kennedy's Boston doctors, gastrointestinal specialist Sara Jordan, concluded that his problem was not a serious physical illness but an emotional malaise affecting his intestines. The death sentence was now lifted, but Jack now received a vaguer psychiatric sentence. His father was ambivalent, writing Jordan that "one of the things I am a little disturbed about is that he may get to thinking he is a sick boy—I see some signs of this—and I want him to get away from that idea as quickly as possible." And in another note: "One thing I want to be sure of is that he doesn't develop into a hypochondriac. So, if there isn't anything seriously the matter with him let's tell him that everybody has a few disturbances now and then." In later years, Kennedy would learn the secret of all his medical problems: he had Addison's disease (now known to be mainly an autoimmune illness in which one's adrenal glands stop producing steroid hormones). Throughout his later life, unwilling to publicly acknowledge his real illness, Kennedy fended off lifelong whispers of hypochondriasis.

ONE REASON WHY young John Kennedy kept going, despite his severe bouts of illness, was his hyperthymic temperament. Here I again will examine the four sources of evidence for a psychiatric diagnosis: symptoms, family history, course of illness, and treatment.

Kennedy's *symptoms*, though well known, have not been previously seen as evidence of hyperthymia. When not ill with Addisonian episodes, young JFK possessed a huge libido. His letters abound with sexual innuendo, and he engaged in extensive sexual activity, including visiting prostitutes and probably contracting venereal diseases. Even before steroid treatment, Kennedy had high energy levels when not in an Addisonian crisis, and was extremely sociable.

This sociability and energy were not limited to his youth. Evelyn Lincoln began to work for the young new senator from Massachusetts in January 1953 (by which time he had only recently begun to use steroids), and describes a highly energetic, driven multitasking machine: "Senator Kennedy evidently woke up each morning bursting with new ideas. Many mornings, as soon as he opened the door, he would begin, 'I have several things for you to do. First . . . second . . . third . . .' and so on, all while he was taking off his overcoat." The young senator was a dynamo: "I had never seen anyone with so much energy," his harried new secretary noted. He was constantly dictating letters and memos, speaking rapidly in his thick Boston accent, making accurate transcription difficult. Lincoln proved more adept at dictation than others, and soon became Kennedy's chief secretary. (Years later, President Kennedy's mania for dictation had not changed. "When you see the President," a senator remarked, "you have to get in your car and drive like blazes back to the Capitol to beat his memo commenting on what you told him.") One anecdote Lincoln provides captures the young senator's energy and routine recklessness—his frenzied approach to automobile and air travel:

> He usually sat in his office . . . until I gave him the standard warning signal: "Twenty minutes till takeoff, Senator." . . . I am told, for thank God I never experienced it myself, that their trips to the airport were like riding in a police car on the chase. The Senator liked to take the wheel and race through the streets, barely missing red lights. Cops would whistle, cars would honk, but he ignored everything . . . Muggsie [his driver] . . . would invariably report that they pulled away the steps to the plane as soon as the Senator climbed on. . . . I fully expected to get a call someday with the news that they had failed to make one of those curves on their way to National Airport.

The same hyperactivity was there in the new president, documented in a contemporaneous book by the perceptive writer William Manchester. After Kennedy's arrival in the White House, the change from Eisenhower was palpable. The ambassador to Russia, who rarely met with Eisenhower alone for more than ten minutes at a time, suddenly found himself having repeated two-hour private meetings with the new president. Kennedy kept up his senatorial pace. He "continued to vibrate with energy. He would pace corridors, read on his feet, dictate rapidly, dart out for brisk constitutionals around the monument, and return in a sprint, snapping his restless fingers." Manchester, spending time in the president's private quarters, noticed plenty of presidential nervousness. His right hand constantly moved, thrumming the arm of his chair. His feet and legs squirmed; he was physically restless, despite the reputation for emotional cool. The physical movement took its toll on the presidential furniture: "Two White House chairs have collapsed under the

stress. Once . . . in the middle of a conference with congressional leaders . . . he was fidgeting away, and the next moment there was an explo-
sion, a hail of ancient splinters, and a loud thump as the Chief Executive
sprawled at the feet of his astonished Vice-President."

One day Manchester counted about one hundred people who
entered and left the Oval Office. After one meeting, Kennedy issued
seventeen directives. The action was fast, as "two months after taking
the oath the new Chief Magistrate had issued thirty-two official messages and legislative recommendations—Eisenhower had issued five in
his first two months—while delivering twelve speeches, promulgating
twenty-two Executive Orders and proclamations, sending twenty-eight
communications to foreign chiefs of state, and holding seven press
conferences." Kennedy's Senate office had been open weekends; the
new president and his brother were shocked that executive offices
closed on Saturdays. Employees received personal notes of thanks from
the attorney general if they came to work on Saturdays.

Though not as extreme as Roosevelt's logorrhea, Kennedy liked to
talk. "I need information" he said, and he sought it everywhere. The
novelist Henry James once called Washington "the city of Conversation," and Manchester dubbed JFK the "conversationalist-in-chief."
Said his family friend Gore Vidal, "He's really a great gossip"—
"terrifically interested" in hearing what others have to say. Even
strangers got presidential attention: Kennedy would reply two hundred times per day to the thousands of daily letters he received.

BESIDES HIGH ENERGY and sociability, a sense of humor is also a sign of
hyperthymic personality, as noted earlier in relation to Roosevelt. Kennedy's wit was famous; entire books have been devoted to it. A few examples
will remind us of his gift, and show how he used it to strategic advantage.

At the Democratic convention in 1960, Kennedy sat quietly as his
opponent, Lyndon Johnson, tried to convince delegates that he should
be nominated for president. The Texan went on and on about all he had

achieved in his years in Congress. Cheers rang out when he finished. Kennedy stepped to the rostrum. Looking at Johnson sheepishly, he said he agreed: Lyndon was doing such a great job as Senate majority leader, he should stay there.

Kennedy, like FDR, gave many press conferences, and he used his charm to great advantage with reporters. Once, during his trying first year, he was asked whether he would have sought to be president, knowing what he then knew, and whether he would recommend the presidency to others. He immediately replied with a smile, "Well, the answer to the first is yes, and the answer to the second is no. I don't recommend it to others, at least not for a while."

His classic style was self-deprecatory; asked during a 1960 campaign press conference about the impact of being Catholic on a reticent voting public, Kennedy replied, "I feel as a Catholic I'll get my reward in my life hereafter, although I may not get it here."

THE *COURSE* OF Kennedy's hyperthymic symptoms was constant, not episodic, consistent with personality traits (rather than a full-blown disease like mania). His own self-medication, seeking to enhance his hyperthymic traits, as described in the next chapter, provides *treatment* evidence in support of hyperthymic personality. This leaves *family history*, still a touchy aspect of John Kennedy's increasingly exposed life. Bipolar disorder in the family would support Kennedy's hyperthymic personality; the two conditions are inherited together in families.

Psychiatrically speaking, living people are more difficult to examine than the dead: those who are alive naturally want to protect their privacy; the dead cannot do so. Now we come to the controversial tale of John's sister Rosemary. Did she too have a mental illness? The standard story is that she was born with mental retardation that worsened over time, leading to being institutionalized from her mid-twenties until her death in 2005 at age eighty-six. Her sister Eunice, in a widely read 1962 article, revealed Rose's mental retardation.

Decades later, historians discovered that when she was twenty-three years old Rosemary received a frontal lobotomy from the founders of psychosurgery, neurologist Walter Freeman and neurosurgeon James Watts. This revelation raised the question of whether Rosemary had, like most lobotomy cases, preexisting mental illness. In retrospect, Rosemary probably had mild mental retardation from birth, with delayed developmental stages (walking, talking) uncommon in mental illnesses. The mildness of the retardation is shown by her ability to do arithmetic and to write adequate English composition as a teenager. Before their passing, unfortunately, Eunice and Ted Kennedy did not respond to interview requests regarding Rosemary; one journalist managed to track down the ninety-year-old neurosurgeon, Dr. Watts, who recalled that she was treated for "agitated depression." Another researcher scoured all the records and correspondence of Walter Freeman and found no reference at all to Rosemary Kennedy. It seemed that Freeman carefully avoided documentation about her.

Rose Kennedy, in her 1974 memoir, describes her daughter's anger, rather than mental retardation per se, as the cause of lobotomy. Rosemary "was upset easily and unpredictably. . . . Some of these upsets became tantrums or rages, during which she broke things or hit out at people. Since she was quite strong, her blows were hard." Sent to a convent in Washington, D.C., she would sneak out at night and return disheveled; the nuns worried that she was having nocturnal sexual encounters. Some friends of the family saw Rosemary, at the time, as mentally ill, not just mentally retarded.

In one medical evaluation, during Congressman John Kennedy's first hospitalization at George Washington University in 1950, a doctor noted, as part of the routine family history, "Sister is insane." How this history was obtained, who gave it to the doctor, and what it meant are unclear. Could it be that this touchy history was briefly raised early in Kennedy's career, when he was still a little-known congressman, but purposefully ignored or downplayed in future records of the rising senator and president? Or was this isolated bit of information actually a misinterpretation? This note, which I believe has never before been discussed in biographies or articles about Kennedy's health, at least raises the question that perhaps mood disorder was present in the Kennedy family, touching Rosemary severely and John lightly.

And then we have Joseph Kennedy Sr. himself.

WHEN THINKING OF the features of hyperthymia—high energy, elevated libido, workaholism, sense of humor, risk-taking, extraversion, sociability, marked ambition—few match the concept more closely than Joseph P. Kennedy Sr. As with many people with hyperthymic personality, Kennedy's temperament allowed him to achieve great success in the business world, a success that he parlayed into political influence for himself and eventually his entire family.

Born the son of a saloon keeper, Kennedy was among the first Irish Americans to excel in Anglophilic Boston. Elected president of his class at Boston Latin School, he entered Harvard College, where he parlayed his social skills into membership in elite social clubs like the Hasty Pudding. He married above himself, taking to bride the daughter of Boston's mayor, John F. "Honey Fitz" Fitzgerald, whereupon he began breeding the clan of nine children who would become famous. He started by taking over a failing local bank, becoming at age twenty-five the nation's youngest bank president.

Joseph Kennedy became a hyperthymic success. He worked long hours and traveled constantly. He was always planning and scheming, making some money grow into more, wanting some power to become much more. He took risks others would not consider. From the very beginning when he took over a failed bank as his first business move, to plunging into the 1920s stock market and being among the earliest "short" sellers, to getting out (just before the Great Crash of 1929) when everyone else was getting in, to taking over failed Hollywood studios and rebuilding them, to stockpiling liquor when the government prohibited it, Kennedy was a lifelong contrarian, gambling against the conventional wisdom, and he made it work over and over again.

His new wealth went far in the Depression-era 1930s, as he bought real estate everywhere and even dabbled in Hollywood. By the mid-1930s he was rich enough to buy political attention, and he became a prized business supporter of Franklin Roosevelt. Soon FDR appointed Kennedy to office, first to head the new Securities and Exchange Commission, then as ambassador to England before the Second World War. Kennedy's pacifist sympathies ended his career when the war began, but by then he had prepared a straight path to the presidency for his sons.

Hyperthymia can lead to much success, but at the cost of much failure. Openness to experience enhances creativity and often leads to incredible new ideas, but it can also become impulsive risk-taking and result in disaster. For all his successes, Joseph Kennedy also had his failures, and has been accused of more than his share of sins. His libido was famous; he not only had numerous affairs, but he was quite open about them, flaunting his relationship with the Hollywood actress Gloria Swanson, and in later years even trying his luck with the girls who came around his sons. Some have suggested his liquor business included illegal rum-running during Prohibition; some claim he bribed journalists; others append anti-Semitism and pro-Nazi sympathies to his pacifism. Even his business genius, acknowledged even by his critics, is sullied by claims that his millions ensued from Wall Street insider trading that would today be illegal.

The sons were much like the father: highly social, extraverted, libidinous, ambitious. Joseph Kennedy usually is credited with passing along these traits through his paternal devotion and care (or control) of them. It could also be that he passed along those traits through his hyperthymic genes. This probability is supported by an objective assessment of two generations of Kennedys, whose lives, though still often shrouded in privacy, are sufficiently public for some assessment of potential hyperthymic personality or mental illness. There were nine siblings in the first generation (sons and daughters of Joseph Sr. and

Rose Kennedy); there are twenty-seven cousins in the next generation (grandchildren of Joseph Sr. and Rose Kennedy). Of these thirty-six people, excluding two assassinations, one person died of a drug overdose (David Kennedy, son of Robert), four died by accident (three in plane crashes—Kathleen, Joe Jr., and JFK Jr.—and one in a skiing accident—Michael, son of Robert), four had substance abuse problems (alcohol in Edward Kennedy, heroin for RFK Jr., cocaine and prescription opiates for David, alcohol and prescription opiates for Patrick, son of Edward), and two had definite or probable mental illness (Rosemary as above, and Patrick, diagnosed with bipolar disorder).

In all, nine of thirty-six members of the Kennedy clan—exactly 25 percent—experienced at least one of the following: mental illness, substance abuse, or accidental death. This is about twice the risk in the rest of the population for mental illness or substance abuse (about 12 percent: the baseline risk in the normal population of bipolar disorder is about 2 percent, for alcohol or substance abuse in the United States about 10 percent). It is about a hundredfold higher for accidental death (the rate for accidental death by airplane crash or skiing accidents and drug overdose is a fraction of 1 percent in the general population, versus 11 percent in the Kennedy family). Accidental death in particular suggests extreme risk-taking behavior, a key feature of hyperthymic personality, a diagnosis also supported by the presence of mental illness, especially bipolar disorder, somewhere in the family tree.

There is no need to invoke a metaphysical entity—a "Kennedy curse." Nor is mere chance and coincidence statistically probable. There is no Kennedy curse. There is a Kennedy gene—for hyperthymia—that is both a curse and a blessing.

IN SUM, the young John Kennedy was hyperthymic when well, and nearly dead when ill. He had multiple serious medical problems, most of which probably reflected the myriad effects of Addison's disease: autoimmune colitis (with chronic diarrhea and weakness), back pain (mostly from muscular spasms), and repeated Addisonian crises (fever, infection, septic shock, near coma). By 1944, he weighed only 126 pounds on a six-foot-one-inch frame (a near-anorexic body mass index of 16.6). He was completely bedridden. Repeated examinations at the Mayo Clinic and Lahey Clinic (in Boston) continued to be normal. Finally, in November 1944, John F. Kennedy was deemed physically disabled and discharged honorably from the navy. (The full medical report is provided in the endnotes.)

Surprisingly, this chronically sick man decided to run for Congress. Many have credited (or blamed) his father for pushing him. Indeed, without the prodding of Joseph Kennedy Sr., John Kennedy might have lived the life of a rich invalid.

Whatever the reason, after an intervening period of journalism and his usual alternation between hyperactivity and hospitalization for physical illness, John Kennedy entered politics. He did well; in fact, his greatest enemy was his illness rather than other candidates. On June 17, 1946, a hot and steamy final primary campaign day, Kennedy walked five miles in a Boston parade, and at the end collapsed. Observers thought he had experienced a heart attack. His skin turned yellow and blue. He was taken home and received medical attention. The newspapers wrote nothing about it. (This event is still rarely mentioned in Kennedy biographies.) The next day, he won the primary, and later the general election.

A year later, on a visit to London, he probably suffered another infection, and became so weak he couldn't get out of bed. He called his friend Pamela Churchill, Winston's daughter-in-law, who arranged a visit by the physician Sir Daniel Davis, who in turn arranged hospitalization. This is when Kennedy was first officially diagnosed with Addison's disease. Unfortunately, the medical records at that time have never been evaluated by scholars, and the exact means by which Kennedy was diagnosed with this condition is not known, though it was probably not by laboratory tests. The usual view is that Davis made the diagnosis based on the clinical syndrome: repeated episodes of sudden exhaustion associated with fever, infection, near coma, and low blood pressure, along with chronic physical symptoms of bronzing of the skin, facial pallor, and low weight.

John Kennedy received another death sentence: He "hasn't got a year to live," Davis confided to Pamela Churchill.

We don't know how Kennedy reacted to this diagnosis. Maybe he felt relieved to have an explanation for his lifelong travails. Even though there was a risk of death, there was also a new treatment: deoxycortico-sterone acetate (DOCA), a steroid, given as pellets implanted under the skin every three months. Kennedy took DOCA the rest of his life. At the time, though, this treatment for Addison's disease was thought to prolong life for only five to ten years.

In 1950, John Kennedy's death sentence was again commuted. Cortisone, a new steroid pill, arrived; within a decade it became rare to die from Addison's disease. John Kennedy's life finally had been saved.

Despite this progress, he was not a happy man in the early 1950s. It is possible, if not probable, that JFK had clinical depressive episodes more than once in the 1950s, either related to Addison's disease, or due to his genetic susceptibility to bipolar disorder, or both. During this period of chronic depression, he appears to have been suicidal. He was "deeply preoccupied with death," his friend Congressman George Smathers recalled. "He was always talking about dying, about ways of dying, how drowning would be good." He resented his reliance on steroids and was somewhat self-destructive; on a trip to Indochina, for instance, he did not bring cortisone, and soon fell ill with a 106-degree fever. To avoid such future life-threatening negligence, his father arranged for DOCA pellets to be placed in bank safe deposit boxes around the world.

By age thirty, after two decades of serious illness, John Kennedy finally received the correct diagnosis, and even the right treatment. He would spend the rest of his life hiding both. In the meantime, despite steroids, he had a few more near-death episodes to survive before he could become president.

IN 1952, running for Senate, Kennedy was healthier than he had ever been. The underdog against a well-ensconced, wealthy incumbent (Henry Cabot Lodge) in a state that had been consistently Republican for a century, Kennedy campaigned strenuously. Using a state map in campaign headquarters, aides placed a pin in every town he visited. For over a year, he did not stop until the map showed at least two pins in every town. He went everywhere, for anything—Rotary Clubs, school assemblies, church groups. Kennedy was indefatigable. Without steroids, this pace would have been impossible. Family money helped his chances of election, but the other side had plenty of money too; Kennedy won in a Republican state, in a Republican year, mainly because of intrepid campaigning.

Six months later, he was back in the hospital (at George Washington University in Washington, D.C.). He had the usual signs of an Addisonian crisis: an infection (of the throat) followed by high fever, nausea and vomiting, and generalized malaise. His mental state was affected in these crises such that, though not in a coma, he was sleepy. In the pre-steroid era, such episodes could progress to coma and death. By 1953, the GWU doctors, noting throughout his medical chart that he was already diagnosed with Addison's disease, gave penicillin and high-dose intravenous steroids. A few days later he was alert and discharged; few noticed the new senator's brief absence.

Within a year, though, his back pain had gotten worse and was now affecting his legs as well. He was barely able to walk on crutches; the cause, in retrospect, was probably severe muscle spasms (years later his back X-rays repeatedly showed mostly normal bone structure); but some doctors, diagnosing an unstable sacroiliac joint, recommended fusion with a bone graft. Most of his doctors disagreed: few Addisonian patients had ever survived such serious surgery. His father concurred: Even if you are disabled, he argued, Franklin Roosevelt had proven that disability was compatible with political success. JFK decided otherwise, finding a willing surgeon and endocrinologist in New York. Bone was grafted, a metal plate inserted, steroids given continuously throughout a three-hour operation. Kennedy's survival itself was remarkable enough that he was anonymously described in a surgical journal as a case of a good outcome with Addison's disease. (The authors later acknowledged that the case was Kennedy.) In fact, there were many complications. As expected, his immune-compromised condition led to serious infection of the surgical wound within three days. The Addisonian crisis came, he fell into an altered mental state, and this time heavy doses of steroids did not perk him up. He went into a full coma. The last rites of the Catholic Church were administered. His father and his new wife, Jackie, watched helplessly.

Kennedy's near death was no secret. His old friend Vice President Richard Nixon, whose Senate office was across the hall, was especially distressed: "[Kennedy's secretary Evelyn] Lincoln recalled Nixon racing into Kennedy's office, an odd look on his face, wanting to know if the reports were true, that her boss lay mortally ill. 'That poor young man is going to die,' Secret Service agent Rex Scouten would recall Nixon saying on the way home one evening, his eyes filling with tears. 'Poor brave Jack is going to die. Oh, God, don't let him die.'"

The intravenous steroids were increased, and a few days later he woke up.

He left the hospital two months after the operation, worse than he'd been upon entry. The back pain persisted; the metal plate, continually infected, was soon removed; an open hole in his back, large enough to fit a man's fist up to the wrist, drained pus for six months. Every night, his new wife would clean the open wound. For over seven months, the newly elected senator was laid up. JFK was devastated. Suggesting the presence of severe depression, a friend later recalled, "We came close to losing him. I don't just mean losing his life. I mean losing him as a person."

FROM 1953 TO 1957, John Kennedy had seven hospitalizations, mostly at GWU in Washington or at New York Hospital, generally for short stays of a few days, usually caused by various infections, either in the urinary tract, ear, or throat, followed by Addisonian crisis symptoms of fever, malaise, and altered mental status—and later improvement with antibiotics and intravenous steroids. His back pain and irritable bowel symptoms also flared up during these years.

Throughout this medically trying time, the world noticed only that he won the Pulitzer Prize and almost became the Democratic vice presidential nominee. At the 1956 convention, when he heard that the *New York Post* was preparing an article on his Addison's disease, Joe Sr. urged his son to come clean: "It is not a killer as it was eight years ago," he said. Better to admit it now, he advised, and get it over with, rather than have it hang around for future campaigns. Again, JFK overruled his father on the topic of illness. He publicly denied any serious illness, saying he was "fit for anything"; the *Post* killed the story. Kennedy's concern about public misinformation wasn't completely unfounded: as one historian notes, a contemporary movie portrayed a person with Addison's disease, treated with cortisone, as becoming psychotic and then committing murder. Best to avoid the topic, Kennedy judged.

Fast-forward five years. On the night of June 22, 1961, barely five months after he first took office, President Kennedy almost died in the White House. (This episode is documented in his medical records, which have been available to scholars since 2002. No biographer, I believe, has ever written about JFK's near death in 1961. I believe I am the first psychiatrist to review his medical records.) The president and his circle engaged in what David Owen has called a medical cover-up. The stigma of sickness ruled their judgment. But, as is the theme of this book, sickness—of any kind—is no stigma. In fact, it can be a badge of honor, and knowing the depths of Kennedy's diseases only serves to reveal, by contrast, the height of his resilience.

He had been feeling quite ill for about a week, exhausted after the stressful Vienna summit in which Soviet leader Khrushchev bullied and harangued him. Soon after his return from Europe, JFK spiked a fever, stopped eating, and couldn't get out of bed. Aides canceled his appointments and scrambled for an explanation. On June 16, Pierre Salinger typed a memorandum for the press, in the name of the personal physician to the president, Dr. Janet Travell. It read, "The President slept later than usual this morning. . . . He is encouraged about his condition [his infection]. He may start walking for short periods without the crutches soon. . . . I am satisfied with the President's progress. No important facts have been concealed from the press. Janet Travell M.D." Dr. Travell took out a blue marker and crossed out "slept later than usual this morning." She read on and crossed out the last line, "No important facts have been concealed from the press." She wrote on the revised letter, "You don't have to say all that." Then she signed her name in the same blue marker.

Travell had just injected Kennedy with intravenous steroids and antibiotics, given along with high-dose oral steroids. She consulted with the president's endocrinologist, Dr. Eugene Cohen, who told her to also give more steroids intramuscularly. This was followed by more oral steroids later that night.

His doctors had already guessed that there was a systemic infection, which had begun in his urinary tract. Because of his Addison's disease, any infection—whether initially in his bladder, throat, or even ears— could become life-threatening. When he became sick, the infection would spread over his whole body. Untreated, high fever would be followed by low blood pressure ("septic shock"), coma, and death. Doctors then gave even more steroids to help his immune response. And without antibiotics there was no hope of overcoming the infection, so he received plenty.

From June 22 to July 3, he also received higher doses of oral steroids, amphetamines, and his usual daily dose of testosterone. All the penicillin and steroid injections produced great pain in the gluteal and thigh regions, with "marked oozing at puncture sites and ecchymotic [bruising]," for which he received doses of the narcotic codeine. He had also received up to five tablets daily of the narcotic painkiller Darvon.

The press was told that the president had a "mild viral infection."

JUNE 22 WAS the turning point. The president could have died. But at some point all the steroids and penicillin kicked in. He came back to life.

That Kennedy and his aides hid his severe illness is not the point of this story. Kennedy thought the American people wanted a healthy president. He might have learned from FDR that the American people could handle, even admire, a sick president. Despite the cover-up, Kennedy deserves respect for all the suffering he endured, for his mere survival in the face of long odds—for his remarkable resilience. Most normal people with half his medical problems and a fraction of his wealth would have retired to a quiet, easy life.

On June 26, 1961, four days after the president began his turn-around, urine culture finally confirmed the cause of his infection: *Aerobacter cloacae* (today more commonly called *Enterobacter cloacae*). This is a dangerous bug. Even now, fatal in 20 to 40 percent of cases (high mortality in the antibiotic era), it mainly infects those who are immunocompromised, like the hospitalized elderly or small children. John Kennedy, neither elderly nor a baby, was immunocompromised by Addison's disease and chronic steroid treatment. *E. cloacae* is found primarily in hospitals, but Kennedy hadn't been in any hospital recently. Outside hospitals, *E. cloacae* is mainly found in the vaginal flora; it is a sexually transmitted disease.

It's unusual for a middle-aged man to have recurrent urinary tract infections and chronic prostatitis, as Kennedy did. Without anatomic abnormalities of the kidney and bladder (which he didn't have), such infections are sexually transmitted. In the president's medical records, with multiple urinalyses and cultures, I found only two recorded instances of bacterial infections (*E. cloacae*, as described, and *E. coli*, a fecal bacterium that causes UTIs in women). We can't tell whether other documented cultures were absent or removed. (His urologist's records are silent on sexual habits, which urological evaluations typically record in detail.)

Probably JFK was infected repeatedly through sexual intercourse, and after frequent doses of antibiotics he developed resistant bacteria, which almost killed him during his first year in the White House.

SO WE HAVE HERE a story of a lifelong illness, one that was terminal until modern medicine happened upon a lifesaving treatment just when the disease was about to claim a young congressman as its next victim. The young man got a second chance, and he made the most of it, and he did so despite the disease continually coming back and attacking him again and again, not only as he strove to rise in political life, but even after he had reached the presidency. Like his hero Winston Churchill and his predecessor Franklin Roosevelt, John Kennedy never gave up. And all three men were greatly abetted in this perserverance by their manic symptoms, part of their hyperthymic personalities. (Churchill also had recurrent severe depressive episodes, though Kennedy had few of the latter, at least after steroid treatment, and Roosevelt never appears to have had severe depression; they all had hyperthymic cyclothymic personality outside of any depressive periods, however.)

Even while he was alive, many noticed the parallels between the story of John F. Kennedy and that of Franklin Roosevelt. Both men were highly sociable, liked to be liked, were popular with their peers, friendly, attractive, charismatic, witty. They were highly energetic (except when in the throes of an acute medical crisis, such as Addisonian crises or the immediate aftermath of the onset of polio); they were unceasingly thinking, planning, reading, talking. They were movers and shakers, literally, not just in the sense of the cliché. They were very high in the personality trait of openness to experience, which goes along with hyperthymia: they were curious, interested in others, listeners as well as talkers, skeptics of the conventional wisdom. (The man who coined that term, John Kenneth Galbraith, worked for and admired both presidents and saw their similarities.) One can see these traits in other presidents and politicians, who also may have had hyperthymic personality: Bill Clinton and Newt Gingrich come to mind in recent years; more distantly, Theodore Roosevelt fits the bill nicely; Thomas Jefferson scored highest in a psychological study of openness to experience as a personality trait (see chapter 14 endnotes). But Kennedy and Franklin Roosevelt set the standard.

One man knew them both very well, Joseph P. Kennedy Sr. In a sadly ironic comment made a year into the Kennedy presidency, the father remarked on his son's luck and resilience:

> I know nothing can happen to him [JFK]. I tell you, something's watching out for him. I've stood by his deathbed four times. Each time I said goodbye to him, and he always came back. In that respect he is like FDR. Because FDR went to the edge, and he came back too. And afterwards he was unique. It's the same thing with Jack. You can't put your finger on it, but there's that difference. When you've been through something like that back, and the Pacific, what can hurt you? Who's going to scare you?

Their story lines could hardly be closer. A young scion of wealth, marked for glory, is almost felled by illness, and in the process changes for the better. The key difference between them is that whereas Roosevelt was granted more years as president than any other man, Kennedy was given, as was said in his memorials, many gifts from God, except length of years.

But the story is not complete: there is another lesson here beyond the resilience of hyperthymic personality. There are the steroids. The drugs that saved John Kennedy's life would prove a dangerous cure; their mind-altering effects would almost ruin his life, as well as his presidency. Without them, he would never have lived to fail or succeed. With them, he almost failed, and then succeeded spectacularly.

PART FIVE

TREATMENT

CHAPTER 12

A SPECTACULAR PSYCHOCHEMICAL SUCCESS

KENNEDY REVISITED

The story of John Kennedy is instructive in a way that is different from all the other leaders I've discussed so far. JFK was *treated*, with steroids and other agents (amphetamines, barbiturates, cocaine analogues), not just occasionally, but consistently over many years. Those treatments greatly influenced his behavior, for worse and, as we'll see, eventually for better. So too was the case with an unlikely bedfellow, a leader with mental illness whose treatments (mainly intravenous amphetamines) markedly worsened that illness: Adolf Hitler.

John Kennedy abused anabolic steroids. He didn't just take cortisone as a replacement for his body's normal physiological needs. He abused testosterone-based anabolic steroids—literally the same drugs today used by bodybuilders—for their psychiatric effects. In so doing, Kennedy was changing his moods, probably causing manic and depressive symptoms, in a way that, for a while, harmed his ability to lead. Later, when his physicians got control of the president's misuse of anabolic steroids, his medications not only kept him alive—they enhanced his function and contributed to his successes.

Adolf Hitler abused intravenous amphetamines. He had, as we will see, bipolar disorder, with spontaneous severe depressive and manic episodes since his youth. But those mood episodes served him well in many ways, contributing to his charisma and leadership skills, until around 1937, when he began receiving amphetamines as treatment for his depressive periods. Soon he began to abuse those treatments by receiving daily intravenous injections—a practice that continued every day throughout the Second World War, worsening his bipolar disorder, with more and more severe manic and depressive episodes, while he literally destroyed the world.

The great physician William Osler once said that all medicines are toxic; it is how they're used that makes them therapeutic. If used in the wrong setting, in the wrong amounts, they always cause harm; they are dangerous; they kill and maim. The art of medicine is about knowing how and when to use medicines—and when *not* to use them. When doctors give drugs to people with underlying psychiatric illnesses, the potential for harm is exponentially higher. And if such people are political leaders, especially with despotic power, that danger can extend to entire nations, even races.

So we now need to turn to the effects of treatment for mental illness in leaders. And we'll see how those treatments can cause great harm, as well as notable success.

JOHN F. KENNEDY's presidency had two distinct phases: early failure and late success. The early period (1961–1962) included the Bay of Pigs disaster (when Kennedy tried to implement regime change in Cuba based on an Eisenhower-planned CIA coup), a botched summit in Vienna with Soviet leader Khrushchev (in which Kennedy appeared weak), and retreat in Berlin (where Khrushchev constructed the Berlin Wall). Domestically, Kennedy waffled on civil rights and was unable to get most of his election platform passed by a Democratically controlled Congress. Few knew that throughout this time he suffered from poorly controlled Addison's disease, which almost killed him, and, as we will see, from the wayward psychiatric effects of anabolic steroid abuse.

The second phase (1962–1963) included his adroit handling of the Cuban Missile Crisis, a triumphant visit to Berlin, and vigorous support for the civil rights movement. It is this latter Kennedy—peaking in Dallas—whom we mostly recall. Few know that during those last years, Kennedy's medical treatment had vastly improved; his steroids and other treatments now enhanced his resilience rather than impaired it. These are not the only causes of Kennedy's successes. But if victory has a hundred fathers, two of the most important for JFK were his natural hyperthymic personality augmented by the manic-like effects of steroid treatments.

From inauguration day until Dallas, John Kennedy ingested a standard set of daily medications. In 1961, under the care of his personal physician, Janet Travell (consulting with Kennedy's endocrinology, urology, surgery, and gastrointestinal specialists), the president took four kinds of daily steroids (including an anabolic steroid, testosterone). Sometimes, when he requested them, he also took amphetamines and barbiturates. Travell, a specialist in muscle spasm who had treated Kennedy for about eight years, frequently supplemented the above treatments with injections of procaine, an analogue of cocaine. These injections helped his pain, but by constantly puncturing his back and buttocks they weakened his muscles in those areas.

At the same time, on his own and without informing his physicians, Kennedy took mysterious injections from Max Jacobsen, purveyor of amphetamines to a well-heeled Manhattan clientele. When this was discovered by Travell and the official White House physician assigned by the navy, George Burkley, they sought Robert Kennedy's help. The attorney general reluctantly asked the president to drop Jacobsen's injections, or at least submit a sample for DEA testing. "I don't care if it's horse piss," JFK replied. "It works." We now know that Jacobsen's injections probably included testosterone, amphetamines, and possibly narcotics. (In 1971, New York State investigated the doctor's injections, found them medically dangerous, and stripped him of his medical license.)

This was the period when, in physical pain and taking numerous psychoactive treatments of unknown safety, the president almost died. Travell kept up her procaine injections, and the president's muscles kept wasting away. She also injected an anabolic steroid, methyltestosterone, at Kennedy's frequent request, while Jacobsen kept injecting God-knows-what.

At this point, an important and underappreciated event happened in the Kennedy presidency: *a medical coup d'état*. Burkley and the other consultants joined together and, working with Robert Kennedy, weakened Travell and banished Jacobsen. Muscle injections were minimized and a weekly regimen of physical exercise started under a new specialist. Doses of the president's drugs were reduced.

Into 1962, the president became more stable in body and mind. He still took four kinds of daily steroids, and now was prescribed daily doses of amphetamine as well. (He also continued to receive, off and on, antidiarrhea medications, and drugs to prevent urinary tract infections). These low to medium doses of multiple steroids were still sufficient (especially with injectable anabolic supplements) to suppress any natural production of steroids in his body (suggested by gynecomastia, growth of breast tissue, a side effect of anabolic steroids), and to cause steroid-related psychiatric side effects. Few historians have clearly noted that these psychiatric risks were especially high because Kennedy always took *anabolic* steroids (methyltestosterone initially, later Halotestin)—the kinds that make athletes sometimes go crazy—not just adrenal replacement steroids.

This may seem like a lot. It is.

KENNEDY'S ANABOLIC STEROID USAGE is perhaps the most complex, and most elusive, part of his medical history. (Even in 1966, in her oral history, Travell enumerated all of Kennedy's daily medications but pointedly excluded any reference to testosterone or its derivatives.) Kennedy routinely requested extra methyltestosterone injections or other extra steroid doses, along with amphetamines, before events like press conferences, state dinners, or even just on busy days. Travell seemed reluctant, but she obeyed the commander in chief and dutifully administered the shots.

After the medical coup, Burkley switched Kennedy from injections to pills: Halotestin (fluoxymesteron, an oral testosterone derivative) became the anabolic steroid of choice. These days, Halotestin is one of the most commonly abused oral anabolic steroids, especially favored by power lifters. It has nineteen times the muscular effects of testosterone. The doses used by the president (about 10 mg/day) were lower than those used by weightlifters long-term, but athletes take similar doses just before performances to make themselves more "aggressive."

The psychiatric effects of testosterone-derived anabolic steroids are known. At least three double-blind, placebo-controlled studies show that healthy people (with no psychiatric or medical diagnoses) given these agents experience significant psychiatric effects—some beneficial (increased libido, increased energy, euphoric mood) and some harmful (anger, aggression, violent thoughts, distractability). Combining these studies, 12 percent (ten out of eighty-four) of healthy people developed enough manic symptoms to reach the severity of a full manic or hypomanic episode. If someone has bipolar disorder or an underlying susceptibility to it (like hyperthymic personality), an even higher rate should occur. Summaries of large clinical populations treated with steroids find a 6 percent risk of severe psychiatric reactions, and 28 percent risk of mild to moderate psychiatric effects. JFK may have had manic episodes, still hidden from historical documentation, or milder manic symptoms, such as heightening of his already high libido. Or maybe, paradoxically, his Addison's disease protected him from getting too manic on steroids. In studies of people with naturally low steroid levels (as in Addison's disease), steroids improve mood and cause fewer psychiatric side effects.

JOHN KENNEDY HAD many reasons to be psychiatrically ill. He may have had a family history of mental illness; Addison's disease, when severe, itself produces clinical depression; and steroids themselves can cause mania or depression. But after carefully examining the medical records in the JFK presidential archives, I found little medical comment on his mental states. Most records simply do not discuss psychiatric symptoms. There was no documentation that Kennedy ever experienced a clinical depressive or manic episode. However, I found documents that suggest he had at least one instance of depressive symptoms severe enough to warrant medical attention.

In early December 1962, Kennedy developed another viral cold, with sinus and throat symptoms ("a slight sniffle," according to his press secretary, Pierre Salinger). On December 11, concerned about mental depression, Jackie Kennedy called both Dr. Travell and Dr. Burkley. Here is the note in Dr. Burkley's file, with "X" being his notation for the president, and "X-1" meaning the First Lady: "Received a call from Dr. Travell who stated that X had spoken to her and said that he seemed a little depressed. . . . Received a call from X-1 stating that X felt somewhat depressed and that she felt that perhaps the antihistamine drugs were responsible for this. She requested that they be discontinued. . . . I received a second call from X-1 stating that she had called Dr. Boles [Kennedy's gastroenterologist] in Boston and requested that he supply a medication which would be a mood elevator without the possibility of upsetting the gastrointestinal tract and that he had suggested Stelazine as the drug of choice." Kennedy then received a small dose of Stelazine—which is in fact an antimanic/antipsychotic, not an antidepressant—for the next three days, after which his infection improved. This brief but somewhat intense period of depression, probably related to his underlying Addison's disease, is the only available documented instance of explicit psychiatric treatment given to John Kennedy.

Even if they didn't cause full-blown depression or mania, Kennedy's steroids could have caused moderate symptoms of those conditions. If so, the most likely candidate for steroid-induced effects might be the presidential libido. The evidence for Kennedy's hypersexuality is both medical—recurrent urinary tract infections, chronic prostatitis, and documentation of *Enterobacter cloacae* infection in June 1961—and journalistic. The most extensive journalistic work is by Seymour Hersh, who draws on the testimony of numerous independent witnesses, including Secret Service agents. According to these reports, the president had many sexual relationships—some brief, others longer, using the White House swimming pool (later filled in by Nixon) as a favored venue, an ironic usage given that contemporary media often reported how his physical exercise regimen involved daily visits to the pool. The president's schedule tended to have long empty periods in the middle of the day, usually from lunch until 3 or 4 p.m. During those times, he went to the pool, usually with his aides David Powers or Kenneth O'Donnell; the Secret Service kept all (including the First Lady) away, except female visitors, often two White House staffers nicknamed "Fiddle" and "Faddle." Others known to have had liaisons with the president included Mary Meyer (sister-in-law to *Washington Post* editor and Kennedy friend Benjamin Bradlee), Judith Campbell Exner, and a White House intern, among others. Secret Service agents also reported that unknown women, presumed to be prostitutes, visited the president, on the road and in the White House.

I recount this libidinous activity because it is relevant to both hyperthymic personality and steroid-related psychiatric effects. Kennedy's hypersexuality was not limited to his presidential years, but also occurred in his college and congressional years, before and after marriage. JFK always had a high sex drive, probably related to his hyperthymic temperament, and later strengthened by libido-enhancing medications (anabolic steroids and amphetamines).

Kennedy's procaine injections are also a possible source of psychiatric effects. Procaine is similar to—but weaker than—cocaine. In animal studies where rhesus monkeys are offered cocaine or procaine, they prefer cocaine. Yet when given procaine, human cocaine addicts report euphoria and pleasurable feelings similar to those of cocaine. When Kennedy combined procaine with other agents that produce euphoria, like amphetamines and steroids, they all augmented one another, increasing his energy and libido further.

This is an explosive mix of psychiatrically active medications: four types of steroids (including anabolic testosterone-like agents), amphetamines, intramuscular procaine, and intermittent barbiturates. It is hard to accept, biologically, the claim made by Kennedy biographers that none of these medications, nor the illnesses they were meant to treat, had any impact on the president's leadership.

This consensus has been challenged only by Dr. David Owen, the sole physician-scholar to examine the medical records and write about Kennedy's leadership. In his personal review of Kennedy's medical records, Owen concluded that two phases can be discerned. In the early years of his presidency, Kennedy's medications were a mess: the mix was higher in testosterone and frequently changing, as well as combined with Jacobsen's mysterious amphetamine/testosterone injections. This was the time of his greatest failures. In the second half of Kennedy's thousand days, though, Owen believes the reduction of Kennedy's injections and the departure of Jacobsen led to more reasonable treatment, and Kennedy became a more effective leader. Owen's insight makes medical and historical sense, as we'll see.

THE POLITICAL TRANSFORMATION of President Kennedy bears recounting in the context of his steroid treatments and the White House medical coup d'état. A few months after taking office, he faced a proposed CIA covert action in Cuba. When Cuban exiles landed in the Bay of Pigs, however, they were overwhelmed. They called for U.S. Air Force backup. Kennedy, who had been assured repeatedly by the CIA and military brass that no such military intervention would be needed, refused. CIA and military leaders were appalled; they had expected him to take the next step when defeat was the only other option. Eisenhower would not have stopped, they told him. ("When you commit the flag, you commit to win," Eisenhower had said during the 1954 overthrow of Guatemala's government.) Kennedy was shocked. For months thereafter, while struggling to survive his Addisonian crisis, he kept repeating over and over, "How could I have been so stupid?" He brooded on how the CIA and the generals had duped him. ("Those sons-of-bitches with all the fruit salad just sat there nodding, saying it would work." "I've got to do something about those CIA bastards . . .")

In June 1961, reporting to Queen Elizabeth on the Vienna summit, the British prime minister, Harold Macmillan, had compared Kennedy to Neville Chamberlain: "The President was completely overwhelmed by the ruthlessness and barbarity of the Russian Chairman. It reminded me in a way of Lord Halifax or Neville Chamberlain trying to hold a conversation with Herr Hitler. . . . For the first time in his life Kennedy met a man who was impervious to his charm." "Too intelligent and too weak" had been Khrushchev's summary conclusion. "Gentlemen, you might as well face it," Kennedy's own secretary of state, Dean Rusk, told a White House meeting in the summer of 1961, when the president was out of the room, "this country is without leadership." Needing extra testosterone injections even to handle state dinners, Kennedy struggled through his annus horribilis.

As his doctors got better hold on his steroid abuse in 1962, Kennedy's mental and physical state improved. By October of that year, when the Soviets placed missiles in Cuba, Kennedy was ready. Rather than rely on the military or CIA, he made decisions himself. Writes one historian, "Walking out on generals was a Kennedy specialty. 'The uniforms' seemed incapable of listening, or understanding, and they could not stop once they swung into canned briefings. . . . 'I don't want that man near me again,' Kennedy said once after one of his walk-outs on [air force general Curtis] LeMay. [Defense Secretary Robert] McNamara and his men learned not to bring the general's name up. 'He has a kind of fit if you mention LeMay.'" The president of 1962 was not going to make the same mistakes as the president of 1961.

The details of the Cuban Missile Crisis are well known: Khrushchev tested Kennedy by bringing missiles to Cuba. Kennedy ignored his generals, who advised attack; he also ignored his diplomats, who opposed any military action. With his brother Robert as his main confidant, he commenced a naval blockade. For thirteen days in which the world teetered on the precipice of nuclear war, Kennedy stared down Khrushchev. The Soviet leader famously blinked first, and after secret negotiations to remove U.S. missile bases in Turkey, Soviet ships turned back and the missiles came out of Cuba.

Prime Minister Macmillan now opined that if Kennedy did nothing else in his entire presidency, this one victory would mark him as a successful leader, for he had done what Chamberlain had failed to do: during peacetime, he stood up to a military threat, refused to give in, and thereby averted future war. About eight months after the missile crisis, Kennedy made his famous speech in West Berlin. Standing tall in front of the Berlin Wall, he was no longer the weak leader whom Khrushchev had harangued. This John Kennedy had new international stature. The people of Berlin could tell a special leader when they saw one; they reached such a frenzy that Mayor Konrad Adenauer, reminded of the Nazi rallies, murmured, "Does this mean Germany can one day have another Hitler?" These two men—Kennedy and Hitler—were complete opposites politically and personally, of course, but they had their medical similarities (as we'll see); Adenauer intuited more than he could have known.

The military presence in Vietnam, later disastrous, was a mistake made in 1961, when Kennedy was medically ill and psychiatrically erratic. By 1963, Kennedy expressed reservations about further involvement in that conflict. Had he lived, he probably would not have responded the way Lyndon Johnson did; the Kennedy of the late 1960s would not have allowed generals to dictate military policy, to pursue the standard line of adding more troops when the original plan failed, to invade another country just because we could. Kennedy had rejected all this reasoning for Havana, ninety miles from Miami; he would not logically have accepted it for Saigon, continents away. He said as much privately: "The first advice I am going to give my successor is to watch the generals and to avoid feeling that just because they are military men their advice on military matters is worth a damn." Johnson certainly did not follow this advice.

BY 1962, Kennedy had bounced back internationally, but not yet domestically. Congress continually stalled most of his legislation into 1963. JFK then made a bold move. He added to his list of killed bills one more that his politically savvy vice president, Lyndon Johnson, thought had no chance: civil rights. Kennedy came to this conclusion not on political grounds, weighing the possibility of legislative or electoral success, but rather through moral and pragmatic considerations.

Robert Kennedy later described the pragmatic aspect, responding to civil rights marches in the South. We have two options, he said; either we send the military to protect the protesters, or we solve the cause of the protests: segregation laws. As with Cuba, Kennedy preferred political to military solutions.

The moral aspect is little appreciated and more complex. It is often said that JFK had little moral passion about civil rights, that he reacted to events rather than participating in them, that his hand was forced by King and others. There is a modicum of truth here. But it depends on which JFK we mean: the erratic JFK of 1961, or the resilient JFK of 1963?

In May 1961—just after the Bay of Pigs and just before the Vienna summit with Khrushchev—when the new president was at his most vertiginous, Martin Luther King was invited to the White House for a secret visit. King entered the White House through a side door; the men got to know each other personally, but nothing of consequence was decided. Robert Kennedy later reported that the Kennedys urged King to focus on voting rights rather than desegregation. Voting rights would be easier to pass in Congress, and eventually it would end desegregation. King demurred; he wanted desegregation as well as voting rights.

After the meeting, King came to this verdict: "In the election, when I gave my testimony for Kennedy, my impression then was that he had the intelligence and the skill and the moral fervor to give the leadership we've been waiting for and do what no President has ever done. Now I'm convinced that he has the understanding and the political skill but so far I'm afraid the moral passion is missing."

King knew Kennedy was not ideologically opposed to civil rights, but as Kennedy put it, the president might agree with him but the government might not; and the government, specifically the southern-run Congress, was reluctant. King decided to compel Kennedy to lead.

King's Southern Christian Leadership Conference (SCLC) staged protests in Albany, Georgia, for desegregation and voting rights; the Freedom Rides moved throughout the South, challenging segregation directly in restaurants and public spaces; and activists began to integrate the universities. Southern governors sent their troopers to harass and fight the protesters. Kennedy, through his brother Robert, watched carefully, and when needed sent federal government forces, usually National Guard units, to protect the protesters. A dangerous dance of quasi-military conflict was playing out between John Kennedy's federal government and southern states. This dance would soon come to a bloody end.

ON JANUARY 21, 1961, James Meredith, a young black man inspired by Kennedy's inaugural address the previous day, registered to attend the segregated University of Mississippi. After delaying tactics by the university, Meredith prepared to attend his first class on the Oxford, Mississippi, campus in September 1962. He announced that he had just bought a new gold Thunderbird and planned to drive it onto campus. The Mississippi governor sent state troopers to stop him. The president intervened, repeatedly calling the governor. Though Kennedy said he was executing the laws, not making them, everyone knew that presidents for generations, including great ones like Franklin Roosevelt, had not bothered to execute these laws. Indeed, being president involves, among other things, deciding which laws to enforce and which ones to ignore.

Kennedy wondered why the protests were mounting. He turned to his closest black adviser, Louis Martin, a newspaper publisher. "Negroes are getting ideas they didn't have before," Kennedy said. "Where are you getting them?" "From you!" Martin replied.

The Mississippi governor promised that state troopers would be unarmed; Kennedy used a table that belonged to General Ulysses Grant to sign orders for federal troops to be available. ("Don't tell them about General Grant's table," he warned an aide.) A Kennedy aide was on the scene in Oxford, Mississippi, reporting by telephone amid an angry crowd. The president asked what the crowd was chanting.

"Well, sir," his aide stammered, "they're chanting: Go to hell, JFK!" Kennedy, turning to his brother, winced.

Just when Kennedy was about to give a televised address calling for calm, some in the crowd began firing weapons. Meredith was shot in the leg, two bystanders were killed (one a French reporter), and the Mississippi state troopers, unarmed as promised, stood by and watched. Federal troops were nowhere to be seen. The president was furious. He stayed up all night trying frantically to get National Guard troops to the scene. "I haven't had such a good time since the Bay of Pigs," he noted sarcastically. He called the nearest military base in Memphis, Tennessee. "People are dying in Oxford," he told the general. "This is the worst thing I've seen in forty-five years."

The president placed a phone call to Dr. Max Jacobsen, the "horse-piss" provider whom he had been secretly seeing since 1960. Come down here, Kennedy told him, this one is a ball-breaker. Jacobsen got on a private jet provided by the president and arrived at the White House that day.

THE MEREDITH SHOOTING was followed by the Birmingham protests and police chief Bull Connor's loosing of the dogs and fire hoses. All the world was watching. By June 1963, with another university showdown in process, this time in Alabama with Governor George Wallace literally standing in the schoolhouse door, Kennedy decided on something dramatic. Robert Kennedy later recounted that the president had planned a speech on civil rights, though he had not decided exactly when or how to deliver it. As with his second try in Cuba, JFK was better prepared in Alabama than he had been in Mississippi; this time federal troops were all over the campus. Five hundred state national guardsmen, mobilized by Wallace, drilled in front of the governor, shouting, "Yankee go home!" Legally, the president could take control of the National Guard from a governor, and JFK didn't hesitate to do so. He signed orders placing the National Guard under federal command; they now had to protect the students. If they did not, Kennedy had four hundred federal soldiers with helicopters waiting to be airlifted immediately to the scene. Wallace stood in the doorway; Robert Kennedy's deputy, Nicholas Katzenbach, walked up and asked him to stand aside. Wallace gave a speech—and then stood aside.

Now that Alabama had desegregated its university without violence, the president decided to take advantage of the moment and give his long-awaited civil rights speech. The problem was, with all that had been happening, his staff hadn't prepared a speech. Wallace had stepped aside about noon. Kennedy would be on television at 8 p.m. In the intervening hours, the president, Robert, speechwriter Ted Sorensen, and Burke Marshall, a civil rights aide, frantically worked on the speech that, as Sorenson said later, they knew would be their most important since the inauguration.

They didn't finish in time. By 8 p.m., the speech was mostly done, but some of it was still on the back of envelopes; Kennedy went ahead with a plan to ad-lib as needed.

He began by recounting the events of the day in Alabama, and then continued, "I hope that every American, regardless of where he lives, will stop and examine his conscience about this. . . . When Americans are sent to Viet Nam or West Berlin, we do not ask for whites only. . . . This is not a sectional issue. . . . Nor is this a partisan issue. . . . This is not even a legal or legislative issue alone. . . . We are confronted primarily with a moral issue. It is as old as the Scriptures and as clear as the American Constitution."

He made a clear appeal based on political empathy, the core of King's philosophy: "If an American, because his skin is dark, cannot eat lunch in a restaurant open to the public, if he cannot send his children to the best public schools available, if he cannot vote for the public officials who represent him . . . then who among us would be content to have the color of his skin changed? Who among us would then be content with the counsels of patience and delay? We face, therefore, a moral crisis as a country and as a people." He then dropped a bombshell, calling for new civil rights laws that would end segregation and extend voting rights to blacks. He had not prepared any such legislation; he announced it before he wrote it. This was an act of passion—moral passion. King's original hopes for JFK had been fulfilled at last.

That night, four hours after Kennedy's speech, Medgar Evers, the head of the NAACP in Mississippi, was murdered.

Kennedy knew there was no way he could pass desegregation and voting rights in the Congress. He knew he would lose the southern states in 1964. This was no political calculation. Kennedy knew what he was giving up. This bold move was simply bad politics. Said Burke Marshall, "Every single person who spoke about it in the White House—every one of them—was against President Kennedy sending up that bill; against his speech in June; against making it a moral issue; against the March on Washington." The exception, Marshall said, was

Robert Kennedy: "He urged it, he felt it, he understood it. And he prevailed. I don't think there was anybody in the Cabinet—except the President himself—who felt that way on these issues, and the President got it from his brother."

Within a few weeks, after Evers's funeral, the president invited his widow and his young children to stay at the White House. Another emotional move from the hyperthymic president: If you kill a black man out of hatred for his race, Kennedy was saying, I'll invite his family to the White House.

IN THE SUMMER of 1963, after finally sending federal troops to support civil rights marches in Alabama and Mississippi, Kennedy initially tried to dissuade civil rights leaders from conducting a planned March on Washington to pressure the Congress to pass Kennedy's new civil rights bill. Too much could go wrong: Kennedy remembered Oxford, Mississippi. But when he couldn't stop them, Kennedy decided to join them. The White House practically took over the whole affair. Kennedy and his staff identified the site for the speeches at the Lincoln Memorial, not just for its symbolism but because, surrounded by water on three sides, it was an ideal venue for crowd control. Kennedy's men installed and controlled the sound system so that they could cut it off at a moment's notice. The White House established the route of the march, keeping it very short, from the Washington Monument to the Lincoln Memorial, and completely limited to the National Mall area, with police on all sides. Kennedy insisted the event occur on a Wednesday, so as to avoid spilling into the weekend, and that it be relatively short, from noon to 4 p.m., with each speech limited to seven minutes.

The organizers even invited the president to speak, but wanting deniability in case the march went awry, he declined. Still, Kennedy himself reviewed and even edited the addresses of the speakers. He changed a line in student leader John Lewis's speech from "We cannot support the Administration's civil rights bill" to "It is true we support the Administration's Civil Rights bill in Congress. We support it with great reservations, however." He also asked Lewis to remove an analogy between the civil rights marchers and General Sherman marching through the South.

Each speaker stuck to the seven-minute limit—except the last. Martin Luther King went on for nineteen rapturous minutes, and when he had finished detailing his mesmerizing dream, the president, watching on television, commented, "He's damned good . . . Damned good!"

Thirty minutes later, King and the other leaders were in the White House. Roy Wilkins, leader of the NAACP, gave credit to Kennedy: "You made the difference. You gave us your blessings. It was one of the prime factors in turning it into an orderly protest to help our government rather than a protest against our government." Three months later, after the president was dead, King revised his earlier judgment about Kennedy's lack of moral passion. JFK "frankly acknowledged that he was responding to mass demands," said King, but that was not all. Kennedy could have ignored or impeded the protesters; instead he helped them "because he thought it was right to do so," King concluded. "This is the secret of the deep affection he evoked. He was responsive, sensitive, humble before the people, and bold on their behalf."

No one could know that this moment of triumph was to be a bittersweet coda. Kennedy thanked the march leaders—and Bull Connor—for making it all possible. Then the president turned to King, extended his hand, and whispered, "I have a dream."

It was a dream conjured up by a depressed leader, and realized by a manic one.

IN HER 1966 ORAL HISTORY, Dr. Janet Travell took offense when Ted Sorensen used the word "drugs" for Kennedy's medications; they were physiological replacements of his normal bodily chemicals, she said. We should set the historical record right, Travell insisted, falsely: John Kennedy never took "drugs." Not only did John Kennedy take drugs, he took plenty of them, many with psychotropic properties; and he eventually benefited from them. Doctors know that drugs are not inherently good or bad; it is *how* they are used—for what purposes and in what doses—that makes them beneficial or harmful. For Kennedy in his last years, under the watchful eye of Dr. Burkley, the benefits outweighed the harms.

Perhaps the most honest judgment was made in a brief, peculiar comment in the last note written, on November 29, 1963, after the president's death, by his urologist, William Herbst. After Travell requested that he send the president's medical records, Herbst expressed some resistance, and then penned one brief final note on the records, presumably for posterity: "It is my considered opinion," he wrote, "that John F. Kennedy experienced a profound psychochemical influence for the better in a spectacular way. This is not an uncommon clinical phenomenon."

Like FDR, John Kennedy had hyperthymic personality, probably biologically related to mental illness in his family. He also suffered from Addison's disease, which almost killed him several times and was tenuously kept at bay with steroids. Yet Kennedy used more drugs than he needed, abusing anabolic steroids for manic-like enhancement of his physical and sexual energy. Left to himself, he overused those agents to the point of becoming erratic and error-prone in his judgment. When his regimen was finally better regulated by some of his doctors, the drugs instead magnified his personality strengths, pharmacologically enhancing his natural hyperthymic resilience.

The results are well known; Kennedy is revered with reason. The sources of his abilities, long shrouded in mystery, include hyperthymic personality and the right mix of steroids. Dr. Herbst was right. John F. Kennedy was indeed a spectacular psychochemical success.

CHAPTER 13

HITLER AMOK

What about Hitler? More than one reader might have posed this question by now. Adolf Hitler would appear to be the most obvious counterexample to my theses: he seems so outrageously insane and abominably evil—far from empathic, realistic, creative, or resilient. I was fully prepared to find this the case and to write him off as an exception. Maybe his case would support the Goldilocks principle: he was too crazy to derive any benefit from mental illness. But in my study of the Hitler literature (in which I found much more psychiatric documentation than I'd expected), I came to a rather different conclusion.

(Given the unfathomably evil Nazi experience, I appreciate that this analysis is delicate. Many who went through the Holocaust still live, as well as many more whose parents or grandparents suffered or perished as a result of it. The memory of those who perished is justifiably cherished, and the subsequent sensitivity of those who remain is understandable. Rather than avoid this topic, however, I think this historical experience is a central modern trauma with which my theme must grapple. I only ask that what I write here be read in the spirit intended, that of seeking the truth, whatever it is, and without any intended moral or political inferences in favor of or against anyone.)

The question, asked in one form or another for generations, is this: Was Hitler mad?

Corollary questions are: Were the Nazi leaders mentally ill? Was the German nation, as a whole, deranged?

The usual answers are: for Hitler, yes; for most Nazi leaders, probably; for Germany, probably not. The minority dissenting view, that none of the above were crazy, was advanced most famously in 1963 by Hannah Arendt (student, friend, and follower of the psychiatrist/ philosopher and leading anti-Nazi thinker Karl Jaspers), who coined the phrase "banality of evil" to express the notion that ordinary people can commit atrocious acts. One perspective sees the fanatic Nazi leaders, and the German masses, as crazy; the other sees them as evil but rational ideologues at worst, conformist acolytes at best. The historical question, for both the leaders and the masses, is important. Was Nazism an aberration of the sick minds of a few men in a weird place, or was it something that could have happened anywhere, or could still happen in the future?

I will discuss other Nazi leaders in a later chapter, but here I hope to show that Adolf Hitler himself had a mental illness, most probably bipolar disorder. I choose to examine him because, as with John Kennedy, his drug use—and abuse—is key to understanding the nature of his leadership. In Hitler's case, intravenous amphetamines *interacted* with his baseline bipolar disorder to worsen his manic-depressive symptoms. Psychiatrists and historians have never previously understood this interaction: they said Hitler either abused amphetamines or not. They never understood that the amphetamine use was really harmful mainly because his underlying bipolar disorder was worsened by it. Kennedy's leadership was eventually enhanced by steroids, interacting with his hyperthymic personality; Hitler's leadership was eventually destroyed by amphetamines interacting with his bipolar disorder.

LET'S RETURN to the four validators of psychiatric diagnosis. Beginning with *symptoms*, Hitler had clear manic and depressive episodes throughout his life. Excellent evidence exists from the memoirs of his closest friend from young adulthood (written ten years after Hitler's death), August Kubizek, who described "dangerous fits of depression. I knew only too well those moods of his, which were in sharp contrast to his ecstatic dedication and activity, and realized that I couldn't help him. At such times he was inaccessible, uncommunicative and distant. . . . Adolf would wander around aimlessly and alone for days and nights in the fields and forests surrounding the town. . . . This state lasted several weeks."

I will rely on Kubizek heavily because his recollections cover Hitler's young adulthood, before his political prime. (Most historians accept the general veracity of Kubizek's account.) These descriptions are psychiatrically important because they show presence of such symptoms outside of the political contexts that some might use to "explain" them.

Hitler's manic symptoms included overtalkativeness, grandiosity, euphoric mood, decreased need for sleep, and hyperactivity, all occurring episodically, and in alternation with depression, as occurs in bipolar disorder. Examples of those symptoms follow.

Kubizek frequently remarked upon Hitler's overactivity: "He walked always and everywhere. . . . I recall him always on the go. He could walk for hours without getting tired." "I cannot remember a time when he had nothing to do or felt bored even for a single hour." "Once he had conceived an idea he was like one possessed. Nothing else existed for him—he was oblivious to time, sleep and hunger." Hitler's mania focused especially on his love of architecture; he was constantly imagining renovations of Linz, Austria, where he then lived: "Here he could give full vent to his mania for changing everything, because a city always has good buildings and bad. He could never walk through the streets without being provoked by what he saw. Usually he carried around in his head half a dozen different building projects, and sometimes I could not help feeling that all the buildings of the town were lined up in his brain like a giant panorama." (Three decades later, Hitler in fact renovated Linz much in the way he had described to his friend Kubizek.)

Kubizek also offers much evidence of distractibility and probable flight of ideas: "When Adolf and I strolled through the familiar streets of the good, old town [Linz]—all peace, quiet, and harmony—my friend would sometimes be taken by a certain mood and begin to change everything he saw. That house there was in a wrong position. . . . That street needed a correction. . . . Let's have a free vista to the Castle. Thus he was always rebuilding the town. But it wasn't a matter of building. A beggar, standing before the church, would be an occasion for him to hold forth on the need for a State scheme for the old. . . . A peasant woman coming along with her milk cart drawn by a miserable dog—occasion to criticize the Society for Prevention of Cruelty to Animals for their lack of initiative. . . . [His restlessness] was a supernatural force, comparable to a motor driving a thousand wheels." Hitler would begin many projects, such as writing plays, but never end them. He would take up a project for which he was unprepared, such as writing a new Wagnerian opera, work on it full steam for an extended time, and then give it up for no reason, without ever returning to it. "I had long since known this behavior of his, when a self-imposed task engrossed him completely and forced him to unceasing activity; it was as though a demon had taken possession of him. Oblivious of his surroundings, he never tired, he never slept. He ate nothing, he hardly drank . . . this ecstatic creativeness."

And there is ample indication of Hitler's overtalkativeness: "He used to give me long lectures about things that did not interest me at all. . . . He just had to talk." He liked to attend sessions of parliament as part of the audience. Then he would lecture Kubizek at night for hours: "Hysterically he described the sufferings of his people, the fate that threatened it, and its future full of danger. He was near tears. But after these bitter words, he came back to more optimistic thoughts. Once more he was building the Reich of all the Germans."

A markedly irritable and unstable mood can mark manic periods, and here again Hitler's behavior matches the bipolar diagnosis: "Adolf was exceedingly violent and high-strung. Quite trivial things, such as a few thoughtless words, could produce in him outbursts of temper which I thought were quite out of proportion to the significance of the matter."

As we saw with Hitler's renovaton of Linz, mania can generate creative and compelling ideas, which, even if outlandish at the time, can still exert an influence long after the manic episode has ended. Kubizek describes one such episode in rich detail. One night, he and Hitler went to see a Wagner opera. Usually, Hitler would critique a show in detail while there and afterward. But on this occasion he left the performance silently and walked rapidly, with Kubizek following him, to the top of the Freinberg mountain overlooking the city.

Adolf stood in front of me; and now he gripped both my hands and held them tight. He had never made such a gesture before. . . . His eyes were feverish with excitement. . . . Never before and never again have I heard Adolf Hilter speak as he did in that hour, as we stood there alone under stars. . . . I cannot repeat every word that my friend uttered. . . . It was as if another being spoke out of his body. . . . I rather felt as though he himself listened with astonishment and emotion to what burst forth from him with elementary force. . . . It was a state of complete ecstasy and rapture. . . . Like flood waters breaking their dykes, his words burst forth from him. He conjured up in grandiose, inspiring pictures his own future and that of his people. Hitherto I had been convinced that my friend wanted to become an artist, a painter, or perhaps an architect. Now this was no longer the case. . . . Now he was talking of a mandate which, one day, he would receive from the people . . . a special mission which one day would be entrusted to him. . . . His words were followed by silence. We descended into the town.

It was 3 a.m. The friends departed and never discussed that night again until over thirty years later, when, in 1939, the Führer invited his old friend to see a Wagner opera in Bayreuth, the site of the composer's annual festival. Kubizek recounted that special night in their youth. Hitler was moved. Later, when they both visited Wagner's widow in her home, Hitler took a turn retelling the story, concluding, "In that hour it began."

I THINK there can be little doubt that these behaviors represented manic episodes, and if someone ever has a manic episode, it is 90 percent likely that he will also have depressive episodes. Hitler too had periods of behavior that meet our current definition of clinical depression, especially when he would suffer setbacks in life, such as being turned down twice by the Vienna Academy of Arts. At that time, Kubizek recalls:

> His mood worried me more and more as the days went by. I had never known him torment himself in this way before. On the contrary! In my opinion, he possessed rather too much than too little self-confidence. But now things seemed to change round. He wallowed deeper and deeper in self-criticism. Yet it only needed the slightest touch . . . for his self-accusation to become an accusation against the times, against the whole world; choking with his catalogue of hates, he would pour his fury over everything, against mankind in general who did not understand him, who did not appreciate him and by whom he was persecuted. I see him before me, striding up and down the small space in boundless anger, shaken to his very depths.

Hitler himself admitted some of the depression in *Mein Kampf:* "As the Goddess of Misery took me in her arms and so often threatened to break me, the Will to Resist grew, and in the end the Will triumphed."

Kubizek notes one more significant personality trait in Hitler: obsessionality. While this trait is unrelated to his bipolar disorder, it's worth mentioning here because we can use it to mark his later decline. This obsessionality was reflected in Hitler's attention to personal hygiene and correct behavior. Even when he was poor, as he was when Kubizek knew him, he was always well groomed and fastidiously dressed. At night he placed his trousers under his mattress to give them a sharp crease the next day. He also was polite in social situations and had good manners.

His obsessive rigor went well beyond personal appearance and cleanliness. Kubizek recounted that "the most outstanding trait in my friend's character was . . . the unparalleled consistency in everything he said and did. There was in his nature something firm, inflexible, immovable, obstinately rigid, which manifested itself in his profound seriousness and was at the bottom of all his other characteristics. Adolf simply could not change his mind or his nature. . . . I remember what he said to me when we met again in 1938 after an interval of thirty years. 'You haven't changed, Kubizek, you have only grown older.' If this was true of me, how much more was it of him! He never changed."

On that point, Kubizek was wrong. Starting in the late 1930s, Hitler would begin abusing drugs in a way that would alter his habits and unhinge his mind.

WE WILL SOON SEE how these symptoms manifested themselves during Hitler's years in power, but now we'll examine his *family history*, which also supports a diagnosis of bipolar disorder.

The identity of Adolf Hitler's paternal grandfather has long been open to question, which makes it hard to determine how closely related Adolf was to members of the Heidler clan (the family name before his father changed it), some of whom were insane. But Adolf's father, Alois, himself displayed manic symptoms, at least as hyperthymic personality.

A civil servant with liberal political beliefs, he had a temper, beat his sons (though maybe not beyond the norms of his time), was obstinate and energetic (like his son Adolf), and hypersexual (unlike Adolf). Alois Hitler fathered at least two children out of wedlock, and had three marriages, the last to Klara, Adolf's mother, his second cousin and housekeeper. The father was restless, constantly moving his family; in one town, they had twelve different addresses. Even after he retired, he moved five times; Adolf attended five schools before dropping out as a teenager. Describing all this, Kubizek stumbled upon the likely cause: "[Alois Hitler] often moved from a decent dwelling to a poorer one. The house was not the important thing; rather the moving. How can one explain this strange mania?"

That Hitler's parents were cousins would intensify their children's susceptibility to illness, whether physical or mental. (Alois and Klara had to obtain a papal dispensation to marry.) They had much family tragedy: their first three children before Adolf died, as did a younger brother when Adolf was eleven. Hitler's only surviving full sibling was his younger sister Paula, a Vienna housemaid, who, under her married name, Wolf, lived without fanfare even during Hitler's rule. She was not known to be mentally ill.

Hitler had half siblings and relatives from Alois's other wives. One half brother, Alois Hitler Jr., was a petty criminal and moved frequently, like his father, living in England briefly and siring a child there (a British citizen, William Patrick Hitler). Adolf's half sister, Angela, had a daughter, Geli, to whom Hitler was quite attached; some historians infer a romantic relationship. Geli, then about twenty, died of a gunshot wound while living with Hitler in 1931. It was ruled a suicide, but some think Hitler shot her in a (lover's?) quarrel, others that he had her killed because she was planning to leave him.

In all, Hitler's family history supports mental illness, especially with the reasonably strong evidence for hyperthymic personality in his father, combined with inbreeding that would have heightened Hitler's risk for bipolar disorder.

REGARDING THE *COURSE* of Hitler's potential bipolar disorder, manic and depressive episodes began in his late teens and early twenties, as documented by his friend Kubizek. These symptoms were episodic, lasting days to weeks, and in some cases (with his most severe depressive periods) months. There are four lost years, beginning in 1910 at age twenty, when Kubizek lost contact with Hitler, until the outbreak of the First World War. These were Hitler's years of most dire poverty, when he lived in a men's hostel in Vienna and sold postcards for a living. There is little record of this period, during which some authors think he suffered from severe depression. Four years of war revived Hitler. He fought bravely, earning the Iron Cross, First Class, which was rarely given to enlisted men. He earned the respect, though not close friendship, of his fellow soldiers. After the war, he joined the new National Socialist Party, and by 1921 was elected its president. After a putsch attempt in 1923, Hitler spent five months in jail, which enhanced his political reputation, and wrote *Mein Kampf*. Though at times of great political risk, such as the putsch, he would repeatedly threaten to shoot himself, he in fact never tried to kill himself before his 1945 suicide. Hitler's influence grew as Germany wallowed in political and economic strife. He emerged with a strong national party that did well in the 1932 elections, and after some intrigue he became chancellor, and then dictator. The revival of the German economy earned him even greater plaudits and more power.

Hitler continued to have manic and depressive periods in the 1930s, though they were briefer than in previous decades. This was the period of his greatest success. A penniless nobody in peacetime, he had risen to the top during a period of great domestic crisis. In this period his close political aides describe him as intelligent, able to listen to others, endowed with a prodigious memory, flexible in thinking, and decisive.

If we had stopped with the prewar leader, Hitler's illness would not seem much more severe than Churchill's. Prewar Hitler was resilient and creative. He was an extremely astute, realistic politician, as historian Alan Bullock has shown in his classic work about Hitler's rise to power. Prewar Hitler wasn't particularly empathic, obviously (though even there he always viewed himself as siding with the oppressed masses of Germany). He was violent from the start (killing political opponents and even some allies), despotic (introducing a new absolutist state), and harshly anti-Semitic (from the beginning of his rule, he restricted the ability of Jews to live and work). But he had not yet invaded any other countries, nor had he turned genocidal.

IN 1937, Hitler began using amphetamines. Before then, his bipolar disorder seemed manageable; either his moods didn't affect him much in the 1930s, or they only added to his productivity and creativity. After that date, a gradual decline began, with worsening manic and depressive episodes that impaired his leadership. Hitler's psychotropic *treatment* history, his amphetamine use, combined with his bipolar disorder, has not been adequately described in previous attempts to "explain" him.

(This story was first fully revealed by the psychiatrist Leonard Heston, a prominent researcher in the genetics of schizophrenia, who along with his German-speaking wife, Renate, published a complete medical study of Hitler in 1980. At that time, the Hestons not only reviewed all available documentation of Hitler's medical records, but they also interviewed his still living doctors and many other people who knew about Hitler's medical care. Their personal interviews are important sources of documentation that, with the passage of time, will only increase in value.)

The year 1937 was when Hitler began treatment with the man who would remain his personal physician until his final days, Theodor Morell. Morell's exclusive practice catered to wealthy Berliners with nonspecific neurotic complaints who loved the doctor's magic injections. We now know these injections sometimes literally were placebos (diluted sugar—20 percent glucose in medical terms), and frequently were potent "natural" tissue extracts, like adrenal glands or ground bull testes. Morell liberally injected not only Hitler but many of the Nazi elite, such that Hermann Goering jokingly titled the doctor *"Herr Reich Injektion Minister*—the Injection Minister of the Reich. After he was captured by American forces, Morell admitted to giving Hitler twenty-eight different treatments, though he probably understated how frequently. A few stand out (and are similar to the injections that John Kennedy would later receive from Max Jacobsen): "Orchikrin," described as "a combination of all hormones of males. Potency is increased by the addition of extracts of testis, seminal vesicles and prostate of young bulls . . . to combat fatigue and depression"; "Prostakrimum," "an extract of seminal vesicles and prostate. Used to prevent depressive moods"; and a steroid derived from ground-up adrenal glands, "Cortiron," "Desoxycoticosteronacetate [*sic*] . . . used for muscle weakness." These descriptions are further proof, based on treatment, that Hitler experienced depression.

In the 1930s, Hitler (again like Kennedy) was racked with horrible gastrointestinal problems: eating produced sudden pain, followed by diarrhea. In retrospect these symptoms are consistent with gastritis, possibly ulcers, or perhaps irritable bowel syndrome (all of which are common in mood disorders). Hitler had already restricted his diet, becoming completely vegetarian, without avail. He called Morell, who eventually prescribed synthetic opiate narcotics and anticholinergic drugs, known to slow diarrhea. (The narcotic given was Eukodal, which is oxycodone, the same ingredient in the highly addictive drug OxyContin.) Hitler improved, and Morell became part of the Führer's inner circle.

Hitler's chronic insomnia was the next target. With constant anxiety and frequent mood episodes, he had developed, like Churchill, reversed sleep cycles. He stayed awake late into the night, talking and working inordinately, but slept each morning until noon. Hitler wanted morning pep and evening sleep. Morell had just the thing.

The insomnia was easy to treat. Barbiturates were used extensively

(Churchill also received them); in his American interrogation, Morell admitted to prescribing a barbiturate for sleep (Brom-Nervacit, which contained a bromide sedative, and Barbital, also called Veronal, the first commercially marketed barbiturate). He likely prescribed it to Hitler for nightly use from 1939 onward.

Morell had made progress: Hitler's stomach was quieted with an opiate; his sleep improved with a barbiturate. Now there was only the problem of pep. Amphetamine would be the solution.

AMPHETAMINES, first marketed in 1928 as Benzedrine (dl-amphetamine), were quite popular. Prescribed initially for narcolepsy, they quickly became the first widely used psychiatric treatment for depression. (By 1971, there were over thirty-one amphetamine preparations marketed in the United States, mostly used for depression.) Morell saw that his patient suffered from depression, anxiety, and insomnia—the kinds of symptoms he frequently saw in his rich Berlin clientele. He decided to prescribe a new antidepressant, methamphetamine.

Heston believes that Hitler's use began in 1937, based on the first reported changes in his behavior. Hitler was less friendly, more withdrawn, more suspicious of others. These changes weren't brief, as in his past depressive episodes, but more consistent. They were especially noted by Albert Speer, the Führer's confidant and a consultant to the Hestons, and by Heinrich Himmler, Hitler's close deputy, who, convinced that Hitler must have neurosyphilis, began collecting a medical file on him. (Hitler had repeated negative tests for syphilis.) Even the Italian king, Victor Emmanuel III, wondered aloud to his court, after seeing Hitler in May 1938, whether he was taking amphetamines.

More definitive evidence that Hitler received amphetamines dates to late 1942, right after the Germans' defeat at Stalingrad, when he became markedly depressed. In the 1970s, the Hestons interviewed Hitler's valet, Heinz Linge, who served him from 1935 onward, and who still admired his old leader. Linge described a daily morning intravenous injection, given by Morell, documented in Linge's appointment books. Morell admitted giving Hitler injections of "Vitamultin-Ca," a mixture of vitamins. Linge describes results never associated with vitamins, though: "The effects were instantly apparent—not minutes later, but while the needle was still in the arm. The effect on Hitler was obviously alerting: he felt 'fresh,' alert, active, and immediately ready for the day." By the middle of 1943, Hitler began to have the injections, according to Linge, multiple times daily, with the same results. The Hestons interviewed other Hitler aides who described similar effects: Hitler was immediately rendered "extremely alert and talkative," a "rejuvenating" effect; after the injections, he was "cheerful, talkative, physically active, and tended to stay awake long hours into the night."

Morell kept the ingredients a jealously guarded secret; despite Himmler's repeated entreaties, Morell cited confidentiality, saying only that it was "a mixture specially compounded for the Führer." Due to his link to Hitler, Morell now ran numerous pharmaceutical factories. Hitler's preparation was secretly made to Morell's specific order, with oral tablets wrapped in gold foil and intravenous injections delivered to Morell himself.

Hitler's other physicians were suspicious of Morell. Dr. Ernst-Günther Schenck, a nutrition inspector for the Waffen-SS, interviewed by the Hestons in the 1970s, reported that in 1943 he managed to obtain a gold-foil-wrapped tablet prepared for Hitler. He analyzed its chemical contents and found, besides vitamins, methamphetamine. Schenck gave the report to his superior, the Reich health minister, who showed it to Himmler. Schenck said that Himmler ordered him to drop the matter. Later assigned to the bunker after the Führer dismissed Morell in the final days, Schenck would be the last physician to see Hitler alive. After ten years in a Russian prison camp, Schenck revealed the story about methamphetamine, which he repeated in his own memoirs and in interviews until his death in 1998. According to Linge, Hitler took about five of these gold-foiled methamphetamine tablets daily, supplemented by continual sucking on over-the-counter candy, called "Cola-Dalmann," which contained appreciable doses of caffeine. (Hitler did not drink alcohol, coffee, or tea, however.) Like Kennedy's doctors, some of Hitler's, such as the highly regarded Karl Brandt, tried to act to restrain the use of harmful drugs, attempting a medical coup d'état against Morell; unlike Kennedy's doctors, they failed.

In sum, Hitler was constantly taking three kinds of psychoactive drugs: opiates, barbiturates, and amphetamines, of which the amphetamine use was most potent since it was given both intravenously and orally. We don't know how much intramuscular anabolic steroids (from the ground-up bull testes, prostate, and adrenal glands) were given, but it is plausible that (like John Kennedy in 1961–1962) Hitler also received anabolic steroids regularly. Kennedy's doctors were able to get his psychopharmacological mix under control after banishing his quack Dr. Jacobsen; Hitler's doctors were never able to oust Morell. If Kennedy's mix eventually became a "spectacular psychochemical success," Hitler's was a much more spectacular disaster.

GIVING AMPHETAMINES every day, intravenously, to a man with untreated bipolar disorder is likely to have a grave effect on his decision-making processes. Even oral amphetamines, being powerful antidepressants, cause mania in about half of people with bipolar disorder, especially if mood stabilizers like lithium (which weren't available in Hitler's time) aren't given as well. If such is the case with oral amphetamines that are less potent than what Hitler took, then the chances someone with bipolar disorder would become manic with *intravenous* amphetamine are much higher than 50 percent, so high that we can't even test the notion: no contemporary hospital ethics committee would ever allow such a risky study; it would be blatant abuse of patients' rights. Yet Adolf Hitler took such abuse every day. Rats treated this way, with daily intramuscular amphetamine for months, are used as an animal model of psychosis. In sum, these are dangerous drugs, especially when given to people with severe mental illnesses.

Hitler had relatively severe bipolar disorder, like Churchill or Sherman; but unlike them, he received daily intravenous amphetamine treatment for the last four years of his life, supplemented with oral amphetamines and caffeine (and mixed with consistent barbiturates and opiates, and intermittent anabolic steroids). A normal person would have a tough time remaining sane with this concoction. (In contrast, Churchill's amphetamines came only in pill form, and not consistently. Kennedy never received intravenous injections of steroids, to our knowledge, only intramuscular, and he did not have full-blown bipolar disorder, but hyperthymic personality, which would make him less susceptible to mania or psychosis. Also, his amphetamines were always oral and low-dose.) To call Hitler a time bomb would be to understate matters. Morell lit a fuse that exploded the entire world.

Hitler changed in those final years in many ways. Though he had always been an angry man, especially when manic, he had been generally courteous and proper in social settings, able to exercise good self-control when needed. But by 1942 he routinely screamed at generals during military meetings. Many observers noted that his rages were much worse than they had been in the 1930s. On one occasion in December 1942, he shouted nonstop for three hours. That anger was not limited to military matters. Once, for instance, after the death of an opera singer (Hitler loved opera), he was indignant at what he thought was insufficient newspaper coverage and exploded in "a frenzy of rage against the press. His fury lasted for hours and made him literally incapable of work for the rest of the day." By December 1943, Himmler, convinced that Hitler had a "sick mind," disobeyed some orders, such as one to execute all prisoners of war. On at least two occasions (in 1938 and 1942) several generals tried to persuade prominent psychiatrists to commit Hitler to a mental asylum. (The doctors refused.)

Speer notes that whereas Hitler used to ask intelligent questions of his generals and then listen to their responses, the Führer increasingly refused to listen to anyone. "No retreat" became his mantra, whatever the specific military circumstances. For instance, Hitler previously had enjoyed reports of General Erwin Rommel's successes in North Africa, especially his tactic of the "fighting retreat and counterattack." But in November 1942, in the great battle of El Alamein, Hitler refused to allow Rommel to move his troops as he wished; no retreat, came the orders. Rommel was demolished. On July 20, 1944, military plotters failed in their attempt to bomb Hitler. Some of the plotters eventually confessed that Rommel was an ally, and as Hitler tracked down and executed officers implicated in the plot, Rommel concluded that his Führer was insane. ("That pathological liar has gone completely mad!" he told an aide.) By October, the regime gave Rommel two options: quietly commit suicide or be executed along with his family. The Nazis said he had died of a heart attack, and arranged a solemn burial with full military honors.

EARLIER IN HIS CAREER, Hitler had no trouble delegating authority. He set broad policies and let his domestic and military advisers enact them. Now he became obsessed with details, telling his commanders what to do at every turn. No order could be given without Hitler's specific approval. Said Field Marshal von Rundstedt, "The only troops I could move without permission were the sentries outside my door." Here too amphetamines may be relevant. Hitler likely had, as previously noted, obsessive tendencies, reflected in his fixation on personal hygiene and cleanliness. This trait may have worsened with amphetamine use, which is well known to cause or worsen symptoms of obsessive-compulsive disorder.

While he was taking amphetamines, Hitler's moods cycled more quickly and severely than before. When he was depressed, he slept longer, refusing to talk about the war as much as possible. He ate alone, he couldn't concentrate, he was indecisive, and, unusually for a man famous for his great memory, he was absentminded. In 1943, Morell even publicly revised his prior diagnosis from (only) depression to manic depression. Morell was no psychiatric expert, but he was correct if he truly said and meant this. (The source for this citation is from a contemporary book by a Swedish journalist.) Morell intensified the amphetamine treatments, which probably only worsened Hitler's mania. Speer reports that from then onward, Hitler never seemed depressed again until the final days in the Berlin bunker. Instead, he was increasingly unrealistic and overoptimistic: "The more inexorably events moved towards catastrophe, the more inflexible he became, the more rigidly convinced that everything he decided on was right." Linge, Hitler's valet, told the Hestons that this was correct, except that Hitler had brief depressive periods, usually lasting days to weeks, when he would get tearful and wish that he would die. The Hestons date such brief periods to August 1944, February 1945, and again at the end of Hitler's life in April 1945. It is probable that the extensive intravenous amphetamine injections, perhaps augmented by steroids, were causing Hitler to "cycle" into and out of his manic and depressive episodes more and more quickly. In his final two years, Hitler probably never experienced a day of normal mood.

His world was collapsing; his mind already had.

WAS HITLER PSYCHOTIC? That is, did he have hallucinations or delusions? This question is worth considering because it reflects a common assumption among both historians and the rest of us. As noted above, it's natural to believe that atrocities as extreme as Hitler's could only be the products of a thoroughly deranged mind—one that has abandoned reality and inhabits an unreal world of delusion and hallucination. This assumption is bolstered in Hitler's case by some evidence that could be viewed as indicative of psychosis.

Hearing voices (auditory hallucination) is one symptom of psychosis, and in 1918, when he was in a military hospital, Hitler heard a voice telling him that he was to be Germany's savior. (Some think his experience occurred under hypnotic suggestion, and that he actually was hearing the voice of his psychiatrist, Dr. Edmund Forster.) Throughout his career, Hitler frequently spoke of following his "inner voice"; but then again, so did Gandhi. Using the word "voice" metaphorically is not the same as hearing an actual voice. During World War II, Hitler claimed to hear orders from God, but such voices were less likely the result of inborn psychosis than years of IV amphetamine use.

As for delusions, psychiatrists sometimes define them as involving fixed false beliefs held against incontrovertible evidence to the contrary, with markedly illogical thought processes. For instance, I might believe the world will end tomorrow because Martians have begun to eat my entrails. That is a clear delusion. But Hitler's extreme anti-Semitism is not delusional, partly because he belonged to a culture where anti-Semitism was hardly unusual. Such an attitude was undoubtedly wrong—both morally and factually—but it was common enough to fall within the realm of normal behavior for Hitler's time. And while he was paranoid toward a world of enemies, his paranoia wasn't necessarily delusional, because he in fact had many enemies. He was paranoid about the German military, but that was not irrational, because German generals repeatedly tried to remove him from power. He had grandiose ideas. He thought he alone would save Germany, but this was not a delusion: many other people thought he could too. He also had a constant phobia about syphilis, fearing that he might have contracted it. But he had many obsessions, including a strong desire to be clean and a fear of germs. This abnormal thinking is more consistent with obsessions than delusions. Toward the end of World War II, he may have had delusions; he was known to issue orders to nonexistent armies. But again, by then he'd been taking intravenous amphetamines for several years, which alone or in combination with his underlying bipolar disorder could produce delusions.

So Hitler wasn't just plain crazy, in the sense of outright psychosis, though he may have been made crazy by a nightmarish mixture of drugs and mania.

AS I DISCOVERED, the literature on Hitler's psychiatric condition is immense, and it offers up a welter of theories about his mental state. We should examine those theories in light of the evidence we've gleaned about his symptoms and drug use.

The most common psychiatric diagnosis given to Hitler is antisocial personality disorder, but this condition involves such features as cruelty to animals, breaking the law, and complete absence of empathy. Yet Hitler loved animals, never broke the law before his political activities, and clearly had much empathy for his mother, his childhood friend Kubizek, his half niece Geli, and others. Other personality disorders, such as borderline personality, also don't correspond with Hitler's life. (There is no evidence he was sexually abused, for instance, and he never cut himself or otherwise attempted suicide before his death—all of which are cardinal features of borderline personality.)

We also can put aside the myriad psychoanalytic histories, for reasons given earlier in this book. Calling Hitler a "paranoid destructive prophet," a typical psychoanalytic diagnosis, fails to clarify his condition or explain his actions. He was paranoid, yes, but that was likely the result of mania and depression rather than unprovable speculations that his father beat him too much or his mother loved him too much. Psychohistory has been rightly rejected by historians on both sides of the Hitler debate—those (like Alan Bullock) who view him as a politically skilled scapegrace who was simply evil, and those (like Hugh Trevor-Roper) who view him as an ideologue who, while certainly evil, believed he was doing good. But rejecting psychoanalytic diagnoses shouldn't prompt us to ignore his clear manic and depressive episodes.

Hitler certainly had many anxiety symptoms (high neuroticism) and obsessions, and he probably experienced post-traumatic stress disorder (PTSD) from World War I, for which he may have received his only official psychiatric treatment in his entire life. This is a controversial topic, because Hitler and the Nazis went to great lengths to deny or try to cover up any documentary evidence that he might have had mental illness. When he was hospitalized at the end of World War I, he claimed he had gone temporarily blind from mustard gas. It seems more likely he had hysterical blindness, a kind of PTSD, and he apparently was treated by the psychiatrist Dr. Edmund Forster, with a kind of hypnotic suggestion. Forster apparently later felt guilty, believing that he may have accidentally inspired Hitler's megalomania; there is some evidence that Forster may have given Hitler's psychiatric records to German exiles in a 1933 Paris meeting, after which he committed suicide or was killed. U.S. intelligence records document this possible scenario, as do some recent researchers who interviewed people who knew Forster. Researchers who have studied Hitler's probable PTSD have drawn simplistic conclusions, however, such as the notion that this condition may have somehow "invented" the Führer—transforming him from a harmless apolitical artist to the grandiose anti-Semitic despot. But, as discussed in chapter 9, PTSD doesn't just occur in a vacuum; one's preexisting personality traits greatly influence one's likelihood of suffering this disorder. Although Hitler likely had PTSD, he also had plenty of mood episodes before the First World War that more cogently prefigure his behavior and actions later in life.

To say Hitler didn't suffer from depression and mania would require ignoring both reliable historical documentation and discounting the knowledge base of psychiatry. One might accept such a diagnosis and still ask whether it makes any difference; does it help us at all to understand Hitler as a historical figure? I believe it does. Up to 1937, I think his moderate bipolar disorder influenced his political career for the better—fueling his charisma, resilience, and political creativity. After that date, the harmful effects of daily intravenous amphetamine—to which he was especially susceptible because of his bipolar disorder—worsened his manic and depressive episodes, impairing his leadership skills with catastrophic effects.

Though he was ultimately one of the worst leaders the world has ever known, Hitler's story supports the basic view of this book that mental illness, especially in its mild to moderate forms, enhances crisis leadership. The Goldilocks principle applies in Hitler's case. An absence of mania might have reduced his ambition and creativity; too much mania made him unrealistic, bordering on psychotic, in his final, amphetamine-driven years.

THE DRAMATICALLY DIVERGENT trajectories of Hitler and Kennedy show us how important it is to factor in the role of drugs when assessing the nature and effects of anyone's mental illness. In leadership, and in life generally, drugs can make a major difference. If anything, this is more true now than it was half a century ago, because many more psychiatric drugs are available and millions of people are taking them. While we know much more now about the relationship between drugs and mental illness, it is still a challenging interaction to manage successfully. But in our time, as in Kennedy's, the right doctors and the right treatment can markedly improve a leader's effectiveness.

Still, given the challenges, some might well ask: Why take the risk? Why not just exclude the mentally ill from positions of power? As we've seen, such a stance would have deprived humanity of Lincoln, Churchill, Roosevelt, and Kennedy. But there's an even more fundamental reason not to restrict leadership roles to the mentally healthy: they make bad leaders in times of crisis—just when we need good leadership most.

PART SIX

MENTAL HEALTH

CHAPTER 14

HOMOCLITE LEADERS

BUSH, BLAIR, NIXON, AND OTHERS

Sanity is rightly seen as healthy, conducive to personal happiness and success in life. But it does not always, or even usually, produce good leadership. Some readers, sympathetic until now with the basic theme of this book—that mental illness enhances leadership in crisis situations—might yet balk at its corollary, that mental health hinders crisis leadership. I've mentioned some examples of sane leaders who faltered in crises—Chamberlain, McClellan—but there are counterexamples; and what, in any case, can explain the counterintuitive notion that mental health can hamper leadership?

About half a century ago, one of Sigmund Freud's last pupils decided to study mental health. The psychiatrist Roy Grinker—editor of the *Archives of General Psychiatry*, chairman of a department of psychiatry—had already spent decades studying mental illness when he began to wonder about mental health. Freud had written little about mental health. He and his followers saw neurosis as part of being human, and thus we were all more or less ill, so Freudians essentially avoided the concept of mental health. Grinker decided to take on this task.

In search of normal men, he turned to a YMCA-run college in his home city of Chicago; there he received permission to give psychological tests to half the student body of 343 people, from whom he selected sixty-five men who screened smack in the middle of the healthy range. Grinker interviewed them each personally and repeatedly over two years, and gradually assembled a detailed list of ingredients that make for mental health.

THE STUDENTS at George Williams College had been active in their local YMCA, and their connections to that organization, their church, and their communities were long and deep. "Uncertainty about the future is minimal," Grinker noted, among these "upright young men."

They came from white- and blue-collar families in the Midwest. They had slightly above average IQs, average college grades (mostly C's), and no childhood or adolescent conflicts with their families. Two-thirds said they had been disciplined firmly by their parents, with well-established boundaries for conduct, but they saw these constraints as beneficial and reasonable. Except for four people with abnormal mood states (two with hypomania and two with depression), two stutterers, two people who displayed paranoid thinking, and one person with recurrent nightmares, the great majority (85 percent) lacked even the mildest mental abnormality.

Grinker noted that though the subjects enjoyed team sports in high school, "only sometimes did one claim to be the leader of a social, work, or sport group." These men were better designed to be followers than leaders: "The average subject has had practically no trouble with those in authority" and even "maintains that he would abide by rules which he considered to be unfair." Overall there is a "picture of an individual who would be submissive to authority, but not slavishly."

Searching for a term less loaded than "normal" to describe these people, Grinker called them *homoclites*, a Latinate term he invented to indicate "those who follow a common rule."

WRITING IN 1962, Grinker anticipated the Nixonian concept of the "Silent Majority": "Within the general population of the United States this group is relatively silent. Its members are goal-directed, anxious only in striving to do their jobs well in which they will have moved up from their fathers' positions, but with little ambition for upward social or economic mobility. By the nature of their aspirations *to do well, to do good*, and *to be liked* they plan to carry on their lives quietly in simple comfort, marry and raise their families, and retire on small pensions plus social security." (italics in original)

He saw the cultural benefits of homoclites: "People like the George Williams students form a solid steady core of stability. They are the middle-of-the-roaders in every way, neither liberal nor conservative, neither hoarders nor speculators, neither grimly tight lipped nor high-steppers. Without them the ambitious, fast-moving climbers would slip into the mire of political, social, and economic chaos. They are not only Kansas . . . they are America."

He also observed how unsuited they were to leadership: "To have a population of relative stability is necessary for the activity of those who possess creativity. . . . Every American boy *could* become President of the United States, but those that do need the common citizen to elect him and for him to govern. Every country needs its proletariat, using the word in Toynbee's sense. It constitutes the majority which is led by the creative individual who withdraws from his society, returning to lead it in the light of his discoveries." (italics in original)

Roy Grinker identified a previously understudied biological specimen—the normal American male. Yet his colleagues were unsatisfied: "I often described my subject-population to various social and professional groups characterized by driven social upward-mobile or prestige-seeking people, who, although outwardly serene, were consumed with never-satisfied ambitions. The invariable comment was 'those boys are sick, they have no ambition.'"

Grinker's concept of mental health described the average person; but health—especially mental health—is often assumed to mean a more ideal state of well-being. He was well aware of this disparity, observing that at least three kinds of mental health can be defined. Some people represent the *norm*, the statistical average. Some represent the *normal*, meaning absence of illness. And some represent the *ideal*, meaning a "standard of perfection." Grinker's homoclites met the standards of the norm and normal, but not ideal, mental health.

Of course, making these distinctions presumes that there is an ideal of mental health. If so, there is no consensus about what it is. As noted above, psychoanalysis held the concept of mental health to be almost meaningless because most of us are abnormal. Since neurosis, defined as unconscious emotional conflicts, is an inherent part of the human lot, we are all more or less neurotic. Hence Sigmund Freud's dictum that every normal person is only approximately normal, and Anna Freud's teaching that a "normal" adolescent, if defined as being free of crisis and conflict, will grow up to become an abnormal adult.

In this case, the Freuds had it right. No *ideal* standard of mental health works scientifically. Or, in the eloquent words of Leston Havens, "Standards of health on the basis of admirable traits ignore the way human situations can call up the need for the most bizarre qualities." If this is true, then mental health can only be scientifically defined in its *norm* and *normal* standards, as defined above. Only Grinker's homoclites—average but not ideal—are mentally healthy. Searching for cultural references to help illustrate his newly defined class of people, Grinker called to mind a fictional depiction of "muscular Christian" normality, from a Thornton Wilder novel:

The hero, who is a missionary, religious, unrealistic, and not very intelligent, goes around the country doing good, converting people, and accepting no return. He says:

"George Brush is my name
America's my nation
Ludington's my dwelling place
and Heaven's my destination."

One couldn't have invented this irony—only the letter "r" in George Brush's name separates fiction from recent reality. In that coincidence we see a hint of what happens when homoclites rule.

WE'LL DISCUSS George Bush and Tony Blair as likely examples of the nature and pitfalls of homoclite leadership. But living leaders can easily arouse strong feelings in us, their contemporaries, that might cloud our understanding of the drawbacks of mental health in crisis situations. So first let's look back in history to other homoclite leaders who provide a sharp contrast to the insane leaders we've already encountered. We'll contrast Neville Chamberlain with his friend and fellow conservative politician Winston Churchill, and we'll explore the telling contrast between bipolar success William Tecumseh Sherman and homoclite failure George McClellan. This is not meant to be stick-figure compare-and-contrast history; Churchill and Sherman were often quite sane; they were not mad twenty-four hours every day all their lives. Similarly, Chamberlain and McCellan were not monochrome homoclites, devoid of emotional and psychological nuance. However, when we apply general definitions of these terms, the great leaders were clearly mentally ill, and their failed counterparts were mentally healthy. This is either a strange coincidence or it is quite meaningful.

What we'll find is that homoclite leaders tend to make bad decisions in crisis situations: they make war when they shouldn't; and they don't make war when they should.

Let's begin with the distinctions between Churchill and Chamberlain. Unlike Churchill, who rose to fame through his war exploits and an aristocratic lineage, Chamberlain was a commoner who worked his way up in municipal politics in industrial Birmingham. Lloyd George, prime minister during the First World War, commented that though Chamberlain would have made "a good mayor of Birmingham in a lean year," he was not up to being prime minister. Others viewed him in much the same light; the future prime minister Harold Macmillan saw him as "a nice man . . . very, very middle class, and very, very narrow in view." He was something of a geek, with hobbies of entomology and ornithology. Chamberlain had entered the family manufacturing business; in college, he studied metallurgy and engineering. He managed well the family business, which consisted of making ships' berths, and his workers viewed him as "a model employer." He married somewhat late, at age forty-one—a happy marriage with two children. His successes in business led him to active civic life, as leader of the Chamber of Commerce, fundraiser for the University of Birmingham, and founder of the city's orchestra. His older half brother, Austen, had entered politics, and Chamberlain followed suit. He ran for city council, then alderman, then lord mayor, and finally entered Parliament in 1918. Austen, already an MP, helped Neville come to the attention of the Conservative leadership, whom he impressed with his efficiency and seriousness of purpose. Lloyd George, prime minister at the time, later reflected on him as a man of "rigid competence," "indispensable for filling subordinate posts at all times," though he would be "lost in an emergency or in creative tasks at any time." He became minister of health in 1923, and successor to Churchill as chancellor of the Exchequer in 1924.

Unlike Churchill, Chamberlain earned a reputation as a successful steward of the British economy; during a period of postwar prosperity, he helped Baldwin promote a "new Conservatism," one that undercut the Labour Party's appeal by giving the working class progressive social reforms. By 1929, Chamberlain had led twenty-five reform laws to fruition. By 1931, when Labour's MacDonald took over the national unity government, Chamberlain was seen as indispensable. Remaining as chancellor of the Exchequer, he would guide Britain through the Great Depression.

THE CONTRAST BETWEEN Churchill's and Chamberlain's approach to Nazism is well known. As previously noted, Chamberlain wanted to establish personal relations with Hitler and rationally *convince* him of the need to avoid war. This was appeasement, the optimistic and misguided attempt to confront tyranny with logic: "If Germany could obtain her desiderata by peaceable methods there was no reason to suppose that she would reject such a procedure in favor of one based on violence."

Had Chamberlain retired in 1937, people would have hailed him as a success. He wasn't a buffoon; he was the wrong kind of leader. Or perhaps more accurately, he was a good politician, but not a good leader. In peacetime he was perfect, but when war loomed ever larger he was horrendous. The two aspects may go together. Churchill, his opposite—terrible in peace, sublime in war—captured the truth in his generous eulogy at Chamberlain's funeral, which occurred in the darkest period of 1940, barely a year after the war had begun: "In one phase men might seem to have been right: in another they seem to have been wrong, and when the perspective of time lengthened, all stood in a different setting."

Until Munich, their peers saw Churchill as unstable, and Chamberlain as eminently sane. The question then becomes: Was Churchill's insanity linked to his wisdom? Was Chamberlain's sanity linked to his blindness? Sanity prevented realistic assessment and rational decision making; one had to be somewhat depressed, a bit out of the mainstream, a contrarian rebel—as Churchill was—to see what was coming. In the storm of crisis, complete sanity can steer us astray, while some insanity brings us to port.

AS I MENTIONED in chapter 1, the American Civil War provides another close pairing—between William Sherman and George McClellan—whose divergent trajectories suggest the perils of sanity for leaders in crisis. As much as Sherman failed in peacetime, McClellan succeeded; as much as McClellan failed in war, Sherman triumphed. McClellan was second in his class at West Point, with hardly any demerits. Sherman was sixth in his class, but with many demerits. In the 1850s, the decade of Sherman's despondency, McClellan was the beau of the American military.

As with Sherman, we have important insights into McClellan's mental states based on near-daily letters to his wife. These letters weren't fully appreciated as a whole and made public until recent decades, and they provide a good record of his thoughts and emotions throughout much of his life. McClellan rarely, if ever, expressed any doubts about himself; his usual attitude was to blame others; he almost never expresses a hint of sadness or anything resembling depression of any kind. If sanity means not being mentally ill, and lacking anxiety and unhappiness, then George McClellan was an eminently sane man.

The son of a Philadelphia surgeon, raised in a wealthy family, McClellan entered the University of Pennsylvania at age thirteen and graduated in only two years. At fifteen he entered West Point, which waived its minimum age requirement of sixteen years. After years of private schooling among the elite in America's most prominent city, McClellan easily handled the academic work of West Point.

He served in the Mexican War under General Winfield Scott and Captain Robert E. Lee, and then, as a twenty-one-year-old veteran, returned to West Point as faculty, becoming a devotee of an unofficial postgraduate officers' course (called the "Napoleon Club") on the recent Napoleonic conflicts. McClellan prepared two papers, one on the battle of Wagram, and a 111-page tome on the Russian campaign of 1812. The core of this Napoleonic teaching was the notion that wars were won by strategy (rapid marching and flanking movements) combined with massive direct assaults focused on the enemy at one point. In Napoleon's era, these tactics were needed partly because the main weapon of war, the musket, was inaccurate. Many soldiers had to line up side by side and shoot in the same direction if they had any hope of hitting a target; a single soldier could not aim and hit a specific target. Movements of masses of men, and concentration of those forces, were needed.

After the Crimean War of 1854, the secretary of war, Jefferson Davis, sent McClellan (then age twenty-nine) and two senior West Point officers on a yearlong tour of Europe to study the conflict. The young McClellan had audiences with Napoleon III in Paris and Tsar Alexander II in Russia. He visited the Crimean battlefields and studied the siege of Sevastopol. He became fluent in French and German, taught himself Russian, and translated the first Russian military textbook into English. Yet his long military report did not recognize the key novelty of the Crimean War, soon to be tragically proven in the American Civil War: the rifle was now much more accurate than muskets had been a generation before. Soldiers could kill with much greater accuracy, making Napoleonic mass assaults nothing but scenes of slaughter. McClellan saw the immense losses in Russian assaults but did not appreciate their cause.

When McClellan returned to America, the booming railroad industry courted the young officer, offering him a far higher salary than the military. He became chief engineer and vice president of the Illinois Central Railroad. In 1857, when the financial crash ruined Sherman's banks, the railroad industry endured. By 1860, McClellan, then president of the Ohio & Mississippi Railroad, was wealthy and had just married a high-society wife.

Unlike Sherman, McClellan's career before the war was a series of unbroken successes.

AFTER THE NORTHERN LOSS at Bull Run, McClellan, who had succeeded in skirmishes in friendly West Virginia against Robert E. Lee, was brought to Washington, promoted to major general, and given command of the main Union army force. At age thirty-four, he was second in rank to his old chief, the now aged General Scott. McClellan chalked up one more triumph, writing to his wife, Ellen, "I almost think that were I to win some small success now I could become Dictator or anything else that might please me—but nothing of that kind would please me—therefore I won't be Dictator. Admirable self-denial." He settled in a large house in Washington and shared formal dinners with dignitaries like Prince Napoleon, the cousin of Napoleon III, with whom he conversed in fluent French.

General Scott had already prepared a war strategy: conduct a naval blockade of the South, preventing any imports or exports, thus weakening the Southern economy over time; focus military attack on control of the Mississippi River, attacking through Tennessee down through Georgia toward New Orleans, thereby dividing the South in two and further impairing any commerce within the region. Northern newspapers dubbed this the "Anaconda" plan, since Scott seemed to want to strangle the South from the periphery, like a snake, rather than to attack it at its heart. The Northern press preferred the latter approach, calling for a direct assault on Richmond, the Confederate capital.

The loss at Bull Run increased fears that Northern morale might not withstand the protracted conflict that Scott's strategy envisaged. When Lincoln asked him to provide his own plan of attack, McClellan came down strongly against Scott. Proposing a Napoleonic strategy of maneuver followed by direct assault, McClellan returned to what he had learned in West Point. He told Lincoln that the North needed to raise 500,000 troops, most of whom would be put under McClellan's command. With the center of operations in Virginia, the simple plan was to "crush the rebellion in one campaign" by taking the Southern capital, followed by South Carolina and Savannah, then moving through the deep South, and ending in New Orleans. In the face of Scott's resistance, McClellan argued, "Shall we crush the rebellion at one blow, terminate the war in one campaign, or shall we leave it as a legacy for our descendants?" All other military activity in the western regions of the South would be merely diversionary to the main focus on the eastern coast. One historian summarized this strategy: "One Napoleonic grand army, perfectly prepared; and one grand campaign, perfectly executed and with nothing left to chance, and the secession impulse would be crushed."

Lincoln vacillated at first, partly in response to the opposition of Secretary of State Seward, before going with McClellan's plan. Referring to Seward, McClellan wrote his wife, "How does he think that I can save this country when stopped by General Scott—I do not know whether he is a dotard or a traitor!—that confounded old General always comes in the way—he is a perfect imbecile." And again: "I am here in a terrible place—the enemy have 3 to 4 times my force—the President is an idiot, the old General in his dotage—he cannot or will not see the true state of affairs."

McClellan, never having failed in anything, was certain he knew what to do.

HISTORY RECORDS MCCLELLAN to be a dismal failure; his defeats are rather commonplace in Civil War history. Here I will briefly summarize. When he first took command, he sought to flank Richmond by a sea route, moving troops down the Virginia coast to advance on the rebel capital from the east. In this Peninsular Campaign, he proved adept at moving and organizing troops, but he failed when the moment of battle came. His attacks were weak and ill-timed, easily repulsed by the new Southern leader, General Robert E. Lee. After a few losses, McClellan packed up and came back to Washington. Lee, in contrast, rapidly moved into counterattack mode, sending Stonewall Jackson up the Shenandoah Valley to threaten Washington, winning the Second Battle of Bull Run. McClellan, by then removed as commander, watched as new Union generals tried to directly attack Lee, losing repeatedly in the process (at Fredericksburg and

Chancellorsville). Lee, as usual, followed defensive victories with offensive attacks, entering Maryland in late 1862. Others having failed, Lincoln reluctantly reappointed McClellan to repulse Lee from the north. Luck gave McClellan Lee's written orders, which a Confederate officer had dropped and a Union soldier found, so McClellan knew exactly what Lee would do and when. Still, at the bloody one-day battle of Antietam, all McClellan could manage was a draw. Lee withdrew to Virginia, and Lincoln practically did somersaults trying to get McClellan to counterattack. The cautious general refused, and Lincoln fired him again, this time for good.

In all, McClellan rarely won a battle, infrequently attacked the enemy successfully, and barely held off Lee while on his own ground, with superior numbers and the enemy's written battle plan in hand.

Like many healthy failures (such as Richard Nixon, see below), McClellan commonly is judged, in retrospect, in unflattering terms: historians call him grandiose, paranoid, narcissistic. Like Nixon, McClellan may have approximated such epithets—like most healthy, normal people would in such circumstances—because he suffered from the hubris of power. He had not failed enough to realize that he was really not as great as everyone said he was. The historian James McPherson has documented McClellan's foibles well. For instance, early in the war, McClellan judged Lee as follows: "Cautious and weak under grave responsibility . . . likely to be timid and irresolute in action." As McPherson points out, "A psychiatrist could make much of this statement, for it really described McClellan himself. It could not have been more wrong as a description of Lee." I believe that McClellan was too healthy—not depressed enough (unlike Lee, who seems to have been dysthymic in his baseline personality) to be realistically accurate in such judgments.

McClellan started out as the new Napoleon; he ended as a comedic shadow of the tragic original, called "McNapoleon" by his detractors. The crisis and strain of war would prove his undoing. Until he was tested by battle, McClellan's claim on power went unchallenged. One is reminded of Plutarch's comment about a failed ancient ruler: had he not become king, no one would have doubted his fitness to rule.

THIS ANALYSIS of failed homoclite leaders is convincing, I hope, but I realize that some readers may be thinking of counterexamples: what about Reagan, Eisenhower, Truman? They all seemed levelheaded and relatively successful. I would say they were homoclites, but that their presidential successes did not include handling major crises, like World War II (almost over when Truman took office), or nuclear standoff (Reagan never faced a Cuban Missile Crisis), or the civil rights crisis (Eisenhower briefly intervened in Little Rock, and otherwise avoided conflict).

Readers may also be thinking of another sort of counterexample—the insane failure. In American politics, the standout here is probably Richard Nixon. His fall is legendary, and so is the popular perception of him as paranoid, depressive, and even delusional. But in fact he was none of these things, except during a relatively brief period at the end of his presidency, when he was engulfed in a crisis of his own making. Before that crisis, he might well have been called successful and, as I will show, mentally healthy.

A problem here is that I will need to prove a negative: that Nixon was *not* mentally ill or abnormal. By trying to rule out one after another diagnosis, I will be making no positive diagnosis. We will be left with normality. That leftover conclusion will not satisfy some readers; but that is all we can do when trying to "prove" normality in general. In the process, I will admit that Nixon was not a classic homoclite: he was not in the middle of the normal range for most personality traits; he had his quirks. But he was not highly abnormal either. He still falls within normal variations of personality, and he certainly did not have a mental illness.

Richard Nixon had the misfortune to become president at the cultural peak of psychoanalysis. During the 1970s, six books and a dozen professional journal articles were devoted to psychoanalytic interpretations of him. In August 1973, when he shoved and yelled at his press secretary in public, *Newsweek* wrote that he was "on the naked edge of a nervous breakdown." One psychiatrist was quoted in *Time* magazine as saying that Nixon's behavior was consistent with schizophrenia. No president before or since has ever received such unwanted psychoanalytic attention.

Historian David Greenberg summarized all this Nixon psychoanalysis thus: "Almost uniformly, Nixon's psychobiographers saw him as a narcissist with a frail ego who lashed out when he felt wounded." A sometimes violent father instilled fear in young Dick, who then "identified with the aggressor." The doctors discovered oral-anal meanings in a school project Nixon had prepared when he was ten years old. They unearthed unconscious aggressive impulses in his childhood fondness for mashing potatoes. Psychoanalytic writers agreed, Greenberg writes: "Each painted Nixon as an insecure, narcissistic personality whose childhood injuries instilled a drive to achieve, a sense of guilt over his success, and a frail ego to which small injuries triggered angry outbursts."

This jibberish is scientifically meaningless. "Narcissism," in particular, is just a Greek myth translated into English; it has no scientific meaning, unlike the law of gravity, or the synaptic stimulation of dopamine receptors (or even clinical depression or mania; or the temperament trait of extraversion). Narcissism has never been empirically validated as a psychiatric diagnosis or mental illness, using scientific methods; it is an idea, a belief, like any Greek myth, but not a scientific diagnosis. The failures of Nixon's psychobiographers were the failures of their psychoanalytic presumptions—belief systems with little scientific grounding—as relevant today for psychiatry as the Marxist theory of surplus value is to economics.

As a psychiatrist, I would have to agree with Richard Nixon's denigration of psychiatrists. The psychobiographers of his day, like Freud himself, used speculative notions to advance their own political agendas. Nixon's verdict on Freud's biography of Woodrow Wilson—"so outlandish as to be downright silly"—is now widely accepted. Whatever one's political views, psychological honesty supports the plea of Gore Vidal (whose politics were hardly Nixonian): "Do not inflict this Freudian horseshit on Nixon, my Nixon."

Putting pejorative psychoanalytic labels aside, the right question is whether Richard Nixon possessed any major mental illness, or any extreme (scientifically valid) personality traits.

Of the four validators of psychiatric diagnosis (symptoms, family history, course of illness, and treatment), psychobiographers focused on symptoms. But *family history* is relevant: there is no documented evidence of mental illness in Nixon's family. *Course of illness* is key: he did not have recurrent mood episodes throughout his life. Toward the end of his presidency he was depressed, even suicidal, and drank excessively, but if this was a clinical depression, it was his only one ever. Unlike King and Gandhi, who also experienced serious depression in later life, Nixon had a normal childhood and adolescence, with no suicide attempts or prior mood episodes.

Regarding *treatment*, we now know that from 1954 onward, Nixon saw a New York internist who was also a psychoanalyst (Arnold Hutschnecker). In the midst of the scandal that led to his famous "Checkers" speech, agonizing over whether he should resign the vice presidency, Nixon suffered from tension, insomnia, and gastrointestinal symptoms, which the psychosomatic doctor rightly associated with stress-related anxiety. Sleeping pills were prescribed (probably barbiturates, which Kennedy also took), and Nixon likely received psychiatric counseling during his regular visits to Hutschnecker. Though Nixon insisted the treatment was for medical, not psychiatric, purposes, his doctor did not distinguish between the two. Hutschnecker, though publicly denying a relationship with Nixon at the time, could not resist self-satisfied psychoanalytic speculation after Watergate, writing in an op-ed article,

"I cannot help thinking if an American president had a staff psychiatrist, Watergate would not have happened."

I wouldn't be so sure. Psychiatry may not be the solution when sanity—not illness—is the problem.

SKEPTICS STILL might not be convinced. Yes, Nixon was depressed, drinking, perhaps even suicidal in the spring and summer of 1974, as he agonized over whether to take a humiliating and unheard-of step: resigning the presidency. Nixon's mental state during Watergate was certainly not calm. Reporters watched for the ultimate mental collapse; afraid to whisper the word "insane," they allowed Nixon's enemies to give them quotes, like labor leader George Meaney's comment that Nixon suffered from "dangerous emotional instability." One journalist, Hunter S. Thompson, was explicit: Nixon was "crazy with rage and booze and suicidal despair." Even friends like Barry Goldwater (speaking before the Watergate tapes were discovered) saw problems: Nixon sounded "as if he were a tape with unexpected blank sections. . . . His mind seemed to halt abruptly and wander aimlessly away. . . . Nixon appeared to be cracking." Nixon was reported to be conversing with White House presidential portraits. Alexander Haig, his military aide, told Nixon's physicians to remove his sleeping pills for fear of suicide.

Yet Nixon's drinking, in particular, appears to have been exaggerated. Numerous aides report that the man, raised as a Quaker to avoid alcohol, tolerated no more than a few drinks without inebriation. Nixon may have been drunk, but it was on a few, not dozens, of glasses.

Lacking close friends (as Reagan did), and introverted (as was Carter), Nixon knew his limitations. "I think I've got a lousy personality," he once commented. He cursed horribly: favored phrases, revealed in White House tapes, included "cocksucker" and "damn Jews." (For Kennedy, "screw" and "fuck" were preferable, while Johnson, holding staff meetings from the presidential loo, favored metaphors of urination and defecation; but when poor polite George McGovern told a heckler to kiss his ass, the media made a fuss.)

None of this indicates mental illness or even an especially abnormal personality. Given that Nixon was faced with the stresses of Vietnam and Watergate, psychiatrist and Holocaust survivor Viktor Frankl would have known what it all was: a normal response to an abnormal situation.

Nixon was not routinely vindictive, as many believe. Throughout his years in and out of power, he showed generosity to his foes, especially the Kennedys. Nixon constantly encouraged the sick JFK of the 1950s personally, and they supported each other politically on anticommunism. They were close enough that when Democratic liberal icons like Eleanor Roosevelt and Harry Truman tried to prevent JFK from winning his party's nomination in 1960, Joseph P. Kennedy Sr. sent word to Nixon that if JFK was not nominated, Nixon could count on the elder Kennedy's support for president. (Robert Kennedy, who served Adlai Stevenson as a campaign aide in 1956, nonetheless quietly voted for Eisenhower and Nixon that year.) After the Bay of Pigs, when Kennedy appealed to Republicans for help, Nixon made phone call after phone call, cajoling Republicans to support a president in crisis. "I just saw a crushed man today," Nixon remarked. "He needs our help. I told him to go upstairs and have a drink with his wife." After JFK's assassination, Nixon invited the widow and her two children for a White House visit. In 1971, Nixon graciously shared dinner with Jackie, JFK Jr., and Caroline. The kids toured the White House, romped around as they wished, and slept overnight in the Lincoln Bedroom. The visit was kept entirely confidential.

NIXON'S CAREER DISPLAYS the hallmark of homoclite leadership: like McClellan and Chamberlain, he was a success in peacetime, a failure in crisis. His failures are most remembered, but often in simplistic terms; his successes also deserve recounting.

To start with the failures first, the grandest is Watergate, leading to the only resignation of a sitting president. This failure, by far his worst, came, ironically, at the crest of his political power. In fact, it seems to fit rather nicely the paradigm of the Hubris syndrome (which I explain below in relation to Tony Blair). Nixon had finally achieved all he had hoped for: he had been elected president, and reelected with a landslide. He was the undisputed leader of his party, his nation, and the free world. His foreign policy successes, still legendary, reflect the homoclite leader at his best during times of political stability and economic prosperity: the opening to China, détente with Brezhnev's Soviet Union, the beginnings of a Middle East peace process. Nixon showed good diplomatic skills, an outgrowth of the social skills of the proficient homoclite. He succeeded at home and abroad, in large measure, because of his abilities as an excellent homoclite leader. By 1973, he was at the pinnacle of his power. And then he seemed to feel that he could abuse that power, to go beyond what the law allowed even the president to do. His goals were minor: to cover up attempts to hassle his Democratic enemies during the 1972 campaign. But it all blew up, as the president refused to listen to the advice of his close associates, as he tried to ignore Congress. Faced with the greatest crisis of his political life, he handled it the way an average homoclite would handle it: he lied, and he dug in, and he fought. He could not humbly admit his errors; he could not realistically see the limits of his power; he could not weather the stress without succumbing to a typically normal all too human response: blaming others rather than himself (hence the claim of "paranoia" so often leveled against him).

This grand failure is best understood in the light of his many earlier successes, for Nixon's earlier career of non-crisis homoclite leadership success is itself remarkable.

It was 1946; communism was the new enemy, and young educated veterans were ideal political protoplasm, ready for old pols to mold them for a new generation. Kennedy ran in Boston, Nixon in Whittier. Unlike JFK's father, Nixon's grocer father could not advise like an ambassador. Kennedy, aided by family connections and finances, won an open race in a Democratic district. Facing a long-standing Democratic incumbent, Nixon won on his own.

Almost. He really won with the essential help of his new political father, Murray Chotiner, a Beverly Hills public relations man whom Nixon hired for $500 a month. Chotiner would be Nixon's Svengali until the day Chotiner died (in 1974, three weeks before Nixon's resignation, in a car accident in my hometown of McLean, Virginia, in front of Ted Kennedy's house; Kennedy called the police to report the wreck).

Chotiner taught Nixon attack politics, summarized thus by Chris Matthews: "Chotiner had two working precepts. The first held that voting was a negative act: People don't vote for someone; they vote against someone. Chotiner's second rule was that voters possessed the mental capacity for grasping just two or three issues at one sitting. The goal of every campaign was therefore to limit the number of issues to two or three, all of them tied to the opponent, all of them negative. 'I say to you in all sincerity that if you do not define the opposition candidate before the campaign gets started,' Chotiner taught his disciples, 'you are doomed to defeat.'"

Richard Nixon was a good student. Facing a popular incumbent, he had little chance to win—until he claimed that his foe had ties to a communist-influenced labor union. That one issue, repeated and rehashed, with much raising of the voice, was enough: Nixon pulled the upset.

Soon, on the House Un-American Activities Committee, Nixon faced State Department diplomat Alger Hiss, who was accused of being a Soviet spy. With the support of senior diplomats, Hiss denied it all dismissively. When Nixon once mentioned Hiss's Harvard Law School education, Hiss interrupted: "I understand yours was Whittier." Nixon sensed a cover-up and proved it well enough to win a perjury conviction. Hiss went to jail, and Nixon became a national celebrity.

Thus began, as some have remarked, McCarthyism before McCarthy.

By the time the Wisconsin senator was in full throttle, Nixon had turned his attention to higher office. First, in 1950, he won a Senate seat, destroying his opponent (an actress who was also Lyndon Johnson's mistress) as the "Pink Lady." (Nixon never impugned her, or later Kennedy, for sexual misbehavior; despite JFK's concerns that Nixon would assail him for "girling," Chotiner's pupil focused on political, not personal, attacks.) The vice presidency followed in 1952, at Eisenhower's side, but at the price of a newly created hate-Nixon crowd. The attacker was attacked soon enough, accused of helping his family receive kickbacks. Eisenhower wanted to dump Nixon. The "Checkers" speech followed, in which Nixon denied the charges and acclaimed his dog. The homoclites of America recognized one of their own, and Eisenhower relented.

After eight years as vice president, Nixon's string of successes ended. In 1960, loss of the presidency. In 1962, loss of the California governorship. Nixon was washed up at age forty-nine. But Chotiner had good advice: Go to New York, make money as a corporate lawyer, deepen your financial connections, stay active in the party behind the scenes, sit out 1964, campaign hard for others in 1966, collect political debts, come back in 1968. By then, America was at war and torn apart. Republicans had their radicals (like Goldwater or Reagan) and their liberals (Nelson Rockefeller and George Romney). Nixon stood in the middle, appealing to all sides.

He promised peace in Vietnam, but with honor; as author Rick Perlstein puts it, he was the peacenik of the Silent Majority—or, which is to say the same thing in my view, the homoclite answer to the hippies.

WE NEED RICHARD NIXON to be sick, because we believe we are healthy. *If mental health means being a homoclite, then mental health has a considerable drawback: conformity.* The Nazi leaders were mostly homoclites, as we will see; so were, by definition, the German people; so are the American people. So was Richard Nixon. So am I, and so, probably, are you. Nixon realized that he shared the average American's vices, not just their virtues. He believed that "you've got to be a little evil to understand those people out there [meaning average Americans]. You have to know the dark side of life to understand those people."

Three decades of psychoanalytic suspicion have taken on a life of their own. Concludes David Greenberg: "The notion of Nixon as a madman, narcissist, or dangerous neurotic lived on in the political culture." This history is not at all consistent with the psychoanalytically based presumptions of some historians. When Theodore White wrote that Nixon's presidency was "a study in psychiatric imbalance," and that Nixon "became unstable as the great forces of history bore down on his character flaws," one has to wonder what White would have made of Kennedy's obsession with dying, the psychiatric impact of his steroid abuse, and his life-threatening hypersexuality. Richard Nixon took no dangerous medications, nor did he engage in any dangerous behaviors. If Nixon was psychiatrically unstable, then John Kennedy would have to be deemed outright insane.

In truth, Nixon was rather normal, and Kennedy mildly abnormal— hence the failures of the first and the resilient successes of the second.

Even the best reporters were psychiatric amateurs. In 1975, James Reston of the *New York Times* asked, "How is the nation to be protected from irrational presidents?" William Safire, having newly joined the *Times* after recently serving as a Nixon aide, saw no reason to claim irrationality: "A man harassed, tortured, and torn, but of sound mind, came to a rational decision to resign." Safire knew something was wrong with Reston's question, though he did not know its psychiatric basis: "There is a delicious inconsistency in the Nixon story: How could an intelligent man, a canny politician, blunder so egregiously in covering up a foolish crime—unless he had lost all his marbles? The historian who figures this out might earn a niche in history himself."

Historians have not figured it out, because they have not realized that, in this case, their man was not crazy. I believe I have solved Safire's riddle: *A mentally healthy homoclite would do what Nixon did.*

NOW WE COME TO our living homoclite leaders, George W. Bush and Tony Blair, two men who ruled when the great crisis of September 11, 2001, ushered in a new political world. I have already acknowledged the challenges of examining the mental state of leaders who are our contemporaries, but I believe it's possible to do so with these two figures because we've already established a detailed context in which to view them (that is, all the other mentally ill and healthy leaders we've considered thus far). And I believe it's valuable to look at the performance of these men, because their immediacy underscores the potentially tragic consequences of homoclite rule during times of crisis.

George W. Bush follows Grinker's model closely: he was solidly religious, upright, middle-of-the-road in his personality traits. He was sociable but not too extraverted, entrepreneurial but not an excessive risk-taker, easygoing (with neither too much nor too little anxiety or neuroticism). Under normal circumstances, like the midwestern homoclites of Grinker's study, he should have spent his years in Midland, at the side of his librarian wife, raising his two girls, watching the Texas Rangers, relaxing in Crawford on vacation. Without a president for a father, a senator for a grandfather, and family ties to Yale and Harvard, he probably wouldn't have gotten as far as he did. But he did as well as he did because of his own efforts too. With the social status that happened to be his lot, George W. Bush was a very successful homoclite, a fine peacetime leader, and a failed crisis leader.

It may seem odd to some readers, especially those who are critical of him, that I will insist that Bush was mentally healthy. In fact, I would diagnose mental health, or the absence of illness, in most leaders.

It is, in fact, a reflection of the deep stigma against mental illness, even among mental health professionals, that critics of his policies or actions should have trouble accepting that George W. Bush might be mentally healthy. Many of us have trouble envisioning someone we disagree with on fundamental issues as being entirely sane. It is harder, as I said earlier, to do psychological history with living leaders, not because of them, but because of our *own* feelings about them. Our feelings—yours and mine, politically based and deep-seated—interfere with objective psychiatric evaluations. The longer a leader is dead, the more objective we can be. Hindsight is clarifying. Chamberlain we can admit as healthy and weak as a leader; Bush and Tony Blair feel, to their critics, unhealthy and weak. But all of them could and should be seen as homoclites.

A KEY CHARACTERISTIC of a homoclite leader is that he or she is effective and successful in peacetime or prosperity, but fails during war or crisis. Let's see how successful George Bush was before he became president.

As a young man, he was widely viewed by friends as amiable and appealing. "He was Huck Finn and Tom Sawyer all in one," one friend recalled. "When you met him, you thought, 'I'd like to be around him.'" He was well liked, and had many friends. He suffered losses, like most people do at some point in life. Perhaps the greatest loss was the death of his older sister from leukemia, when George was only seven years old. His mother has written about how George's parents hid the severity of the illness from the young boy; he found out she was seriously sick only after she had died. Barbara Bush does not describe anything resembling depression in her son, only a questioning about why he had not known earlier. Barbara, on the other hand, suffered much, as most mothers would. She describes how she realized she needed to move on when she overheard George tell a friend that he could not come to play because his mother was grieving. Some might point to this experience as unusual, marking Bush as in some way psychologically abnormal as a result. In fact, about 15 percent of all adults in the

U.S. population lose a parent or a sibling before age twenty, making this a relatively common phenomenon. Fifty years ago, when medical treatment for illnesses like leukemia was much less effective than it is now, one would expect even higher rates of early sibling loss. Although childhood parental loss in particular increases the risk of depression when a person reaches adulthood, some studies show that most people who experienced losses during childhood correlate with people being *more* resilient as adults. Thus the experience of his sister's death does not necessarily, or even probably, imply that Bush would have become in some way psychologically abnormal as a result.

Bush had the best education, attending the elite Andover boarding school and then Yale. At the end of high school, his SAT score was 1280 (adjusted for today's test), which puts him well above the average score of 1026, and approximates to an IQ of about 120, average for a college graduate (and similar to John Kennedy), and notably higher than the norm of 100. So much for the claim that he is unintelligent. He was extremely socially adept; he joined a jock fraternity at Yale and was soon elected its president. He showed not only his pure intelligence but his "emotional intelligence" when during a fraternity ceremony he was asked to name as many of the new pledges as he could. Most people could name at most a dozen of their fraternity brothers, mostly new acquaintances; Bush named all fifty. His social ability is also highlighted by his election to elite societies, like the famed Skull and Bones. Even later political enemies, like the Clinton operative Lanny Davis, who was a Yale classmate, commented on Bush's interpersonal abilities. Some have used his average college grade of C to demean his intellectual skills, but a C at Yale is no mean feat. Bush's grades at Yale were in fact slightly higher than Franklin Roosevelt's, and similar to John Kennedy's, at Harvard.

In all, this history of childhood and young adulthood indicates a thoughtful, sociable, intelligent, "well-adjusted" man. Even so, this period also marks the start of Bush's drinking, and many of Bush's detractors would cite his alcoholism as an indication that he must at least be mentally abnormal in that regard. Bush doesn't hide this aspect of his past; indeed, he begins his memoir *Decision Points* by discussing it. He appears to have begun drinking in college, and according to his college friends later interviewed by the journalist Ronald Kessler, he drank no more than was typical in his social circle. But while vacationing with his family in Maine, the twenty-one-year-old was arrested for drunk driving, an event that later came to light one week before the 2000 election, producing the public perception that Bush had a severe alcoholic past that he had been hiding. In the police station, his blood alcohol level was found to be 0.10. This is legally drunk, but it is a level that is achieved by having four drinks. If this reflects psychological abnormality, then the majority of the U.S. population would qualify as abnormal at one time or another. Bush had no other legal or medical problems with alcohol, though he continued to drink for the next two decades. In his memoir, he describes quitting right after his fortieth birthday, when he was bothered by a hangover the day after drinking wine with friends.

A key factor appears to have been increasing anger related to drinking. One public event occurred in 1986, when a tipsy Bush confronted the journalist Al Hunt, who was dining with his wife, Judy Woodruff, and their four-year-old daughter in a Dallas restaurant. Hunt had written an article predicting that Bush's father would not be the 1988 Republican presidential nominee; George W. was livid, and swore at Hunt in public. His wife, Laura, pressured him to quit drinking, and the morning after the fortieth birthday bash, he apparently did. He says he has not had a drink since.

This history is actually the best possible outcome in anyone with alcohol problems, as well described in a fifty-year study of the natural history of alcoholism by the psychiatrist George Vaillant. As part of a larger study that young men entered around age twenty, Vaillant's group followed about six hundred normal men throughout their lives, many into their seventies. Of this group, eighty-nine people developed alcoholism (about 15 percent) over fifty years of follow-up. In fact,

Bush's history is typical: among Vaillant's subjects, alcoholism usually began in the twenties, and increased until about age forty, at which point it decreased by about 2 to 3 percent of persons per year. But two features mark Bush as different from a typical alcoholic: he quit cold turkey, without any formal treatment; and he has never relapsed, as best as we can tell. In contrast, Vaillant found that only about one-third of the people in his study managed to stop drinking completely, and 95 percent of them relapsed at some point after quitting.

Thus Bush can be seen as different from a homoclite in that he has had alcohol problems in the past, something that does not occur in about 85 percent of the population. But Bush's problem with alcohol was not severe and did not meet addiction diagnostic criteria: he had no symptoms of withdrawal or physical dependence, and his only legal problem occurred with a minimally high level of alcohol. Further, he was able to stop cold turkey and never relapsed, which makes him unlike 95 percent of alcoholics.

All this is to say that Bush's purported alcoholism is perhaps the strongest argument against simple homoclite status, but it also was a highly unusual kind of alcohol problem, one that was mild and easily solved, in such a way that rarely happens in those with alcoholism. Placed in the larger context of a great deal of evidence of mental health, as described above, Bush's past alcohol problems seem smaller and less central to who he is than many of his critics suppose.

THE REST OF BUSH'S pre-presidential life also strongly supports the notion of him as a homoclite. After graduating from Yale and Harvard Business School, he decided to join the oil business in Texas, like his father. This was a wise move; the 1970s oil boom was creating plenty of millionaires; it has been estimated that one person in five in Bush's hometown of Midland was a millionaire. Bush started with limited funds, $15,000 given to him from a trust fund owned by his father. He lived frugally: he was known for being cheap, and he often wore secondhand clothes. He used his social abilities to talk neighbors and friends into investing in drilling on West Texas land. Sometimes he succeeded, sometimes he didn't, but all in all, he was a typical 1970s Texas oil entrepreneur.

His grandfather having been a senator and his father a congressman, George W. seems to have caught the family bug for politics, and after a few years in the oil business he ran for Congress in 1977, beating another man in the Republican primary, but losing the general election to a Democrat who painted Bush (ironically, we might think in hindsight) as an eastern liberal. He returned to the oil business, but, like many others, suffered when oil prices fell in the 1980s. Bush's company lost money, along with most in his industry. By then his father was vice president; this fact did not hurt when Bush's indebted company was bought in 1984 by another oil company, Harken Oil and Gas. Bush's debts were paid as part of the deal, and Harken hired him as a consultant.

Five years later, Bush took the step that was his best success: he joined a group that bought the Texas Rangers baseball team. By then his father was president, no doubt a helpful fact; Bush put up much less money, most of it borrowed, than his fellow investors. But because of his high profile, Bush became the face of the Rangers, the most active and publicly visible leader, hiring and firing personnel, attending games, interacting with players and fans. He helped arrange for a new stadium, partly taxpayer-funded, that attracted more fans, and by the time Bush and his investors sold the team a decade later its value had risen greatly, making him a multimillionaire. By then he had also won the governorship in 1994, defeating the popular incumbent Ann Richards. Bush ran as a self-made businessman, in the oil business, but more important, in the sports business. His baseball success was key to establishing his political value: It "solved my biggest political problem in Texas," Bush would later say. "My problem was, 'What's the boy ever done?'"

Here's what he did. Born to a wealthy and politically connected family, which gave him excellent private schooling, he nonetheless started life with little personal income beyond a small inheritance. He married a local librarian and had two girls, whom they raised in middle-class comfort. He entered the oil business and did well during a boom and poorly during a bust. He ran for Congress and was a popular figure in his community. His family connections helped him segue into the baseball business, and he turned a financially faltering team into a profitable one. He then ran for governor and won. All in all, an impressive track record. Even without becoming president, he would be considered a success in life.

BUSH'S RISE WAS NOT EASY, but it was not very hard either. The key period was the 1980s, when his oil company failed, but he survived. His father's political power was central to the son's progress. The homoclite does not fail often, and when he does, he learns little. If he fails too much, he disintegrates rather than grows from the experience. Rarely having been tested in his youth, he hasn't had a chance to develop the resilience that might see him through later hardships. Having suffered little, he can't empathize with those who do. Having lived a secure life, he cannot recognize and react to hazards.

A homoclite makes a good friend, but a risky leader.

When the Twin Towers fell in 2001, Bush responded as the average subject in Grinker's study might have responded. They attacked us; we must attack them. They threatened us; we must invade them. As discussed in chapter 1, one sign of creativity is "integrative complexity," the ability to see things from multiple perspectives. The typical homoclite does not think this way; he tends to see things more simply, as Grinker argued. If someone attacks you, you strike back. This is simple logic; it is not inherently vindictive. It is straightforward, not empathic or complex. In his memoirs, Bush reflects little on his thought processes after 9/11, beyond the basic notion that we were attacked and we had to respond. Tony Blair, describing that period, emphasizes Bush's lack of complexity (albeit admiringly): "I would be at a press conference with him, in the epicentre of those world-changing events, and I would think 'George, explain it; don't just say it.'" But Bush felt little need to explain. In *Decision Points*, he only takes about two pages to describe the aftermath of the failure to find weapons of mass destruction (WMD) in Iraq, and even then he only describes his feelings briefly: "No one was more shocked and angry than I was when we didn't find the weapons. . . . I had a sickening feeling every time I thought about it. I still do." His rationale was one-track: "I remembered the shattering pain of 9/11, a surprise attack for which we had received no warning. This time we had a warning like a blaring siren. Years of intelligence pointed overwhelmingly to the conclusion that Saddam had WMD. He had used them in the past. He had not met his responsibility to prove their destruction. He had refused to cooperate with the inspectors, even with the threat of an invasion on his doorstep. The only logical conclusion was that he was hiding WMD. And given his support of terror and his sworn hatred of America, there was no way to know where those weapons would end up." Blair, in contrast, devotes more than a hundred pages in his memoir to describing his thoughts about the matter, and though he agrees with Bush, he does acknowledge other ways of thinking about the risks of invading Iraq.

Bush's administration strove to rationalize an invasion of Iraq; when this rationale proved wrong, we invented other reasons to stay. When we started to lose, we tried harder, consistent with Santayana's dictum that fanaticism consists of redoubling your efforts after losing sight of your goals. Bush showed no evidence of the complex integrative thinking that characterized the better generals of the Civil War. He did not empathize wth his enemies, as King and Gandhi (and even Sherman) had. He did not realistically assess the dangers of Saddam Hussein's weapons of mass destruction. He did not prepare (as Kennedy had during the Cuban Missile Crisis) a creative response that avoided war as a last resort. Bush made all options other than war untenable.

Bush's defenders will offer more complex rationalizations for the invasions of Afghanistan and Iraq, some of which might be valid. But the invasion of Iraq clearly was based on false claims. Rather than admit error, as Kennedy had in the Bay of Pigs, and withdraw, Bush did what Kennedy refused to do: send in even more troops and stay even longer.

This is quite normal. In psychological terms, Bush can't be faulted for thinking this way. Most of us think and act similarly. Most people have a hard time admitting error, apologizing, changing our minds. It takes more than a typical amount of self-awareness to realize that one is wrong and to admit it.

At least George Bush wasn't lonely. In his unshakable certainty, the conservative American homoclite was joined by his liberal British counterpart.

A HOMOCLITE PERSONALITY is not uniquely midwestern, or Texan, or American; nor is it exclusively conservative. Homoclites can also be liberal, cosmopolitan Europeans. Tony Blair and George Bush differed in political belief and personal style, but they were similar in psychological makeup.

Blair was a classic British amalgam, born to an Irish mother and an English father in the capital of Scotland. His father, Leo, taught law, and for a few years the family followed Leo's career to Australia. Leo came from a poor background, a foster child raised in Glasgow. He joined the army in the Second World War and then obtained a law degree. He worked hard all his life, attaining solid middle-class status, and, as a self-made man, identified with the Conservative Party. Eventually he settled in the city of Durham, and even planned to run for Parliament as a Tory, before he suffered a stroke in his mid-forties. Leo survived and recovered, but he had to give up his political hopes. Tony Blair's mother, Hazel, was a religious woman who took her children every summer to her ancestral home in Donegal, Ireland, for vacation; she was apparently extremely pleasant, shy, and a devoted mother. When Tony was twenty-two and at Oxford, his mother died of cancer, the first blight on an otherwise stable childhood. Leo Blair gave his three children all the advantages that he had never enjoyed: private schooling and a healthy family life. Tony attended Fettes College as a teenager, Scotland's premier boarding school. He did not enjoy the strict rules at Fettes, and he rebelled mildly, but not much. He excelled most in acting, and he enjoyed rock music. When he got to Oxford, he became a leader in his social circle and, like Bush, was highly amiable and sociable. He sang and played guitar in a rock band, the Ugly Rumours, studied hard, apparently never tried marijuana (which was de rigueur during his college years in the early 1970s), and talked plenty of politics and religion with his classmates. A circle of friends influenced him greatly, including an Australian Marxist who would be a lifelong friend, and an Australian priest who strongly influenced the young Blair in the direction of embracing his mother's religious example rather than his father's secular one. Blair was introduced to the writings of a Scottish liberal Christian theologian, John MacMurray, a man he would credit throughout his life as a major intellectual guide. With this background, Blair essentially came to a mild Labour social-ism from the perspective of Christian ethics. It was fair and just, spiri-tually and ethically, to fight poverty. This became Blair's road to leftist politics, a different end, but similar rationale to that which lay behind George Bush's compassionate conservatism. Like many homoclites, both men saw religion as a central feature of who they were.

In sum, Blair came from classic homoclitic stock, solidly middle class, soundly religious. He worked his way up productively and suc-cessfully in peacetime, as healthy people do, winning leadership with moderate Labour policies by means of appreciable interpersonal charm and oratorical gifts. After graduating from Oxford, Blair became a law-yer and married Cherie Booth, also a lawyer, who had been raised in working-class Liverpool in a religious Roman Catholic and highly pro-Labour family. In 1980, just when Margaret Thatcher had buried Labour in elections the previous year, Tony Blair joined the Labour Party and began looking for a place to run for Parliament. The party took him as a sacrificial candidate in a safe Tory district; Blair lost. Then, in 1983, he approached Labour leaders who were vetting candidates for a new constituency in Sedgefield, one that was considered to be a safe Labour seat. Many candidates wanted the plum; when Blair knocked on the doors of the local party offices, he was greeted by a half dozen men engrossed by European Cup soccer matches. As one of them, John Burton, recalled much later, Blair settled down to watch and enjoy the sporting event; beer and snacks were shared.

Blair won the seminal political contest of his career by *literally* passing the having-a-beer test.

Said Burton, "It was his manner that won us over. He had a presence about him that I knew instinctively could win elections. There was a kindred spirit." Homoclites recognized one of their own, and they knew that the homoclite masses would respond to him as they had.

Once Blair had his safe Sedgefield seat, he could focus on internal Labour politics. He worked his way up quickly, especially after Neil Kinnock became Labour leader and began to modernize the party. Instead of trade unionists who focused on workers only, Kinnock began to move Labour toward meeting the needs of the middle classes more broadly. Blair and another new young member of Parliament, Gordon Brown, became Kinnock's posse, the new leaders in waiting. Labour kept losing, and Blair and Brown kept rising through the ranks, until finally, after the sudden death of Labour leader John Smith in 1993, Blair was elected the new leader. In 1997, his party finally won.

Like Bush, Blair won power from the opposing party in a time of peace and plenty, convincing the British public through his likable persona and moderate politics. Labour had been out of power for almost two decades. Margaret Thatcher had remade British society, making classic welfare policies unpopular. Blair found a way to make "New Labour" attractive. Much as Bill Clinton had co-opted some of Reagan's rhetoric ("the era of big government is over"), Blair conceded on some policies, while arguing for a compassionate support of those aspects of the welfare state that Britons valued (like the National Health

Service). Blair was likable, polite, centrist, even religious—all homoclite traits. He succeeded beyond expectation, the only Labour leader in modern times to be elected three times, leader of Great Britain for ten full years (1997–2007). And he used this electoral success to achieve important political successes, most notably finally attaining, through the kind of tireless negotiation he would later display in the Middle East, a durable peace in Northern Ireland. As his press secretary Alastair Campbell aptly summarized in his memoir, "Progress in Northern Ireland alone should stand as historic testimony . . . but there were many others—an independent Bank of England, a Scottish Parliament and Welsh Assembly, elected mayors, a reformed House of Lords, regenerated cities, something close to full employement, a minimum wage, improved investment in reformed schools and hospitals." And he goes on and on, legitimately.

Like many other homoclite leaders, Tony Blair was—before the greatest crisis of his political life—a notable success story.

ALL THIS CHANGED after 9/11. Here we have extensive evidence of Blair's homoclite mindset, because, as mentioned, he provides over a hundred pages of introspection on the topic in his memoir (in contrast to Bush's two).

The key issue is how he responded to the crisis of 9/11. At least as he explains it in his recent memoir, Blair was not completely unrealistic; he could at least fathom rational attitudes other than his own (something that George Bush has not explicitly allowed). Blair admits "only" two ways of dealing with 9/11: one was to "manage" the problem, leaving the Taliban and Saddam in power, maintaining and strengthening economic and military sanctions. Blair calls this "soft-power"; Gandhi and King might have called it nonviolent resistance. To his credit, Blair admits its rationality: "Some indeed advocated this strategy (though not many did so on 12 September), and I do not dismiss it. It is the true alternative to what we actually did. . . . So we would have been provoked to war; and resisted the provocation." Isn't that exactly what King preached over and over again? (This reminds us, despite the January holiday hagiography, how hard it is for us to truly follow King's principles in foreign policy.)

The other option was the "hard-power" approach, most forcefully and purely advocated by Dick Cheney; that was the route Blair and Bush took. Says Blair now, "The other way, the way we chose, was to confront it [terrorism] militarily. I still believe that was the right choice, but the costs, implications and consequences were far greater than any of us, and certainly me, could have grasped on that day." Blair goes on to say that he now knew that this was not a merely or purely military decision; it required "geopolitical" context; it required "nation-building," something Bush had previously ridiculed, something that Blair now fully accepts.

So we have come full circle, to the foreign policy of one of Blair's favorite historical predecessors—back to the nineteenth-century liberal imperialism of William Gladstone. In an interview with journalist Philip Stephens in 2004, after Stephens notes that "what puzzled many people, even close cabinet colleagues, was his certainty that he was right about Iraq," Stephens asked Blair about whether his "moral sureness" was based on his Christian faith. Blair dodged the reference to Christianity but insisted on the need to "follow through on the values you have." He went on to expound on Saddam's excesses and tyranny, with "thousands of young kids dying" all the time. "We are interventionists," Blair admitted, saying that it matters to him, as a "progressive politician," if people are dying in Iraq or in Sierra Leone or Zimbabwe or Burma. He realized the obvious retort, that he only invaded one of those countries, one which happened to have oil wealth: "Of course, there is going to be a limit to what you can do . . . but our value system has got to be hard-edged, it can't be just soft."

To his credit, Blair maintains a somewhat open mind: "Who knows which [option] is right? No one. We will only know later. . . . In such circumstances . . . the only course is to follow instinct and belief. There is nothing more to do." This is true. The problem is that in such circumstances, in conditions of crisis, the instincts and beliefs of the homoclite leader tend to be wrong. It takes the mentally ill leader—the depressive realist, the creative manic—to apply the right instincts and correct beliefs.

Blair, unlike Bush, keeps talking, keeps justifying: "All these years on and still fighting, people look at the situation and ask: What went wrong? This ignores the possibility that it is not so much a case of 'what went wrong,' as that the nature of the struggle means that it will turn and twist and evolve over time."

In the end, Tony Blair has come to a drastic conclusion. In his view, his error lay not in his decision, but in the original rationale for his decision. He had sold it as a response to terrorists, a fringe group in the world of Islam. Take out the cancer in Iraq and Afghanistan, the thinking went, and the healthy Islamic body politic would respond well. But the cancer wasn't a single tumor that could be removed with one swift, decisive operation. It was an extensive mass that had metastasized throughout the world of Islam, with no clear beginning and no end. To excise the cancer, one had to harm "normal" Muslims too: "The battle is not, I'm afraid, between a small, unrepresentative group of extremists and the rest of us. . . . It is also a fundamental struggle for the mind, heart and soul of Islam." To preserve the rationale for our decision, we have to blame others even more. Not Muslim extremists, but Islam itself is the problem. In this, the George Bush who often decried "Islamo-fascism" would agree.

TONY BLAIR'S BIOGRAPHY reads like a case from Roy Grinker's study. He was again sociable but not extremely extraverted (unlike FDR), calm but not overly or insufficiently anxious, curious but not a risk-taker (unlike JFK). Even his earnest attitude to religion is consistent with homoclite psychology.

In sum, Tony Blair was a mentally healthy, homoclite leader. He rightly objects to assertions, based on stigma attached to mental illness, that he must be mentally unwell: "Friends opposed to the war think I'm being obstinate; others, less friendly, think I'm delusional. To both I may say: Keep an open mind." To both, I would say, your conclusions are right, but your premises are wrong. His political enemies think there is something wrong with Blair—morally, politically, psychologically. If Blair was politically mistaken, the cause was not any mental abnormality; it was mental health. Tony Blair had many problems, but mental illness was not one of them. His main problem, like Bush, may have been that he was too mentally healthy to handle the crises thrust upon him.

BLAIR AND BUSH praise each other for their "integrity," for standing up to popular disapproval, then and now. This may not be unreasonable. Indeed, none other than John Kennedy wrote a book, *Profiles in Courage*, which argued that political courage meant just this: to do what was right, what was in the people's best interests, rather than what was popular. But if Bush and Blair are wrong, then their steadfastness is not a measure of integrity or political courage. It is hubris.

So concludes David Owen, foreign minister in the British Labour government of the late 1970s, founder and leader of the Social Democratic Party in the 1980s, and a trained physician and neurologist. In recent years Owen has published books on the health and illnesses of twentieth-century political leaders, many of whom he met and knew personally. In his book *In Sickness and in Power*, he recounts having dinner with Tony Blair on December 18, 1998. The two men and their wives gathered at a table in the kitchen of No. 10 Downing Street. It was the third evening of a four-day bombing blitz against Iraq jointly authorized by President Clinton and Prime Minister Blair in which the United States and UK dropped more than 600 bombs and launched 415 cruise missiles on Iraqi targets, killing an estimated 1,400 members of Iraq's Republican Guard. At the time Congress had passed a resolution calling for the overthrow of Saddam Hussein. Owen recalls a pleasant wide-ranging conversation with detailed discussion on Iraq and the euro currency. Throughout the conversation, Blair was respectful and thoughtful—a good listener.

In July 2002, the two couples had dinner again in the same surroundings. The people were the same; the room was the same; the food was similar. But the social interaction could hardly have been more different. In the time since their previous dinner, Blair was now a veteran leader, having been in office five years, and he was embroiled in planning for an upcoming war in Iraq. Though the circumstances of the meal were quite similar, Blair himself had changed considerably. He no longer listened; he ignored viewpoints that challenged his opinion on Iraq. An open mind had been replaced by closed neural pathways, it seemed. Owen was struck by the transformation, and his wife summed it up during the drive home by describing Blair as "messianic," a term later commonplace, but then rarely applied to him.

The Blair of 1998 was a highly realistic politician who had plumbed the wishes of the British electorate. The Blair of 2002 was a premier living in a world that contrasted sharply with the real one, and yet he could no longer appreciate the discordance, or even be open to hearing about it from allies. What happened to Blair between the two dinners?

One might have predicted this outcome, based on the Goldilocks principle. Too much illusion is dangerous, and one has to make some effort to avoid sliding down that dangerous slope. Psychologist Shelley Taylor credits the real world itself: the world around us will correct us if we start to become too illusory. We will start to get negative feedback from friends and from harsh reality itself, which will punish us with setbacks: "The world provides sources of physical and social feedback that may keep illusions from becoming too extreme." Unless you're prime minister.

David Owen calls it "Hubris syndrome" and considers it a disorder of power. He has observed leaders at the highest ranks of international politics for decades, and he believes that prolonged exposure to power makes many of them unwilling and even unable to accept criticism or correctly interpret events that diverge from their own beliefs. Hubris syndrome worsens with the duration and absoluteness of one's rule. Owen has even identified specific features of the syndrome, which is completely independent of depression, mania, or abnormal personality. According to Owen, such leaders become unresponsive to opposing views, speak in the royal "we," presume the beneficial judgment of history or God, ignore public opinion, demean dissent, and rigidly hold their beliefs against evidence to the contrary.

Normally, people and events around us prevent us from developing too many illusions about the state of the world. We hear criticism or suffer setbacks that show that our approach to a particular situation is misguided, and we correct our course as best we can. But leaders often lack that useful check on their illusions. Their position gives them the power to ignore negative messages, or—more likely—they're less likely to get those messages in the first place. Yes-men abound in the corridors of power. Once leaders attain power, the world gives them less and less realistic feedback, and they're better able to exert their own power to suppress or dismiss such unhappy reactions.

As we saw earlier in our examination of depressive realism, mentally healthy people are insulated from some of the world's travails by their positive illusion—the belief that they and the world are actually better than they are. Generally speaking, positive illusion is a good thing, but I believe that power magnifies positive illusion into the Hubris syndrome. In this instance, we might apply the Goldilocks principle again: some illusion is beneficial, too much is dangerous—for the homoclite leader and especially for the society he leads. There are several possible antidotes to Hubris syndrome—term limits and "checks and balances" are two methods many democracies use to limit a leader's power. But clearly such measures aren't always effective by themselves. Another possible antidote might be having a leader who is not too mentally healthy. People who suffer from depression also benefit from a depressive realism that should protect them from the illusion-enhancing effects of power.

In his memoir, Tony Blair [TB] himself indirectly confirms Dr. Owen's diagnosis:

The difference between the TB of 1997 and the TB of 2007 was this: faced with this opposition across such a broad spectrum in 1997, I would have tacked to get the wind behind me. Now I was not doing it. I was prepared to go full into it if I thought it was the only way to get to my destination. "Being in touch" with opinion was no longer the lodestar. "Doing what was right" had replaced it.

But what if you are not right?

BUSH AND BLAIR were normal; so too, mostly, was Nixon; so too were one last group of leaders commonly assumed to be abnormal: Nazis. I have already discussed Hitler, whose bipolar illness is consistent with the thesis of this book. Helpful initially, it became a detriment when combined with years of intravenous amphetamine treatment. We are left with the other Nazis. Weren't they sick men?

In the Nuremberg trials, the Allies subjected about two dozen Nazi leaders to two years of evaluation by multiple psychiatrists and psychologists, with extensive personal interviews and psychological tests. These evaluations concluded that those Nazi leaders were normal men, mentally healthy, not insane. This may seem a banal confirmation of Hannah Arendt's thesis of the banality of evil. If it is, it at least tells us that no Nazi leader was mentally ill except possibly the three who committed suicide (Hitler, Himmler, and Goebbels). The list of those who were found to be normal is not in itself unimpressive: Hermann Goering (Luftwaffe chief), Joachim von Ribbentrop (foreign minister), Franz von Papen (vice chancellor), Hans Fritzsche (chief deputy to Goebbels), Alfred Rosenberg (editor of the Nazi newspaper), Rudolf Hess (Hitler's secretary, his cellmate from the 1923 prison, and a Nazi party leader from its inception), Albert Speer (armaments chief and, more important given Hitler's original life goal, a prominent architect), and others such as the leader of the Hitler Youth, ministers of justice and economics, and the governors of occupied Poland and Austria. If one believes that the Nazi tragedy reflected the mental illness of much of its leadership, at least some of these Nazi leaders should have been mentally ill. None was.

The consistency of the mental health of these men especially disturbed one of the psychiatrists who examined them, Dr. Douglas Kelley. Kelley had developed close relationships with the prisoners, and he was convinced they were normal healthy men, which made the whole process of Nazism that much harder to understand. For instance, Goering was Hitler's second in command and later committed suicide by taking potassium cyanide just before he was to be hanged. After much evaluation, Kelley concluded that Goering had a "normal basic personality," although he was "cynical and filled with a mystical fatalism." (Goering also had an IQ of 138, which is nearly at the "genius" level of 140 or above; even so, he was only third highest in IQ among the Nuremberg Nazi leaders. So much for the nineteenth-century biologist Sir Francis Galton's thesis that intelligence is the hallmark of greatness.) When Kelley was transferred, Goering gave him a signed photograph as a gift, and Alfred Rosenberg, the intellectual leader of the group, wrote a farewell letter: "Your excellency Major Kelly! I regret the fact that you are leaving Nuremberg, and the comrades imprisoned with me certainly also regret it. I thank you for your human attitude and for your endeavors to understand *our* motives as well. . . ." Just before his hanging, Goering managed to obtain a potassium cyanide pill and commit suicide. A decade later, Dr. Kelley killed himself the same way.

TO GIVE READERS a sense of the evidence on which these observations are based, I will now describe briefly the results of the Rorschach tests of the Nazi leaders. Though open to Freudian interpretations,

Rorschach tests can be interpreted descriptively, comparing results between different groups. The Nazi Rorschachs were not published for decades, and were first reported to demonstrate mental illness galore: "[The authors] unequivocally conclude that 'The Nazis were not psychologically normal or healthy individuals.' . . . With few exceptions, [they] describe the Nazi leaders as vicious psychopaths, opportunistic villains, and morally and emotionally bankrupt bigots who experienced no real guilt for their instrumental roles in the slaughter of millions of Jews and other victims of Nazi terror." This initial report was discredited when another psychologist "blinded" the tests, hiding the Nazis' identities and mixing in psychiatric patients and normal controls. Blinded experts could not distinguish the Nazi tests from the other two groups; sometimes Nazi results were judged pathological, but other times they were described as completely normal, even commendably well-adjusted.

A follow-up analysis in 1976 compared the Nazi results with other control groups: patients with schizophrenia and depression, a 1930s sample of German common criminals, a normal control of Kansas state troopers, and a second normal control group of medical students in the 1970s. The average Nazi leader showed little empathy, much positive emotion (e.g., self-confidence, self-esteem, happy mood), and normal amounts of negative emotion (e.g., sadness, anger). His overall cognitive style was deemed to be "integrative/holistic" (in other words, he tended to interpret the inkblot picture as a whole, as opposed to analyzing its parts). Most important, in comparison with the psychiatric and antisocial controls, the Nazi leaders demonstrated *no* evidence of psychosis at all, and hardly any antisocial personality traits. Indeed, the group that they approximated most closely was the "normal" Kansas state troopers.

The most unusual response, found only in some Nazi Rorschachs (five of them), and never in any of the other groups, was what the researchers called an "eerie" finding. Among animal shapes reported in the inkblots, only Nazis reported seeing a chameleon, suggesting perhaps a tendency to accommodate themselves to the powers that be (four of the five chameleon Nazis were acquitted at trial).

In sum, the Nazi leaders were much more normal than otherwise. They most closely resembled American state troopers, a finding that may say much more about the kind of person who seeks power over others than anything specific about Nazi ideology.

One might ask whether the Nazi leaders fooled the test giver, or consciously provided material that they thought would show them in the best light while on trial. This is possible, but as regards antisocial traits the 1930s German criminals also would have had similar motivations. Also, if one truly has psychosis, it is rather difficult to fake not having it. Depression, and to a lesser degree mania, might have been consciously masked to some extent, but even there, complete success at minimizing all symptoms is difficult.

One aspect of the unfortunate normality of the Nazi evil was that, like most mentally healthy homoclite leaders, the Nazis could not learn from their mistakes, even after their evident failure. Here is how the prosecutor of the Nuremberg trials, FDR's old friend Robert Jackson, described it:

> I have yet to hear one of these men say that he regretted he had a part in starting the war. Their only regret is at losing it. Not one sign of contrition or reform has appeared, either in public testimony or private interrogation of the twenty-one men in the dock. Not one of them has condemned the persecution of the Jews or of the Church—they have only sought to evade personal responsibilities. Not one has condemned the creation of the concentration camps; indeed, Hermann Goering testified they are useful and necessary. Not one has indicated that, if he were free and able, he would not do the same thing over again.

Psychiatrist Robert Lifton, in his many interviews with Nazi doctors, confirms that the highest-ranking leaders were mentally healthy, even in many ways admirable, men. Karl Brandt, for instance, a prominent academic physician, a member of an aristocratic family, educated in the best universities, one of Hitler's close doctors, was a leader of the medical euthanasia of mentally ill patients. Yet he was highly respected even by anti-Nazi leaders. Said one, "You must not picture Professor Brandt as a criminal, but rather as an idealist." Everyone Lifton interviewed spoke of Brandt as "decent, straightforward, and reliable. One doctor who knew him quite well described him as 'a highly ethical person . . . one of the most idealistic physicians I have ever met.'" Lifton saw Brandt as the prototype of the "decent Nazi": ethical in his personal relationships, upright and opposed to the extremism of "crude Nazis." Yet decent Nazis were Nazis nonetheless, believers in racial hygiene and the tools Hitler used to implement his genocide. Brandt never repudiated Hitler or Nazism throughout his Nuremberg trial, even though at the very end of the war, when Brandt declined to commit suicide, Hitler had repudiated him. Just before his hanging in 1948, Brandt could earnestly say these last words: "I have always fought in good conscience for my personal convictions and done so uprightly, frankly and openly."

The homoclite leader, suffering from hubris, rarely admits failure. If this kind of evil is banal in the sense of being commonplace, awareness of it is hardly common. Without these homoclite leaders, as Lifton concluded, the Nazi mass murders would never have happened.

IF THE CONCEPT of homoclites is scientifically correct, then it can be universally applied. All masses of people, including the German populace, are, by definition, homoclites: the average of a statistical mean of psychological traits—which constitutes a scientific definition of mental health. Their main weakness, as explained in the previous chapters, is conformity, which can be manipulated by demagogues; and yet they are hardy, resilient stock, able to survive such manipulation and then create a better world. In contrast, as I've tried to show, most Nazi leaders were not mere followers, nor were they insane; they were true believers, ideologues, rational fanatics—but from a psychiatric perspective they were mentally healthy.

While it is natural for laymen to see Hitler and the Nazis as insane, historians have struggled with the moral consequences of whatever judgments one makes about the mental states of Hitler and the Nazi leaders. The path of least resistance is to just avoid the topic, and this is what many do. They assume that Hitler and the Nazi leaders were more or less normal and thus responsible for their acts, and so too for the German people. If Hitler had a mental illness, then he could be made a scapegoat, or in some sense relieved of responsibility for his crimes—the ultimate insanity defense.

This is a simplistic mistake. To identify presence of mental illness with lack of moral responsibility is an expression of major ignorance about what mental illness is; yet I find this assumption in prominent historical works on Hitler and the Nazis. One can have mental illness, even the most severe, like schizophrenia, and still fall far short of the legal standard of innocence by insanity. In fact, in the vast majority of cases, those with mental illnesses are legally responsible for their actions, even when they commit the most heinous crimes. The *medical* and *legal* meanings of mental illness hardly overlap at all.

Medically, Adolf Hitler was a mentally ill man, with bipolar disorder and many abnormal personality traits, worsened markedly by years of treatment with intravenous amphetamine. Legally, he knew what he was doing, and he intended to do it; thus he was fully responsible for all his actions, despite having a mental illness and taking treatments that worsened that illness. There is no strong legal case in favor of Hitler from a psychiatric point of view as regards his historical crimes, as historian Martin Kitchen describes well. But this fact does not change the reality of his mood episodes or his intravenous amphetamine treatment, nor the effects of that illness and that treatment on his behavior.

No Hitler, no Holocaust, it is said. And yet Hitler did not create and maintain the Nazi regime all by himself. He was helped along by many other Nazi leaders who were, we now know, quite mentally healthy.

They were homoclite leaders, devout followers of an ideology that they truly accepted. Banality does not do justice to this fact. Though they were disciples of the dictator, these Nazi leaders enjoyed great freedom of action for most of the Nazi regime. They were indispensable to Hitler, his eyes and ears and arms and hands. Without the second-rank Nazi leaders, no one man could have run such a totalitarian state. We must face the paradox: they were ghastly creatures, but they were mentally healthy, normal homoclites. It might seem that the term "homoclites" should not be used for such monsters, but only for nice, upright people like the students of Grinker's YMCA college. But many Nazi leaders had also been nice, upright people most of their lives, before they became fanatic adherents of a racist doctrine. This disconcerting possibility may hold within it a dangerous wisdom about human psychology: the violence that lurks within even the healthiest of us.

And we can't let the German people off this hook. Most historians would argue rightly that Hitler and the Nazis have to be understood within their wider social context. Here the homoclite masses of Germany become relevant. When the masses yearn for community and conformism, and respond to the charisma of a manic-depressive supreme leader, and are prodded along by second-rank homoclite leaders, in a world where other countries don't respond to what is happening, and where poverty is rampant—one has an explosive mix.

We must not underestimate the dangers of homoclite psychology. It is not a matter of Hitler or the Nazi leaders or the German people just going bananas. The German people were mentally healthy, as were most of the Nazi leaders, and for most of his life Hitler's bipolar disorder was helpful to his leadership and his charisma, despite its drawbacks. There is much more mental health here than illness. Germany and its Nazi leaders were not much different, psychologically, from any nation or any leaders. And that's the scary part.

CHAPTER 15

STIGMA
AND POLITICS

We are left with a dilemma. Mental health—sanity—does not ensure good leadership; in fact, it often entails the reverse. Mental illness can produce great leaders, but if the illness is too severe, or treated with the wrong drugs, it produces failure or, sometimes, evil. The relationship between mental illness and leadership turns out to be quite complex, but it certainly isn't consistent with the common assumption that sanity is good, and insanity bad.

The thesis of this book runs counter to a deep cultural stigma accompanying mental illness. I suspect that it may be among our species' deepest biases, more so than even racism or sexism. Even those who realize the problem of psychiatric stigma, like doctors, cannot escape their inherent stigma. Some studies show that physicians attach as much stigma to mental illness as the general population. Even mental health professionals, who attach the least stigma to mental illness, have negative attitudes toward some mental illnesses, especially schizophrenia and bipolar disorder. And even some mentally ill people themselves harbor stigmatizing beliefs about mental illness.

This stigma is the basis, I think, for most of the intuitively negative reactions that readers may have to this book's theme. Those who have tried to argue otherwise have always noted this bias. Writing in late-nineteenth-century Italy, the psychiatrist Cesare Lombroso noted that a "proud mediocrity" resists the notion that what is common, and thus normal, may not be best. In 1930s Germany, the psychiatrist Ernst Kretschmer observed the same stigma and called it out as a "prejudice" of psychiatric "inferiority"; it is "agreeable" to be sane, he noted, but "a sound mind is possessed by the man who is emotionally in a state of stable equilibrium and who has a general feeling of well-being. Peace of mind and restful emotions, however, have never been spurs to great deeds." The same held in 1960s England when Lord Moran published his medical diaries about Churchill, revealing the great man's depression. Churchill's wife could not accept it ("It shows Winston in a completely false light") and she tried to dissuade Moran from publishing it, citing doctor-patient confidentiality. America in the 1990s was no different. Just as the Churchill family blackballed Moran, the Kennedy family criticized Nigel Hamilton's carefully documented evidence for John Kennedy's youthful hyperthymia (even though Hamilton never claimed a psychiatric diagnosis).

Prejudice against mental illness crosses all societies and all historical epochs. Profound intuitive responses and beliefs have grown out of this stigma over millennia, and they will not change easily or soon.

However deep the stigma may be, the indisputable fact remains that the border between health and illness is porous. Some aspects of mental health are found in even the most severe mental illness, and some aspects of mental illness reside in the most mentally healthy person. In this regard, the Freudians were right; we all are mentally ill to some extent. Harvard psychologist Brendan Maher showed that abnormal, illogical thought processes are common in normal, mentally healthy people. They differ in degree but not in kind from the delusional thinking that characterizes schizophrenics. Researchers have identified a slew of irrational thinking habits—called mental heuristics and biases. These include treating familiar ideas less critically than unfamiliar ones, assuming a causal link between events that happen coincidentally, exaggerating the threat from uncommon risks, and many others. (One source identified thirty-one standard irrational thought processes.) The overlaps between normal sadness and clinical depression, and between normal happiness and mania, have also been much examined by professionals and laypeople. So whether we're considering mood states or thought processes, the line between mental health and mental illness is hardly sharp, and the fuzziness at the borders means that some conditions will overlap each other. Mental illness isn't like being pregnant—you are or you are not—it's more like hypertension, or diabetes, or heart disease, all of which involve gradations of abnormality leading, in extreme cases, to specific events like a stroke, coma, or heart attacks.

Part of the stigma accompanying mental illness comes from our desire to view it as something completely "other"—utterly separate from those of us who are normal. But there is some of this "other" in all of us.

THESE CONSIDERATIONS obviously bear on contemporary politics and psychiatric practice. Regarding politics, recent experience in the United States suggests that stigma is alive and well. The last major national American politician to have admitted to any psychiatric condition was the unfortunate Missouri senator Thomas Eagleton, who was briefly the Democratic nominee for vice president in 1972. Soon after his nomination was announced, word spread that Eagleton had received electroconvulsive treatment (ECT) for depression, a common approach in that era (before most psychiatric drugs became widespread). We now know that he was hospitalized and treated three times between 1960 and 1966. Apparently he also received Thorazine, a medication now used for mania and psychosis (though also for depression in that era; it is similar to the Stelazine that Kennedy briefly received in the White House). Some have concluded that Eagleton may have had not just depression, but mania too, that is, bipolar disorder. After Democratic presidential candidate George McGovern dumped Eagleton from the ticket, despite Eagleton's strong objections, the Missourian returned to the Senate for a long career (1968–1986), during which time he served with distinction and was never known to have been severely depressed or manic. After leaving the Senate, he went on to live another two decades, never once criticizing McGovern in public or seeking retrospective revenge on his critics.

Of course, we know what happened to the mentally healthy Richard Nixon, who beat McGovern by a landslide in 1972.

The Eagleton effect, as we might call it, has had long tendrils. The electorate can, it seems, accept mental illness in political spouses (with depression usually: Rosalynn Carter, Kitty Dukakis, Tipper Gore; sometimes with mania: the wife of Florida governor Jeb Bush); but no serious politician has ever admitted even to being depressed. Abraham Lincoln couldn't become president these days, nor could Winston Churchill become prime minister. Of course Lincoln and Churchill hid their severe depressions from their respective electorates. But will we, as a society, ever evolve to the point where we can seek out our Lincolns and Churchills instead of getting them despite ourselves?

We are not there yet. Even the recent election of Barack Obama suggests persistence of the stigma attached to mental illness. He was elected partly because he seems so calm, steady, and unemotional, particularly in contrast to the perceived volatility of John McCain. The candidate was aware of being normal, all too normal: "[Adviser David Axelrod] said to me he wasn't so sure I'd be a good candidate because I was too normal. . . . Axelrod's right. . . . I'm pretty well-adjusted." "No drama" Obama might be considered the epitome of mental health. We like our presidents moderate and middle-of-the-road—psychologically even more than politically. But psychological moderation is not what marks our great presidents. Can we applaud passion, embrace anxiety, accept irritability, appreciate risk-taking, even prefer depression? When we have such presidents—the charismatic emotional ones, like Bill Clinton—we might have to accept some vices as the price of their psychological talents.

Atop the list of vices might be the one that most offends our Puritan heritage: sexual indiscretion. This vice is particularly applicable to this book's thesis, since hypersexuality is a common symptom of mania—and a common trait among the leaders we've examined. The impeachment of Bill Clinton over his affair with Monica Lewinsky, a White House intern, brought forth years of pontification on sex and politics. The implication was, for Clinton critics, that a good president had to display "good character"—kindness, moral rectitude, self-control, and so on. "Character above all" became the mantra (the title, for instance, of a PBS broadcast subtitled *An Exploration of Presidential Leadership*). When George W. Bush ran for president, he implied as much when he echoed in his victory speech a note he struck often on the campaign trail: "And so, when I put my hand on the Bible, I will swear to not only uphold the laws of our land, I will swear to uphold the honor and dignity of the office to which I have been elected, so help me God." Journalist Ronald Kessler titled his sympathetic biography of Bush *A Matter of Character*, and emphasized how Bush's superior behavior made him a better leader than Clinton. Sexuality was always the underlying theme, but Kessler extended his claim to a more general lack of decorum, especially in how the president treated support staff, from cooks and maids to the Secret Service men Kessler interviewed. "With Bush, there was an instant change," a former Secret Service agent told Kessler. "He was punctual. Clinton was never on time for anything. It was embarrassing. Bush and his wife treated you normally, decently. They had conversations with us. The Clintons were arrogant, standoffish, and paranoid. Everyone got a morale boost with Bush. He was the complete opposite of Clinton."

I agree with the premise, but not the conclusion. Bush had more sexual continence than Clinton; he may have been better behaved with staff; he may have been more normal and decent. But all that might argue *against*, not for, better leadership skills as a president in time of crisis. Personal vices are, after all, much less of a problem than political shortcomings. As the bumper sticker popular during the Iraq war said, "Nobody died when Clinton lied."

I am aware this viewpoint goes against conventional morality and the opinion of at least one founding father, John Adams, who famously said, "Public virtue cannot exist in a Nation without private Virtue." But an excess of virtue is a vice, if we recall that the classical Greek concept of virtue, derived from Aristotle, involved moderation. *Too much* virtue converts courage to recklessness, for instance. It may be legitimate to turn around and flee, rather than fight, under the right circumstances. That's what Aristotle meant by virtue, not some ideal of never-changing steadfastness. Given this perspective, one cannot cleanly separate virtue from vice, for the virtue of courage sometimes involves fighting, sometimes retreating, sometimes charging—each action interpretable as vices of violence, cowardice, and recklessness. Lincoln understood. "It's my experience," he once said, "that folks who have no vices have generally very few virtues."

There is a link between this Puritan fusion of private virtue with political leadership and the problem of stigma accompanying mental illness: the insistence on making simplistic Manichean judgments about people's behavior. One is a moral conflation, the other a psychological one. In this book, I am strongly suggesting that political skill on the one hand, and psychological health or even moral merit on the other, are unrelated in most cases, and in some instances may even be inversely related. A "normal" character is not inherently conducive to crisis leadership. In fact, once the benefits of mental illness are appreciated, then we have to accept that "abnormal" personal character traits may indicate better political leadership, irrespective of what our moral beliefs may tell us.

It's not just about sex. As we've seen, the greatest leaders have committed an array of sins. Like alcoholism: Churchill definitely tended toward the extreme there. Or violence: Sherman was darkly savage in many ways. Like dishonesty: King and Kennedy were apparently not open with friends and family about their sexual affairs. Or coldness: Gandhi gave his family little attention or personal sympathy. Or arrogance: FDR had to endure polio before he achieved any measure of humility. Or recklessness: Ted Turner risked his fortune more than once. Some of these sins were unavoidable: hypersexuality and alcoholism, for instance, often arise in those with mood disorders. Other sins were intrinsic to the success of those who commited them. These weaknesses were also strengths.

Our leaders cannot be perfect; they need not be perfect; their imperfections indeed may produce their greatness. The indelible smudges on their character may be signs of brilliant leadership.

We make a mistake, however instinctive, when we choose leaders like us. This is our own arrogance, as normal homoclitic people. We overvalue ourselves; we think, being normal, that we are wonderful. We stigmatize those who differ from us, whether because of race, sex, habits, culture, religion—or, perhaps more viscerally, because of mental illness or abnormal behaviors.

I don't mean to claim that it always takes a disturbed person to have a nuanced and humble view of life and the world. Many probably mentally healthy leaders are also complex and insightful: I would be inclined to include people like Harry Truman, Jimmy Carter and Nelson Mandela on such a list. My claim is that mental illnesses, like depression, do not detract from such abilities, but in fact can enhance them.

As we have seen throughout this book, the greatest leaders are often abnormal, even flat out mentally ill. We should accept, even celebrate, this possibility. Being normal is great in a friend and a spouse and in one's daily life; but leaders of nations and armies and businesses are faced with tasks and crises that no one else faces in normal life. For abnormal challenges, abnormal leaders are needed.

We are far from accepting severe depression or mania in our leaders.

But there is reason for hope. In 1990, Florida senator Lawton Chiles, running for governor, admitted to depression, which was successfully treated with Prozac. He was elected. Congressman Patrick Kennedy, the last political scion of that great clan, has been entirely open about his bipolar disorder and substance abuse, and he has made the stigma attached to mental illness the focus of his political career.

Stigma is not all or nothing: these days Prozac carries less stigma than ECT, and depression carries less stigma than in the past. But bipolar disorder remains highly stigmatized, and mania sounds scary to many. We have taken a few steps away from stigma, but many more remain to be taken.

THESE DAYS WE HAVE many more treatments for mental illnesses than we used to. Now we can not only improve but, perhaps more important (as seen with the cases of Hitler and Kennedy), worsen mental illnesses, raising some important questions about how the ideas in this book relate to treatment of conditions like depression and mania.

To be clear, I believe that untreated depression and bipolar disorder can be dangerous and deadly. All patients should be treated, in my view, when their symptoms are severe. Many should be treated even when their symptoms are mild or moderate, or even when they have no symptoms, in the case of conditions like bipolar disorder, where the most effective treatment is prevention of future episodes with mood stabilizers like lithium.

We needn't worry that drugs will deprive mentally ill leaders of the traits that make for great crisis leadership. Frankly, our drugs don't work that well. Most people who take medications still have mood episodes and symptoms; it's just that the medications can make them less frequent or less severe, thus preventing the suicide or psychosis that might otherwise result.

But sometimes, especially with mild depression, we should strive to see beyond the therapeutic imperative, and to realize that life is not all about banishing every symptom. The symptoms of depression might be an inescapable—and sometimes a beneficial—part of life.

This view contradicts the beliefs of many mental health professionals, especially those in the cognitive-behavioral therapy (CBT) school of thought. As I mentioned in the introduction, they believe that depression makes one more unrealistic than normal people. Many mental health professionals, especially psychiatrists, reject depressive realism in favor of CBT. But these perspectives are not necessarily contradictory. As with illusion—where the Goldilocks principle suggests that some is good and none or too much is bad—so it may be with depression. Some of it enhances realism, but none at all, or too much, may lead to distorted, illusory thinking.

This perspective is still relevant to all kinds of depression, even the more severe kinds. The depressive person isn't at his most realistic when he's in the deep throes of a depressive episode, but rather just before and just after. Beforehand, many people with depressive illness persist at a mildly depressed baseline, not so severe as to diagnose a clinical "major" depressive episode, but also not completely well. Afterward, once the severe episode is over, some people have mild leftover depression, and they can become even more insightful about their lives.

TOWARD THE END of his life, broke and broken, F. Scott Fitzgerald wrote a letter to his daughter, who was about to go to college, in which he advised her "to form what, for lack of a better phrase, I might call the wise and tragic sense of life. . . . By this I mean the thing that lies behind all great careers, from Shakespeare's to Abraham Lincoln's, and as far back as there are books to read—the sense that life is essentially a cheat and its conditions are those of defeat, and that the redeeming things are not 'happiness and pleasure' but the deeper satisfactions that come out of struggle."

For most of us, thankfully, life is not as tragic as it is for those with severe depression. Yet there are lessons for us all in the lives of those whose depression (sometimes aided by mania) spurred them onward to a realistic sense of the world's hazards, empathic concern for others, creative approaches to problems, and the resilience to survive and thrive. Our normal mild self-illusion often serves us well in the course of our daily lives. As Ralph Waldo Emerson said, we need to aim slightly above if we wish to hit the mark. But such normal illusion also hides important realities. When the crises of daily life come, we realize that we had been living a forgetful life, unaware of some basic truths. Then some depression may help us see what has happened and what we must do. And then we might be able to meet the challenges of life, and maybe even attain some happiness in the process.

Quite a paradox it is: being open to some depression may allow us, ultimately, to be less depressed.

EPILOGUE

The general approach I take in this book might be called psychological history, an attempt to apply our most scientific current standards in psychology and psychiatry to the study of historical leaders. This approach has its own historical roots in the Freudian "psychohistory" discussed in the introduction, but as described there, my approach is quite different. In this new procedure, one does not "pathologize." Health is diagnosed all the time, but it is seen to have limitations that are unhelpful. Illness, on the other hand, when present, is often helpful. These views are the reverse of stigma-based intuitions of both common sense and previous psychohistories: the "abnormal" is not necessarily a problem; the "normal" is not inherently a benefit. The new psychological history, for the first time, tries to get beyond stigma, consciously and clearly.

This new approach is scientific, not hypothetical; empirical, not theoretical. It has its roots in research in psychology and politics that originated with the classic work of the psychologist Hans Eysenck, *The Psychology of Politics*, later developed in the lifelong statistical research of psychologist Dean Keith Simonton, and in recent years advanced by psychologists Kay Jamison and Drew Westen, and cognitive scientist George Lakoff. It recently has begun to influence a minority of professional historians, like Michael Fellman in his biography of Sherman, and journalists like Joshua Shenk in his biography of Lincoln. But many, especially in academia, might still balk at such a new discipline.

Some people—especially among academics in the humanities and social sciences—doubt whether there is such a thing as mental illness. Some flatly deny its existence. Others allow for the reality of mental illness but argue that such illness is experienced in different ways in different eras, and thus any attempt to reconstruct mental illness anytime before our own era would simply involve transporting our own concepts into previous times. This would be the psychiatric equivalent of imposing our values when we assess why George Washington or Thomas Jefferson owned slaves.

The words academics use for this critique is "social construction." Either mental illness is a complete social construction, a creation of human societies as a means of controlling those who deviate from the mainstream, or it is at least socially relative (the same illness is experienced and expressed differently over time and in different cultures). Both of these critiques have merit, but they don't constitute a reason to dismiss psychological history as invalid, just as they don't invalidate psychiatry as a practice. That social factors are relevant to mental illness (and thus to both psychiatry and psychological history) is nothing new; in fact, social factors are relevant to many illnesses. (Can we understand diabetes or hypertension without considering social factors?) The presence of social factors does not mean that illness is *nothing but* a social construction.

Rather, these critiques highlight the importance of paying attention to cultural and historical differences in the experience of illness, just as one does in contemporary psychiatry when assessing patients from different ethnic groups. Some illnesses vary so much by culture and by century that indeed they seem highly socially constructed; contemporary examples might include eating disorders and attention deficit disorder. Other conditions, however, seem reasonably stable over time and across cultures. Schizophrenia is found in almost all societies these days, and its current definition is based on similar descriptions from over a hundred years ago in Germany. Manic-depressive illness also seems stable across cultures, and has been described in the same manner for at least as long. The core constructs of these conditions, delusions in the case of schizophrenia and mania/melancholia in the case of manic-depressive illness, have been consistently described (the claims of some postmodernist historians notwithstanding) in human history dating back to ancient Greece and Rome. These conditions are not just socially constructed.

My conclusion is that psychological history should focus on these major mental illnesses—schizophrenia and manic-depressive illness (or bipolar disorder and recurrent severe depression, in current lingo). In these realms, historians and psychiatrists can share knowledge and interpret facts in a way that is both fertile and accurate.

NOW WE COME to what I expect will be the most common objection to the notion of psychological history.

Most of us have a universal belief: because I can explain why I feel or act a certain way, then those explanations must explain those feelings or actions. This especially holds for psychiatric labels: if I can explain why I am depressed or manic, then I am not ill with the diseases of depression or mania. Coming up with reasons makes everything "normal." History can live without psychiatry, it might be argued, if reasons can be found that explain the actions of historical actors. But there are (wrong) reasons, and there are (right) *reasons*. There are always reasons; I imagine that if all books on history are examined, rare will be the place where a historian says, "We really don't know why X did Y." So it is in life. Rare are the occasions where we admit about ourselves, or others, that we really don't know why we feel or act certain ways. More often, we come up with plausible guesses; then we mistake these for reality. The Jewish philosopher Maimonides once said that if one can only learn to say, "I don't know," he will prosper.

In the daily work of psychiatry, it is typical to hear patients say, "Doctor, I'm not sick. I'm depressed because of X." "I'm not bipolar. I acted that way because of Y." It would be a poor psychiatrist who would accept the reasons of every patient at face value; in fact, no professional training in medicine or psychology would be needed if one took that approach. Indeed, neurological research on epilepsy patients who have surgery separating the two hemispheres of the brain ("split-brain" research) shows that people always come up with reasons for how they feel, even when the reasons are patently false. The most valid approach is neither to accept what patients say as truths nor to reject them as untruths, but rather to see everything as a half-truth, and to keep investigating until the whole picture comes together.

Historians routinely make this commonsense mistake of not accepting mental illness if a "cause" can be found. For instance, regarding General Sherman, historian Stephen Ambrose writes, "The manic-depressive goes into a mood for no reason at all; Sherman became exhilarated or depressed for excellent reasons." Scientifically, this is simply a false statement. Mania and depression routinely are triggered ("caused," if you like) by life events. And yet it is false to simply say, therefore, that the mania or depression does not happen, or that it can be reduced away to the life events. This has been proven by decades of excellent twin studies looking at genetic and environmental causes for depression in particular in thousands of persons.

Some psychiatric colleagues who read my chapter on Martin Luther King, despite their psychiatric knowledge, still made this common-sense mistake. King was not depressed because he "had" the illness of depression, this colleague remarked; he was depressed because of the extreme stress of living with the danger of death daily. This may be, or it could be that he had the disease of depression, or both.

This problem can't be easily dismissed: it is a profound dilemma that has exasperated philosophers for at least three centuries, since the philosopher David Hume starkly laid out this "problem of causation." X happens; then Y happens; X happens; then Y happens; X happens; then Y happens. At some point, we conclude that X *causes* Y. But as Hume points out, this idea of "cause" only means the *constant conjunction* of X and Y. Someday, Y might not follow X, and our assumption of cause would be proven incorrect. But we cannot know whether this will happen or not. So in the meantime, we presume causation. In sum: saying something causes something else is always a probabilistic statement; one can never be 100 percent certain.

So it is with all knowledge: with philosophy, science, psychiatry, and history.

Historians have tended to dismiss any psychological studies of historical figures; they often suggest that psychiatric judgments are made too quickly, too easily. Yet these same historians implicitly make psychiatric judgments of normality as the default alternative, without providing strong grounds for doing so. The universal assumption of psychiatric normality seems to be worth questioning, and the careful assessment of psychiatric abnormality, within a wider context of mental health in most leaders, seems to be worth considering.

THERE IS ANOTHER important problem I need to acknowledge and address. It is not enough to say that some leaders may have had mental illnesses; they may have had carbuncles as well, and influenza, and hemorrhoids. What matters is showing how their mental illnesses affected their leadership skills, and whether these effects helped or hurt them as leaders. This kind of effort will inevitably be limited by the state of our knowledge regarding psychology and psychiatry (and of the biographical facts), but as long as we stick with accepted standards of science in interpreting psychology and psychiatry, this kind of psychological history will be as valid as any other interpretation of history. We should keep in mind that the historian, at least one who seeks to write narrative history, is always engaging in psychological history.

The historian seeks to understand why leaders did what they did; he does so by trying to determine the mindset of that person in his context—his family, culture, society. The historian, in a way, puts himself in the place of the historical actor and empathizes, or understands from within. In that sense, psychological history already happens all the time. But because some historical figures were mentally ill, this empathic procedure doesn't always work. We cannot simply understand such a figure as if he or she were sane and rational, like us (presumably). Here is where some knowledge of psychiatry is not only helpful, but necessary. Here is where the old psychohistory ends and a new psychological history needs to begin.

There will always be an element of uncertainty, nonetheless, to any inferences one might make about the direct relation between a psychopathological state and a leadership skill. For instance, when I related Churchill's depression to his realistic assessment of Nazism, this inference cannot be directly proven. We wouldn't even be able to prove such an inference definitively had Churchill himself said, somewhere, something like, "I think I understand Hitler's true nature better than the rest of you because I have had severe depression and in those periods I have gained important insights into the world, especially into people like him."

This problem also has a long and profound history. Philosophers have agonized over this matter almost as long as they have lost sleep over Hume and causation. Once we accept a probabilistic notion of "cause" like Hume's, we are then faced with the conundrum of whether such notions of cause apply the same way to all fields of knowledge. Is it the same thing to speak of "cause" when Newton's apple falls to the ground, or when Einstein's atoms collide, as when we speak of what caused Napoleon to invade Russia? Is "cause" the same thing in physics and history, in chemistry and psychology? Is it the same, in short, when we study nature versus when we study human beings who love, and hate, and believe, and doubt? The German philosopher Wilhelm Dilthey spent his entire life asking, and trying to answer, this question.

And his answers, though profound, are still not widely accepted, or even understood.

This is not a simple question whose answer we can base on our commonsense beliefs. Dilthey suggests one solution: what we mean by "cause" is different in history and psychology than it is in biology and physics. There is overlap; the scientific concept of cause—involving counting, statistics, controls, and so on—can certainly be applied to human psychology. And we have used that kind of research throughout this book. But such scientific standards do not fully explain human history or psychology. People seem to draw meanings out of their experiences, and these meanings affect their actions. In history and psychology, we not only have to "explain" the facts; we have to "understand" the meanings of what people feel and what they do. We need to know not just "how" but "why."

HISTORY ISN'T molecular biology. History involves the interpretation of people's motives and intentions. Psychiatry also entails interpreting people's motives and intentions. The only difference between history and psychiatry, in this sense, is mortality—psychiatrists examine the living, historians the dead, but both in the same manner. The average historian seeks to interpret motives based on common sense and rational judgment and empathic intuition. All this is defensible, as long as a logical and persuasive rationale is provided. Yet the same defensibility holds for the psychological historian who seeks to interpret motives based on psychopathology and psychiatric research, again as long as a logical and persuasive rationale is provided. Kretschmer noted in 1931 that we ignore the positive aspects of mental illnesses for historical figures, although we see them around us on a daily basis: "Whilst thus many men of genius themselves prize madness and insanity as the highest distinction of the exceptional man—the biographer stands with uplifted hands before him and guards him from desecration by the psychiatrist!" There is no inherent reason why legitimate psychiatric concepts should be banished from history, as has mostly been the case until now.

At bottom, the new approach to psychological history comes up against that deep human bias: the stigma of mental illness. In taking this approach, our stigmatizing intuitions continually will rise against us, just as racist and sexist intuitions bedeviled past historians. Psychological history can have this benefit too: it can begin the process of leading us, as a society, toward a more objective and fair understanding of mental illness, no longer as just darkness and doom—something purely negative, to be feared and avoided, or "socially constructed" away—but, without denying its harms and dangers, also as the source of some of the best qualities in humankind.

ACKNOWLEDGMENTS

Over a decade ago, Michael Fellman's biography of General Sherman launched me on this project. Years later, after I published, with the editorial help of Paige Williams, an article on Sherman in *Atlanta* magazine, Michael became a central guide, adviser, and friend. I also benefited greatly from the friendship of Joshua Shenk, whose work on Lincoln catalyzed my thinking. Drew Westen generously introduced me to his agent, Susan Arellano, who provided critical hands-on help with my book proposal. Authors typically thank their editors profusely; I now understand why. Eamon Dolan not only gave me the opportunity to publish, but he sensitively guided both the content and style of the manuscript; I learned much in the process.

Others were kind in responding to queries on specific chapters, reading chapter drafts, or sharing ideas: Lauren Alloy, Ross Baldessarini, Carl Bell, Ed Diener, Frederick Goodwin, Stephen Kinzer, Martin Kitchen, Howard Kushner, Ed Mendelowitz, Godehard Oepen, Rick Perlstein, Ronald Pies, Alvin Poussaint, Dean Keith Simonton, Shelley Taylor, Tom Wootten, and my mother-in-law, Suzanne Hewitt. I especially thank Lord David Owen, whose ideas, encouragement, and example were vital. Elizabeth Whitham and Niki Holtzman assisted with sources, as did Sairah Thommi, who also helped with the endnotes and bibliography. Sergio Barroilhet assisted with research in the John F. Kennedy Presidential Library archives, whose efficient and professional staff I also acknowledge. Of friends who supportively followed the progress of this project, one is missing: James Hegarty, MD. Jim walked the streets of Gettysburg with me while we talked about these ideas, and he lived out Churchill's creed of never giving up.

Acknowledgment is an unsatisfactory word for my deepest debts. My father, Kamal Ghaemi, MD, bequeathed to me loves of apparently incompatible things: history, politics, and philosophy on one hand; medicine, science, and psychology on the other. A cloud of family witnesses deserve gratitude: especially my mother, Guity Kamali Ghaemi, my late grandfather, Mohammad Mehdi Kamali, and my late aunt, Golnoush Kamali, who bore severe mental illness with nobility of soul. My family—my wife, Heather, and my children, Valentine and Zane—lived through the very slow gestation of this book; they listened and talked and laughed with me along the way. Heather saw potential in this project long before I did, and steadily encouraged me to keep going with it. In the process, a semicircle of Valentine's Barbies and Zane's Legos and toy soldier regiments, cluttering the office floor, provided pleasant writing company, as did Roscoe. I have one last, old debt. Emerson said a teacher never knows where his influence will end. Decades ago, Thomas Bott—my sixth-grade teacher at Churchill Road Elementary School in McLean, Virginia—sparked my interest in Civil War history, applauding dozens of my reports, until finally he said I could stop writing. I never really did.

NOTES

EPIGRAPHS

The epigraph from Aristotle is drawn from Anna Lydia Motto and John R. Clark, trans., "The Paradox of Genius and Madness: Seneca and His Influence," in *Cuadernos de Filología Clásica*, 189–199 (Madrid: Editorial Complutense, 1992). The epigraph from Jack Kerouac is drawn from the Penguin Classics edition (New York, 2002), 5.

INTRODUCTION: THE INVERSE LAW OF SANITY

1 *"In these times it is hard to say":* Michael Fellman, *Citizen Sherman: A Biography of William Tecumseh Sherman* (New York: Random House, 1995), 100.

2 *a genetic link:* Ibid., 98.

2 *the work of historian Michael Fellman: Citizen Sherman.*

3 *Cesare Lombroso defined that link forcefully:* Cesare Lombroso, *The Man of Genius* (New York: C. Scribner's Sons, 1891). Lombroso's work was also later followed by Wilhelm Lange-Eichbaum in *The Problem of Genius* (New York: Macmillan, 1931). Lange-Eichbaum emphasized the role of followers rather than leaders, which I discuss in chapter 14.

3 *Francis Galton . . . the opposing view:* Francis Galton, *Hereditary Genius* (New York: D. Appleton & Co., 1870).

3 *Four key elements of some mental illnesses:* Juan Francisco Galvez, Sairah Thommi, and S. Nassir Ghaemi, "Positive Aspects of Mental Illness: A Review in Bipolar Disorder," *Journal of Affective Disorders* 128, no. 3 (2011): 185–190. See also Hagop S. Akiskal and Kareen K. Akiskal, "In Search of Aristotle: Temperament, Human Nature, Melancholia, Creativity and Eminence," *Journal of Affective Disorders* 100 (2007): 1–6; Kay Jamison, *Touched with Fire: Manic-Depressive Illness and the Artistic Temperament* (New York: Free Press, 1996).

5 *"[Wilson] carried great burdens":* Sigmund Freud and William C. Bullitt, *Woodrow Wilson: A Psychological Study* (Piscataway, NJ: Transaction, 1967), 197.

7 *Four specific lines of evidence have become standard in psychiatry:* Ming Tsuang and Mauricio Tohen, eds., *Textbook in Psychiatric Epidemiology,* 2nd ed. (New York: Wiley-Liss, 2002).

8 *antidepressants can cause mania:* Frederick K. Goodwin and Kay R. Jamison, *Manic-Depressive Illness,* 2nd ed. (New York: Oxford University Press, 2007).

12 *"Mania is extremity for one's friends":* J. Meyers, ed., *Robert Lowell: Interviews and Memoirs* (Ann Arbor: University of Michigan Press, 1988), 7.

13 *"To see a world in a grain of sand":* Alexander Gilchrist and Anne Burrows Gilchrist, *Life of William Blake* (New York: Macmillan, 1863), 94.

14 *"For months / My madness gathered strength":* Ian Hamilton, *Robert Lowell: A Biography* (New York: Random House, 1982), 256. This is an unpublished section of the poem, based on early drafts described by Lowell's biographer Ian Hamilton. The final poem is called "Home After Three Months Away," and it relates to being psychiatrically hospitalized at McLean Hospital soon after the birth of one of his children, with Lowell's heartache at missing his new baby. Lowell removed all except the last line for the final published poem, suggesting perhaps his continuing struggle to understand and accept his manic-depressive illness.

14 *The psychoanalytic view . . . is the most coherent:* David S. Janowsky, Melitta Leff, and Richard S. Epstein, "Playing the Manic Game: Interpersonal Maneuvers of the Acutely Manic Patient," *Archives of General Psychiatry* 22, no. 3 (1970): 252–261.

14 *Mania often occurs without any preceding depression:* Athanasios Koukopoulos and S. N. Ghaemi, "The Primacy of Mania: A Reconsideration of Mood Disorders, *European Psychiatry* 24, (2009): 125–134.

15 *Our basic temperaments are set by the time we reach kindergarten:* A. Caspi and P. A. Silva, "Temperamental Qualities at Age Three Predict Personality Traits in Young Adulthood," *Child Development* 66 (1995): 486–498.

17 *These temperaments were described:* The insights about temperament in the classic work of Kretschmer have since been validated and replicated with numerous empirical studies (although his views about the relation of physical body type to personality have not). Ernst Kretschmer, *Physique and Character* (New York: Harcourt, Brace and Co., 1925). Hagop Akiskal and Kareen Akiskal, "Cyclothymic, Hyperthymic, and Depressive Temperaments as Subaffective Variants of Mood Disorders," in *American Psychiatric Press Review of Psychiatry*, vol. 11, ed. Allan Tasman, 43–62 (Washington, DC: American Psychiatric Press, 1992).

17 *"The brilliant enthusiast, the radical fanatic":* Ernst Kretschmer, *The Psychology of Men of Genius* (London: Kegan Paul; New York: Harcourt, Brace and Co., 1931), 13.

CHAPTER 1. MAKE THEM FEAR AND DREAD US: SHERMAN

23 *asked . . . Liddell-Hart to write a book:* B. H. Liddell-Hart, *Sherman: Solder, Realist, American* (New York: Da Capo, 1993).

24 *"There is many a boy here":* John Marszalek, *Sherman: A Soldier's Passion for Order* (Carbondale: Southern Illinois University Press, 2007), 447.

24 *This task was taken up by Michael Fellman:* Lee W. Formwalt, "An American Historian North of the Border: A Conversation with Michael Fellman," *Organization of American Historians Newsletter* 36 (2008).

25 *Fellman discovered depressive tendencies in Robert E. Lee:* Michael Fellman, *The Making of Robert E. Lee* (Baltimore: Johns Hopkins University Press, 2003).

25 *outright mental illness in General Sherman:* Michael Fellman, *Citizen Sherman: A Biography of William Tecumseh Sherman* (New York: Random House, 1995).

25 *"think of many different and unusual uses":* Richard S. Mansfield and Thomas V. Busse, *The Psychology of Creativity and Discovery* (Chicago: Nelson-Hall, 1981), 4.

26 *a two-phase process:* Ibid.

26 *"Exuberant behavior and emotions":* Kay R. Jamison, *Exuberance: The Passion for Life* (New York: Knopf, 2004), 150–151.

27 *one study found that Robert E. Lee set the standard:* Dean Keith Simonton, *Greatness: Who Makes History and Why* (New York: Guilford, 1994), 80.

27 *One who has tried is Tom Wootton:* Tom Wootton, *Bipolar in Order* (Tiburon, CA: Bipolar Advantage Publishing, 2009).

28 *leaving him bankrupt:* Fellman, *Citizen Sherman*, 60–68.

28 *"I am of course used up root and branch":* Ibid., 63.

29 *"I am doomed to be a vagabond":* Ibid., 66.

29 *He saw fault on both sides:* Ibid., 77–83.

29 *Sherman declined to vote:* Marszalek, *Sherman*, 135.

30 *In* Citizen Sherman, *Fellman describes:* Fellman, *Citizen Sherman*, 95.

30 *"lapse into long silent moods":* Ibid., 96.

30 *"I am up all night":* Ibid., 96–97.

31 *"He has had little or no sleep:* Ibid., 98.

31 *Sherman's brother John:* Ibid.

31 *"I see no hope at all":* Ibid., 106.

31 *"such nervousness that [Sherman] was unfit for command":* Ibid., 100.

31 *"I should have committed suicide":* Ibid., 107.

32 *"an abrupt spiritual rebirth":* Ibid., 117.

32 *"We are absolutely stripping the country":* Ibid., 145.

32 *"To secure the safety":* Ibid., 147–148.

32 *"He stood by me when I was crazy":* R. W. Johnson, *A Soldier's Reminiscences in Peace and War* (Philadelphia: J. B. Lippincott Co., 1886), 308.

33 *In his* Memoirs, *Grant credits Sherman:* Ulysses S. Grant, *Memoirs and Selected Letters* (New York: Literary Classics of the United States, 1990), 652–653.

33 *"The unprecedented measure you propose":* Fellman, *Citizen Sherman*, 186.

33 *"You might as well appeal against the thunder-storm":* Reprinted in William Tecumseh Sherman, *Memoirs of General William T. Sherman*, vol. 2 (New York, 1875), 600–602.

34 *Said the . . .* Army and Navy Gazette: Irwin Silber, ed., *Songs of the Union* (Mineola, NY: Dover Publications, 1995), 15.

35 *When Sherman was close to Savannah:* John George Nicolay and John Hay, *Abraham Lincoln: A Memoir* (New York: The Century Company, 1890).

35 *"If the people raise a howl":* Fellman, *Citizen Sherman*, 180.

35 *"War is cruelty":* Ibid., 182.

35 *"My aim then was to whip the rebels":* Ibid., ix.

36 *"a marvelous talk about a march to the sea":* Lee Kennett, *Sherman: A Soldier's Life* (New York: HarperCollins, 2002), 257.

36 *"I attach much more importance":* Sherman, *Memoirs*, 1008.

36 *Wrote a Michigan soldier:* Fellman, *Citizen Sherman*, 224.

37 *"bore their afflictions with some manliness":* Ibid., 231.

37 *"It might be well to instruct your brigade commanders":* Ibid., 232.

37 *Lee himself may have been dysthymic:* Michael Fellman, *The Making of Robert E. Lee*.

CHAPTER 2. WORK LIKE HELL—AND ADVERTISE: TURNER

40 *In his recent autobiography:* Ted Turner, *Call Me Ted* (New York: Grand Central, 2008).

40 *"I was a restless kid":* Ibid., 4.

40 *"Today's schools would probably jump to the conclusion":* Ibid., 4–5.

41 *narrowly missed being run over by a train:* Ibid., 37.

41 *"I have always had a lot of energy":* Ibid., 259.

41 *"As a result of his upbringing":* Ibid., 329.

41 *"The fall of 1962 was an exciting time":* Ibid., 56.

42 *"My father knew the billboard business":* Ibid., 56.

42 *"He said they were for 'his nerves' ":* Ibid., 56–57.

43 *"I'd had some problems with mood swings":* Ibid., 263–264.

43 *about 40 percent of people with bipolar disorder were misdiagnosed:* S. Nassir Ghaemi, Erica E. Boiman, and Frederick K. Goodwin, "Diagnosing Bipolar Disorder and the Effect of Antidepressants: A Naturalistic Study," *Journal of Clinical Psychiatry* 61 (2000): 804–808.

44 *as documented in Jane Fonda's memoir:* Jane Fonda, *My Life So Far* (New York: Random House, 2005).

44 *"lithium is a miracle"* . . . : A 1992 *Time* magazine article reported thus: "If Turner can sound lighthearted about his death obsession, it is because he does feel much better about life these days. One of the main reasons is that at the urging of his second wife Janie, who was hoping to save their marriage, he began to see an Atlanta psychiatrist, Dr. Frank Pittman, in 1985. Pittman did two important things for Turner. The first was put him on the drug lithium, which is generally used to treat manic-depression as well as a milder tendency toward mood swings known as a cyclothymic personality. Turner's colleagues and J. J. Ebaugh, the woman for whom he left Janie, suddenly saw an enormous change in his behavior. "Before, it was pretty scary to be around the guy sometimes because you never knew what in the world was going to happen next. If he was about to fly off the handle, you just never knew. That's why the whole world was on pins and needless around him," says Ebaugh. "But with lithium he became very even tempered. Ted's just one of those miracle cases. I mean, lithium is great stuff, but in Ted's particular case, lithium is a miracle." Priscilla Painton, "The Taming of Ted Turner," *Time*, January 6, 1992. http://www.time.com/time/magazine/article/0,9171,974622-2,00.html#ixzz1I1LwlHeh (accessed Apirl 4, 2011).

44–45 *"On several occasions, the German general attacked the British":* Turner, *Call Me Ted*, 182.

45 *"We had already invested about $100 million":* Ibid., 194–197.

46 *"Confronted with a problem":* Ibid., 21.

46 *taking chances that may or may not work out:* Shelley Taylor, personal email communication, October 20, 2009.

47 *Arthur Koestler called this kind of executive the Commissar:* Arthur Koestler, *The Yogi and the Commissar, and Other Essays* (New York: Collier, 1961).

48 *"defined almost exclusively in terms of growth":* "In Sickness and in Power: Hubris Syndrome and the Business World," speech by Right Honorable Lord David Owen at the Association of British Neurologists Joint Annual Meeting, Liverpool, England, June 25, 2009, written transcript, 13. As we'll see in chapter 14, Owen thinks that poor leaders suffer from a "Hubris syndrome," where they increasingly lose touch with reality and make harmful decisions. My view is that this outcome occurs more in the mentally healthy "normal" leader than in the mentally abnormal leader.

CHAPTER 3. HEADS I WIN, TAILS IT'S CHANCE

51 *decided to test it on undergraduates:* L. B. Alloy and L. Y. Abramson, "Judgment of Contingency in Depressed and Nondepressed Students: Sadder but Wiser?" *Journal of Experimental Psychology* 108 (1979): 441–485.

52 *Ellen Langer and Jane Roth:* Ellen J. Langer and Jane Roth, "Heads I Win, Tails It's Chance: The Illusion of Control as a Function of the Sequence of Outcomes in a Purely Chance Task," *Journal of Personality and Social Psychology* 32 (1975): 951–955.

53 *"positive illusions":* Shelley E. Taylor and David A. Armor, "Positive Illusions and Coping with Adversity," *Journal of Personality* 64 (1996): 873–898.

54 *One study even quantified this principle:* Robert A. Cummins and Helen Nistico, "Maintaining Life Satisfaction: The Role of Positive Cognitive Bias," *Journal of Happiness Studies* 3 (2002): 37–69.

CHAPTER 4. OUT OF THE WILDERNESS: CHURCHILL

58 *the "sex goddess" of Victorian England:* John Pearson, *The Private Lives of Winston Churchill* (New York: Simon and Schuster, 1991), 68.

58 *Lord Randolph's son Winston had a different mental illness:* Ibid., 130. "Mrs. Diana Churchill 'Suicided,'" *The Age* (Melbourne, Australia), October 25, 1963, http://news.google.com/newspapers?id=wVARAAAAIBAJ&sjid=EJUDAAAAIBAJ&pg=5979, 4123402 (accessed February 26, 2011).

59 *"For two or three years the light faded":* Baron Charles McMoran Wilson Moran, *Churchill: The Struggle for Survival, 1940–1965* (Boston: Houghton Mifflin, 1966), 179.

59 *"I don't like standing near the edge of a platform":* Ibid.

59 *"I don't like sleeping near a precipice like that":* Ibid., 309.

60 *His friend Lord Beaverbrook noted:* William Manchester, *The Last Lion: Winston Spencer Churchill; Visions of Glory, 1874–1932* (New York: Little, Brown, 1983), 24.

60 *"He is a mass of contradictions":* David Owen, *In Sickness and in Power: Illnesses in Heads of Government During the Last 100 Years* (Westport, CT: Praeger, 2008), 41.

60 *Numerous physicians who knew Churchill:* Anthony Storr, *Churchill's Black Dog, Kafka's Mice* (New York: Ballantine, 1990). W. Russell Brain, "Encounters with Winston Churchill," *Medical History* 44 (2000): 3–20. Owen, *In Sickness and in Power.*

60 *"the drive and vitality and youthfulness of a cyclothyme":* Brain, "Encounters with Winston Churchill."

60 *"We are all worms":* Quoted in Lord David Owen, "Winston Churchill and Franklin Roosevelt: Did Their Health Problems Impair Their Effectiveness as World Leaders?" Churchill Lecture Series, Churchill Museum and Cabinet War Rooms, May 5, 2009, written transcript, 9.

61 *"You know, that was Churchill's idea":* Frances Perkins, *The Roosevelt I Knew* (New York: Viking Press, 1946), 383.

61 *The course of his depressive episodes:* Pearson, *The Private Lives of Winston Churchill.* Moran, *Churchill.* Martin Gilbert, *In Search of Churchill* (New York: Wiley, 1994).

62 *"The PM was in a crazy state of exultation":* John Harvey, *The War Diaries of Oliver Harvey* (London: Collins, 1978), 274.

62 *"great fluctuation of mood":* Owen, *In Sickness and in Power,* 42.

62 *"He felt that everything he had done":* Pearson, *The Private Lives of Winston Churchill,* 416.

62 *"I have achieved a great deal":* Storr, *Churchill's Black Dog,* 19.

62 *gave Churchill amphetamines:* Richard Lovell, "Lord Moran's Prescriptions for Churchill," *British Medical Journal* 310 (1995): 1537.

62 *"I have taken more out of alcohol":* Chris Wrigley, *Winston Churchill: A Biographical Companion* (Santa Barbara, CA: ABC-CLIO, 2002), 13.

62 *His daily routine involved:* www.winstonchurchill.org (accessed December 16, 2010).

63 *Once, when he was hit by a car:* Winston Churchill, correspondence with Dr. Otto C. Pickhardt, January 1932, http://www.christies.com/LotFinder/lot_details.aspx?int ObjectID=5382265 (accessed February 26, 2011).

63 *"In 1940 when all the odds were against Britain":* Storr, *Churchill's Black Dog*, 4–5.

64 *the Duke of Westminster:* Lynne Olson, *Troublesome Young Men: The Rebels Who Brought Churchill to Power and Helped Save England* (New York: Macmillan, 2008), 67–69.

64 *"an Austrian Joan of Arc":* Ibid., 68.

65 *"a born leader":* Ibid., 69.

65 *"It was no business of ours":* Ibid., 66.

65 *"When Winston was born":* Martin Gilbert, *Winston Churchill: The Wilderness Years* (Boston: Houghton Mifflin, 1984), 155.

66 *"In spite of the hardness and ruthlessness":* Robert C. Self, *Neville Chamberlain: A Biography* (Farnham, UK: Ashgate, 2006), 573.

66 *"How could honourable men with wide experience":* Gilbert, *Winston Churchill*, 234.

66 *"Winston has always been a 'despairer' ":* Storr, *Churchill's Black Dog*, 16.

CHAPTER 5. BOTH READ THE SAME BIBLE: LINCOLN

68 **Lincoln's Melancholy:** Joshua Wolf Shenk, *Lincoln's Melancholy* (Boston: Houghton Mifflin, 2005).

68 *"In early January 1841":* Ibid., 56.

69 *"Lincoln 'told me that he felt like committing suicide often' ":* Ibid., 19.

69 *"was the victim of terrible melancholy":* Ibid., 22.

69 *"often got the 'blues' ":* Ibid., 12.

69 *"His great-uncle once told a court of law":* Ibid., 12–13.

70 *Regarding the* course *of his illness:* Ibid., passim.

70 *Dr. Anson Henry:* Ibid., 57.

70 *"The Doctors say he is within an inch of being a perfect lunatic":* Ibid., 58.

71 *prescribed mercury tablets . . . also bled Lincoln:* Ibid., 59.

71 *"I am now the most miserable man living":* Ibid., 62.

71 *"fun and hilarity without restraint":* Ibid., 23.

71 *"As a nation, we began by declaring that 'all men are created equal' ":* Sean Wilentz, ed., *The Best American History Essays on Lincoln* (New York: Palgrave Macmillan, 2009), 139.

73 *"I would like to have God on my side":* Ibid., 219.

73 *"you and we are different":* Ibid., 76.

74 *"Here comes my friend Douglass":* Ibid., 80.

74 *Some historians think the war changed Lincoln:* Ibid., 79.

75 *"Whenever I hear anyone arguing for slavery":* Ibid., 81.

75 *"Both read the same Bible":* Lincoln's second inaugural address, transcript of original manuscript, http://www.ourdocuments.gov/doc.php?doc=38&page=transcript (accessed February 26, 2011).

76 *General James Longstreet:* William L. Richter, "James Longstreet: From Rebel to Scala-wag," *Louisiana History: The Journal of the Louisiana Historical Association* 11 (1970): 215–230.

CHAPTER 6. MIRROR NEURON ON THE WALL

80 *the English translation . . . captures this usage:* E. B. Titchener, *Lectures on Experimental Psychology of the Thought Processes* (New York: Macmillan, 1909).

80 *Karl Jaspers made empathy central to psychiatry:* Karl Jaspers, *General Psychopathology* (Baltimore: Johns Hopkins University Press, 1997).

80 *Thomas Insel and associates at the National Institute of Mental Health:* T. R. Insel and L. E. Shapiro, "Oxytocin Receptor Distribution Reflects Social Organization in Monog-amous and Polygamous Voles," *Proceedings of the National Academy of Sciences USA* 89 (1992): 5981–5985.

81 *The next hint about empathy came from studying macaques:* Reviewed in V. Gallese and A. Goldman, "Mirror Neurons and the Simulation Theory of Mind-Reading," *Trends in Cognitive Sciences* 2 (1998): 493–501.

82 *Similar research has since shown:* One British study, also using PET scanning, involved two conditions: either the research subject received a painful stimulation through an electrode on the back of her hand, or the same painful electrical stimulation was given to the subject's partner, seated next to her. The brain regions that became more active with the subject's own experience of pain were the somatosensory cortex (neurons directly connected to pain receptors in the hand), as well as the mirror neurons of the insula, and the cingulate gyrus. When observing her partner's painful stimulation, the subject's brain activity increased in the same mirror neuron regions (insula and cingu-late gyrus), but not the somatosensory cortex. T. Singer et al., "Empathy for Pain Involves the Affective but Not the Sensory Components of Pain," *Science* 303 (2004): 1157–1162.

82 *Psychologists divide empathy into different parts:* S. G. Shamay-Tsoory, "Empathic Pro-cessing: Its Cognitive and Affective Dimensions and Neuroanatomical Basis," 216–232, and C. D. Batson, "These Things Called Empathy: Eight Related but Distinct Phenomena," 3–16, both in Jean Decety and Willam Ickes, eds., *The Social Neuroscience of Empathy* (Cambridge, MA: MIT Press, 2009).

83 *It is generally estimated that at least one-half of human communication is nonverbal:* Albert Mehrabian and Susan R. Ferris, "Inference of Attitudes from Nonverbal Com-munication in Two Channels," *Journal of Consulting Psychology* 31 (1967): 248–252.

83 *severely depressed patients had much higher scores:* L. E. O'Connor et al., "Guilt, Fear, Submission, and Empathy in Depression," *Journal of Affective Disorders* 71 (2002): 19–27.

84 *patients with various psychiatric illnesses:* E. Knott and L. M. Range, "Does Suicidal History Enhance Acceptance of Other Suicidal Individuals?" *Suicide and Life-Threatening Behavior* 31 (2001): 397–404.

85 *patients' ratings of their psychotherapists' empathy:* D. D. Burns and S. Nolen-Hoeksema, "Therapeutic Empathy and Recovery from Depression in Cognitive-Behavioral Therapy: A Structural Equation Model," *Journal of Consulting Clinical Psychology* 60 (1992): 441–449.

CHAPTER 7. THE WOES OF MAHATMAS: GANDHI

87 *identification with his mother:* Erik H. Erikson, *Gandhi's Truth: On the Origins of Militant Nonviolence* (New York: Norton, 1969), 153–158. While Erikson's analysis is more extensive than presented here, it never engages with Gandhi's depression.

88 *"I watched day after day":* Karen E. James, "From Mohandas to Mahatma: The Spiritual Metamorphosis of Gandhi," *Essays in History* 28 (1984): 5–20, http://www.lib .virginia.edu/area-studies/SouthAsia/gandhi.html.

88 *"was literally praying that God should gather him":* Ibid.

88 *"He was very shy and withdrawn":* Erikson, *Gandhi's Truth*, 99.

89 *"Our want of independence began to smart":* Mohandas K. Gandhi, *Autobiography: The Story of My Experiments with Truth* (New York: Dover, 1983 [1948]), 22–23.

89 *"I decided at last to write out the confession":* Ibid., 23.

90 *only about 2 percent of children try to kill themselves:* Ronald C. Kessler, Guilherme Borges, and Ellen E. Walters, "Prevalence of and Risk Factors for Lifetime Suicide Attempts in the National Comorbidity Survey," *Archives of General Psychiatry* 56 (1999): 617–626. David M. Fergusson and Michael T. Lynskey, "Childhood Circumstances, Adolescent Adjustment, and Suicide Attempts in a New Zealand Birth Cohort," *Journal of Child and Adolescent Psychiatry* 34 (1995): 612–622.

90 *Indeed, 90 percent of children who attempt suicide:* David Shaffer, Madelyn S. Gould, Prudence Fisher, Paul Trautman, Donna Moreau, Marjorie Kleinman, and Michael Flory, "Psychiatric Diagnosis in Child and Adolescent Suicide," *Archives of General Psychiatry* 53 (1996): 339–348. Fergusson et al., "Childhood Circumstances."

90 **(or possibly, given some hypersexuality, cyclothymia):** Based on incomplete and debated evidence, it is also possible that Gandhi's baseline temperament consisted of cyclothymia. Some observers report that Gandhi sometimes had a high amount of energy, as exemplified by his habit of taking long, vigorous walks (Fischer, *Gandhi: His Life and Message for the World*, 1954). There is also some evidence of possible hypersexuality: for instance, in his *Autobiography*, Gandhi describes very high libido when he first got married; he describes marked guilt because he was engaged in sexual intercourse with his wife at the very moment his father died. He felt he could not control his urges even enough to stay by his father's deathbed. Freud once remarked that a major prohibition usually reflects a profound instinctual urge. In this sense, Gandhi's later emphasis on celibacy may reflect a strong sexual instinct. In his later life, there was also a controversy around the fact that Gandhi slept with his young niece. Some close aides even left the Mahatma over that scandal. Gandhi claimed he was only testing his vow of celibacy, and that he was literally sleeping, not having sex. If these controversies and claims are correct, then these behaviors are not consistent with pure dysthymia but may reflect periods of high energy and hypersexuality, which would make a cyclothymic temperament more likely. I did not make that diagnosis in the text because the veracity of these claims is not entirely clear to me. At least Gandhi had dysthymic temperament, I would conclude, but he possibly had cyclothymic temperament instead. Bal Ram Nanda, *Gandhi and His Critics* (New York: Oxford University Press, 1994), 14–17. Jad Adams, *Gandhi: Naked Ambition* (London: Quercus Publishing, 2011).

90 *"I was a coward":* Gandhi, *Autobiography*, 17.

90 *"I always felt tongue-tied":* Ibid., 55.

91 *"I felt the illness was bound to be prolonged":* Ibid., 407–408.

92 *the unfortunate life of Gandhi's eldest son:* Chandulal Bhagubhai Dalal, *Harilal Gandhi: A Life* (Chennai, India: Orient Longman, 2007).

93 *"My attitude towards the English":* Louis Fischer, *The Essential Gandhi* (New York: Vintage, 1983), 192–193.

93 *"We can do nothing without Hindu-Moslem unity":* Ibid., 253.

94 "Three-fourths of the miseries and misunderstandings in the world": Ibid., 255–256.

95 *"Europe has sold her soul":* Richard Grenier, "The Gandhi Nobody Knows," *Commentary*, March 1983, 59–72.

95 *"Let them take possession of your beautiful island":* Ibid.

95 *They repeat the conventional wisdom:* This viewpoint was later repeated by Erik Erikson in conversations with Huey P. Newton, the founder of the Black Panther Party in the 1960s, and a critic of King's nonviolence. Erik H. Erikson and Huey P. Newton, *In Search of Common Ground* (New York: Norton, 1973).

96 *Gandhi tried to persuade Nehru and other Hindu leaders:* Documents online at http://www.oocities.org/sadna_gupta/Extra6A_1940to43offersofJinnahPMship.html (accessed February 26, 2011).

96 *to give Pakistan £44 million:* Bal Ram Nanda, *Gandhi and His Critics* (New York: Oxford University Press, 1994), 109.

97 *"There was a time when people listened to me":* Fischer, *The Essential Gandhi*, 355–356.

97 *"He said, there was a time when India listened to him":* Arthur Koestler, *The Yogi and the Commissar, and Other Essays* (New York Collier, 1961), 267.

97 *"what he had mistaken for Satyagraha":* Ibid., 266.

97 *"Where do congratulations come in?":* Fischer, *The Essential Gandhi*, 362.

98 *"The woes of Mahatmas":* Gandhi, *Autobiography*, 215.

98 *"a dark and deadly future":* Fischer, *The Essential Gandhi*, 368.

CHAPTER 8. PSYCHIATRY FOR THE AMERICAN SOUL: KING

99 *"For several minutes, Gandhi and his guests discussed Christianity":* Lerone Bennett, *What Manner of Man: A Biography of Martin Luther King Jr.* (Chicago: Johnson Publishing Company, 1964), 3–4.

100 *American black leaders had become deeply interested in satyagraha:* Vijay Prashad, "PropaGandhi Ahimsa in Black America," *Little India*, 2002, http://www.littleindia.com/march2002/PropaGandhi%20Ahimsa%20in%20Black%20America.htm (accessed January 17, 2011).

100 *"The black workers led by young, educated ministers":* William Edward Burghardt DuBois, *W. E. B. DuBois: A Reader* (New York: Macmillan, 1995), 92.

100 *"The American Negro is not yet free":* Ibid.

101 *An edited collection of his papers, published after his death:* Clayborne Carson, ed., *The Autobiography of Martin Luther King Jr.* (New York: Warner Books, 1991).

101 Time *magazine reported in its 1963 "Man of the Year" article:* Available at http://www.time.com/time/subscriber/personoftheyear/archive/stories/1963.html (accessed September 3, 2010).

101 *"The first incident occurred":* Bennett, *What Manner of Man*, 18.

102 *Jesse Jackson recalls:* Jesse Jackson, online oral interview, http://www.thehistorymakers.com/programs/dvl/files/Jackson_Jessef.html (accessed January 17, 2011).

102 *This MLK was too radical for many:* Vincent Harding, *Martin Luther King: The Inconvenient Hero* (Maryknoll, NY: Orbis Books, 1996).

103 *"By 1968, King was working at a frenzied pace":* Stephen B. Oates, *Let the Trumpet Sound: A Life of Martin Luther King, Jr.* (New York: Harper and Row, 1982), 440.

103 *"'Bayard,' King said [to Rustin]":* Ibid., 444–445.

104 *"After the Meredith march, there were fewer marches":* Author interview with Alvin Pouissant, Boston, January 29, 2010.

104 *"What I have been doing is giving, giving, giving":* David Garrow, *Bearing the Cross: Martin Luther King, Jr., and the Southern Christian Leadership Conference* (New York: HarperCollins, 2004), 125.

105 *Dr. Poussaint . . . gave me a firsthand assessment:* Author interview with Alvin Pouissant, January 29, 2010.

107 *some of King's aides urged their leader to get psychiatric help:* Oates, *Let the Trumpet Sound,* 440.

107 *"Psychologists would say that a guilt complex":* The King Papers Project, Stanford University, http://mlk-kpp01.stanford.edu/primarydocuments/Vol4/27-Oct-1957_InterviewByAgronsky.pdf (accessed September 3, 2010).

107 *"put our outrage into perspective":* Andrew Young, *A Way Out of No Way* (Nashville: Thomas Nelson, 1994), 63.

107–108 *Bevel's insight was hard earned:* Les Carpenter, "A Father's Shadow: A Civil Rights Hero and the Daughter He Abused," *Washington Post Magazine,* May 27, 2008, available at http://www.washingtonpost.com/wp-dyn/content/discussion/2008/05/22/DI2008052202148.html (accessed February 27, 2011).

108 *"By nonviolence, we were trying to cure":* Author interview with Alvin Poussaint.

108 *"a sort of aesthetic or romantic love":* Martin Luther King, *Strength to Love* (Minneapolis: Fortress Press, 1977), 52.

109 *"What do nonviolent fighters do":* Bennett, *What Manner of Man,* 210–211.

109 *The answer, as King would later tell Poussaint:* Author interview with Alvin Poussaint.

110 *"war without violence":* Krishnalal Shridharani, *War Without Violence: A Study of Gandhi's Method and Its Accomplishments* (New York: Harcourt, Brace and Co., 1938).

110 *"My creed of nonviolence is an extremely active force":* http://www.mkgandhi.org/nonviolence/phil8.htm (accessed September 3, 2010).

110 *"The nonviolent resister is just as opposed to the evil":* http://mlk-kpp01.stanford.edu/index.php/encyclopedia/documentsentry/non_aggression_procedures_to_interracial_harmony/ (accessed September 3, 2010).

110 *King did not reject violence per se:* From his 1957 interview with Martin Agronsky:

[*Agronsky:*] Gandhi, Dr. King, dramatized and defined the technique of nonviolence. And yet, he also said that the only alternative to fear is violence. And that if that were the alternative, he would have to choose violence. Do you subscribe to that judgment of Gandhi, or would you disavow violence under any condition?

[*King:*] Well, I think I would have to somewhat interpret Gandhi at this point. I don't think he was setting forth violence as the—as an alternative. I think he was emphasizing, or rather, trying to refute, an all-too-prevalent fallacy. And that is, that the persons who use the method of nonviolence are actually the weak persons, persons who don't have the weapons of violence, persons who are afraid.

> And I think that is what Gandhi was attempting to refute. Now in that instance, I would agree with Gandhi. That if the only alternative to violence—to fear is violence, and vice versa, then I would say fight. But it isn't the only alternative.

The King Papers Project, Stanford University, http://mlk-kpp01.stanford.edu/primary documents/Vol4/27-Oct-1957_InterviewByAgronsky.pdf (accessed September 3, 2010).

110 *in a 1967* **New York Times Magazine** *article:* Alvin Poussaint, "A Negro Psychiatrist Explains the Negro Psyche," *New York Times Magazine,* August 20, 1967.

111 *Another black political leader:* Frantz Fanon, *The Wretched of the Earth* (New York: Grove Press, 1965).

111 *He called it "constructive assertiveness":* Poussaint, "A Negro Psychiatrist Explains the Negro Psyche."

111 *Shortly afterward, when King visited Boston:* Author interview with Alvin Poussaint, January 29, 2010.

111 *the coming together of . . . Frantz Fanon and Martin Luther King:* Years later, Erik Erikson, who had published a careful study of Gandhi, made this connection as he tried to understand the ideas of the leader of the Black Panther Party, Huey Newton. Erikson wrote, "There is a relationship between violence and nonviolence which is rarely considered by those who have not studied the question. . . . [Gandhi's] point . . . was that nonviolence doesn't just mean abstention from a violence which one would not have the means to carry through anyway, but the renunciation of armed tactics one would well know how to use. In this sense, the meaningful opposition is not that of arbitrary violence versus fragmented nonviolence, but that of disciplined violence versus disciplined nonviolence." Erik H. Erikson and Huey P. Newton, *In Search of Common Ground* (New York: Norton, 1973), 49–50.

112 *"Martin always felt that anger was a very important commodity":* Oates, *Let the Trumpet Sound,* 274.

112 *"Many people fear nothing more terribly":* King, *Strength to Love,* 21.

113 *"you have to be a little crazy":* Available on iTunes: http://deimos3.apple.com/Web Objects/Core.woa/Browse/new.duke.edu.1293697282.01293697292.1874801640? i=1201849001 (accessed July 15, 2010).

CHAPTER 9. STRONGER

118 *"good outcomes in spite of serious threats":* Ann Masten, "Ordinary Magic: Resilience Processes in Development," *American Psychologist* 56 (2001): 227–238.

118 *a "steeling" effect:* Michael Rutter, "Implications of Resilience Concepts for Scientific Understanding," *Annals of the New York Academy of Sciences* 1094 (2006): 1–12.

120 *Harry Stack Sullivan:* Helen Swick Perry, *Psychiatrist of America: The Life of Harry Stack Sullivan* (Cambridge, MA: Belknap Press, 1982). M. S. Allen, "Sullivan's Closet: A Reappraisal of Harry Stack Sullivan's Life and His Pioneering Role in American Psychiatry," *Journal of Homosexuality* 29 (1995): 1–18.

120 *"low-grade morons," "psychopaths":* Ben Shephard, *A War of Nerves: Soldiers and Psychiatrists in the Twentieth Century* (Cambridge, MA: Harvard University Press, 2000), 199.

120 *By 1943, 112,500 enlisted men had been discharged:* Ibid., 201.

120 *"To the specialists":* Ibid., 202.

121 *This is the case with all hysteria:* Paul McHugh, *The Mind Has Mountains* (Baltimore: Johns Hopkins University Press, 2006).

121 *In a classic example from medical history:* Edward Shorter, *From Paralysis to Fatigue: A History of Psychosomatic Illness in the Modern Era* (New York: Free Press, 1992).

122 *most people who experience trauma do* not *develop PTSD:* Ronald C. Kessler, Amanda Sonnega, Evelyn Bromet, Michael Hughes, et al., "Posttraumatic Stress Disorder in the National Comorbidity Survey," *Archives of General Psychiatry* 52 (1995): 1048–1060.

The above study is the largest and most definitive U.S. community psychiatric diagnostic study. It documented a lifetime PTSD rate of 7.8 percent, twice as high in women (10 percent) as in men (5 percent). If one includes other traumas besides physical and sexual abuse (such as crime, war, major auto accidents), about half of the American population experienced a major traumatic event (60.7 percent of men and 51.2 percent of women). Thus only about 10 percent of individuals who experience a major trauma later develop PTSD.

These are averages. With more severe trauma, such as repeated and intense childhood sexual abuse, as opposed to one occurrence, the PTSD rates rise. In the aftermath of September 11, 2001, the general PTSD rate in New York City was 6–8 percent; but if persons had been physically injured during the attack, it was 26 percent. Among Vietnam veterans, chronic PTSD appears to be present in 9 percent; in those with the most combat exposure, it is 28 percent. Studies rarely find full PTSD present in more than one-third of any sample, even with the most severe trauma. Milder PTSD symptoms that may not meet the full definition ("subsyndromal" PTSD) occur, but still only in a minority. For instance, after September 11, 2001, with syndromal PTSD present in 6–8 percent of the population, subsyndromal PTSD symptoms were found in another 17 percent. (S. Galea et al., "Psychological Sequelae of the September 11 Terrorist Attacks in New York City," *New England Journal of Medicine* 346 [2002]: 982–987.) In sum, with typical traumas, even under the worst conditions, at least one-third of persons have no PTSD symptoms at all—ever. (G. A. Bonanno and A. D. Mancini, "The Human Capacity to Thrive in the Face of Potential Trauma," *Pediatrics* 121 [2008]: 369–375.)

The same holds in the absolute human trauma—death. Each of us must face the deaths of loved ones, and, eventually, ourselves. Grief after the death of a beloved person is a universal human experience. Chronic grief, however—a grief of such severity that it involves long-term depression and PTSD-like symptoms—only happens in about 10 percent of persons. (W. Middleton, P. Burnett, B. Raphael, and N. Martinek, "The Bereavement Response: A Cluster Analysis," *British Journal of Psychiatry* 169 [1996]: 167–171.) Even when a death is unexpected and especially painful, chronic PTSD-like grief does not occur in most persons.

122 *Bonanno identifies four major types:* George A. Bonanno, "Loss, Trauma, and Human Resilience," *American Psychologist* 59 (2004): 20–28.

122 *they recovered repressed memories:* This is what Freud's first patient famously called "the talking cure"—a staple of Freudian dogma. All sorts of unconscious emotions exist within us, some related to childhood trauma; our current neuroses, anxieties, and depressive symptoms flow from those repressed unconscious emotions. This view has not been without controversy: feminists later attacked Freud for repressing the theory of repression, fearing the consequences of revealing the sexual abuse of young girls in

a male-dominated Victorian world; others see the whole concept of repression as a fabrication, mere suggestion by psychotherapists with their own ideologies (sometimes fantastically so, as in the theory of sexual abuse by aliens from outer space). The repressed memory debate has led to lawsuits and delirium, with some probable unjust accusations, and some legitimate cases dismissed as unprovable.

123 *Similarly, in Gulf War veterans:* P. B. Sutker et al., "War Zone Stress, Personal Resources, and PTSD in Persian Gulf War Returnees," *Journal of Abnormal Psychology* 104 (1995): 444–452.

124 *strong social supports:* Michael Rutter, "Resilience in the Face of Adversity: Protective Factors and Resistance to Psychiatric Disorder," *British Journal of Psychiatry* 147 (1985): 598–611.

124 *Some psychologists call this "ordinary magic":* Masten, "Ordinary Magic: Resilience Processes in Development."

124 *Similarly, in studies on World War II veterans:* K. A. Lee, G. E. Vaillant, W. C. Torrey, and G. H. Elder, "A 50-Year Prospective Study of the Psychological Sequelae of World War II Combat," *American Journal of Psychiatry* 152 (1995): 516–522.

124 *In an uncommon project:* Stephan Collishaw et al., "Resilience to Adult Psychopathology Following Childhood Maltreatment, *Child Abuse and Neglect* 31 (2007): 211–229.

124 *psychologist Dean Keith Simonton found:* Dean Keith Simonton, *Greatness: Who Makes History and Why* (New York: Guilford, 1994).

125 *are usually set by age three or so:* A. Caspi and P. A. Silva, "Temperamental Qualities at Age Three Predict Personality Traits in Young Adulthood," *Child Development* 66 (1995): 486–498.

125 *Adults who have higher neuroticism scores experience more PTSD:* Lee et al., "A 50-Year Prospective Study."

125 *one study examined . . . terrorist attacks in Russia:* V. S. Yastrebov, "PTSD After-effects of Terrorist Attack Victims," in *The Integration and Management of Traumatized People After Terrorist Attacks,* ed. S. Begec, 100–107 (Amsterdam: IOS Press, 2007).

126 *study of forty-six college students:* Barbara L. Frederickson, Michael M. Tugade, Christian E. Waugh, and Gregory R. Larkin, "What Good Are Positive Emotions in Crisis? A Prospective Study of Resilience and Emotions Following the Terrorist Attacks on the United States on September 11th, 2001," *Journal of Personality and Social Psychology* 84 (2003): 365–376.

126 *in young adults with childhood sexual abuse:* Bonanno, "Loss, Trauma, and Human Resilience."

126 *Genetic studies with identical versus fraternal twins:* Kenneth Kendler and Carol Prescott, *Genes, Environment and Psychopathology* (New York: Guilford, 2006).

126 *George Vaillant . . . concluded:* George Vaillant, *Adaptation to Life* (Boston: Little, Brown, 1977).

127 *followed children of the Great Depression:* Rutter, "Implications of Resilience Concepts for Scientific Understanding."

127 *a project . . . with which I was associated, at Massachusetts General Hospital:* Mark H. Pollack et al., "Persistent Posttraumatic Stress Disorder Following September 11 in Patients with Bipolar Disorder," *Journal of Clinical Psychiatry* 67 (2006): 394–399.

127 *a study of well-being in two thousand adults:* M. D. Seery, E. A. Holman, and R. C. Silver, "Whatever Does Not Kill Us: Cumulative Lifetime Adversity, Vulnerability, and Resilience," *Journal of Personality and Social Psychology* 99 (2010): 1025–1041.

127 *in seventy-eight women who had experienced a serious life event:* Allison S. Troy, Frank H. Wilhelm, Amanda J. Shallcross, and Iris B. Mauss, "Seeing the Silver Lining: Cognitive Reappraisal Ability Moderates the Relationship Between Stress and Depressive Symptoms," *Emotion* 10 (2010): 783–795.

128 *Resilience grows out of exposure to . . . risk:* Rutter, "Implications of Resilience Concepts."

CHAPTER 10. A FIRST-CLASS TEMPERAMENT: ROOSEVELT

130 *"Get down, you fool!":* Alexander Woollcott, "Get Down, You Fool," *Atlantic Monthly* 161 (1938): 169–173.

131 *"blow your trumpet" and "give the order to charge":* G. Edward White, *Justice Oliver Wendell Holmes: Law and the Inner Self* (New York: Oxford University Press, 1995), 470.

131 *"A second-class intellect, but a first-rate temperament":* The aide thought Holmes was referring to FDR, and this is the standard view; but some historians now claim the statement referred to Theodore Roosevelt. Paul Boller, *Not So! Popular Myths About Americans from Columbus to Clinton* (New York: Oxford University Press, 1996), 102–103. This phrase has been repeated in various combinations: "second-rate mind," "second-class mind," "first-class temperament." The most commonly cited original usage appears to be what is in the text, and the original source was the aide, Thomas Corcoran, who reported it verbally afterward.

131 *FDR's first-rate temperament . . . was hyperthymic:* In what follows I describe symptom evidence for hyperthymia, but I did not come across in my research evidence for full manic episodes or for clinical depressive episodes. The closest evidence for a possible clinical depression comes toward the end of FDR's life, when he had suffered from severe hypertension for years and was about to die of a massive stroke. Alen Salerian, an FBI psychiatric consultant, has suggested that Roosevelt might have been clinically depressed during the Yalta conference in 1945. David Owen, reviewing medical records of the time, could not confirm this impression. In any case, depression at that time would most likely be attributable to Roosevelt's cerebrovascular disease, especially since there is no evidence of a prior pattern of depressive episodes throughout his life. David Owen, *In Sickness and in Power: Illnesses in Heads of Government During the Last 100 Years* (Westport, CT: Praeger, 2008), 47.

131 *"Obviously that man has never had indigestion":* John Gunther, *Roosevelt in Retrospect* (New York: Harper and Brothers, 1950), 23.

131 *the State Department asked him to brief the president:* Ibid., 24–28.

132 *"FDR's extreme loquaciousness":* Ibid., 55.

132 *"My own method":* Ibid.

132 *"The simplest way to get at the President":* Ibid.

132 *"asking somebody who had never been in Latin America":* Ibid., 56.

132 *after Pearl Harbor:* Ibid., 31.

132 *"His vitality was . . . practically unlimited":* Ibid., 63.

132 *he made 399 trips by rail:* Ibid., 139.

132 *"The Roosevelt family is completely superhuman":* Marion Elizabeth Rodgers, *Mencken: The American Iconoclast* (New York: Oxford University Press, 2005), 434.

133 *TR needed only six hours' sleep:* Gunther, *Roosevelt in Retrospect*, 8.

133 *he had only two sleepless nights:* Ibid., 32.

133 *"He was often restless":* Ibid., 33.

133 *He spent about a quarter of the working day on the telephone:* Ibid., 125.

133 *"You know, a man will do a lot of right things":* Ibid., 130.

133 *"incurably sociable":* Frances Perkins, *The Roosevelt I Knew* (New York: Viking Press, 1946).

134 *"It was here that Roosevelt was irresistible":* Robert H. Jackson, *That Man: An Insider's Portrait of Franklin D. Roosevelt* (New York: Oxford University Press, 2003), 135.

134 *"[Wilson] refused to see most of them":* Ibid., 135–136.

134 *"There was always considerable conflict":* Ibid., 111.

135 *"Roosevelt certainly was not accomplished as an administrator":* Ibid., 111.

135 *not "a careful, direct-line administrator":* Perkins, *The Roosevelt I Knew*, 384.

135 *"Mr. President, you know you've got to let the cattle graze":* Ibid., 135.

136 *why not just shoot forty-nine thousand instead?:* Jackson, *That Man*, 149.

136 *"My fellow immigrants . . .":* Gunther, *Roosevelt in Retrospect*, 67.

136 *about 60 to 80 percent of newspapers opposed him:* Graham J. White, *FDR and the Press* (Chicago: University of Chicago Press, 1979), 70.

136 *"You know, we had to buy that fucking paper":* Robert Dallek, *An Unfinished Life: John F. Kennedy* (Boston: Little, Brown, 2003), 172.

137 *almost a thousand press conferences in all:* Gunther, *Roosevelt in Retrospect*, 134–136.

137 *"Innovations never frightened him":* Ibid., 64–66.

137 *He loved to read:* Ibid., 118–119.

137 *After Yalta, FDR was headed to Saudi Arabia:* Perkins, *The Roosevelt I Knew*, 88–89.

138 *"You sometimes find something pretty good in the lunatic fringe":* Gunther, *Roosevelt in Retrospect*, 115.

138 *once writing a memorandum:* Ibid., 115.

138 *"That fellow in the White House":* Ibid., 115.

138 *"Mr. President, are you a Communist?":* Perkins, *The Roosevelt I Knew*, 330.

139 *Roosevelt . . . read some of Kierkegaard's works:* Ibid., 146–148.

139 *FDR scribbled . . . China's coastal contours:* Jackson, *That Man*, 13.

139 *Family history provides some evidence:* Gunther, *Roosevelt in Retrospect*, 156–161.

140 *in some genetic studies of bipolar disorder:* Sermin Kesebira, Simavi Vahipa, Fisun Akdeniza, Zeki Yüncüa, Müge Alkana, and Hagop Akiskal, "Affective Temperaments as Measured by TEMPS-A in Patients with Bipolar I Disorder and Their First-Degree Relatives: A Controlled Study," *Journal of Affective Disorders* 85 (2005): 127–133. S. G. Simpson, S. E. Folstein, D. A. Meyers, F. J. McMahon, D. M. Brusco, and J. R. DePaulo Jr., "Bipolar II: The Most Common Bipolar Phenotype?" *American Journal of Psychiatry* 150 (1993): 901–903.

140 *"I have one wish for you":* Gunther, *Roosevelt in Retrospect*, 168.

141 *"It's ridiculous to tell me":* Ibid., 238.

141 *he fell, or almost fell, about five times:* Ibid., 236.

142 *the "ultimate humility":* Perkins, *The Roosevelt I Knew*, 44–45.

142 *"When he reached the top":* Gunther, *Roosevelt in Retrospect*, 267–268.

142 *was the worst aspect of his disability:* Ibid., 236.

142 *"an untried rather flippant young man":* Ibid., 242

142 *Roosevelt was disciplined by his illness:* Jackson, *That Man*, 171.

143 *"Roosevelt underwent a spiritual transformation":* Perkins, *The Roosevelt I Knew*, 29.

143 *"This is the Happy Warrior":* Gunther, *Roosevelt in Retrospect*, 245–250.

144 *"A governor does not have to be an acrobat"*: Ibid., 253.

144 *"Ten years ago, Governor Roosevelt suffered an attack"*: Ibid., 266.

144 *"nothing in human judgment is final"*: Perkins, *The Roosevelt I Knew*, 164.

145 *"recovery was not enough"*: Gunther, *Roosevelt in Retrospect*, 289.

145 *a government "that cannot take care of its old"*: Ibid., 289.

145 *"We can't sell the United States short in 1980"*: Perkins, *The Roosevelt I Knew*, 294.

145 *"Isn't this Socialism?"*: Ibid., 299.

145 *FDR did not take a class with James:* At my request, my colleague at Harvard Dr. Eugene Taylor examined the registrar's records there for Roosevelt's college years of 1900–1904 and documented that Roosevelt was never a student in a class taught by William James.

146 *"the greatest political personality of the century"*: John Kenneth Galbraith, *Name Dropping* (Boston: Houghton Mifflin, 1999), 43.

146 *"He would certainly have been President"*: Gunther, *Roosevelt in Retrospect*, 243.

CHAPTER 11. SICKNESS IN CAMELOT: KENNEDY

147 *"If that crazy Muckers club had been mine"*: Christopher Matthews, *Kennedy and Nixon: The Rivalry That Shaped Postwar America* (New York: Simon and Schuster, 1996), 23.

147 *"I do not think it particularly helpful"*: January 22, 1963, JFK Presidential Archives, Box 1, Choate School Archives.

148 *an IQ of 119:* Robert Dallek, *An Unfinished Life: John F. Kennedy* (Boston: Little, Brown, 2003), 33.

148 *"a very able boy":* James N. Giglio, "Growing Up Kennedy: The Role of Medical Ailments in the Life of JFK, 1920–1957," *Journal of Family History* 31 (2006): 362.

148 *At age thirteen he was hospitalized:* Giglio, "Growing Up Kennedy," 361. Dallek, *An Unfinished Life*, 34.

148 *Robert joked that if a mosquito bit Jack:* Arthur Schlesinger, *Robert Kennedy and His Times* (Boston: Houghton Mifflin, 2002), 13.

148 *At age seventeen, he had his worst infection ever:* Giglio, "Growing Up Kennedy," 361. Nigel Hamilton, *JFK: Reckless Youth* (New York: Random House, 1993), 101–105. Dallek, *An Unfinished Life*, 35.

149 *He was diagnosed with fatal leukemia:* Dallek, *An Unfinished Life*, 77. Giglio, "Growing Up Kennedy," 363.

149 *His father, unwilling to accept this death sentence:* Joseph P. Kennedy to George St. John, September 15, 1934: "About the early part of the summer we sent Jack to Mayo's and he remained there a month. A thorough investigation of his physical condition . . . unable to find the cause of Jack's illness during the winter. If there is the slightest tendency to a relapse he would have to be taken out of school for a year." JFK Presidential Archives, JFK Personal Papers, Box 1. They had discovered that he had many allergies— to "animal hair, house dust, and certain foods, including lamb, pork, and to a lesser extent, whole milk, beef, and various grains." Giglio, "Growing Up Kennedy," 363.

149 *a month of testing at the Mayo Clinic:* Dallek, *An Unfinished Life*, 73.

149 *"they have not found out anything as yet"*: Giglio, "Growing Up Kennedy," 365.

149 *"Joe's blood count was 9400"*: Ibid.

149 *"one of the things I am a little disturbed about"*: Ibid., 367.

149 *"One thing I want to be sure of":* Ibid., 368.

150 *Kennedy fended off lifelong whispers of hypochondriasis:* In the oral history interview between Kennedy's close adviser Ted Sorensen and Kennedy's personal White House physician, Janet Travell, Sorensen asks, "Did you ever feel that he complained, or did not complain but suggested maladies that perhaps weren't something he had—that he had any tendencies toward being hypochondriac?" Travell responds, "Oh, no, he was the opposite of a hypochondriac. It was difficult to get him to state his complaints, unless they were very acute." (JFK Presidential Archives, Oral History Collection, interview of Janet Travell by Ted Sorensen, January 20, 1966.) The association of ulcers and colitis (today called irritable bowel syndrome) with psychiatric or emotional causes is now, perhaps paradoxically, less strongly held than it was in the 1930s. Peptic ulcer disease, long considered a classic psychosomatic illness, is due in many persons to a previously unrecognized bacterial infection, and treatable with an antibiotic. Irritable bowel syndrome seems more common in those with psychiatric conditions, like depression, and improves somewhat with antidepressants, but it also occurs in persons without psychiatric diagnoses and improves with nonpsychiatric medications too. It is important to note that an autoimmune inflammatory disease of the bowel called celiac disease can mimic irritable bowel syndrome and is often misdiagnosed.

We cannot know for sure the cause of John Kennedy's lifelong gastrointestinal illness; perhaps it was partly psychosomatic and due to his nervous and anxious and active temperament; partly, or even fully, it might have been part of a larger autoimmune disorder, which manifested a bit in his allergies, more in his irritable bowel syndrome, and even more, soon thereafter, in his near-fatal Addison's disease.

150 *evidence of hyperthymia:* Hamilton, *Reckless Youth,* 131–133. Long before he took steroids, he was seen as extremely sociable, charismatic, and energetic, getting elected by his peers "most likely to succeed," which was, as Hamilton notes, "a complete travesty of his record at Choate."

150 *visiting prostitutes and probably contracting venereal diseases:* Ibid., 153–158, 341–342.

150 *"Senator Kennedy evidently woke up each morning":* Evelyn Lincoln, *My Twelve Years with John F. Kennedy* (New York: Bantam, 1966), 3.

151 *"When you see the President":* William Manchester, *Profile of a President* (London: Michael Joseph, 1967), 26–27.

151 *"He usually sat in his office":* Lincoln, *My Twelve Years,* 25.

151 *He "continued to vibrate with energy":* Manchester, *Profile of a President,* 26–27.

151 *"Two White House chairs have collapsed":* Ibid., 144.

152 *"two months after taking the oath":* Ibid., 26–27.

152 *"He's really a great gossip":* Ibid., 49.

152 *would reply two hundred times per day:* Ibid., 54.

152 *Kennedy's wit was famous:* Bill Adler, ed., *The Kennedy Wit* (New York: Citadel, 1967).

153 *Lyndon was doing such a great job:* Lincoln, *My Twelve Years,* 125.

153 *"I hear you're losing Ohio":* Manchester, *Profile of a President,* 131.

153 *"Well, the answer to the first is yes":* Helen Thomas, *Thanks for the Memories, Mr. President* (New York: Simon and Schuster, 2003), 23.

153 *"I feel as a Catholic":* Adler, *The Kennedy Wit,* 40.

153 *a widely read 1962 article:* Eunice Kennedy Shriver, "Hope for Retarded Children," *Saturday Evening Post,* September 22, 1962, available at http://www.eunicekennedy shriver.org/articles/print_article/148 (accessed February 27, 2011).

154 Rosemary received a frontal lobotomy: Ronald Kessler, "Rosemary Kennedy's Inconvenient Illness," http://newsmax.com/RonaldKessler/Rosemary-Kennedy/2008/06/17/id/324146 (accessed February 16, 2010). Jack El-Hai, *The Lobotomist* (New York: Wiley, 2005), 171. Hamilton, *Reckless Youth*, 409–412.

154 "agitated depression": Kessler, "Rosemary Kennedy's Inconvenient Illness."

154 Freeman carefully avoided documentation about her: El-Hai, *The Lobotomist*, 174.

154 Rose Kennedy, in her 1974 memoir: Rose Kennedy, *Times to Remember* (New York: Doubleday, 1974), 286.

154 nocturnal sexual encounters: Kessler, "Rosemary Kennedy's Inconvenient Illness." Hamilton, *Reckless Youth*, 409–412. Access to Rosemary Kennedy's personal file, within Joseph Kennedy Sr.'s personal papers at the JFK Presidential Archives, is more restricted than access to the president's medical records. I was not able to obtain permission to see Rosemary's file.

154 mentally ill, not just mentally retarded: Kessler interviewed Dr. Bertram Brown, who was a member of the president's panel on mental retardation, and Dr. Brown stated that he and his colleagues at that time had believed that she had mental illness. In retrospect, he believes that the Kennedys downplayed her mental illness in reaction to social stigma being higher for that condition than for mental retardation. Kessler also found that FBI records quoted Joseph Kennedy's Boston attorney at the time as saying that Rosemary had mental illness.

154 "Sister is insane": The entry is by a Dr. "E. Price." JFK Presidential Archives, Box 45, dated December 14, 1950.

155 touching Rosemary severely: It is often now stated that Rosemary worsened due to a "botched" lobotomy. There is no evidence that this was the case. Dr. Watts later described the surgery as uncomplicated. Rather than being botched, lobotomy simply did not work for those with mental illness plus mental retardation. In 1941, Rosemary Kennedy was only the sixty-sixth person in the United States to receive frontal lobotomy; hundreds of thousands would eventually get it. Unfortunately, Joseph Kennedy Sr. was too far ahead of the curve; the best medical treatment of the time, one that would receive a Nobel Prize within the decade, was disastrous: "Because of the lobotomy, she had the development of a 2-year-old. She could not wash or dress herself or put her shoes on. She had to be supervised at all times." (Kessler, "Rosemary Kennedy's Inconvenient Illness.") Standing in line at Ted Kennedy's memorial viewing at the JFK Library, I spoke with a union activist from Wisconsin. He told me that he and his family worked in the institution that housed Rosemary, and that he had observed that for years, without media coverage, Ted Kennedy quietly flew every month from Washington to visit Rosemary in the Wisconsin institution.

155 Born the son of a saloon keeper: The next three paragraphs draw from Ronald Kessler, *The Sins of the Father* (New York: Warner, 1996).

156 numerous affairs . . . trying his luck with the girls: Garry Wills, *The Kennedy Imprisonment* (Boston: Back Bay, 1994).

156 Wall Street insider trading: Kessler, *The Sins of the Father*.

156 an objective assessment of two generations of Kennedys: This section represents my summary of publicly known facts regarding reasons for death or substance abuse or diagnosed mental illness in the Kennedy family. It might be said that Joe Jr. died in combat. And couldn't the other two plane crashes be attributed to the Kennedys' access via their wealth to small-plane travel, which is more dangerous than commercial plane travel? Perhaps the same could be said for the skiing accident? Skiing is a sport associated with wealth. These many explanations could be true, but violate Occam's razor. When we need many reasons to avoid a simpler explanation, perhaps the simpler explanation is right. Joe Jr. accepted a dangerous flying mission that he did not have to take. Kathleen agreed to fly in bad weather against her pilot's objections and despite grounding of all commercial flights. Michael's skiing accident occurred while playing ski football without any helmet, while skiing down Copper Bowl, a steep slope in Aspen, Colorado.

Could it be that excessive risk-taking, an aspect of hyperthymia, lies behind some of these unfortunate happenings? A *Time* article noted on the death of Michael Kennedy, "As a teenager, Michael jumped off a 75-ft. cliff above the Snake River in Wyoming during a rafting trip. Brother Robert, while at Harvard, leaped 10 feet between two six-story dorms on a dare. He was arrested in 1983 for heroin possession. Joe II drove his jeep off the road in 1973, paralyzing family friend Pam Kelley. Brother David died in 1984 of a drug overdose." http://www.time.com/time/magazine/article/0,9171,987634-3,00.html#ixzz1FCPl6rMg (accessed February 27, 2011).

157 *the baseline risk . . . of bipolar disorder . . . for alcohol or substance abuse . . . for accidental death:* Ronald C. Kessler, Olga Demler, Richard G. Frank, Mark Olfson, Harold Alan Pincus, Ellen E. Walters, Philip Wang, Kenneth B. Wells, and Alan M. Zaslavsky, "Prevalence and Treatment of Mental Disorders, 1990 to 2003," *New England Journal of Medicine* 352 (2005): 2515–2523.

157 *a fraction of 1 percent in the general population:* National Vital Statistics Report 59, no. 2, http://www.cdc.gov/nchs/data/nvsr/nvsr59/nvsr59_02.pdf (accessed February 27, 2011).

158 *The full medical report:* Here I present, verbatim for the first time, important extracts from Kennedy's medical records. Although they are now available for study by scholars, the JFK Presidential Library does not allow photocopying of John Kennedy's medical records. Furthermore, they are open to study only by scholars who are physicians or who are accompanied by physicians. I personally transcribed the full medical report of Kennedy's naval discharge. I believe this is the first time that the verbatim transcript of the following report has been made publicly available. The same holds for other verbatim transcriptions of Kennedy's medical records, such as his back X-ray reports (see pages 298–299) and nursing notes on his near-fatal 1961 infection in the White House (see pages 300–301).

US Naval Hospital Chelsea Mass 16 October 1944

Report of Medical Survey

Diagnosis: Hernia, intervertebral disc

Disability is not the result of his own misconduct and was incurred in line of duty

Existed prior to enlistment: No

Present condition: Unfit for Duty. Probable future duration: Indefinite

This 27-year old Lt., USNR, was admitted to this hospital on 11 June 1944 with the complaint of pain in the lower back referred down the left leg. This dated from a fall aboard ship on 1 August 1943. In addition he had lower abdominal pain increased on defecation. By permission of the BuMed & S he was granted leave to report to the Lahey Clinic. While there an oxygen spinogram was interpreted as demonstrating a herniation of the fifth lumbar intervertebral disc. On 23 June 1944 an operation was performed by Dr. James L. Poppen at the Lahey Clinic in which some of the abnormally soft disc interspace material was removed and it was noted that there was very little protrusion of the ruptured cartilage present.

Investigation of the gastro-intestinal complaints by Dr. Sara M. Jordan of the Lahey Clinic revealed on x-ray examination spasm and irritability of the duodenum without a definite ulcer crater but . . . suggestive of a duodenal ulcer scar. Spasm of the colon was also demonstrated. Anti-spasmodic medication was prescribed.

He returned to this activity on 4 August 1944. The pain in the back and in the left leg continued as did the lower abdominal pain. The neurosurgeon at this hospital did not feel that the operation had corrected the condition and that some other cause might underlie the neuritis of the left sciatic nerve. An orthopedic consultant injected procaine into the left sciatic nerve with considerable relief of symptoms. Review of the films from the Lahey Clinic by the roentgenologist here failed to reveal any definite abnormality of the G.I. tract or in the spine.

. . . On 3 October 1944 his back and leg pain had improved but there was continuation of the abdominal pain. . . . Because of continued symptoms and the necessity of further time to regain strength and weight lost while on combat duty, the Board recommends that he be retained for further study and treatment.

P. P. Henson, Comdr. MC V (S) USNR, P. B. Snyder Lt. Comdr. MC V (S) USNR, W. J. Jinkins, Jr. Lt. MC V (S) USNR

158 *hospitalization for physical illness:* After resting in Arizona for a few months, Kennedy felt better and decided to work as a journalist, first in San Francisco at the United Nations conference, then in Berlin for the Potsdam conference, and later in England, where he covered the elections that ousted Churchill. Kennedy was back to his old self: energetic, active, sexual. But as usual, he had another relapse. His pattern seemed to be one serious illness episode per year, lasting about two to three months, followed by six to nine months of normal health and heightened energy. In London, Kennedy had his usual high fever, malaise, and gastrointestinal pain. He was hospitalized for two days. Giglio, "Growing Up Kennedy," 374.

158 *walked five miles in a Boston parade:* Lee Mandel, "Endocrine and Autoimmune Aspects of the Health History of John F. Kennedy," *Annals of Internal Medicine* 151 (2009): 350–354.

158 *a visit by the physician Sir Daniel Davis:* Some biographers assume that Dr. Davis was an expert in Addison's disease. He was not. He appears to have been simply a successful physician, with relationships with many members of the British upper classes. Giglio, "Growing Up Kennedy," 375. Dallek, *An Unfinished Life*, 105.

159 *chronic physical symptoms:* It is clear, though, that all of Kennedy's Lahey Clinic doctors and his later doctors accepted and concurred with the Addison's disease diagnosis. Sara Jordan, for instance, wrote a 1952 letter clearly saying so and explaining the condition to Joseph Kennedy; she made it clear at that time that John Kennedy's main medical problem (all the previous gastrointestinal diagnoses notwithstanding) was

Addison's disease of the adrenal glands. (Giglio, "Growing Up Kennedy," 376.) I could not find any evidence that Kennedy was ever rediagnosed with laboratory tests in the 1950s, but such testing would likely not have been definitive anyway since he constantly received steroid treatment throughout the rest of his life.

159 *"hasn't got a year to live":* Giglio, "Growing Up Kennedy," 375.

159 *Kennedy took DOCA the rest of his life:* Giglio, "Growing Up Kennedy," 375–376. Dallek, *An Unfinished Life,* 76.

159 *"deeply preoccupied with death":* Matthews, *Kennedy and Nixon,* 48.

159 *on a trip to Indochina:* JFK always traveled with a medical bag including his steroids. Once in the 1960 election, his bag was lost and Kennedy went to great lengths to contact political allies so as to find it. Giglio, "Growing Up Kennedy," 377.

160 *aides placed a pin in every town:* Kenneth P. O'Donnell and David F. Powers, *Johnny, We Hardly Knew Ye* (Boston: Little, Brown, 1972), 78–80.

160 *Without steroids, this pace would have been impossible:* Before his Senate run, Kennedy put out a press release attributing his hospitalizations to malaria. He had already begun treatment with his first endocrinologist, Dr. Elmer Bartels of Boston, who had started to treat him with DOCA and later cortisone, as noted earlier in the text. Bartels warned Kennedy that despite such treatment, he would always be prone to Addisonian crises triggered by infections of any sort. Giglio, "Growing Up Kennedy," 376.

160 *Six months later, he was back in the hospital:* JFK Presidential Archives, Medical Records, John F. Kennedy Personal Papers (hereafter PP), Box 45. Giglio, "Growing Up Kennedy," 377.

160 *noting throughout his medical chart that he was already diagnosed with Addison's disease:* JFK Presidential Archives, Medical Records, PP, Box 45.

160 *X-rays repeatedly showed mostly normal bone structure:* Ibid. My assessment of these medical files conflicts with the conclusion drawn by Robert Dallek and his medical collaborator that Kennedy had some osteoporosis, which would be expected with long-term steroid use. (Dallek, *An Unfinished Life,* 81.) As late as 1962, Kennedy's back X-rays did not show osteoporosis or osteoarthritis or any other bony explanation for his pain. Here is a summary by Dr. George Burkley, White House physician, who concluded from this evidence that most of the president's back pain was due to muscular spasm, not bony arthritis: "The lumbar-sacral X-rays were examined in New York and were found to show very little difference from those taken in 1958. In other words no increase in the lesion in the left sacral iliac region and there was no evidence of any change in the intervertebral spaces, no evidence of osteoarthritis in any area. The X-rays indicate that there has been no bony change since 1958. I recommend that the exercise be continued as they are done now and to be increased in the judgment of Dr. K." JFK Presidential Archives, Medical Records, PP, Box 48, March 19, 1962.

Here is the full report on the back X-ray from 1962, located in JFK Presidential Archives, Medical Records, PP, Box 45:

Xray: Lumbar spine and pelvis, 14 March 1962, by John H. Cheffey and L. T. Brown, Captains MC USN. "The available projections demonstrate the distal three thoracic and the upper four lumbar vertebrae to be normal. Interspaces between these vertebrae have been well maintained; the interspace between L4 and L5 is normal. The interspace between L5 and S1 is narrow. Contiguous bony surfaces are increased slightly in density at L5-S1 except for the posterior-inferior half of L5 where loss of clarity of the surface is apparent. There appears to be minor subchondral dissolution of bone at L5-S1. In oblique projections, apophyseal joint space between L5 and S1 [is] incompletely obliterated but definite loss of clarity exists, especially on the left. Evidence of fusion is shown posteriorly between L5 and the upper sacrum.... The fusion is solid.... The right sacroiliac joint is slightly narrowed. The left sacroiliac joint is irregular in contour. Particularly in the middle portion of the joint contiguous bony surfaces present pronounced sclerosis. Several irregular areas of radiolucency are shown in this region, apparently in the sacrum particularly. Changes demonstrated in this region are compatible with those to be seen following operative intervention and are not inconsistent with findings to be seen with bone infection.... Hip joints as shown in a single frontal projection are normal in appearance. Soft tissues and other bony structures as they are seen are within normal limits."

160 *His father concurred:* Giglio, "Growing Up Kennedy," 377.

161 *a three-hour operation:* Ibid., 377–378.

161 *"Lincoln recalled Nixon racing into Kennedy's office":* Matthews, *Kennedy and Nixon*, 99.

161 *large enough to fit a man's fist up to the wrist:* O'Donnell and Powers, *Johnny, We Hardly Knew Ye*, 114–116

161 *"We came close to losing him":* Giglio, "Growing Up Kennedy," 378.

162 *seven hospitalizations:* JFK Presidential Archives, Medical Records, PP, Box 45.

162 *"It is not a killer":* Giglio, "Growing Up Kennedy," 379. Dallek, *An Unfinished Life*, 300.

162 *a contemporary movie portrayed a person with Addison's disease:* Giglio, "Growing Up Kennedy," 385.

162 *This episode is documented in his medical records:* JFK Presidential Archives, Medical Records, PP, Box 45. This matter is ignored increasingly by historians. One of the first Kennedy books (Hugh Sidey, *John F. Kennedy, President* [Greenwich, CT: Fawcett, 1964]), written just one year after Kennedy's death, discusses the matter at reasonable length (one page, 98), describes real concern about Kennedy's condition among journalists and politicians (one Republican commented, "Now we've got an invalid for a President"), and even describes Travell's treatment with intravenous steroids and antibiotics. Sidey had been taking notes for something like an authorized biography of JFK for six years, and thus his records on this event were likely shared with the president. Travell herself, in her 1966 oral history, near the end of the medical part of her interview with Ted Sorensen, volunteered the June 1961 crisis as an important part of Kennedy's medical history, and considered it the most serious episode of illness during his presidency. "Interesting," Sorensen commented, and then the interview went in a different direction. Robert Dallek (*An Unfinished Life*) received much praise for being the first biographer to gain access to more medical records, and to write a biography greatly built around Kennedy's illnesses. Yet he did not refer to this episode at all. Richard Reeves (*President Kennedy: Profile of Power* [New York: Simon and Schuster, 1993]), who wanted to describe what it was like to be president on a day-by-day basis, titled his chapters by dates, usually within days or a week of each other. In this period, he jumps from June 17 to July 19, skipping altogether the weeks of Kennedy's near-fatal illness, without comment. Evelyn Lincoln (*My Twelve Years with John F. Kennedy*) does not

mention it at all in her diary of the Kennedy years, even though she was an active participant in JFK's health care. The Travell files are full of notes describing how extra steroid or amphetamine doses were given to "Mrs. L" to give to the president.

163 *"The President slept later than usual this morning"*: JFK Presidential Archives, Medical Records, PP, Box 45, typed memorandum dated June 16, 1961.

163 *Travell had just injected Kennedy:* IV solucortef 100 mg given with 1.8 million units penicillin + tetracycline, hydrocortisone 40 mg orally. JFK Presidential Archives, Medical Records, PP, Box 45, June 16, 1961.

163 *give more steroids intramuscularly:* Cortisone acetate 50 mg IM. JFK Presidential Archives, Medical Records, PP, Box 45.

163 *more oral steroids later that night:* Hydrocortisone 10–20 mg. Ibid.

163 *From June 22 to July 3:* In the week of June 22–29, he received intramuscular doses of 600,000 units of procaine penicillin twenty-seven times. He also received oral steroids (hydrocortisone 10 mg in the morning and 20 mg in the afternoon daily; 0.125 mg daily of Florinef), amphetamines (2–4 tablets of dextroamphetamine, "Dexatabs," daily), and his usual daily dose of testosterone (10 mg daily of methyltestosterone tablets). Ibid.

164 *received doses of the narcotic codeine:* Codeine phosphate 750 mg, and codeine sulfate 500 mg. Ibid.

164 *"mild viral infection"*: Ibid., June 22, 1961.

164 *He came back to life:* Ibid. Dr. Travell's handwritten note on June 21, 1961, was ominous, describing a fever of 104.5 and "shivering," blood cultures being drawn at 3:15 a.m., and symptoms of being "very chilly" and "perspiring profusely." The next morning, his personal nurse's neatly handwritten notes were unfiltered (edited below only for clarity and repetition; we have no available nurse's notes for the nights of June 21 and into the early morning of June 22):

> June 22
>
> 830 AM—perspiring moderately. Complete sponge bath given. Pajamas and linen changed.
>
> 9 AM—seen by doctors
>
> 920 AM—infusion of 500 cc 5% dextrose and saline [solucortef omitted] started in right hand by Dr T
>
> 930 AM—president asleep
>
> 10 AM—another infusion started . . . perspiring moderately
>
> 1010 AM—P asleep
>
> 1020 AM—P awake. Examined by Drs. [four physicians, Dr. Preston Wade, an orthopedic surgeon from New York, Cohen, Travell, and George Burkley, a naval physician who conducted the president's laboratory tests and filled in for Dr. Travell as needed]
>
> 1030—seen by Mrs Kennedy
>
> 1100—infusion running
>
> 1120—President still awake. Appears to be feeling more comfortable.
>
> 1125—Dozing lightly
>
> 1130—Turned to left side.
>
> 1135—President asleep
>
> 1205—President awake. Stated he was cold. . . . Perspiring moderately

1210—Patient appears to be sleeping.
1255—President awake
100—Mrs Kennedy with patient
115—Penicillin G 600K units given in left deltoid . . . backrub given . . . perspiration much less
130—infusion running well
135—President sleeping
200—asleep
245—President still asleep
310—P awake . . . states he feels much better
315—Hydrocortisone tablet 1 20 mgm po taken
330—sitting up
430—President appears to be feeling much better. Shaved
530—Mrs Kennedy with president
715—Penicillin
730—Dinner—ate with hearty appetite
815—Temp 97.8

The next day, he resumed his evening barbiturate sleeping pill (Tuinal), and Dr. Travell documented the amphetamine/narcotic/steroid/testosterone regimen that he mostly continued throughout his presidency ("AM: Dexatab 2 tab, Cod[eine] s[ulfate] 2 tab = 65 mg, Testosterone 25 mg IM by request, For pm today Dexatab 2 tab, [vitamin] C 500, Fl[orinef] pink 0.1 mg, HC [hydrocortisone] 10 mg, Cod[eine] S[ulfate] 32 mg"). The president recovered and went to Hyannisport for July Fourth. On the eighth, he had a chill at four in the afternoon, then at 6:10 p.m., according to Travell's notes, a fever of 103.2 and a high pulse of 120. At 6:30 p.m., he again received intravenous steroids and intramuscular antibiotics ("Infusion saline glucose started + solucortef 50 mg, streptomycin penicillin im given"). Two hours later, he received 25 mg of cortisone intramuscularly. The next day, his temperature was 97.0: "Slept well no complaints," wrote Travell. Another Addisonian relapse averted.

164 *urine culture finally confirmed . . .* **Aerobacter cloacae:** Ibid. Dr. Travell's handwritten note is as follows: "June 24—T note: Urine: aerobacter resistant to strep and pen . . . many mucus threads, much amorphous, straw hazy, rbc 2–4 phf wbc 1–3 phf." On June 26, a urine culture laboratory report states growth of the following organism: "Aerobacter cloacae."

164 *fatal in 20 to 40 percent of cases:* Michael E. Ellis, *Infectious Diseases of the Respiratory Tract* (Cambridge, UK: Cambridge University Press, 1998), 140.

164 *mainly found in the vaginal flora:* Sebastian Faro, *Sexually Transmitted Diseases in Women* (Baltimore: Lippincott Williams & Wilkins, 2003), 98.

165 *His urologist's records are silent on sexual habits:* JFK Presidential Archives, Medical Records, PP, Box 45, Dr. Herbst's notes, 1954–1955.

166 *Galbraith . . . and admired both presidents:* John Kenneth Galbraith, *Name Dropping* (Boston: Houghton Mifflin, 1999).

166 *Jefferson scored highest:* Dean Keith Simonton, *Greatness: Who Makes History and Why* (New York: Guilford, 1994), 271–276.

166 *"I know nothing can happen to him":* Seymour Hersh, *The Dark Side of Camelot* (Boston: Little, Brown, 1997), 15–16.

CHAPTER 12. A SPECTACULAR PSYCHOCHEMICAL
SUCCESS: KENNEDY REVISITED

170 *William Osler once said:* William Osler, *Aequanimitas* (Philadelphia: P. Blakinson's Son & Co., 1914).

171 *Kennedy ingested a standard set of daily medications:* Florinef 0.25 mg, hydrocortisone 20 mg, methyltestosterone 10 mg, and Meticorten 2.5 mg, Lomotil (a narcotic-derived antidiarrheal agent), thyroid hormone, and sometimes penicillin. JFK Presidential Archives, John F. Kennedy Personal Papers (hereafter PP), Medical Records, Boxes 45 and 46.

171 *he also took amphetamines and barbiturates:* Dextroamphetamine (Dexatabs) and Tuinal (an equal mixture of secobarbital sodium and amobarbital sodium). Ibid.

171 *injections of procaine:* Ibid., Box 46. David Owen, *In Sickness and in Power: Illnesses in Heads of Government During the Last 100 Years* (Westport, CT: Praeger, 2008), 161.

171 *Kennedy took mysterious injections from Max Jacobsen:* Owen, *In Sickness and in Power,* 164–170. Robert Dallek, *An Unfinished Life: John F. Kennedy* (Boston: Little, Brown, 2003), 398–399. Richard Reeves, *President Kennedy: Profile of Power* (New York: Simon and Schuster, 1993), 146–147.

171 *"I don't care if it's horse piss":* Dallek, *An Unfinished Life,* 399.

171 *New York State investigated the doctor's injections:* Owen, *In Sickness and in Power,* 165.

172 *injected an anabolic steroid, methyltestosterone, at Kennedy's frequent request:* JFK Presidential Archives, Medical Records, PP, Boxes 45 and 46.

172 *a medical coup d'état:* The medical coup d'etat was not a one-day affair. David Owen best discusses the timeline (*In Sickness and in Power,* pp. 176–177). The process began in October 1961, when Admiral Burkley, the naval officer assigned as the official White House physician, decided to take on Travell, Kennedy's personal physician. Burkley had the important support of Dr. Eugene Cohen, a New York endocrinologist who was Kennedy's prime consultant for Addison's disease. Burkley and Cohen had decided that Travell's many injections needed to be replaced by a physical exercise and muscle-training regimen, for which they enlisted a New York specialist, Hans Kraus, MD. Travell opposed the proposal, but, over a year, Burkley and Cohen, apparently with the support of Robert Kennedy, gained the president's approval for the change. By October 1962, Owen notes, the medical coup d'etat was complete, and Travell, though still nominally personal physician to the president, was greatly weakened. The animosity and distrust between Travell and Burkley can be seen in a medical note in Burkley's records: "3 February 1962 Requested the medical records on X [the president] for the last six months. Dr. Travell said she would like to straighten them up before she gives them to me. I said that this was not necessary, but she said she would like to straighten them up. . . . Within the last few days Dr. Travell has been inferring that *all* the recent improvement of X's condition is due to the fact that he is now getting Gamma Globulin and injections of vitamins. Several days ago while discussing the chair for the helicopter a very obvious effort to cover information on the upper part of the sheet by covering it with an additional paper. Contents were not divulged to me" (JFK Presidential Archives, PP, Box 48). Burkley had the upper hand as the official physician, backed by the military and the White House bureaucracy; Travell had been hired by the president alone. Over time, Travell remained in the White House but was closely watched and controlled by Burkley. This is captured in a note by Jackie Kennedy to Burkley in late 1963: "Memo for Dr Burkley: August 21, 1963 I have asked

Dr. Travell to put suitable bulbs and reading lights in all the places where the President and I read in the White House. So, please, let's not get excited if you see her tip-toeing up to our floor in the elevator! JBK" (JFK Presidential Archives, PP, Box 48).

172 *He still took four kinds of daily steroids:* As above except methyltestosterone injections were replaced by oral Halotestin 10 mg daily.

172 *suggested by gynecomastia:* This is documented as early as 1955 during one of JFK's hospitalizations. JFK Presidential Archives, PP, Medical Records, Box 45. New York Hospital admission note, August 29, 1955: "Gynecomastia, unknown etiology."

172 *Kennedy always took* **anabolic** *steroids:* Later Halotestin. JFK Presidential Archives, Medical Records, PP, Box 46.

172 *in 1966, in her oral history:* JFK Archives, Oral History Program, interview of Janet Travell by Ted Sorensen.

173 *but she obeyed the commander in chief:* For example, November 14, 1961: "Hypo Testosterone aq. Susp. 37.5 mg.im right buttock . . . requested med. For trip given to Dave Powers Requested MT. 25 q.d." Or September 21, 1961: "7:15 pm Asked me to come up . . . back still aches. More tired today . . . asks if his medication has been cut back. . . . Pulse fast very keyed up and just back from pool. Given fluorinef 0. 1 stat. Also box of codeine 32 mg. Ritalin 5 mg. to take just before leaving shortly for state dinner, or during evening." JFK Presidential Archives, Medical Records, PP, Box 46.

After the somewhat haphazard care he had received in early 1961, culminating in his Addisonian crisis of June of that year, Kennedy's doctors began to keep better track of his testosterone use, and they have left us monthly summaries of his total dosages for ten months from August 1961 onward. (JFK Presidential Archives, Box 46, Travell notes.) I have added up those doses, keeping in mind that for the first eight months he received methyltestosterone, and in the last two months (beginning May 1962) he was switched to Halotestin. In the first eight months, he received a total dose of 3010 mg of methyltestosterone, either orally or intramuscularly; this is about 12.5 mg of methyltestosterone daily. In the final two months tallied, he received 610 mg of Halotestin, or about 10 mg daily. These are not exceedingly high doses of anabolic steroids, but they are consistent and chronic.

173 *athletes take similar doses . . . to make themselves more "aggressive":* http://www.steroid.com/Halotestin.php (accessed February 11, 2010).

173 *At least three double-blind, placebo-controlled studies:* F. Talih, O. Fattal, and D. Malone, "Anabolic Steroid Abuse: Physical and Psychiatric Costs," *Cleveland Clinic Journal of Medicine* 74 (2007): 341–352.

173 *Summaries of large clinical populations:* T. P. Warrington and J. M. Bostwick, "Psychiatric Adverse Effects of Corticosteroids," *Mayo Clinic Proceedings* 81 (2006): 1361–1367.

173 *steroids improve mood and cause fewer psychiatric side effects:* Penelope J. Hunt, Eleanor M. Gurnell, Felicia A. Huppert, Christine Richards, A. Toby Prevost, John A. H. Wass, Joseph Herbert, and V. Krishna K. Chatterjee, "Improvement in Mood and Fatigue After Dehydroepiandrosterone Replacement in Addison's Disease in a Randomized, Double Blind Trial," *Journal of Clinical Endocrinology and Metabolism* 85, no. 12 (2000): 4650–4656. E. Ur, T. H. Turner, T. J. Goodwin, A. Grossman, and G. M. Besser, "Mania in Association with Hydrocortisone Replacement for Addison's Disease," *Postgraduate Medical Journal* 68 (1992): 41–43.

174 *"a slight sniffle" . . . "Received a call" . . . a small dose of Stelazine:* JFK Presidential Archives, Medical Records, PP, Box 46. The Stelazine dose was 1 mg twice daily. Note of Dr. George Burkley, December 13, 1962.

175 *The most extensive journalistic work is by Seymour Hersh:* Seymour Hersh, *The Dark Side of Camelot* (Boston: Little, Brown, 1999).

176 *they prefer cocaine:* C. E. Johanson and T. Aigner, "Comparison of the Reinforcing Properties of Cocaine and Procaine in Rhesus Monkeys," *Pharmacology Biochemistry and Behavior* 15, (1981): 49–53.

176 *pleasurable feelings similar to those of cocaine:* Bryon Adinoff, Kathleen Brady, Susan Sonne, Robert F. Mirabella, and Charles H. Kellner, "Cocaine-like Effects of Intravenous Procaine in Cocaine Addicts," *Addiction Biology* 3 (1998): 189–196.

176 *the claim made by Kennedy biographers:* The first historian to see most of Kennedy's medical records (in 2002), Robert Dallek, documented the steroid use and other medications, but concluded that Kennedy, though ill, was unaffected in his role as president. As summarized by another historian, James Giglio, "despite the potential risks, his health seemed to have had no negative impact on his presidential performance." James N. Giglio, "Growing Up Kennedy: The Role of Medical Ailments in the Life of JFK, 1920–1957," *Journal of Family History* 31 (2006): 358–385 (quote on 379).

176 *has been challenged only by Dr. David Owen:* Owen, *In Sickness and in Power,* 141–190.

177 *"When you commit the flag":* Reeves, *President Kennedy,* 71.

177 *"How could I have been so stupid?" . . . "Those sons-of-bitches" . . . "I've got to do something":* All from ibid., 103.

177 *"The President was completely overwhelmed":* Ibid., 174.

177 *"Too intelligent and too weak":* Ibid., 166.

177 *"Gentlemen, you might as well face it":* Ibid., 196.

177 *"Walking out on generals was a Kennedy specialty":* Ibid., 182.

178 *"Does this mean Germany":* Dallek, *An Unfinished Life,* 624.

179 *"The first advice I am going to give my successor":* Benjamin Bradlee, *Conversations with Kennedy* (New York: Pocket Books, 1976), 117.

179 *Robert Kennedy later described the pragmatic aspect:* JFK Presidential Archives, Oral History Program, interview of Robert F. Kennedy by Ted Sorensen, 1966.

179 *Martin Luther King was invited to the White House:* Reeves, *President Kennedy,* 100.

180 *"In the election, when I gave my testimony":* Harris Wofford, *Of Kennedys and Kings* (Pittsburgh: University of Pittsburgh Press), 128–129.

181 *"Negroes are getting ideas":* Reeves, *President Kennedy,* 357.

181 *"Don't tell them about General Grant's table":* Ibid., 359.

181 *"Go to hell, JFK!":* Ibid., 360.

181 *"People are dying in Oxford":* Ibid., 363.

181 *The president placed a phone call to Dr. Max Jacobsen:* The role of Jacobsen is documented well by Dallek (*An Unfinished Life*) and Owen (*In Sickness and in Power*). Jacobsen first saw Kennedy in 1960. Owen documents the high likelihood that Jacobsen's injections involved amphetamines and steroids. In fact, when the Bureau of Narcotics and Dangerous Drugs interviewed Jacobsen in 1969, it noticed track marks on his arms, and the doctor admitted to injecting himself with 25 mg of methamphetamine every two to three days (Owen, 165).

There appears to have been a gradient of medical competence. Burkley and Cohen saw Travell as incompetent, and they all thought Jacobsen was a dangerous quack.

Thus, in 1961, before the break between Travell and Burkley, all the White House physicians were banding together to get a handle on Jacobsen. In the JFK Library Archives, I believe I have found the first probable documentation of this effort involving Travell and the others. The following note by Travell refers to the president; GGB stands for George G. Burkley: "April 11 1962, 6:00 pm. Went upstairs early to rest. Did not swim, and said that he was too tired to do exercises. Creep in town, left White House about 8 PM. (GGB),—also yesterday PM" (JFK Presidential Archives, PP, Box 46). If we can infer that "Creep" refers to Jacobsen, then it appears that Burkley had discovered that Jacobsen had visited the president and had informed Travell. As with the medical coup d'etat, Jacobsen was not ousted overnight because the president resisted. However, Jacobsen's visits became less frequent and faced overt opposition by the White House medical staff, Travell included. Robert Kennedy, as in many other matters, had a major impact, and his June 1962 intervention against Jacobsen was likely the beginning of the end. Thus, though Jacobsen injected the president as late as September 1962, his injections were less frequent and thus likely influenced the president for the worse to a lesser degree than had been the case in 1961.

David Owen has reviewed Jacobsen's unpublished memoirs and reports that Jacobsen mainly describes visits to the president on a frequent basis in the spring and summer of 1961, in the new administration's first year, when Kennedy was at his worst politically and at his sickest physically and mentally. Jacobsen saw Kennedy less frequently in 1962, and it is highly probable that his last visit was during the Oxford, Mississippi, crisis of September 1962 (Owen, 169; Dallek, 582).

The Jacobsen story, so similar to Hitler's relationship with Theodor Morell, which is discussed in the next chapter, first came out in the media in 1972, but many of the facts were unknown at that time. Dallek's 2003 biography first broke the story in detail. Owen's book in 2008 first made the link to Kennedy's performance.

181–182 *Come down here, Kennedy told him:* Reeves, *President Kennedy*, 364.

183 *"I hope that every American":* Ibid., 521.

183 *He knew he would lose the southern states:* Robert Kennedy was later asked in an oral history whether the Kennedys thought they would gain any political or electoral advantage with their new policy. (JFK Presidential Archives, Oral History Program, interview of Robert F. Kennedy by Ted Sorensen, 1966.) No, he recounted; they did not expect that black voting rights would change elections in the South for years to come, perhaps in the 1970s or later, but not so soon as to have any effect on JFK's reelection. They fully expected to lose the South, even Johnson's Texas, during the 1964 election, Robert said; they might even lose the whole election. They knew their civil rights plan would mean electoral losses to some extent, but they were also savvy enough to have Lou Harris polling in the North and Midwest, with increasing support for Kennedy's civil rights position. JFK had made a dangerous gamble, the first Democrat since the Civil War to do so: he would enter reelection, he had decided, with a plan to win by taking all of the country except the South. In fact, with the exception of Jimmy Carter, Democrats have only won the presidency since JFK by peeling off, barely, a few southern states either because of personal roots or special circumstances. Of the ten standard southern states—Virginia, North and South Carolina, Georgia, Tennessee, Alabama, Mississippi, Louisiana, Arkansas, and Texas—Lyndon Johnson, riding a wave of post-assassination sympathy, won only five; Bill Clinton won four in 1992 and three in 1996; and Barack Obama, even with a major black turnout, won only one. Only Jimmy Carter was successful, winning all southern states but Virginia in 1976. In fact, since JFK, no white non-southern Democrat has won the presidency.

183 *"Every single person who spoke about it":* Wofford, *Of Kennedys and Kings,* 172.

184 *The White House practically took over:* Reeves, *President Kennedy,* 580–582.

184–85 *He changed a line in . . . John Lewis's speech . . . asked Lewis to remove an analogy:* Ibid., 581–582.

185 *"He's damned good":* Ibid., 584.

185 *"You made the difference":* Ibid., 585.

185 *JFK "frankly acknowledged that he was responding to mass demands":* Wofford, *Of Kennedys and Kings,* 177.

185 *"I have a dream":* Reeves, *President Kennedy,* 584.

185 *In her 1966 oral history:* JFK Presidential Archives, Oral History Program, interview of Janet Travell by Ted Sorensen, 1966:

> Sorensen: Did he ever express concern that he was dependent on too many drugs or that they might have some unknown effects on his system?
> Travell: These were not drugs.
> Sorensen: Pills.
> Travell: That's right. . . . He really didn't take any drugs. . . . He didn't take sleeping pills. He wouldn't take medication for pain. He didn't want it. I think the record should be perfectly clear that the things that he did take were normal physiological constituents of the body, almost entirely.

186 *"It is my considered opinion":* JFK Presidential Archives, Medical Records, PP, Box 45, November 29, 1963.

CHAPTER 13. HITLER AMOK

188 *was advanced . . . by Hannah Arendt:* Hannah Arendt, *Eichmann in Jerusalem: A Report on the Banality of Evil* (New York: Viking, 1963). Arendt previously had been a student and mistress of the philosopher Martin Heidegger, who later became pro-Nazi. Arendt, who was Jewish, then rejected Heidegger's ideas and maintained close personal and intellectual ties to Jaspers.

189 *the memoirs of his closest friend from young adulthood:* August Kubizek, *The Young Hitler I Knew* (Boston: Houghton Mifflin, 1955; Norwalk CT: MBI Publishing Company, 2006).

189 *Most historians accept the general veracity:* Some historians express concern that Kubizek's memoir may not be entirely valid, partly because some have claimed that it was commissioned by the Nazi Party, a claim vehemently denied by Kubizek and by his publisher Stocker Verlag. Though a party member in 1942, Kubizek had not joined in previous years and was never an active member. He also turned down Hitler's offers of special positions throughout the Nazi period. Another critique is that Kubizek's claim that Hitler was anti-Semitic early in his life has not been corroborated, apparently, from other sources. With such caveats, most historians accept the broad outline of Kubizek's memoir. (Martin Kitchen, personal email communication, July 31, 2010.)

189 *"He walked always and everywhere":* Kubizek, *The Young Hitler I Knew,* 39.

189 *"I cannot remember a time when he had nothing to do":* Ibid., 62.

189 *"Once he had conceived an idea":* Ibid., 105.

189 *"Here he could give full vent to his mania":* Ibid., 105.

190 *"When Adolf and I strolled":* Ibid., 55.

190 *"I had long since known this behavior of his":* Ibid., 194.

190 *"He used to give me long lectures":* Ibid., 32.

190 *"Hysterically he described":* Ibid., 226.

191 *"Adolf was exceedingly violent and high-strung":* Ibid., 32.

191 *"Adolf stood in front of me":* Ibid., 117.

192 *"In that hour it began":* Ibid., 116.

192 *it is 90 percent likely . . . depressive episodes:* Frederick Goodwin and Kay Jamison, *Manic-Depressive Illness,* 2nd ed. (New York: Oxford University Press, 2007).

192 *"His mood worried me more and more":* Kubizek, *The Young Hitler I Knew,* 158.

192 *"As the Goddess of Misery took me":* Adolf Hitler, *Mein Kampf* (Delhi: Jaico Publishing, 2008).

193 *"the most outstanding trait":* Kubizek, *The Young Hitler I Knew,* 49.

193 *his* **family history:** Fritz Redlich, *Hitler: Diagnosis of a Destructive Prophet* (New York: Oxford University Press, 1998), 255–257. Ron Rosenbaum, *Explaining Hitler* (New York: Random House, 1998), 19–21. Leonard L. Heston and Renate Heston, *The Medical Casebook of Adolf Hitler* (New York: Stein and Day, 1980), 63–67.

194 *"[Alois Hitler] often moved":* Kubizek, *The Young Hitler I Knew,* 54.

195 *Regarding the* **course:** Jablow Hershman and Julian Lieb, *A Brotherhood of Tyrants* (New York: Prometheus, 1994), 69–82. Heston and Heston, *The Medical Casebook of Adolf Hitler,* 67–72.

196 *his classic work about Hitler's rise to power:* Alan Bullock, *Hitler: A Study in Tyranny* (New York: Harper and Row, 1964).

196 *In 1937, Hitler began using amphetamines:* Heston and Heston, *The Medical Casebook of Adolf Hitler,* 82–83.

196 *previous attempts to "explain" him:* Rosenbaum in his book (*Explaining Hitler*) never mentions Heston's work. Redlich (*Hitler: Diagnosis of a Destructive Prophet*) discusses the amphetamine story only briefly, but never engages with it in terms of what it means psychiatrically.

196 *published a complete medical study of Hitler:* Leonard L. Heston and Renate Heston, *The Medical Casebook of Adolf Hitler* (New York: Stein and Day, 1980).

196 *the man who would remain his personal physician:* Robert Kaplan, "Doctor to the Dictator: The Career of Theodor Morell, Personal Physician to Adolf Hitler," *Australasian Psychiatry* 10 (2002): 389–392.

197 **"Herr Reich Injektion Minister":** Heston and Heston, *The Medical Casebook of Adolf Hitler,* 85. D. Doyle, "Adolf Hitler's Medical Care," *Journal of the Royal College of Physicians of Edinburgh* 35 (2005): 75–82.

197 *Morell admitted to giving Hitler twenty-eight different treatments:* Heston and Heston, *The Medical Casebook of Adolf Hitler,* 162. Doyle, "Adolf Hitler's Medical Care."

197 **"Orchikrin"** . . . **"Prostakrimum"** . . . **"Cortiron":** Heston and Heston, *The Medical Casebook of Adolf Hitler,* 162. Transcript of interrogation of Dr. Morell by Allied investigators, November 29, 1945.

197 *the narcotic given was Eukodal:* Heston and Heston, *The Medical Casebook of Adolf Hitler,* 75.

198 *a barbiturate for sleep . . . Brom-Nervacit:* Ibid., 79, 162.

198 *By 1971, there were over thirty-one amphetamine preparations:* http://www.druglibrary.org/schaffer/library/studies/cu/cu36.html (accessed February 27, 2011). Methamphetamine was also widely distributed to German and U.S. troops during the war.

198 *They were especially noted by Albert Speer:* Heston and Heston, *The Medical Casebook of Adolf Hitler,* 72.

198 *Himmler . . . began collecting a medical file:* Ibid., 138.

198 *repeated negative tests for syphilis:* Ibid., 115.

198 *the Italian king . . . wondered aloud to his court:* Ibid., 138.

198 *the Hestons interviewed Hitler's valet:* Ibid., 82–83.

199 *"a mixture specially compounded for the Führer":* Ibid., 16.

199 *Schenck . . . analyzed its chemical contents:* Ibid., 85–86. Schenck's confirmation is the most definitive documentation that Hitler took methamphetamine, which raises the question: Was Hitler simply a crystal meth addict? Is his behavior merely attributable to methamphetamine addiction? I would say no, for the following reasons: although methamphetamine is the same ingredient as in crystal meth, the pill form is quite different from the injected crystal form. Each pill of methamphetamine, called Pervitin in Hitler's day, contained 3 mg of active drug. (Andreas Ulrich, "Hitler's Drugged Soldiers," *Der Spiegel,* 5/6/2005; http://www.spiegel.de/international/0,1518,354606,00.html [accessed April 11, 2011]). Thus Hitler's use added up to 15 mg/day, which is notably lower than the usual minimum composition of crystal meth (100 to 1000 mg). Also, oral use is much less addicting than intravenous. Depending on how much daily intravenous amphetamine Hitler also received, and whether it was the methamphetamine form, his usage might have begun to approach the low end of crystal meth addiction. It is more likely, though, that the harmful amphetamine effects for Hitler had to do with the fact that, especially when the drug is given intravenously, it is likely to destabilize mood episodes in bipolar disorder.

199 *Schenk . . . repeated in his own memoirs:* E. G. Schenck, *Patient Hitler. Eine medizinische Biographie* (Düsseldorf, 1989). "Hitler's Life: Hitler's Doctor—Interview with Ernst Günther Shenck," http://www.onlinefootage.tv/video/show/id/4430 (accessed February 27, 2011).

199 *According to Linge:* Heston and Heston, *The Medical Casebook of Adolf Hitler,* 82–83.

200 *Like Kennedy's doctors, some of Hitler's:* Finally intervening in 1944, when Hitler was declining mentally, Hitler's other doctors chose the wrong drug: noting that Morell's gastrointestinal preparations included traces of strychnine, they accused Morell of trying to poison the Führer. The doses were tiny, however, and of dubious risk; Hitler dismissed Morell's enemies. Kaplan, "Doctor to the Dictator," 392.

200 *Even oral amphetamines . . . cause mania:* A. P. Wingo and S. N. Ghaemi, "Frequency of Stimulant Treatment and of Stimulant-Associated Mania/Hypomania in Bipolar Disorder Patients," *Psychopharmacology Bulletin* 41, no. 4 (2008): 37–47.

201 *he shouted nonstop for three hours:* Heston and Heston, *The Medical Casebook of Adolf Hitler,* 40.

201 *Himmler, convinced that Hitler had a "sick mind":* Ibid., 42.

201 *several generals tried to persuade prominent psychiatrists to commit Hitler:* Redlich, *Diagnosis of a Destructive Prophet,* 337.

202 *"That pathological liar has gone completely mad!":* Charles F. Marshall, *Discovering the Rommel Murder* (Mechanicsburg, PA: Stackpole Books, 2002), 259.

202 *"The only troops I could move":* Alan Wykes, *Hitler* (New York: Ballantine, 1970), 120.

202–203 *Morell even publicly revised his prior diagnosis:* Hershman and Lieb, *Brotherhood of Tyrants,* 79. Heston and Heston, *The Medical Casebook of Adolf Hitler,* 46.

203 *The source . . . a Swedish journalist:* G. T. Pihl, *Germany: The Last Phase* (New York: Knopf, 1944).

203 *"The more inexorably events moved":* Albert Speer, *Inside the Third Reich* (New York: Simon and Schuster, 1997), 292.

203 *Linge . . . told the Hestons:* Heston and Heston, *The Medical Casebook of Adolf Hitler,* 46.

203 *The Hestons date such brief periods:* Ibid., 47.

203 *"cycle" into and out of his manic and depressive episodes:* Ibid., 139–140.

203 *his mind already had:* In addition to manic depression, it is hard to avoid another illness: Hitler is well known to have had parkinsonian symptoms in his final years, a common side effect of amphetamines, especially when used in their potent forms and intravenously, as with Hitler. Parkinson's disease starts on average at age sixty. Onset in one's forties is considered early, and usually due to external causes, like head trauma or drugs. Hitler's parkinsonian symptoms began around age fifty. If it was naturally occurring, concurrent amphetamine use also may have worsened the condition. E. Gibbels, "Hitler's Neurologic Disease—Differential Diagnosis of Parkinson Syndrome," *Fortschritte der Neurologie-Psychiatrie* 57 (1989): 505–517. Original article in German.

203 *Hitler heard a voice:* This was first described in *Mein Kampf.* It has been discussed by Hershman and Lieb, *Brotherhood of Tyrants,* 62. Except for those authors, most historians and physicians have viewed Hitler's experience as a metaphorical, rather than actual (and hence psychotic), "voice." Robert George and Leeson Waite, *The Psychopathic God: Adolf Hitler* (New York: Da Capo, 1993), 378. This was also the conclusion of the official U.S. intelligence psychiatric profile of Hitler, conducted from a psychoanalytic perspective by Walter C. Langer in 1942–1943. He interviewed a number of sources who knew Hitler somewhat well. This was a very psychoanalytically oriented evaluation, and it applied numerous Freudian concepts to explain Hitler, such as projection and narcissism. It labeled him neurotic, not psychotic, but beyond that judgment it is not diagnostically valuable. Walter C. Langer, *The Mind of Adolf Hitler: The Secret Wartime Report* (New York: Basic Books, 1972). One might claim that Hitler had "overvalued ideas," such as Aryan superiority and Jewish conspiracy, but these views, shared by many in his culture, would not meet most psychiatric definitions of delusional.

203–204 *Some think his experience occurred under hypnotic suggestion:* David Lewis, *The Man Who Invented Hitler* (London: Headline Publishing Company, 2003).

205 *a "paranoid destructive prophet":* Redlich, *Diagnosis of a Destructive Prophet.*

205 *But rejecting psychoanalytic diagnoses:* We can draw from three full books about Hitler written by psychiatrists who are prominent researchers or academics but not psychoanalysts (Hershman and Lieb, Heston and Heston, Redlich). Supplementing those works with memoirs and other historical material, Hitler's story is rather well documented. The three psychiatric writers disagree among themselves (one sees Hitler as having no mental illness but mainly affected by amphetamine-induced psychosis, another sees him as having pure manic-depressive psychosis, and a third sees him as having neither condition but rather a kind of political personality disorder of paranoid destruction). All these sources provide the same evidence, described above, which seems to show rather clearly that Hitler had manic and depressive episodes, a likely family history of manic symptoms, a typical course for bipolar disorder, and treatment for depression. The likely diagnosis of bipolar disorder seems solid.

206 *apparently was treated by . . . Dr. Edmund Forster:* Lewis, *The Man Who Invented Hitler*. Lewis presents the following story: There is some evidence that Hitler was examined and apparently treated by a psychiatrist at Pasewalk Hospital in present-day Poland, where he had been sent in late October 1918. This was a hospital known to be used for psychiatric cases, six hundred miles away from where Hitler had been involved in a mustard gas attack in France; all his other companions injured in the attack were treated at medical hospitals nearby. Hitler was sent far away, suggesting a psychiatric problem. Also, Hitler's complete and immediate recovery from mustard gas is biologically implausible. On this evidence, it seems reasonable to conclude, as did U.S. intelligence during World War II, that Hitler suffered from something like PTSD, manifested as hysterical blindness. Naval intelligence records from 1943, declassified in 1973, report, according to Dr. Karl Kroner, who saw Hitler immediately after the blindness, that Hitler was transferred to the care of a psychiatrist, Dr. Edmund Forster. Exactly during the period when the armistice occurred, Forster treated Hitler with what might today be called a species of psychodrama, sometimes used in French and German psychiatry of the nineteenth century for hysteria (excellent examples are found in the most prominent ninenteenth-century psychiatric text written by Philippe Pinel). According to Dr. David Lewis's book on Forster, the psychiatrist made strong hypnotic suggestions to Hitler that he had much to see and live for, including helping Germany. One week after the armistice, Hitler recovered his eyesight and was discharged from the army as unfit for duty. He never again had any difficulty with his vision. Years later, after Hitler came to power in 1933, Forster, a known anti-Nazi, took his psychiatric records to France and reportedly gave them to German exiles there, including Eduard Weiss, who, according to Lewis, later posthumously published the content in fiction form. Soon thereafter, Forster either committed suicide or was killed. After the naval report was released, Rudolph Binion, an American-German professor, tracked down some persons who were present in the reported Paris meeting with Forster, and they confirmed the events. Forster's notes have never been found, though, leading to doubt on the part of other observers.

This is the only known official psychiatric evaluation or treatment of Hitler in his life. While Lewis and others make the mistake, in my view, of thinking that Forster's hypnotic suggestion "invented" the grandiose Führer, the overall story of PTSD is consistent with Hitler's many psychiatric symptoms and his high level of anxiety (which is called the personality trait of neuroticism), a well-established risk factor for PTSD.

In 1923, after the Munich putsch, Hitler was again psychiatrically examined, though this time by the chief physician of Landsberg prison, Dr. Joseph Brinsteiner, who was not a psychiatrist. Documented in a January 8, 1924, report titled "Report of the Mental Condition of Prisoner Adolf Hitler," it was described as follows by one biographer: "The doctor, who was obviously very impressed by his prisoner, wrote very general comments stressing that he was a man of very high intelligence, extraordinary range of knowledge and great oratorical ability. At the time of his arrest, Hitler was very depressed, the doctor said, and suffering from 'a very painful neurosis' (*sehr schmerzhaften Neurose*). No details are given. The report emphasizes the ephemeral nature of the condition and that the prisoner was soon in excellent spirits." Robert G. L. Waite, *The Psychopathic God: Adolf Hitler* (New York: Basic Books, 1977), 350. A prison guard, Otto Lurker, who later published in 1933 a hagiographic memoir of Hitler's time in jail, called "Hitler Behind Fortress Walls," reported that the painful neurosis diagnosed by Dr. Brinsteiner was due to a shoulder dislocation Hitler suffered when hurt during the melee of the putsch. Lurker quotes Brinsteiner as telling the court, while attesting that Hitler was mentally fit to stand trial, "The patient . . . has no symptoms of psychic disorders or psychopathic tendencies." Quoted in Milan Hauner, *Hitler: A Chronology of His Life and Time*, 2nd ed. (London: Palgrave Macmillan, 2008). Yet the earlier possibility of psychiatric diagnosis and treatment for PTSD would be consistent with the known fact that the chairman of psychiatry at the University of Heidelberg, Karl Willmans, had stated publicly that Hitler had suffered a hysterical reaction during World War I. In 1933, Willmans was forced to resign. Ruth Lidz and Hans-Rudolph Wiedemann, "Karl Wilmanns (1873–1945) einige Ergänzungen und Richtigstellungen," *Fortschritte der Neurologie-Psychiatric* 57 (1989): 161–162.

CHAPTER 14. HOMOCLITE LEADERS: BUSH, BLAIR, NIXON, AND OTHERS

211 *Grinker decided to take on this task:* Roy R. Grinker Sr., Roy R. Grinker Jr., and John Timberlake, " 'Mentally Healthy' Young Males (Homoclites)," *Archives of General Psychiatry* 6 (1962): 405–453.

213 *"Within the general population of the United States":* Ibid., 445–446.

213 *"People like the George Williams students":* Ibid., 446.

213 *"To have a population of relative stability":* Ibid., 448.

213 *"I often described my subject-population":* Ibid., 446.

214 *Sigmund Freud's dictum:* Ibid., 448.

214 No ideal *standard of mental health works scientifically:* Karl Jaspers, *General Psychopathology* (Baltimore: Johns Hopkins University Press, 1997). S. Nassir Ghaemi, *The Rise and Fall of the Biopsychosocial Model: Reconciling Art and Science in Psychiatry* (Baltimore: Johns Hopkins University Press, 2009).

214 *"Standards of health on the basis of admirable traits":* Leston Havens, *A Safe Place: Laying the Groundwork of Psychotherapy* (Cambridge, MA: Harvard University Press, 1989), 28.

214 *"muscular Christian" normality:* Grinker, " 'Mentally Healthy' Young Males," 444.

215 *what happens when homoclites rule:* Grinker's work gives us a framework to understand mental health, and if applied to leaders it would head us in the direction of looking at personality and seeing whether our leaders are similar to or different from the rest of us in their personality traits. Historians and psychologists have worked out ways to do this, not only for personality traits, but also for intelligence, another psychological attribute commonly seen as important for leadership. (Dean Keith Simonton, *Greatness: Who Makes History and Why* [New York: Guilford, 1994].) For intelligence, this involves quantifying leaders' achievements in childhood and early adulthood, such as grades and academic degrees, and correlating those achievements with population averages. Assuming a population IQ norm of 100, one can then infer higher or lower levels of intelligence for historical figures. This method has been used in psychology research now for over eighty years. For personality traits, historians and scholars are given biographical data—anonymized and altered enough to try to remove specifics that would identify the individuals—based on which they complete assessments of major personality traits, as in the NEO scale, which assesses the three major personality traits of neuroticism (one's baseline level of anxiety), extraversion (one's sociability

and outgoingness), and openness to experience (one's willingness to take risks or tendency to follow routines or habits). These estimates are then correlated with objective (number of bills passed, reelection) and subjective (consensus of historians) estimates of presidential success. (In the normal population, we all score somewhere on each of these traits, and we do so in a way that statistically is called the "normal" curve, also referred to as the bell curve. Most of us score in the middle, while 2.5 percent of us score at either extreme—very high or very low—on each trait. These traits can also be translated into the abnormal temperaments discussed previously. Thus those with hyperthymic personality will tend to be very high on extraversion and openness to experience.)

When applied to presidents (Simonton, 2006), these studies of intelligence and personality support, in my view, the idea that most presidents are homoclites, and that the most successful of them are the least homoclitic. Using the above methods, about one-half of presidents (twenty-three out of forty-three) had IQ estimates in the average, but not gifted, range (100–120). (The average college graduate has an IQ of 120, while the population norm is 90–110, above average is 110–120, gifted is 120–140, and above 140 is considered "genius" level.) Among twelve recent presidents from FDR onward, only four score in the gifted range (FDR, Kennedy, Carter, and Clinton). For those presidents considered by some as not particularly intelligent, like George W. Bush (IQ estimate 111) or Reagan (IQ estimate 118), estimated intelligence is above the population average (though not greater than the average college graduate). These are not stupid men, nor are they highly intelligent; they are just normal. (Just to show that intelligence is overrated as a measure of success, by the way, one might note that the estimated IQ for George Washington was 125, lower than Clinton or Carter.)

Personality seemed a more robust predictor of presidential success. Specifically, of the three traits in the NEO (Simonton, 2006), only openness to experience correlated with presidential success, and even this was not straightforward. The three highest-rating presidents for openness to experience were Thomas Jefferson, John Quincy Adams, and Lincoln; yet Adams is generally seen as ineffectual. Clinton and Kennedy ran distant seconds on this personality trait, and some presidents viewed as successful, like Reagan and Washington, scored low on it. I would turn the usual interpretation of these personality tests around. The standard view is that these studies show that neuroticism, for instance, is "irrelevant" to presidential personality. Rather, it would be more accurate to say that extremes of neuroticism, and indeed all personality traits, are not found in our presidents. They are mostly average in their personality traits, and even their intelligence. Much as we yearn for heroes, our presidents are, by and large, normal people—homoclites like you and me. And yet when one picks out those who are extreme on any of these features, whether personality or intelligence, one finds names like Jefferson and Lincoln and Franklin Roosevelt and Kennedy—those who are seen as the "best" presidents, the ones full of charisma and creativity. They are not "normal" people: they are the ones with abnormal temperaments, like hyperthymic personality, or even frank mental illness.

Most presidents, however, are normal and thus homoclites. Hence research about the psychological basis of political beliefs in the general population (who are also homoclites) might help us understand the psychology of these homoclite leaders. The classic work in this area is that of British psychologist Hans Eysenck (*The Psychology of Politics* [London: Routledge and Kegan Paul, 1954]), who observed that the left/right theory of politics could not account for the many similarities between communism and fascism—apparent extreme opposites. Eysenck interviewed middle-class and working-class persons in 1950s England and classified their political beliefs along the above labels; he then gave them NEO-like personality tests. (Eysenck himself was a founding father of personality research.) Statistically grouping people with similar political beliefs versus their personality traits, Eysenck found another factor besides political ideology (left-wing versus right-wing) that seemed to relate to how practical versus how idealistic people tended to be. In other words, political behavior needed to be seen on two dimensions, the first being political ideology, as is commonly accepted, and the second not being political at all, but psychological, correlating with personality traits, which (borrowing from the philosopher William James) Eysenck labeled *tender-mindedness* versus *tough-mindedness*. This produces a new two-dimensional picture, when combined with the original dimension of political ideology. Over the years, numerous genetic studies on identical twins have repeatedly confirmed that Eysenck was right: *temperament is an important biological predictor of political beliefs* (Lindon Eaves, Hans Eysenck, and Michael Neale, *Genes, Culture, and Personality: An Empirical Approach* [London: Academic Press, 1989]).

Eysenck's thesis may help explain why apparently opposite political figures, like Bush and Blair, could find so much common ground: their personalities were similar—they were tough-minded "normal guy" leaders, taking pride in their toughness, arms swaying beside them as they strode to a press conference podium together, like two gunslingers at a shootout. Other homoclite leaders, differing in the normal range of personality traits, will be tender-minded instead, and thus likely to make different political judgments. It goes beyond available evidence to speculate how these considerations apply to other recent or contemporary leaders, like Bill Clinton or Barack Obama, but Eysenck's theory provides testable hypotheses for historians and psychologists to assess.

216 *Chamberlain was a commoner:* Nick Smart, *Neville Chamberlain: A Biography* (London: Routledge, 2009).

216 *"a good mayor of Birmingham":* George Lichtheim, *Thoughts Among the Ruins* (Piscataway, NJ: Transaction, 1973), 177.

216 *"a nice man":* Robert C. Self, *Neville Chamberlain: A Biography* (Farnham, UK: Ashgate, 2006), 97.

216 *"rigid competence," "indispensable for filling subordinate posts":* Peter Rowland, *David Lloyd George: A Biography* (New York: Macmillan, 1976), 707.

217 *"If Germany could obtain her desiderata":* Ibid., 219.

217 *"In one phase men might seem to have been right":* Graham Macklin, *Chamberlain* (London: Haus, 2006), 97.

218 *The son of a Philadelphia surgeon:* Most of the material on McClellan is drawn from Stephen Sears, *George B. McClellan: The Young Napoleon* (New York: Da Capo, 1999).

220 *"I almost think":* Ibid., 95.

220 *"Shall we crush the rebellion":* Ibid., 99.

221 *"One Napoleonic grand army":* Ibid.

221 *"How does he think":* Ibid., 103.

221 *"I am here in a terrible place":* Ibid.

222 *"Cautious and weak" . . . "A psychiatrist could make much":* James McPherson, *Crossroads of Freedom: Antietam* (New York: Oxford University Press, 2004), 44.

222 *unlike Lee, who seems to have been dysthymic:* Michael Fellman, *The Making of Robert E. Lee* (Baltimore: Johns Hopkins University Press, 2003).

223 *what about Reagan, Eisenhower, Truman?:* Historians may disagree. Truman did have to deal with Korea. And at the end of World War II, he had to make the massive decision to bomb Hiroshima and Nagasaki. Whether the latter decision in particular was the correct one, and the mark of a successful crisis leader, is something about which Japanese and American readers may have differences of opinion. Reagan certainly has his fans, as did Eisenhower. I cannot and do not attempt to cover every major leader of the twentieth century in this book, and I especially try to avoid recent ones. The most recent leader I study in detail is Nixon. As for the others, I can only make tentative comments while awaiting the clarifying impact of time and distance. This all depends, of course, on historians' having open enough minds to even consider some of these theses.

224 *six books and a dozen professional journal articles:* David Greenberg, *Nixon's Shadow* (New York: Norton, 2004), 235.

224 *"on the naked edge of a nervous breakdown":* Ibid., 256.

224 *"Almost uniformly":* Ibid., 235.

224 *"Each painted Nixon":* Ibid., 244–245.

224 *Narcissism has never been empirically validated:* The concept of narcissism was heavily used by Freud, and is a psychoanalytic belief. It is often used pejoratively. Though it can be operationalized and identified in populations (Robert Raskin and Howard Terry, "A Principal-Components Analysis of the Narcissistic Personality Inventory and Further Evidence of Its Construct Validity," *Journal of Personality and Social Psychology* 54, no. 5 [1988]: 890–902), it is not validated as a distinct and separate personality trait or personality disorder or unique personality condition. By validation, I mean scientific standards as described in this book: being distinct from other conditions in the four validators of symptoms, course of illness, family history, and treatment response. In such studies, it is poorly separable from a host of other claimed personality disorders. Andrea Fossati, Theodore P. Beauchaine, Federica Grazioli, Ilaria Carretta, Francesca Cortinovis, and Maffei Cesare, "A Latent Structure Analysis of Diagnostic and Statistical Manual of Mental Disorders, Narcissistic Personality Disorder Criteria," *Comprehensive Psychiatry* 46 (2005): 361–367. W. John Livesley, "Diagnostic Dilemmas in Classifying Personality Disorder," in *Advancing DSM: Dilemmas in Psychiatric Diagnosis*, ed. Katharine A. Phillips, Michael B. First, and Harold Alan Pincus, 153–168 (Washington, DC: American Psychiatric Press, 2003).

225 *"so outlandish as to be downright silly":* Greenberg, *Nixon's Shadow*, 238.

225 *"Do not inflict this Freudian horseshit":* Ibid., 253.

225 *Regarding* treatment: Ibid., 242–243.

226 *"I cannot help thinking":* Ibid., 232.

226 *"dangerous emotional instability":* Ibid., 257.

226 *"crazy with rage":* Ibid.

226 *"as if he were a tape":* Ibid., 258.

226 *Haig . . . remove his sleeping pills:* Ibid., 259.

226 *"I think I've got a lousy personality":* Christopher Matthews, *Kennedy and Nixon: The Rivalry That Shaped Postwar America* (New York: Simon and Schuster, 1996), 282.

226 *"cocksucker" and "damn Jews":* Greenberg, *Nixon's Shadow*, 254. Rick Perlstein, *Nixonland: The Rise of a President and the Fracturing of America* (New York: Scribner, 2008), 353.

226 *"screw" and "fuck"*: Nigel Hamilton, *JFK: Reckless Youth* (New York: Random House, 1993), 143. Robert Dallek, *An Unfinished Life: John F. Kennedy* (Boston: Little, Brown, 2003), 172.

226–227 *Johnson . . . favored metaphors of urination and defecation:* In one of my favorites, Johnson once commented to John Kenneth Galbraith as follows: "Did y'ever think Ken that making a speech on economics is a lot like pissing down your leg? It seems hot to you, but it never does to anyone else." John Kenneth Galbraith, *A Life in Our Times* (New York: Ballantine, 1981), 450.

227 *McGovern told a heckler:* Perlstein, *Nixonland,* 739.

227 *Victor Frankl would have known:* Said Frankl, "An abnormal reaction to an abnormal situation is normal behavior." Viktor Frankl, *Man's Search for Meaning* (Boston: Beacon, 2000), 32.

227 *Nixon constantly encouraged the sick JFK:* Matthews, *Kennedy and Nixon,* 87–102.

227 *Joseph P. Kennedy Sr. sent word to Nixon:* Ibid., 132.

227 *Robert Kennedy . . . quietly voted:* Ibid., 113.

227 *"I just saw a crushed man today":* Matthews, *Kennedy and Nixon,* 199. Garry Wills, *Nixon Agonistes* (New York: Signet, 1969), 40.

227 *to invite the widow and her two children:* Matthews, *Kennedy and Nixon,* 292–297.

228 *It was 1946:* What follows is based on Matthews, *Kennedy and Nixon.*

229 *"Chotiner had two working precepts":* Ibid., 35.

229 *"I understand yours was Whittier":* Ibid., 61.

230 *as author Rick Perlstein puts it:* Perlstein, *Nixonland,* 435.

231 *"you've got to be a little evil":* Tom Wicker, *One of Us: Richard Nixon and the American Dream* (New York: Random House, 1991), 686.

231 *"The notion of Nixon":* Greenberg, *Nixon's Shadow,* 263.

231 *"a study in psychiatric imbalance":* Ibid., 261.

231 *In truth, Nixon was rather normal:* Three authors who appear to come to similar conclusions based on journalistic and historical evidence are Wicker (*One of Us*), Wills (*Nixon Agonistes*), and Perlstein (*Nixonland*).

231 *"How is the nation to be protected":* Greenberg, *Nixon's Shadow,* 261.

231 *"A man harassed, tortured, and torn" . . . "There is a delicious inconsistency":* Ibid., 262.

232 *the Hubris syndrome identified by David Owen:* David Owen, *In Sickness and in Power: Illnesses in Heads of Government During the Last 100 Years* (Westport, CT: Praeger, 2008).

233 *As a young man:* The material in this paragraph is drawn from Ronald Kessler, *A Matter of Character: Inside the White House of George W. Bush* (New York: Sentinel, 2004).

233 *"He was Huck Finn and Tom Sawyer":* Ibid., 16.

233–234 *about 15 percent of all adults . . . lose a parent or a sibling:* http://www.disabled-world .com/communication/community/parent-loss.php (accessed February 27, 2011).

234 *childhood parental loss . . . increases the risk of depression:* Kenneth Kendler and Carol Prescott, *Genes, Environment and Psychopathology* (New York: Guilford, 2006).

234 *some studies show that . . . losses during childhood:* Norman F. Watt, James P. David, Kevin L. Ladd, and Susan Shamos, "The Life Course of Psychological Resilience: A Phenomenological Perspective on Deflecting Life's Slings and Arrows," *Journal of Primary Prevention* 15 (1995): 209–246.

234 *SAT score was 1280 . . . IQ of about 120:* Kessler, *A Matter of Character,* 23.

235 *his memoir* **Decision Points:** George W. Bush, *Decision Points* (New York: Crown, 2010).

235 *his blood alcohol level was found to be 0.10:* Kessler, *A Matter of Character,* 35.

235 *pressured him to quit drinking . . . he apparently did:* A psychiatrist colleague has told me that he knew a Bush family member who claimed that Bush continues to drink and has even been drunk at times at family meals, as recently as just before the 2000 presidential election. However, according to my colleague, that person was not willing to make that accusation publicly, and since I cannot confirm the source or corroborate the claim, I cannot present it as probably or even possibly true.

235 *This history is actually the best possible outcome:* George E. Vaillant, *The Natural History of Alcoholism Revisited* (Cambridge, MA: Harvard University Press, 1995).

237 *"solved my biggest political problem":* Kessler, *A Matter of Character,* 54.

238 *one sign of creativity is "integrative complexity":* Simonton, *Greatness,* 80,

238–239 *"I would be at a press conference with him":* Tony Blair, *A Journey: My Political Life* (New York: Knopf, 2010), xiv.

239 *"No one was more shocked and angry than I":* Bush, *Decision Points,* 262.

239 *"I remembered the shattering pain of 9/11":* Ibid., 252.

239 *Santayana's dictum that fanaticism:* This view does not undermine my assertion that Bush was mentally healthy. I do not see fanaticism as a type of mental illness. It occurs most commonly, in fact, in the mental health of homoclites, who do not have much integrative complexity. Grinker's work showed this possibility in his description of how homoclites were similar to "muscular Christianity."

240 *Blair was a classic British amalgam:* These pages on Blair draw mostly from his memoirs, and from Philip Stephens, *Tony Blair: The Making of a World Leader* (New York: Viking, 2004), 2–15.

241 *a major intellectual guide:* Blair, *A Journey,* 80–81. John Burton and Eileen McCabe, *We Don't Do God: Blair's Religious Belief and Its Consequences* (London: Continuum, 2009), 4–8.

242 *"It was his manner that won us over":* Burton and McCabe, *We Don't Do God,* 20.

242 *became Kinnock's posse:* Alastair Campbell, *The Blair Years* (New York: Knopf, 2004).

242 *likable persona and moderate politics:* Stephens, *Tony Blair.*

243 *"Progress in Northern Ireland":* Campbell, *The Blair Years,* xxix.

243 *"Some indeed advocated this strategy":* Blair, *My Journey,* 349.

244 *"The other way, the way we chose":* Ibid.

244 *liberal imperialism of William Gladstone:* Stephens, *Tony Blair,* 16.

244 *"We are interventionists":* Ibid., 215–219.

244–245 *"Who knows which [option] is right" . . . "All these years":* Blair, *My Journey,* 349.

245 *"The battle is not":* Ibid., 348.

246 *"Friends opposed to the war":* Ibid., 380.

247 *"The world provides sources":* Shelley E. Taylor and David A. Armor, "Positive Illusions and Coping with Adversity," *Journal of Personality* 64 (1996): 873–898.

249 *"The difference between the TB of 1997":* Blair, *My Journey,* 651.

250 *"normal basic personality" . . . "mystical fatalism":* Jack El-Hai, "The Nazi and the Psychiatrist," *Scientific American,* January 5, 2011, available at http://www.saloforum.com/index.php?threads/the-nazi-and-the-psychiatrist-goering-and-kelley.286/ (accessed May 1, 2011). Authors have previously wondered whether Kelley committed suicide because of his desperation in realizing how the Nazi horror happened at the hands of normal, ordinary men and thus could happen again anywhere, anytime. El-Hai, who has interviewed Kelley's son and conducted new research, notes that

Kelley had alcohol problems and that he killed himself impulsively while in the midst of an argument with his wife. His son believes that Kelley swallowed the cyanide pill by accident.

250 *Goering also had an IQ of 138:* El-Hai, "The Nazi and the Psychiatrist."

250 *"Your excellency Major Kelly!":* John Michael Steiner, *Power Politics and Social Change in National Socialist Germany* (New York: Walter de Gruyter, 1976), 395. The original text of the letter is presented by Steiner in both English and German. The English translation begins, "Dear Major Kelly," but the original German reads, "*Sehr geehrter Major Kelly!*" The literal translation for the German salutation is "Your excellency"; I've altered the English translation on this point to capture the respect in which the Nazi leaders held Dr. Kelley.

250 *the Rorschach tests of the Nazi leaders . . . A follow-up analysis:* Barry A. Ritzler, "The Nuremberg Mind Revisited: A Quantitative Approach to Nazi Rorschachs," *Journal of Personality Assessment* 42 (1978): 344–353. Molly Harrower, "Rorschach Records of the Nazi War Criminals: An Experimental Study After Thirty Years. *Journal of Personality Assessment* 40 (1976): 341–351.

252 *"I have yet to hear one of these men say":* Robert H. Jackson, *That Man: An Insider's Portrait of Franklin D. Roosevelt* (New York: Oxford University Press, 2003), 170.

253 *"You must not picture Professor Brandt as a criminal":* Robert Lifton, *The Nazi Doctors: Medical Killing and the Psychology of Genocide* (New York: Basic Books, 1986), 116–117.

254 *in prominent historical works on Hitler and the Nazis:* John Lukacs, *The Hitler of History* (New York: Vintage, 1998).

254 *as historian Martin Kitchen describes well:* Martin Kitchen, *The Third Reich: Charisma and Community* (London: Pearson Longman, 2008). Martin Kitchen, "Hitler Bewitcher or Hitler Bewitched?" in *Creativity and Madness: An Interdisciplinary Symposium,* ed. J. D. Keehn, 93–108 (York, ON: University Press of Canada, 1987).

254 *No Hitler, no Holocaust:* Ron Rosenbaum, *Explaining Hitler* (New York: Random House, 1998), 348.

CHAPTER 15. STIGMA AND POLITICS

256 *a deep cultural stigma accompanying mental illness:* Paul Jay Fink and Allen Tasman, eds., *Stigma and Mental Illness* (Washington, DC: American Psychiatric Publishing, 1992).

256 *physicians attach as much stigma:* William R. Dubin and Paul Jay Fink, "Effects of Stigma on Psychiatric Treatment," in Fink and Tasman, eds., *Stigma and Mental Illness.*

256 *Even mental health professionals:* David Kingdon, Tonmoy Sharma, and Deborah Hart, "What Attitudes Do Psychiatrists Hold Towards People with Mental Illness?" *Psychiatric Bulletin* 29 (2004): 401–406.

257 *a "proud mediocrity":* Cesare Lombroso, *The Man of Genius* (New York: C. Scribner's Sons, 1891), 2.

257 *a "prejudice" of psychiatric "inferiority":* Ernst Kretschmer, *The Psychology of Men of Genius* (London: Kegan Paul; New York: Harcourt, Brace and Co., 1931), 6.

257 *"It shows Winston in a completely false light":* Lord David Owen, "Winston Churchill and Franklin Roosevelt: Did Their Health Problems Impair Their Effectiveness as World Leaders?" Churchill Lecture Series, Churchill Museum and Cabinet War Rooms, May 5, 2009, written transcript, 36.

257 *the Kennedy family criticized Nigel Hamilton's . . . evidence:* http://www.huffington post.com/nigel-hamilton/the-kennedys_b_810465.html (accessed February 27, 2011).

257 *Brendan Maher showed:* Brendan Maher, "Delusional Thinking and Cognitive Disorder," *Integrative Physiological and Behavioral Science* 40 (2005): 136–146.

258 *mental heuristics and biases:* Stuart Sutherland, *Irrationality* (London: Pinter and Martin, 2007).

258 *identified thirty-one standard irrational thought processes:* http://www.acceleratingfuture.com/michael/works/heuristicsandbiases.htm (accessed February 27, 2011).

258 *the unfortunate Missouri senator Thomas Eagleton:* http://chipur.com/i-want-relief/thomas-eagleton-heartbeat-depressed-president/ (accessed February 27, 2011).

259 *"[Adviser David Axelrod] said to me":* Dan Balz and Haynes Johnson, *The Battle for America 2008: The Story of an Extraordinary Election* (New York: Penguin, 2009), 18.

260 *"Character above all":* http://www.pbs.org/newshour/character/ (accessed February 27, 2011).

260 *"And so, when I put my hand on the Bible":* http://www.4president.org/speeches/bush cheney2000convention.htm (accessed February 27, 2011).

260 *"With Bush, there was an instant change":* http://old.nationalreview.com/interrogatory/kessler200408090855.asp (accessed February 27, 2011).

261 *"Nobody died when Clinton lied":* http://www.nobodydied.com/ (accessed February 27, 2011).

261 *"Public virtue cannot exist":* John Adams, Samuel Adams, and James Warren, *Warren-Adams Letters* (Boston: Massachusetts Historical Society, 1917), 22.

261 *"It's my experience":* Abraham Lincoln, Marion Mills Miller, and Henry Clay Whitney, *Life and Works of Abraham Lincoln: Speeches and Presidential Addresses, 1859–1865* (New York: Current Literature Publishing Company, 1907), 282.

264 *"to form what, for lack of a better phrase":* Matthew Joseph Bruccoli and Scottie Fitzgerald Smith, *Some Sort of Epic Grandeur: The Life of F. Scott Fitzgerald* (Columbia: University of South Carolina Press, 2002), 443.

EPILOGUE

266 *the classic work of the psychologist Hans Eysenck:* Hans Eysenck, *The Psychology of Politics* (London: Routledge and Kegan Paul, 1954).

266–267 *Simonton . . . Westen . . . Lakoff:* Dean Keith Simonton, *Psychology, Science, and History: An Introduction to Historiometry* (New Haven, CT: Yale University Press, 1990). Drew Westen, *The Political Brain* (New York: Public Affairs, 2007). George Lakoff, *The Political Mind* (New York: Viking, 2008).

267 *Michael Fellman in his biography of Sherman:* Michael Fellman, *Citizen Sherman: A Biography of William Tecumseh Sherman* (New York: Random House, 1995).

267 *Joshua Shenk in his biography of Lincoln:* Joshua Wolf Shenk, *Lincoln's Melancholy* (Boston: Houghton Mifflin, 2005).

267 *does not mean that illness is* nothing but *a social construction:* S. Nassir Ghaemi, *The Rise and Fall of the Biopsychosocial Model: Reconciling Art and Science in Psychiatry* (Baltimore: Johns Hopkins University Press, 2009).

268 *the claims of some postmodernist historians notwithstanding:* For some of my debates with postmodernist oriented colleagues, see http://metapsychology.mentalhelp.net/poc/view_doc.php?type=book&id=4504, http://metapsychology.mentalhelp.net/poc/

view_doc.php?type=book&id=4440, and alien.dowling.edu/~cperring/aapp/bulletin_
v_17_2/21.doc (accessed February 27, 2011).

269 *"split-brain" research:* Michael Gazzaniga, *Mind Matters: How Mind and Brain Interact to Create Our Conscious Lives* (Boston: Houghton Mifflin, 1988). In some epilepsies, where seizures do not respond well to medications, as a last resort a kind of surgery is sometimes used where the fibers, called the corpus callosum, connecting the right and left hemisphere are cut. After corpus callectomy, seizures that begin on one side of the brain at least do not travel to the other side, and full-blown convulsions are thus prevented. This kind of surgery began a few decades ago, and in the intervening time researchers have observed an important thing about these patients: living with two halves of a brain no longer communicating with each other, they seem to have two brains, not one. Not much is noticeable in terms of personality or behavior; interacting on the street or in stores, one cannot tell someone with a split brain, after corpus callectomy, apart from the rest of us. With neuropsychological tests, however, important abnormalities emerge.

The right hemisphere of the brain controls the left visual field; the left hemisphere controls the right visual field. In all right-handed persons, language is fully controlled by the left hemisphere. (In left-handed persons, language is partly controlled by both hemispheres.) Thus in right-handed patients after split-brain surgery, the split between language and vision can be tested. If an image is shown to the right hemisphere (in the left visual field) of, say, a woman talking on a phone, the experimenter who asks the patient—What do you see?—will get an answer, a wrong answer, but an answer nonetheless. "I see a friend," the subject might say. "What is the friend doing?" "Cooking dinner." Then with a phone nearby, the experimenter can ask the subject, "Show me what you saw." The subject will pick up the phone.

The split-brain epilepsy patient "knows" what is seen by the right hemisphere, but she cannot speak it. What is most interesting is that she does not say, "I do not know," or "I am unsure," or some such. Even when prompted before the experiment by the researcher saying, "Now remember, you have had split-brain surgery for your seizures, keep that in mind when you answer my questions," patients rarely say that they do not know what they saw, or why they feel as they do about what they saw. They never admit ignorance; they always make something up. That is the way our brains operate: our brains are *rationalizing machines;* we are designed, by God or evolution, to come up with plausible explanations for what we experience. We *never* say we do not know.

269 *Stephen Ambrose writes:* Stephen Ambrose, "William T. Sherman: A Reappraisal," *American History Illustrated* 1 (1967): 6–7.

269 *decades of excellent twin studies:* Kenneth Kendler and Carol Prescott, *Genes, Environment and Psychopathology* (New York: Guilford, 2006).

270 *David Hume starkly laid out this "problem of causation":* David Hume, *An Enquiry Concerning Human Understanding* (Cambridge, UK: Cambridge University Press, 2007).

271 *The German philosopher Wilhelm Dilthey:* Rudolf Makkreel, *Dilthey: Philosopher of the Human Studies* (Princeton, NJ: Princeton University Press, 1992). S. Nassir Ghaemi, *The Rise and Fall of the Biopsychosocial Model* (Baltimore: Johns Hopkins University Press, 2009).

272 *"Whilst thus many men of genius themselves":* Ernst Kretschmer, *The Psychology of Men of Genius* (London: Kegan Paul; New York: Harcourt, Brace and Co.), 4.

BIBLIOGRAPHY

Adams, Jad. *Gandhi: Naked Ambition.* London: Quercus, 2011.

Adams, John, Samuel Adams, and James Warren. *Warren-Adams Letters.* Boston: Massachusetts Historical Society, 1917.

Adinoff, Bryon, Kathleen Brady, Susan Sonne, Robert F. Mirabella, and Charles H. Kellner. "Cocaine-like Effects of Intravenous Procaine in Cocaine Addicts." *Addiction Biology* 3 (1998): 189–196.

Adler, Bill, ed. *The Kennedy Wit.* New York: Citadel, 1967.

Akiskal, Hagop S., and Kareen K. Akiskal. "In Search of Aristotle: Temperament, Human Nature, Melancholia, Creativity and Eminence." *Journal of Affective Disorders* 100 (2007): 1–6.

———. "Cyclothymic, Hyperthymic, and Depressive Temperaments as Subaffective Variants of Mood Disorders." In *American Psychiatric Press Review of Psychiatry*, vol. 11, ed. Allan Tasman. Washington, DC: American Psychiatric Press, 1992.

Allen, M. S. "Sullivan's Closet: A Reappraisal of Harry Stack Sullivan's Life and His Pioneering Role in American Psychiatry." *Journal of Homosexuality* 29 (1995): 1–18.

Alloy, L. B., and L. Y. Abramson. "Judgment of Contingency in Depressed and Nondepressed Students: Sadder but Wiser?" *Journal of Experimental Psychology* 108 (1979): 441–485.

Ambrose, Stephen. "William T. Sherman: A Reappraisal." *American History Illustrated* 1 (1967): 6–7.

Arendt, Hannah. *Eichmann in Jerusalem: A Report on the Banality of Evil.* New York: Viking, 1963.

Balz, Dan, and Haynes Johnson. *The Battle for America 2008: The Story of an Extraordinary Election.* New York: Viking, 2009.

Batson, C. D. "These Things Called Empathy: Eight Related but Distinct Phenomena." In *The Social Neuroscience of Empathy*, ed. Jean Decety and Willam Ickes, 3–16. Cambridge, MA: MIT Press, 2009.

Bennett, Lerone. *What Manner of Man: A Biography of Martin Luther King Jr.* Chicago: Johnson Publishing Company, 1964.

Blair, Tony. *A Journey: My Political Life.* New York: Knopf, 2010.

Boller, Paul. *Not So! Popular Myths About Americans from Columbus to Clinton.* New York: Oxford University Press, 1996.

Bonanno, George A. "Loss, Trauma, and Human Resilience." *American Psychologist* 59 (2004): 20–28.

Bonanno, George A., and A. D. Mancini. "The Human Capacity to Thrive in the Face of Potential Trauma." *Pediatrics* 121 (2008): 369–375.

Bradlee, Benjamin. *Conversations with Kennedy.* New York: Pocket Books, 1976.

Brain, Russell W. "Encounters with Winston Churchill." *Medical History* 44 (2000): 3–20.

Bruccoli, Matthew Joseph, and Scottie Fitzgerald Smith. *Some Sort of Epic Grandeur: The Life of F. Scott Fitzgerald.* Columbia: University of South Carolina Press, 2002.

Bullock, Alan. *Hitler: A Study in Tyranny.* New York: Harper and Row, 1964.

Burns, D. D., and S. Nolen-Hoeksema. "Therapeutic Empathy and Recovery from Depression in Cognitive-Behavioral Therapy: A Structural Equation Model." *Journal of Consulting Clinical Psychology* 60 (1992): 441–449.

Burton, John, and Eileen McCabe. *We Don't Do God: Blair's Religious Belief and Its Consequences.* London: Continuum, 2009.

Bush, George W. *Decision Points.* New York: Crown, 2010.

Campbell, Alastair. *The Blair Years.* New York: Knopf, 2004.

Carson, Clayborne, ed. *The Autobiography of Martin Luther King Jr.* New York: Warner Books, 1991.

Caspi, A., and P. A. Silva. "Temperamental Qualities at Age Three Predict Personality Traits in Young Adulthood." *Child Development* 66 (1995): 486–498.

Collishaw, Stephan, et al. "Resilience to Adult Psychopathology Following Childhood Maltreatment." *Child Abuse and Neglect* 31 (2007): 211–229.

Cummins, Robert A., and Helen Nistico. "Maintaining Life Satisfaction: The Role of Positive Cognitive Bias." *Journal of Happiness Studies* 3 (2002): 37–69.

Dalal, Chandulal Bhagubhai. *Harilal Gandhi: A Life.* Chennai, India: Orient Longman, 2007.

Dallek, Robert. *An Unfinished Life: John F. Kennedy.* Boston: Little, Brown, 2003.

Doyle, D. "Adolf Hitler's Medical Care." *Journal of the Royal College of Physicians of Edinburgh* 35 (2005): 75–82.

DuBois, William Edward Burghardt. *W. E. B. DuBois: A Reader.* New York: Macmillan, 1995.

Dubin, William R., and Paul Jay Fink. "Effects of Stigma on Psychiatric Treatment." In *Stigma and Mental Illness,* ed. Paul Jay Fink and Allen Tasman, 1–7. Washington, DC: American Psychiatric Publishing, 1992.

Eaves, Lindon, Hans Eysenck, and Michael Neale. *Genes, Culture, and Personality: An Empirical Approach.* London: Academic Press, 1989.

El-Hai, Jack. "The Nazi and the Psychiatrist." *Scientific American,* January 5, 2011. http://www.saloforum.com/index.php?threads/the-nazi-and-the-psychiatrist-goering-and-kelley.286/ (accessed May 1, 2011).

———. *The Lobotomist.* New York: Wiley, 2005.

Ellis, Michael E. *Infectious Diseases of the Respiratory Tract.* Cambridge, UK: Cambridge University Press, 1998.

Erikson, Erik H. *Gandhi's Truth: On the Origins of Militant Nonviolence.* New York: Norton, 1969.

Erikson, Erik H., and Huey P. Newton. *In Search of Common Ground.* New York: Norton, 1973.

Eysenck, Hans J. *The Psychology of Politics.* London: Routledge and Kegan Paul, 1954.

Fanon, Frantz. *The Wretched of the Earth.* New York: Grove Press, 1965.

Faro, Sebastian. *Sexually Transmitted Diseases in Women*. Baltimore: Lippincott Williams & Wilkins, 2003.

Fellman, Michael. *The Making of Robert E. Lee*. Baltimore: Johns Hopkins University Press, 2003.

———. *Citizen Sherman: A Biography of William Tecumseh Sherman*. New York: Random House, 1995.

Fergusson, David M., and Michael T. Lynskey. "Childhood Circumstances, Adolescent Adjustment, and Suicide Attempts in a New Zealand Birth Cohort." *Journal of Child and Adolescent Psychiatry* 34 (1995): 612–622.

Fink, Paul Jay, and Allen Tasman, eds. *Stigma and Mental Illness*. Washington, DC: American Psychiatric Publishing, 1992.

Fischer, Louis. *The Essential Gandhi*. New York: Vintage, 1983.

———. *Gandhi: His Life and Message for the World*. New York: Mentor Books, 1954.

Fonda, Jane. *My Life So Far*. New York: Random House, 2005.

Formwalt, Lee W. "An American Historian North of the Border: A Conversation with Michael Fellman." *Organization of American Historians Newsletter* 36 (2008).

Fossati, Andrea, Theodore P Beauchaine, Federica Grazioli, Ilaria Carretta, Francesca Cortinovis, and Cesare Maffei. "A Latent Structure Analysis of Diagnostic and Statistical Manual of Mental Disorders, Narcissistic Personality Disorder Criteria." *Comprehensive Psychiatry* 46 (2005): 361–367.

Frankl, Viktor. *Man's Search for Meaning*. Boston: Beacon, 2000.

Fredrickson, Barbara L., Michele M. Tugade, Christian E. Waugh, and Gregory R. Larkin. "What Good Are Positive Emotions in Crisis? A Prospective Study of Resilience and Emotions Following the Terrorist Attacks on the United States on September 11th, 2001." *Journal of Personality and Social Psychology* 84 (2003): 365–376.

Freud, Sigmund, and William C. Bullitt. *Woodrow Wilson: A Psychological Study*. Piscataway, NJ: Transaction, 1999.

Galbraith, John Kenneth. *Name Dropping*. Boston: Houghton Mifflin, 1999.

———. *A Life in Our Times*. New York: Ballantine, 1981.

Galea S., J. Ahern, H. Resnick, D. Kilpatrick, M. Bucuvalas, J. Gold, and D. Vlahov. "Psychological Sequelae of the September 11 Terrorist Attacks in New York City." *New England Journal of Medicine* 346 (2002): 982–987.

Gallese, V., and A. Goldman. "Mirror Neurons and the Simulation Theory of Mind-Reading." *Trends in Cognitive Sciences* 2 (1998): 493–501.

Galton, Francis. *Hereditary Genius*. New York: D. Appleton & Co., 1870.

Galvez, Juan Francisco, Sairah B. Thommi, and S. Nassir Ghaemi. "Positive Aspects of Mental Illness: A Review in Bipolar Disorder." *Journal of Affective Disorders* 128 (2011): 185–190.

Gandhi, Mohandas K. *Autobiography: The Story of My Experiments with Truth*. New York: Dover, 1983 (1948).

Garrow, David. *Bearing the Cross: Martin Luther King, Jr., and the Southern Christian Leadership Conference*. New York: HarperCollins, 2004.

Gazzaniga, Michael. *Mind Matters: How Mind and Brain Interact to Create Our Conscious Lives*. Boston: Houghton Mifflin, 1988.

George, Robert, and Leeson Waite. *The Psychopathic God: Adolf Hitler*. New York: Da Capo, 1993.

Ghaemi, S. Nassir. *The Rise and Fall of the Biopsychosocial Model: Reconciling Art and Science in Psychiatry*. Baltimore: Johns Hopkins University Press, 2009.

Ghaemi, S. Nassir, Erica E. Boiman, and Frederick Goodwin. "Diagnosing Bipolar Disorder and the Effect of Antidepressants: A Naturalistic Study." *Journal of Clinical Psychiatry* 61 (2000): 804–808.

Gibbels, E. "Hitler's Neurologic Disease—Differential Diagnosis of Parkinson Syndrome." *Fortschritte der Neurologie-Psychiatrie* 57 (1989): 505–517. Original article in German.

Giglio, James N. "Growing Up Kennedy: The Role of Medical Ailments in the Life of JFK, 1920–1957." *Journal of Family History* 31 (2006): 358–385.

Gilbert, Martin. *In Search of Churchill*. New York: Wiley, 1994.

———. *Winston Churchill: The Wilderness Years*. Boston: Houghton Mifflin, 1984.

Gilchrist, Alexander, and Ann Burrows Gilchrist. *Life of William Blake*. New York: Macmillan, 1863.

Goodwin, Frederick, and Kay Jamison. *Manic-Depressive Illness*. 2nd ed. New York: Oxford University Press, 2007.

Grant, Ulysses S. *Memoirs and Selected Letters*. New York: Literary Classics of the United States, 1990.

Greenberg, David. *Nixon's Shadow*. New York: Norton, 2003.

Grenier, Richard. "The Gandhi Nobody Knows." *Commentary*, March 1983, 59–72.

Grinker, Roy R., Roy R. Grinker Sr., and John Timberlake Jr. "'Mentally Healthy' Young Males (Homoclites)." *Archives of General Psychiatry* 6 (1962): 405–453.

Gunther, John. *Roosevelt in Retrospect*. New York: Harper and Brothers, 1950.

Hamilton, Ian. *Robert Lowell: A Biography*. New York: Random House, 1982.

Hamilton, Nigel. *JFK: Reckless Youth*. New York: Random House, 1993.

Harding, Vincent. *Martin Luther King: The Inconvenient Hero*. Maryknoll, NY: Orbis Books, 1996.

Harrower, Molly. "Rorschach Records of the Nazi War Criminals: An Experimental Study After Thirty Years." *Journal of Personality Assessment* 40 (1976): 341–351.

Harvey, John, ed. *The War Diaries of Oliver Harvey*. London: Collins, 1978.

Hauner, Milan. *Hitler: A Chronology of His Life and Time*. 2nd ed. London: Palgrave Macmillan, 2008.

Havens, Leston. *A Safe Place: Laying the Groundwork of Psychotherapy*. Cambridge, MA: Harvard University Press, 1989.

Hersh, Seymour. *The Dark Side of Camelot*. Boston: Little, Brown, 1997.

Hershman, Jablow, and Julian Lieb. *Brotherhood of Tyrants*. New York: Prometheus, 1994.

Heston, Leonard L., and Renate Heston. *The Medical Casebook of Adolf Hitler*. New York: Stein and Day, 1980.

Hitler, Adolf. *Mein Kampf*. Delhi: Jaico Publishing, 2008.

Hunt, Penelope J., Eleanor M. Gurnell, Felicia A. Huppert, Christine Richards, A. Toby Prevost, John A. H. Wass, Joseph Herbert, and V. Krishna K. Chatterjee. "Improvement in Mood and Fatigue After Dehydroepiandrosterone Replacement in Addison's Disease in a Randomized, Double Blind Trial." *Journal of Clinical Endocrinology and Metabolism* 85 (2000): 4650–4656.

Insel, T. R., and L. E. Shapiro. "Oxytocin Receptor Distribution Reflects Social Organization in Monogamous and Polygamous Voles." *Proceedings of the National Academy of Sciences USA* 89 (1992): 5981–5985.

Jackson, Robert H. *That Man: An Insider's Portrait of Franklin D. Roosevelt.* New York: Oxford University Press, 2003.

James, Karen E. "From Mohandas to Mahatma: The Spiritual Metamorphosis of Gandhi." *Essays in History* 28 (1984): 5–20. http://www.lib.virginia.edu/area-studies/South Asia/gandhi.html.

Jamison, Kay R. *Exuberance: The Passion for Life.* New York: Knopf, 2004.

———. *Touched with Fire: Manic-Depressive Illness and the Artistic Temperament.* New York: Free Press, 1996.

Janowsky, David S., Melitta Leff, and Richard S. Epstein. "Playing the Manic Game: Interpersonal Maneuvers of the Acutely Manic Patient." *Archives of General Psychiatry* 22 (1970): 252–261.

Jaspers, Karl. *General Psychopathology.* Baltimore: Johns Hopkins University Press, 1997.

Johanson, C. E., and T. Aigner, "Comparison of the Reinforcing Properties of Cocaine and Procaine in Rhesus Monkeys." *Pharmacology Biochemistry and Behavior* 15 (1981): 49–53.

Johnson, R. W. *A Soldier's Reminiscences in Peace and War.* Philadelphia: J. B. Lippincott Co., 1886.

Kaplan, Robert. "Doctor to the Dictator: The Career of Theodor Morell, Personal Physician to Adolf Hitler." *Australasian Psychiatry* 10 (2002): 389–392.

Kendler, Kenneth, and Carol Prescott. *Genes, Environment and Psychopathology.* New York: Guilford, 2006.

Kennedy, Rose. *Times to Remember.* New York: Doubleday, 1974.

Kennett, Lee. *Sherman: A Soldier's Life.* New York: HarperCollins, 2002.

Kerouac, Jack. *On the Road.* New York: Penguin Classics, 2002.

Kesebira, Sermin, Simavi Vahipa, Fisun Akdeniza, Seki Yüncüa, Müg Alkana, and Hagop Akiskal. "Affective Temperaments as Measured by TEMPS-A in Patients with Bipolar I Disorder and Their First-Degree Relatives: A Controlled Study." *Journal of Affective Disorders* 85 (2005): 127–133.

Kessler, Ronald. *A Matter of Character: Inside the White House of George W. Bush.* New York: Sentinel, 2004.

———. *The Sins of the Father.* New York: Warner, 1996.

Kessler, Ronald C., Guilherme Borges, and Ellen E. Walters. "Prevalence of and Risk Factors for Lifetime Suicide Attempts in the National Comorbidity Survey." *Archives of General Psychiatry* 56 (1999): 617–626.

Kessler, Ronald C., Olga Demler, Richard G. Frank, Mark Olfson, Harold A. Pincus, Ellen Walters, Phillip Wang, Kenneth B. Wells, and Alan M. Zaslavsky. "Prevalence and Treatment of Mental Disorders, 1990 to 2003." *New England Journal of Medicine* 325 (2005): 2515–2523.

Kessler, Ronald C., Amanda Sonnega, Evelyn Bromet, Michael Hughes, et al. "Posttraumatic Stress Disorder in the National Comorbidity Survey." *Archives of General Psychiatry* 52 (1995): 1048–1060.

King, Martin Luther, Jr. *Strength to Love.* Minneapolis: Fortress Press, 1977.

Kingdon, David, Tonmoy Sharma, and Deborah Hart. "What Attitudes Do Psychiatrists Hold Towards People with Mental Illness?" *Psychiatric Bulletin* 28 (2004): 401–406.

Kitchen, Martin. *The Third Reich: Charisma and Community.* London: Pearson Longman, 2008.

————. "Hitler Bewitcher or Hitler Bewitched?" In *Creativity and Madness: An Interdisciplinary Symposium*, ed. J. D. Keehn, 93–108. York, ON: University Press of Canada, 1987.

Knott, E., and L. M. Range. "Does Suicidal History Enhance Acceptance of Other Suicidal Individuals?" *Suicide and Life-Threatening Behavior* 31 (2001): 397–404.

Koestler, Arthur. "Mahatma Gandhi—Yogi and Commissar." In *The Heel of Achilles*, 267. New York: Random House, 1974.

————. *The Yogi and the Commissar, and Other Essays*. New York: Collier, 1961.

Koukopoulos, Athanasios, and S. Nassir Ghaemi. "The Primacy of Mania: A Reconsideration of Mood Disorders." *European Psychiatry* 24 (2009): 125–134.

Kretschmer, Ernst. *The Psychology of Men of Genius*. London: Kegan Paul; New York: Harcourt, Brace and Co., 1931.

————. *Physique and Character*. New York: Harcourt, Brace and Co., 1925.

Kubizek, August. *The Young Hitler I Knew*. Boston: Houghton Mifflin, 1955.

Lakoff, George. *The Political Mind*. New York: Viking, 2008.

Lange-Eichbaum, Wilhelm. *The Problem of Genius*. New York: Macmillan, 1931.

Langer, Ellen J., and Jane Roth. "Heads I Win, Tails It's Chance: The Illusion of Control as a Function of the Sequence of Outcomes in a Purely Chance Task." *Journal of Personality and Social Psychology* 32 (1975): 951–955.

Langer, Walter C. *The Mind of Adolf Hitler: The Secret Wartime Report*. New York: Basic Books, 1972.

Lee, K. A., G. E. Vaillant, W. C. Torrey, and G. H. Elder. "A 50-Year Prospective Study of the Psychological Sequelae of World War II Combat." *American Journal of Psychiatry* 152 (1995): 516–522.

Lewis, David. *The Man Who Invented Hitler*. London: Headline Publishing Company, 2003.

Lichtheim, George. *Thoughts Among the Ruins*. Piscataway, NJ: Transaction, 1973.

Liddell-Hart, B. H. *Sherman: Soldier, Realist, American*. New York: Da Capo, 1993.

Lidz, Ruth, and Hans-Rudolph Wiedemann. "Karl Wilmanns (1873–1945) einige Ergänzungen und Richtigstellungen." *Fortschritte der Neurologie-Psychiatric* 57 (1989): 161–162.

Lifton, Robert J. *The Nazi Doctors: Medical Killing and the Psychology of Genocide*. New York: Basic Books, 1986.

Lincoln, Abraham, Marion Mills Miller, and Henry Clay Whitney. *Life and Works of Abraham Lincoln: Speeches and Presidential Addresses, 1859–1865*. New York: Current Literature Publishing Company, 1907.

Lincoln, Evelyn. *My Twelve Years with John F. Kennedy*. New York: Bantam, 1966.

Livesley, W. John. "Diagnostic Dilemmas in Classifying Personality Disorder." In *Advancing DSM: Dilemmas in Psychiatric Diagnosis*, ed. Katharine A. Phillips, Michael B. First, and Harold Alan Pincus, 153–168. Washington, DC: American Psychiatric Press, 2003.

Lombroso, Cesare. *The Man of Genius*. New York: C. Scribner's Sons, 1891.

Lovell, Richard. "Lord Moran's Prescriptions for Churchill." *British Medical Journal* 310 (1995): 1537.

Lukacs, John. *The Hitler of History*. New York: Vintage, 1998.

McHugh, Paul. *The Mind Has Mountains*. Baltimore: Johns Hopkins University Press, 2006.

Macklin, Graham. *Chamberlain*. London: Haus, 2006.

McPherson, James. *Crossroads of Freedom: Antietam*. New York: Oxford University Press, 2004.

Maher, Brendan. "Delusional Thinking and Cognitive Disorder." *Integrative Physiological and Behavioral Science* 40 (2005): 136–146.

Makkreel, Rudolf. *Dilthey: Philosopher of the Human Studies*. Princeton, NJ: Princeton University Press, 1992.

Manchester, William. *The Last Lion: Winston Spencer Churchill; Visions of Glory, 1874–1932*. New York: Little, Brown, 1983.

———. *Profile of a President*. London: Michael Joseph, 1967.

Mandel, Lee. "Endocrine and Autoimmune Aspects of the Health History of John F. Kennedy." *Annals of Internal Medicine* 151 (2009): 350–354.

Mansfield, Richard S., and Thomas V. Busse. *The Psychology of Creativity and Discovery*. Chicago: Nelson-Hall, 1981.

Marshall, Charles F. *Discovering the Rommel Murder*. Mechanicsburg, PA: Stackpole Books, 2002.

Marszalek, John. *Sherman: A Soldier's Passion for Order*. Carbondale, IL: Southern Illinois University Press, 2007.

Masten, Ann. "Ordinary Magic: Resilience Processes in Development." *American Psychologist* 56 (2001): 227–238.

Matthews, Christopher. *Kennedy and Nixon: The Rivalry That Shaped Postwar America*. New York: Simon and Schuster, 1996.

Mehrabian, Albert, and Susan R. Ferris, "Inference of Attitudes from Nonverbal Communication in Two Channels." *Journal of Consulting Psychology* 31 (1967): 248–252.

Meyers J., ed. *Robert Lowell: Interviews and Memoirs*. Ann Arbor: University of Michigan Press, 1988.

Middleton W., P. Burnett, B. Raphael, and N. Martinek. "The Bereavement Response: A Cluster Analysis." *British Journal of Psychiatry* 169 (1996): 167–171.

Moran, Baron Charles McMoran Wilson. *Churchill: The Struggle for Survival, 1940–1965*. Boston: Houghton Mifflin, 1966.

Motto, A. L., and J. R. Clark. "The Paradox of Genius and Madness: Seneca and His Influence." *Cuadernos de Filología Clásica Estudios Latinos* 2 (1992): 189-200.

Nanda, Bal Ram. *Gandhi and His Critics*. New York: Oxford University Press, 1994.

Nicolay, John George, and John Hay. *Abraham Lincoln: A Memoir*. New York: The Century Company, 1890.

Oates, Stephen B. *Let the Trumpet Sound: A Life of Martin Luther King, Jr*. New York: Harper and Row, 1982.

O'Connor, L. E., et al. "Guilt, Fear, Submission, and Empathy in Depression." *Journal of Affective Disorders* 71 (2002): 19–27.

O'Donnell, Kenneth P., and David F. Powers. *Johnny, We Hardly Knew Ye*. Boston: Little, Brown, 1972.

Olson, Lynne. *Troublesome Young Men: The Rebels Who Brought Churchill to Power and Helped Save England*. New York: Macmillan, 2008.

Osler, William. *Aequanimitas*. Philadelphia: P. Blakinson's Son & Co., 1914.

Owen, David. "Winston Churchill and Franklin Roosevelt: Did Their Health Problems Impair Their Effectiveness as World Leaders?" Churchill Lecture Series, Churchill Museum and Cabinet War Rooms, May 5, 2009. Written transcript.

———. *In Sickness and in Power: Illnesses in Heads of Government During the Last 100 Years*. Westport, CT: Praeger, 2008.

Parker, Richard. *John Kenneth Galbraith: His Life, His Politics, His Economics*. Chicago: University of Chicago Press, 2006.

Pearson, John. *The Private Lives of Winston Churchill*. New York: Simon and Schuster, 1991.

Perkins, Frances. *The Roosevelt I Knew*. New York: Viking Press, 1946.

Perlstein, Rick. *Nixonland: The Rise of a President and the Fracturing of America*. New York: Scribner, 2008.

Perry, Helen Swick. *Psychiatrist of America: The Life of Harry Stack Sullivan*. Cambridge, MA: Belknap Press, 1982.

Pihl, G. T. *Germany: The Last Phase*. New York: Knopf, 1944.

Pollack, Mark H., et al. "Persistent Posttraumatic Stress Disorder Following September 11 in Patients with Bipolar Disorder." *Journal of Clinical Psychiatry* 67 (2006): 394–399.

Poussaint, Alvin. "A Negro Psychiatrist Explains the Negro Psyche." *New York Times Magazine*, August 20, 1967.

Prashad, Vijay. "PropaGandhi Ahimsa in Black America." Originally published in *Little India*, 2002. http://www.littleindia.com/march2002/PropaGandhi%20Ahimsa%20in%20Black%20America.htm (accessed January 17, 2011).

Raines, Howell. *My Soul Is Rested*. New York: Penguin, 1983.

Raskin, Robert, and Howard Terry. "A Principal-Components Analysis of the Narcissistic Personality Inventory and Further Evidence of Its Construct Validity." *Journal of Personality and Social Psychology* 54 (1988): 890–902.

Redlich, Fritz. *Hitler: Diagnosis of a Destructive Prophet*. New York: Oxford University Press, 1998.

Reeves, Richard. *President Kennedy: Profile of Power*. New York: Simon and Schuster, 1993.

Richter, William L. "James Longstreet: From Rebel to Scalawag." *Louisiana History: The Journal of the Louisiana Historical Association* 11 (1970): 215–230.

Ritzler, Barry A. "The Nuremberg Mind Revisited: A Quantitative Approach to Nazi Rorschachs." *Journal of Personality Assessment* 42 (1978): 344–353.

Rodgers, Marion Elizabeth. *Mencken: The American Iconoclast*. New York: Oxford University Press, 2005.

Rosenbaum, Ron. *Explaining Hitler*. New York: Random House, 1998.

Rowland, Peter. *David Lloyd George: A Biography*. New York: Macmillan, 1976.

Rutter, Michael. "Implications of Resilience Concepts for Scientific Understanding." *Annals of the New York Academy of Sciences* 1094 (2006): 1–12.

———. "Resilience in the Face of Adversity: Protective Factors and Resistance to Psychiatric Disorder." *British Journal of Psychiatry* 147 (1985): 598–611.

Schenck, E. G. *Patient Hitler. Eine medizinische Biographie*. Düsseldorf, 1989.

———. "Hitler's Life: Hitler's Doctor—Interview with Ernst Günther Schenck." http://www.onlinefootage.tv/video/show/id/4430 (accessed April 4, 2011).

Schlesinger, Arthur. *Robert Kennedy and His Times*. Boston: Houghton Mifflin, 2002.

Sears, Stephen. *George B. McClellan: The Young Napoleon*. New York: Da Capo, 1999.

Seery, M. D, E. A. Holman, and R. C. Silver. "Whatever Does Not Kill Us: Cumulative Lifetime Adversity, Vulnerability, and Resilience." *Journal of Personality and Social Psychology* 99 (2010): 1025–1041.

Self, Robert C. *Neville Chamberlain: A Biography*. Farnham, UK: Ashgate, 2006.

Shaffer, David, Madelyn S. Gould, Prudence Fisher, Paul Trautman, Donna Moreau, Marjorie Kleinman, and Michael Flory. "Psychiatric Diagnosis in Child and Adolescent Suicide." *Archives of General Psychiatry* 53 (1996): 339–348.

Shamay-Tsoory, S. G. "Empathic Processing: Its Cognitive and Affective Dimensions and Neuroanatomical Basis." In *The Social Neuroscience of Empathy*, ed. Jean Decety and Willam Ickes, 216–232. Cambridge, MA: MIT Press, 2009.

Shenk, Joshua Wolf. *Lincoln's Melancholy*. Boston: Houghton Mifflin, 2005.

Shephard, Ben. *A War of Nerves: Soldiers and Psychiatrists in the Twentieth Century*. Cambridge, MA: Harvard University Press, 2000.

Sherman, William Tecumseh. *Memoirs of General William T. Sherman*. Vol. 2. New York, 1875.

Shorter, Edward. *From Paralysis to Fatigue: A History of Psychosomatic Illness in the Modern Era*. New York: Free Press, 1992.

Shridharani, Krishnalal. *War Without Violence: A Study of Gandhi's Method and Its Accomplishments*. New York: Harcourt, Brace and Co., 1938.

Shriver, Eunice Kennedy. "Hope for Retarded Children." *Saturday Evening Post*, September 22, 1962.

Sidey, Hugh. *John F. Kennedy, President*. Greenwich, CT: Fawcett, 1964.

Silber, Irwin, ed. *Songs of the Union*. Mineola, NY: Dover, 1995.

Simonton, Dean Keith. *Greatness: Who Makes History and Why*. New York: Guilford, 1994.

———. *Psychology, Science, and History: An Introduction to Historiometry*. New Haven, CT: Yale University Press, 1990.

———. "Presidential IQ, Openness, Intellectual Brilliance, and Leadership." *Political Psychology* 27 (2006): 511–526.

Simpson, S. G., S. E. Folstein, D. A. Meyers, F. A. McMahon, D. M. Brusco, and J. R. DePaulo Jr. "Bipolar II: The Most Common Bipolar Phenotype?" *American Journal of Psychiatry* 150 (1993): 901–903.

Singer, T., et al. "Empathy for Pain Involves the Affective but Not the Sensory Components of Pain." *Science* 303 (2004): 1157–1162.

Smart, Nick. *Neville Chamberlain: A Biography*. London: Routledge, 2009.

Speer, Albert. *Inside the Third Reich*. New York: Simon and Schuster, 1997.

Steiner, John Michael. *Power Politics and Social Change in National Socialist Germany*. New York: Walter de Gruyter, 1976.

Stephens, Philip. *Tony Blair: The Making of a World Leader*. New York: Viking, 2004.

Storr, Anthony. *Churchill's Black Dog, Kafka's Mice*. New York: Ballantine, 1990.

Sutherland, Stuart. *Irrationality*. London: Pinter and Martin, 2007.

Sutker, P. B., et al. "War Zone Stress, Personal Resources, and PTSD in Persian Gulf War Returnees." *Journal of Abnormal Psychology* 104 (1995): 444–452.

Talih, F., O. Fattal, and D. Malone. "Anabolic Steroid Abuse: Physical and Psychiatric Costs." *Cleveland Clinic Journal of Medicine* 74 (2007): 341–352.

Taylor, Shelley E., and David A. Armor. "Positive Illusions and Coping with Adversity." *Journal of Personality* 64 (1996): 873–898.

Titchener, E. B. *Lectures on Experimental Psychology of Thought Processes*. New York: Macmillan, 1909.

Thomas, Helen. *Thanks for the Memories, Mr. President*. New York: Simon and Schuster, 2003.

Troy, Allison S., Frank H. Wilhelm, Amanda J. Shallcross, and Iris B. Mauss. "Seeing the Silver Lining: Cognitive Reappraisal Ability Moderates the Relationship Between Stress and Depressive Symptoms." *Emotion* 10 (2010): 783–795.

Tsuang, Ming, and Mauricio Tohen, eds. *Textbook in Psychiatric Epidemiology*. 2nd ed. New York: Wiley-Liss, 2002.

Turner, Ted. *Call Me Ted*. New York: Grand Central, 2008.

Ur, E., T. H. Turner, T. J. Goodwin, A. Grossman, and G. M. Besser. "Mania in Association with Hydrocortisone Replacement for Addison's Disease." *Postgraduate Medical Journal* 68 (1992): 41–43.

Vaillant, George E. *Adaptation to Life*. Boston: Little, Brown, 1977.

———. *The Natural History of Alcoholism Revisited*. Cambridge, MA: Harvard University Press, 1995.

Waite, Robert G. L. *The Psychopathic God: Adolf Hitler*. New York: Basic Books, 1977.

Warrington, T. P., and J. M. Bostwick. "Psychiatric Adverse Effects of Corticosteroids." *Mayo Clinic Proceedings* 81 (2006): 1361–1367.

Watt, Norman F., James P. David, Kevin L. Ladd, and Susan Shamos. "The Life Course of Psychological Resilience: A Phenomenological Perspective on Deflecting Life's Slings and Arrows." *Journal of Primary Prevention* 15 (1995): 209–246.

Westen, Drew. *The Political Brain*. New York: Public Affairs, 2007.

White, G. Edward. *Justice Oliver Wendell Holmes: Law and the Inner Self*. New York: Oxford University Press, 1995.

White, Graham J. *FDR and the Press*. Chicago: University of Chicago Press, 1979.

Wicker, Tom. *One of Us: Richard Nixon and the American Dream*. New York: Random House, 1991.

Wilentz, Sean, ed. *The Best American History Essays on Lincoln*. New York: Palgrave Macmillan, 2009.

Wills, Garry. *The Kennedy Imprisonment: A Meditation on Power*. Boston: Back Bay, 1994.

———. *Nixon Agonistes*. New York: Signet, 1969.

Wingo, Aliza P., and S. Nassir Ghaemi. "Frequency of Stimulant Treatment and of Stimulant-Associated Mania/Hypomania in Bipolar Disorder Patients." *Psychopharmacology Bulletin* 41 (2008): 37–47.

Wofford, Harris. *Of Kennedys and Kings*. Pittsburgh: University of Pittsburgh Press, 1980.

Woollcott, Alexander. "Get Down, You Fool." *Atlantic Monthly* 161 (1938): 169–173.

Wootton, Tom. *Bipolar in Order*. Tiburon, CA: Bipolar Advantage Publishing, 2009.

Wrigley, Chris. *Winston Churchill: A Biographical Companion*. Santa Barbara, CA: ABC-CLIO, 2002.

Wykes, Alan. *Hitler*. New York: Ballantine, 1970.

Yastrebov, V. S. "PTSD After-effects of Terrorist Attack Victims." In *The Integration and Management of Traumatized People After Terrorist Attacks*, ed. S. Begec, 100–107. Amsterdam: IOS Press, 2007.

Young, Andrew. *A Way Out of No Way*. Nashville: Thomas Nelson, 1994.

INDEX